HOMELESSNESS, LIBERTY AND PROPERTY

In *Homelessness, Liberty and Property*, Terry Skolnik establishes a novel theory about the government's duties to end homelessness, maintain public property's value, and legitimize laws that regulate public space. In doing so, Skolnik provides new insight into how the property law system and the regulation of public space limit unhoused persons' freedom and political equality. The book deepens our understanding of how various areas of law, such as constitutional law, legal philosophy, criminal law, and property law, approach the reality of homelessness and advances original arguments to provide new justifications for the right to housing. Skolnik concludes by offering a set of concrete proposals for how the government may better reduce the incidence of homelessness and treat unhoused persons with greater concern and respect. This title is part of the Flip it Open Programme and may also be available open access. Check our website Cambridge Core for details.

Terry Skolnik is a research professor at the Sandra Day O'Connor College of Law, Arizona State University (ASU). He is the executive director of ASU's Academy for Justice. He is also an associate professor at the University of Ottawa, Faculty of Law, Civil Law Section.

Homelessness, Liberty and Property

TERRY SKOLNIK
Arizona State University

CAMBRIDGE
UNIVERSITY PRESS

CAMBRIDGE
UNIVERSITY PRESS

Shaftesbury Road, Cambridge CB2 8EA, United Kingdom

One Liberty Plaza, 20th Floor, New York, NY 10006, USA

477 Williamstown Road, Port Melbourne, VIC 3207, Australia

314–321, 3rd Floor, Plot 3, Splendor Forum, Jasola District Centre,
New Delhi – 110025, India

103 Penang Road, #05–06/07, Visioncrest Commercial, Singapore 238467

Cambridge University Press is part of Cambridge University Press & Assessment,
a department of the University of Cambridge.

We share the University's mission to contribute to society through the pursuit of
education, learning and research at the highest international levels of excellence.

www.cambridge.org
Information on this title: www.cambridge.org/9781009392679

DOI: 10.1017/9781009392631

When citing this work, please include a reference to the DOI 10.1017/9781009392631

First published 2025

A catalogue record for this publication is available from the British Library

A Cataloging-in-Publication data record for this book is available from the Library of Congress

ISBN 978-1-009-39267-9 Hardback

Contents

Acknowledgments

I thank the following people who provided valuable feedback on prior versions of this manuscript: Anna Maria Konewka, Alexandra Flynn, Ben Ewing, Ben McJunkin, Christopher Essert, Ekow Yankah, Evan Fox-Decent, Hamish Stewart, Malcolm Thorburn, Marie-Eve Sylvestre, Marie-France Fortin, Peter Oliver, Sylvia Rich, Vanessa MacDonnell, and Vincent Chiao. I also thank the following colleagues who provided helpful advice and guidance on my book proposal: Hanoch Dagan, Jason Weinrib, Patrick Dumberry, and Paul Daly. I thank the following law students for their excellent research assistance: Alexandre Faubert Charlebois, Jean-François Bélanger, Maya Vacante, and Nicholas Burrell. I thank the following friends and colleagues who helped me refine my arguments and work through difficult ideas throughout the years: Edward Béchard-Torres, Michelle Biddulph, Olga Redko, and William Colish. I thank the Social Sciences and Humanities Research Council of Canada for their generous funding that supported my doctoral research. Lastly, I thank the following institutions and research centers for their support while I drafted and refined this manuscript: Arizona State University's Academy for Justice and the Center for Constitutional Design at the Sandra Day O'Connor College of Law, New York University's Center for Human Rights and Global Justice, The Buchmann Faculty of Law at Tel Aviv University, the Public Law Centre at the University of Ottawa, and the University of Toronto. All mistakes are my own.

This book was adapted from my doctoral dissertation and reproduces some of its arguments, sentences, and footnotes. Additionally, certain arguments advanced in this book are based on academic articles that I published previously and that contain similar sentences, phrasing, and footnotes. The arguments advanced in Chapters 3, 4, and 5 draw largely on my previously published articles entitled: "How and Why Homeless People Are Regulated Differently" (2018) 42 *Queen's Law Journal* 297 and "Freedom and Access to Housing: Three Conceptions" (2018) 35 *Windsor Yearbook of Access to Justice* 226. The arguments advanced in Chapter 6 draw largely on my previously published article entitled: “Rethinking Homeless People’s Punishments” (2019) 22 *New Criminal Law Review* 73. Lastly, the arguments advanced in Chapter 8 draw largely on my previously published article entitled: “Homeless Encampments: A Philosophical Justification” (2022) 36 *Journal of Law and Social Policy* 97.

Introduction

Homelessness and the Regulation of Public Property

Homelessness continues to be one of the most visible social problems of our time. Tent encampments have sprung up in urban parks, on city streets, and in other public places.[1] Some American cities have declared a state of emergency due to the growth of homeless encampments.[2] And these are just some of the most visible examples. Many unhoused persons experience a more hidden form of homelessness.[3] Some stay on friends' couches or sleep in motels.[4] Others are confined to detention centers, are treated in hospitals, or sleep in their cars.[5]

For centuries, governments have attempted to address homelessness through a combination of social assistance and coercion – an approach that continues today.[6] Yet homelessness remains ubiquitous in major US and Canadian

[1] Steve Lopez, "L.A. Homeless Crisis Grows Despite Political Promises, Many Speeches and Millions of Dollars. How Do We Fix This?" LA Times (January 28, 2018), www.latimes.com/local/california/la-me-lopez-homeless-20180128-story.html [perma.cc/J7DW-CMPX]; Joshua Sabatini, "SF Clears 11 Homeless Encampments Since August, Three Later Re-Emerge," SF Examiner (June 6, 2017), www.sfexaminer.com/news/sf-clears-11-homeless-encampments-since-august-three-later-re-emerge/article_c7e3117b-75b5-5139-a260-0dbc7d71836d.html [perma.cc/FXD8-WEW5]; Daniel Duane, "The Tent Cities of San Francisco," NY Times (December 17, 2016), www.nytimes.com/2016/12/17/opinion/sunday/the-tent-cities-of-san-francisco.html [perma.cc/SXN2-FMBM].

[2] Project Homeless, "Three Years into a State of Emergency, What We've Learned about Homelessness," Seattle Times (November 3, 2018), www.seattletimes.com/seattle-news/homeless/three-years-into-a-state-of-emergency-what-weve-learned-about-homelessness; Anh Do, "Santa Ana City Council Declares 'Crisis' over Homeless Encampments in Civic Center," LA Times (September 6, 2016), www.latimes.com/local/lanow/la-me-ln-santa-ana-homeless-20160906-snap-story.html.

[3] Peter Rossi, *Down and Out in America: The Origins of Homelessness* (University of Chicago Press, 1989) at 48 (using the term "hidden homelessness" to imply those staying out of public view); Stephen Gaetz, Tanya Gulliver, and Tim Richter, "The State of Homelessness in Canada: 2014" (2014) Homeless Hub, at 38–39, www.homelesshub.ca/sites/default/files/SOHC2014.pdf [perma.cc/7H3U-9ZF4] (describing hidden homelessness as those staying provisionally with friends).

[4] Tony Robinson and Allison Sickels, "No Right to Rest: Criminalizing Homelessness in Colorado" (April 2015) at 15, Denver Homeless Out Loud, https://wp-cpr.s3.amazonaws.com/uploads/2019/06/homelessness-study.pdf [perma.cc/NVH8-W6AP].

[5] *Ibid.*; Expert Advisory Panel on Homelessness, *A Place to Call Home* (Toronto: Government of Ontario, 2015) at 11–12.

[6] *See, e.g.*, George Nicholls, *A History of the English Poor Law* (London: PS King and Son, 1904) at 36; James Fitzjames Stephen, *History of the Criminal Law England*, Vol. III (London: MacMillan, 1883) at 266.

cities.[7] Interrelatedly, many cities are facing a growing housing crisis.[8] Scholars, lawyers, governments, and the public are all taking notice. For instance, in a 2019 poll, roughly 95 percent of Los Angeles residents ranked homelessness as the most pressing issue for the city (lack of affordable housing came in a close second).[9]

Homelessness matters to those experiencing it, to their friends and family, and to the wider community. Compared to the general population, unhoused persons have a lower life expectancy, are disproportionately subject to physical and sexual violence, and are more likely to have mental health problems and substance use issues.[10] Members of certain communities – such as Indigenous persons, racialized persons, immigrants, members of the LGBTQ community, and veterans – are overrepresented in unhoused populations.[11]

The effects of homelessness extend beyond those without access to housing. In addition to tent encampments, feces, garbage, and syringes have accumulated in the public spaces of certain cities with a high population of unhoused persons.[12] In other cities where homelessness is prevalent, polls reveal that a significant portion of residents report that they feel unsafe.[13] Homelessness can also decrease a city's tourism and lower its revenue.[14] Some elections are won or lost according to how a city plans to respond to homelessness and improve residents' quality of life.[15] Local governments continue to struggle with how to regulate their parks, streets, beaches, and squares so that everyone can use these public spaces on equal terms.[16]

7 US Department of Housing and Urban Development, "2021 Annual Homeless Assessment Report (AHAR) to Congress" (Washington, 2021) at 9, 12, 13; Tristin Hopper, "Canadians Fed Up with Homelessness and Governments Making It Worse: Exclusive Poll," National Post (November 4, 2022), https://nationalpost.com/news/canada/canadians-fed-up-with-homelessness [perma.cc/64WK-QKW3].

8 Conor Dougherty, "The Next Affordable City Is Already Too Expensive," NY Times (February 20, 2022), www.nytimes.com/2022/02/20/business/economy/spokane-housing-expensive-cities.html [perma.cc/JH49-FAQW].

9 Benjamin Oreskes, Doug Smith, and David Lauter, "95% of Voters Say Homelessness Is L.A.'s Biggest Problem, Times Poll Finds. 'You Can't Escape It'," LA Times (November 14, 2019), www.latimes.com/hyjyzuysvia-123 [perma.cc/4SYE-G7YF].

10 Stephen Hwang, "Homelessness and Health" (2001) 164 *CMAJ* 229 at 230–31.

11 City of Ottawa, "Everyone Counts: Ottawa's 2018 Point in Time Count" (Ottawa, 2018) at 1–2.

12 Thomas Fuller, Shaila Dewan, and Kellen Browning, "San Francisco Mayor Declares State of Emergency to Fight City's 'Nasty Streets'," NY Times (December 17, 2021), www.nytimes.com/2021/12/17/us/san-francisco-state-of-emergency-crime.html [perma.cc/E45D-W2WZ].

13 Benjamin Oreskies and David Lauter, "L.A. Voters Angry, Frustrated over Homelessness Crisis, Demand Faster Action, Poll Finds," LA Times (December 1, 2021), www.latimes.com/homeless-housing/story/2021–12-01/la-voters-are-frustrated-impatient-over-persistent-homelessness-crisis [perma.cc/6DTF-MVYA]. According to the poll, four in ten residents reported that they felt unsafe.

14 *Joyce* v. *City and County of San Francisco*, 846 F Supp 843 at 846 (ND Cal 1994) (San Francisco's Mayor's Office of Economic Planning and Development attributed a loss of $173 million in sales due to homelessness).

15 Heather MacDonald, "San Francisco's Matrix Program for the Homeless" (1995) 14:1 *Crim Just Ethics* 78 at 79.

16 This definition of public property is derived from Michael Robertson, "Common Property *Redux*" (2016) 49 *UBC L Rev* 563 at 608.

The State has regulated homelessness and public property in various ways. Historically, vagrancy laws governed public property and homelessness until courts began to strike them down as unconstitutionally vague.[17] Vagrancy statutes were largely replaced by narrowly tailored municipal ordinances (or bylaws) that continue to regulate homelessness and public property.[18] These ordinances became popular in the United States following the Broken Windows Theory's emergence in the 1980s.[19] The Broken Windows Theory posits that cities must tackle low-level incivilities (e.g., public urination, panhandling, littering) to prevent more serious crime and disorder.[20] Canadian and American police forces adopted Broken Windows policing strategies and enforced municipal ordinances harshly.[21] These ordinances prohibit individuals from alleviating their most basic needs on public property.[22] For instance, they proscribe acts such as sleeping on public property, urban camping, public urination and defecation, and more.[23]

Scholars challenge the legitimacy of laws that govern public property on different grounds. Some contend that cities are not just regulating public property, but rather, criminalizing and punishing the condition of homelessness.[24] According to this argument, since unhoused persons must alleviate their basic needs but have no default private place to do so, laws that regulate public property criminalize unhoused persons' survival.[25] Others argue that laws that govern public property are counterproductive and create a vicious cycle of criminalization, punishment,

17 *See, e.g.*, *Papachristou* v. *Jacksonville*, 405 US 156; William J Stuntz, "The Pathological Politics of Criminal Law" (2001) 100:3 *Mich L Rev* 505 at 559–60.

18 *See, e.g.*, Terry Skolnik, "How and Why Homeless People Are Regulated Differently" (2018) 43 *Queen's LJ* 297 at 304–05; Emily Snoddon, "Clarifying Vagueness: Rethinking the Supreme Court's Vagueness Doctrine" (2019) 86:8 *U Chi L Rev* 2301 at 2331.

19 George Kelling and James Wilson, "Broken Windows: The Police and Neighbourhood Safety," The Atlantic (March 1982), www.theatlantic.com/magazine/archive/1982/03/broken-windows/304465/ [perma.cc/MM5T-W4XZ]; Bernard Harcourt and Jens Ludwig, "Broken Windows: New Evidence from New York City and a Five-City Social Experiment" (2006) 73 *U Chi L Rev* 271 at 272, 282.

20 Kelling and Wilson, "Broken Windows."

21 David Garland, *The Culture of Control: Crime and Social Order in Contemporary Society* (University of Chicago Press, 2001) at 181; Marie-Eve Sylvestre, Céline Bellot, and Catherine Chesnay, "Taming Disorderly People One Ticket at a Time: The Penalization of Homelessness in Ontario and British Columbia" (2013) 55:2 *Can J Corr* 161 at 162.

22 NLCHP, "Housing Not Handcuffs: Ending the Criminalization of Homelessness in U.S. Cities" (Washington, 2016) at 8–16, Homeless Law, https://homelesslaw.org/wp-content/uploads/2018/10/Housing-Not-Handcuffs.pdf [perma.cc/3J4X-2NDA].

23 *Ibid.*; Taunya Lovell Banks, "The Disappearing Public Toilet" (2020) 50:4 *Seton Hall L Rev* 1061 at 1073–74 (describing how ordinances prohibit public urination); Ron Hochbaum, "Bathrooms as a Homeless Rights Issue" (2020) 98:2 *NC L Rev* 205 at 208 (noting how ordinances prohibit defecation in public).

24 *See, e.g.*, Maria Foscarinis, "Downward Spiral: Homelessness and Its Criminalization" (1996) 14:1 *Yale L & Pol'y Rev* 1 at 2–3; Maria Foscarinis, Kelly Cunningham-Bowers, and Kristen Brown, "Out of Sight – Out of Mind: The Continuing Trend toward the Criminalization of Homelessness" (1999) 6:2 *Geo J Poverty L & Pol'y* 145 at 151, 156, 164; Donald Saelinger, "Nowhere to Go: The Impacts of City Ordinances Criminalizing Homelessness" (2006) 13:3 *Geo J Poverty L & Pol'y* 545 at 545–46.

25 David M. Smith, "A Theoretical and Legal Challenge to Homeless Criminalization as Public Policy" (1994) 12:2 *Yale L & Pol'y Rev* 487 at 492–97.

and homelessness.[26] Scholars also point out that these laws are enforced disparately against people experiencing homelessness and other marginalized persons.[27]

Others defend the legitimacy of laws that regulate public property. They contend that these laws are necessary to maintain order and preserve public property's shared use for all.[28] They posit that public spaces such as streets and sidewalks must be free from tents and other obstructions to ensure the efficient flow of traffic.[29] And they note that these laws also help maintain a city's attractiveness, economic vitality, and tourism.[30]

Courts, scholars, lawyers, and civil society organizations are increasingly confronted with this tension between homelessness and the regulation of public property. Attorneys have challenged the constitutionality of laws that govern public property. They argue that these laws are vague, overbroad, discriminatory, violate fundamental rights, impose cruel and unusual punishments, and more.[31] Although some of these claims have succeeded, most have failed.[32] Interrelatedly, scholars and civil libertarians have claimed that the Constitution provides a positive right to housing; an argument that courts have rejected.[33]

Legal theorists, for their part, continue to deepen our understanding of homelessness, access to housing, and the regulation of public space. Some examine how homelessness undermines interests such as freedom, political equality, and full citizenship.[34] Others' empirical work demonstrates how the police disparately enforce laws that govern public property against unhoused persons.[35] Certain scholars explore homelessness as a discrete legal condition

26 Allard K. Lowenstein International Human Rights Clinic, *Forced into Breaking the Law: The Criminalization of Homelessness in Connecticut* (New Haven: Yale Law School, 2016) at 2–5.

27 Farida Ali, "Limiting the Poor's Right to Public Space: Criminalizing Homelessness in California" (2014) 21:2 *Geo J Poverty L & Pol'y* 197 at 221.

28 Robert Ellickson, "Controlling Chronic Misconduct in City Spaces: Of Panhandlers, Skid Rows, and Public-Space Zoning" (1996) 105:5 *Yale LJ* 1165 at 1168–70.

29 Robert Teir, "Restoring Order in Urban Public Spaces" (1997–1998) 2:2 *Tex Rev L & Pol* 255 at 257–58.

30 *Ibid.* at 275.

31 For an overview of these challenges, see Kathryn Hansel, "Constitutional Othering: Citizenship and the Insufficiency of Negative Rights-Based Challenges to Anti-Homeless Systems" (2011) 6:2 *Nw JL & Soc Pol'y* 445 at 448–61.

32 *Ibid.* Chapter 2 of this book offers a summary of constitutional challenges to laws that govern public property and summarizes their successes and failures.

33 *Tanudjaja* v. *Canada (Attorney General)*, 2014 ONCA 852; *Lindsey* v. *Normet*, 405 US 56 (1972); Maria Foscarinis, "The Growth of a Movement for a Human Right to Housing in the United States" (2007) 20 *Harv Hum Rts J* 35 at 37.

34 *See, e.g.*, Jeremy Waldron, "Homelessness and the Issue of Freedom" (1991–92) 39:1 *UCLA L Rev* 295; Kathleen Arnold, *Homelessness, Citizenship, and Identity* (Albany: SUNY Press, 2004); Terry Skolnik, "Freedom and Access to Housing: Three Conceptions" (2018) 35 *Windsor YB Access Just* 226.

35 *See, e.g.*, Marie-Eve Sylvestre and Céline Bellot, "Challenging Discriminatory and Punitive Responses to Homelessness in Canada" in Martha Porter and Bruce Jackman (eds.), *Advancing Social Rights in Canada* (Markham: Irwin Law, 2013) at 172; Commission des droits de la personne et des droits de la jeunesse, "The Judiciarization of the Homeless in Montréal: A Case of Social Profiling" (Montreal, November 6, 2009) at 2, www.cdpdj.qc.ca/storage/app/media/publications/Homeless_Summary.pdf.

that results in distinct disadvantages: legal powerlessness, vulnerability, and second-class citizenship.[36]

The intersection between homelessness and the regulation of public property also touches on fundamental criminal law principles and doctrines. Courts analyze whether unhoused persons had no choice but to alleviate their needs on public property and break the law, such that it is unconstitutional to convict and punish them.[37] Judges assess whether some law unconstitutionally criminalizes the status of homelessness, or rather, constitutionally prohibits some unlawful act.[38] Judicial decisions examine whether it is cruel and unusual to criminalize unhoused persons' basic human acts or impose certain punishments.[39]

These criminal law principles and doctrines, though, are inextricably linked to deeper philosophical concepts: the freedom or absence of choice, the distinction between status and acts, and the scope of the State's power to criminalize and punish. When asking whether an unhoused person had a free choice to sleep on public property, one must consider deeper moral questions: When is a choice free, and furthermore, what is freedom?[40] When considering whether unhoused persons' conduct is involuntary, one may draw on the intersecting fields of psychology, philosophy, and physiology – disciplines that raise further questions about human agency and free will.[41] When evaluating whether a law prohibits an act or criminalizes one's status, one must inquire into the connection between a person's capacity, choices, and character, and the extent to which individuals control them.[42] Finally, when assessing whether cities can legitimately prohibit and punish conduct, it leads to broader questions about the breadth of State power, the limits of criminalization, and the legitimacy of punishment.[43]

The regulation of public property also requires courts to theorize about constitutional rights. When defendants attack the constitutionality of laws that govern public property, courts must answer complex questions about the meaning, purpose, and

36 Kevin Bundy, "'Officer, Where's My Stuff?' The Constitutional Implications of a De Facto Property Disability for Homeless People" (2003) 1 *Hastings Race & Poverty LJ* 57 at 67; Christopher Essert, "Property and Homelessness" (2016) 44 *Phil & Pub Aff* 266 at 266; Jane Baron, "Property and 'No Property'" (2006) 42:5 *Hous L Rev* 1425 at 1427.

37 *Jones* v. *City of Los Angeles*, 444 F (3d) at 1118 (9th Circ 2006); Edward Walters, "No Way Out: Eighth Amendment Protection for Do-or-Die Acts of the Homeless" (1995) 62:4 *U Chi L Rev* 1619 at 1628.

38 *Robinson* v. *California*, 370 US 660 (1962); Juliette Smith, "Arresting the Homeless for Sleeping in Public: A Paradigm for Expanding the Robinson Doctrine" (1994–1995) 29:2 *Colum JL & Soc Probs* 293 at 305–06.

39 Benno Weisberg, "When Punishing Involuntary Conduct Violates the Eighth Amendment: Applying the *Robinson* Doctrine to Homelessness and Other Contextual 'Crimes'" (2005) 96:1 *J Crim L & Criminology* 329 at 351.

40 Antony Duff, "Choice, Character, and Criminal Liability" (1993) 12:4 *Law & Phil* 345 at 346–48.

41 Stephen Morse, "Criminal Law and Common Sense: An Essay on the Perils and Promise of Neuroscience" (2015) 99:1 *Marquette L Rev* 39 at 44–45.

42 Michael Moore, "Choice, Character, and Excuse" (1990) 7:2 *Soc Phil & Pol'y* 29.

43 *See generally*, Lindsay Farmer, *Making the Modern Criminal Law: Criminalization and Civil Order* (Oxford University Press, 2016), ch. 3.

scope of these constitutional rights. For instance, does panhandling or sleeping on public property constitute expressive conduct that is protected by the First Amendment?[44] Do urban camping bans violate the fundamental right to travel?[45] Do laws that govern public property discriminate against people experiencing homelessness as a suspect class?[46] To answer these questions, judges must first consider the meaning of "expressive conduct," evaluate the moral underpinnings of the fundamental right to travel, and consider the notion of political equality. These questions and answers force one to think hard about the interests and values that underlie constitutional rights – such as freedom, equality, and dignity – and their interrelationship.[47]

There is more. The intersection between homelessness and laws that govern public property raises broader questions about the nature of rights, the separation of powers, and the role of public institutions in a democracy. Judges analyze whether laws that govern public property respect constitutional rights. As part of their reasoning, they must interpret whether constitutional rights are negative in nature and merely protect individuals against State interference, or rather, are positive in nature and impose affirmative duties on the State to provide access to housing.[48] These inquiries require judges to assess their role in a constitutional democracy, their institutional competence, and their relationship with other branches of government.[49]

For all these reasons, the intersection between homelessness and the regulation of public property matters. So too do legal decisions that attempt to reconcile unhoused persons' fundamental interests with the need to regulate public space. These judicial decisions ultimately dictate where unhoused persons can be, what they can do, and the legal risks associated with living their lives. Moreover, the impact of these decisions spill over into other jurisdictions. When a court decides that some city's municipal ordinance is unconstitutional, a neighboring city may repeal a similar provision.[50] Conversely, when judges uphold the constitutionality of some law that regulates public property, other cities may follow suit and enact

44 *International Soc. for Krishna Consciousness, Inc.* v. *Lee*, 505 US 672 (1992) (begging and expressive conduct); *Clark* v. *Community for Creative Non-Violence*, 468 US 288 (1984) (camping and expressive conduct); Helen Hershkoff and Adam Cohen, "Begging to Differ: The First Amendment and the Right to Beg" (1991) 104:4 *Harv L Rev* 896 at 909.

45 *Allen* v. *City of Sacramento*, 234 Cal App (4th) 41 (App Ct 2015) at 60–61; Paul Ades, "The Unconstitutionality of 'Antihomeless' Laws: Ordinances Prohibiting Sleeping in Outdoor Public Areas as a Violation of the Right to Travel" (1989) 77:3 *Cal L Rev* 595.

46 *Joel* v. *City of Orlando*, 232 F (3d) 1353 at 1357–58 (11th Circ 2000).

47 *See, e.g.*, Alon Harel, *Why Law Matters* (Oxford University Press, 2014), ch. 2.

48 Helen Hershkoff, "Positive Rights and State Constitutions: The Limits of Federal Rationality Review" (1999) 112:6 *Harv L Rev* 1131 at 1135, 1164; Helen Hershkoff and Stephen Loffredo, *Getting By: Economics Rights and Legal Protections for People with Low Income* (Oxford University Press, 2020) at 635.

49 Frank Cross, "The Error of Positive Rights" (2000–01) 48:4 *UCLA L Rev* 857 at 859–60, 880.

50 *Pottinger* v. *City of Miami*, 810 F Supp 1551 at 1558 (SD Florida 1992). As the court observed in *Pottinger*, the City of Miami changed its ordinance regulating public sleeping after a similar

similar offenses. Like homelessness, the regulation of public property remains a complex and enduring issue.

It may seem that scholars have already approached the relationship between homelessness and laws that govern public property from every angle: historical,[51] empirical,[52] philosophical,[53] and constitutional.[54] Each of these approaches has contributed invaluably to our understanding. Yet despite these contributions, we still lack an overarching theory of how the State can treat unhoused persons with equal concern and respect.[55] We also lack a broader account of the State's duties related to homelessness, public property, and the laws that govern its use.

I.1 OVERVIEW OF THIS BOOK AND ITS ARGUMENTS

This book sets out a theory of the State's duties related to homelessness and public property. It argues that the republican theory of freedom and government (or republicanism) provides new insight into homelessness and laws that govern public property.[56] Republicanism also offers a theoretical foundation for why the State has certain obligations related to homelessness and public property. Furthermore, republican theories of freedom and government underpin this book's concrete proposals that aim to help achieve that end.

I.1.1 *Republicanism and Domination*

A brief overview of republicanism is necessary before setting out this book's overarching arguments. The republican theory of freedom (or liberty, the terms are used interchangeably) emerged during the era of the Roman republic.[57] Republican theorists construe freedom as nondomination.[58] The term "domination" implies

ordinance was struck down as unconstitutional in *Hershey* v. *City of Clearwater*, 834 F (2d) at 938, 940 (11th Circ 1987).

51 Charles James Ribton-Turner, *A History of Vagrants and Vagrancy, and Beggars and Begging* (London: Chapman & Hall, 1887).

52 Marie-Eve Sylvestre, "Policing the Homeless in Montreal: Is This Really What the Population Wants?" (2010) 20:4 *Policing & Soc'y* 432; Christine Campbell and Paul Eid, *La Judiciarisation des personnes itinérantes à Montréal: un profilage social* (Montreal: Commission des Droits de la Personne et des Droits de la Jeunesse, 2009).

53 Jane Baron, "Homelessness as a Property Problem" (2004) 36:2 *Urb Law* 273 at 287.

54 For a summary of constitutional approaches, see Hansel, "Constitutional Othering" at 448–61.

55 Ronald Dworkin, *Taking Rights Seriously* (Cambridge: Harvard University Press, 1977) at 218; Philip Pettit, *On the People's Terms: A Republican Theory and Model of Democracy* (Cambridge University Press, 2013) at 78–79.

56 Philip Pettit, *Republicanism: A Theory of Freedom and Government* (Oxford University Press, 1999) at 52–54.

57 Philip Pettit, "Criminalization in Republican Theory" in Antony Duff, Lindsay Farmer, Sandra Marshall et al. (eds.), *Criminalization: The Political Morality of the Criminal Law* (Oxford University Press, 2014) at 136.

58 Pettit, *Republicanism* at 52–54.

that an individual is vulnerable to unilateral threats of interference by others.[59] Individuals enjoy republican freedom when others wield no such unilateral power to interfere with them; they suffer domination when others wield that power.[60]

The republican theory of liberty is typically contrasted with both positive and negative theories of freedom.[61] The positive theory of liberty conceptualizes freedom as self-actualization.[62] Individuals enjoy positive liberty when they reach their potential or attain their higher selves.[63] Positive freedom is concerned with the existence of psychological obstacles – and the lack of access to resources – that affect self-mastery.[64] The negative theory of liberty, on the other hand, conceptualizes freedom as noninterference.[65] Individuals enjoy negative freedom when they do not experience actual interference by others.[66]

Republican freedom is broader than its negative counterpart. Negative liberty theory posits that concrete obstructions are necessary to undermine freedom.[67] Republicanism, in contrast, recognizes that individuals are unfree if they experience domination without interference.[68] More specifically, domination without interference undermines freedom because a person may limit their own liberty to avoid obstructions by others.[69] A dominated person may abandon their preferences, relinquish their authenticity, or become deferential to others to escape such hinderances.[70] Republicanism acknowledges that individuals lack freedom if they must adopt such coping mechanisms.[71] In the republican tradition, domination is typically exemplified by the relationship between master and slave.[72] Yet while negative liberty theory leads to the absurd conclusion that a slave is free if they

59 *Ibid.*

60 Frank Lovett and Philip Pettit, "Preserving Republican Freedom: A Reply to Simpson" (2018) 46:4 *Phil & Pub Aff* 363 at 364–65.

61 Philip Pettit, "Free Persons and Free Choices" (2007) 28:4 *Hist of Pol Thought* 709 at 713; Christian Nadeau, "Non-Domination as a Moral Ideal" in Daniel Weinstock and Christian Nadeau (eds.), *Republicanism: History, Theory, and Practice* (London: Frank Cass, 2004) at 121–22.

62 Isaiah Berlin, "Two Concepts of Liberty" in Henry Hardy (ed.), *Liberty* (Oxford University Press, 2002) at 168–69 (distinguishing positive and negative theories of liberty).

63 *Ibid.* at 178–79.

64 Pettit, "Free Persons and Free Choices" at 713.

65 Berlin, "Two Concepts of Liberty" at 168–70.

66 *Ibid.*

67 *Ibid.*

68 Cécile Laborde, "Republicanism" in Michael Freeden, Lyman Tower Sargent, and Marc Stears (eds.), *The Oxford Handbook of Political Ideologies* (Oxford University Press, 2013) at 519.

69 Pettit, *On the People's Terms* at 64.

70 *Ibid.*

71 *Ibid.*

72 *See, e.g.*, Quentin Skinner, "Freedom as the Absence of Arbitrary Power" in Cécile Laborde and John Maynor (eds.), *Republicanism and Political Theory* (Oxford: Wiley, 2008) at 86; Christian Nadeau, "Republicanism" in Gerald Gaus and Fred D'Agostino (eds.), *The Routledge Companion to Social and Political Philosophy* (New York: Routledge, 2013) at 257.

suffer no concrete interference by their master, republicanism recognizes that the slave's domination grounds their unfreedom.[73]

Domination can exist in various forms.[74] Horizontal domination arises where individuals are subject to unilateral threats of interference by others.[75] Vertical domination takes place where individuals are vulnerable to a unilateral prospect of interference by the State.[76] And double domination occurs where individuals are exposed to horizontal and vertical forms of domination that can mutually reinforce one another.[77]

I.1.2 *Homelessness and Double Domination*

This book demonstrates how unhoused persons experience double domination because they lack private property rights and are uniquely vulnerable to laws that govern public property.[78] As discussed in later chapters, unhoused persons face horizontal domination because they are constantly subject to others' power of exclusion.[79] Private property rights confer a power to exclude others.[80] Individuals must obtain others' permission to access their private property.[81] Yet this permission is also a precondition for individuals to do any act in that space.[82] Since unhoused persons lack private property rights, they continually depend on others' permission to access private property and do any act in that space; they are consistently vulnerable to others' exclusionary power.[83]

This horizontal domination, in turn, accounts for why people experiencing homelessness face two additional forms of domination from laws that govern public property. First, others exert control over unhoused persons' opportunities to obey laws that regulate public property.[84] Like everyone else, people experiencing homelessness must alleviate their needs.[85] They must shelter themselves, sleep, urinate, and defecate, and they cannot abstain from these acts.[86] Although various laws

73 Pettit, *Republicanism* at 22–24, 31.

74 Philip Pettit, *Just Freedom: A Moral Compass for a Complex World* (New York: Norton and Co., 2014) at 5–7.

75 *Ibid.*

76 *Ibid.*

77 *See, e.g.*, Cécile Laborde, *Critical Republicanism: The Hijab Controversy and Political Philosophy* (Oxford University Press, 2008) at 151.

78 *See, e.g.*, Skolnik, "How and Why." Throughout this book, the term "lack of private property rights" refers to a lack of real (or immovable) property rights, such as a private right associated with a house, apartment, condominium, trailer, and more.

79 Essert, "Property and Homelessness" at 266.

80 Morris R. Cohen, "Property and Sovereignty" (1927–28) 13:1 *Cornell LQ* 8 at 12.

81 Waldron, "Homelessness and the Issue of Freedom" at 304.

82 Essert, "Property and Homelessness" at 275–76.

83 *Ibid.* at 266.

84 Skolnik, "How and Why" at 313–19.

85 Waldron, "Homelessness and the Issue of Freedom" at 321.

86 *Ibid.*

prohibit need-alleviating acts on public property, these acts are lawful on private property.[87] The problem is that unhoused persons must receive permission to access others' private property to alleviate their needs and obey these laws.[88] Yet rightsholders and those authorized to act on their behalf – shelter employees, café owners, and others – have the power to exclude unhoused persons from their private property.[89] This refusal limits unhoused persons' freedom to comply with laws that regulate public property. Rightsholders thus exert control over whether people experiencing homelessness can access private property, alleviate their needs behind closed doors, and ultimately, obey the law.[90]

Second, unlike others, unhoused persons must sacrifice their basic interests to obey laws that regulate public property; a concept referred to as "nonegalitarian trade-offs."[91] In some contexts, unhoused persons must stay in a homeless shelter to comply with laws that prohibit sleeping or camping on public property. Yet shelters may be dangerous, overcrowded, or unsanitary.[92] If unhoused persons wish to obey laws that regulate public property and avoid coercion, they must sacrifice their basic interests – such as liberty, security, privacy, and dignity – as the cost of compliance.[93]

Nonegalitarian trade-offs subject unhoused persons to both horizontal and vertical domination.[94] They face horizontal domination when they must sleep in a shelter to obey laws that prohibit sleeping in public or urban camping, yet risk harm, violence, or theft by others in these spaces.[95] They are vulnerable to unilateral threats of interference by others in such contexts. But unhoused persons also experience vertical domination if they refuse to sacrifice their interests to obey the law.[96] Unhoused persons are exposed to coercion by the State if they decline to stay in a shelter, alleviate their needs in public, and risk arrest or punishment because they violate laws that govern public property.[97]

87 Skolnik, "How and Why" at 307.
88 *Ibid.* at 313–19.
89 *See, e.g., ibid.* at 310.
90 *Ibid.* at 309.
91 *Ibid.* at 317.
92 Jana Jasinkski et al., "The Experience of Violence in the Lives of Homeless Women: A Research Report" (2005) at 24, National Institute of Justice, www.ojp.gov/pdffiles1/nij/grants/211976.pdf [perma.cc/N8JG-K53C]; Andrea Elliot and Rebecca Ruiz, "New York Is Removing Over 400 Children from 2 Homeless Shelters," NY Times (February 21, 2014), www.nytimes.com/2014/02/21/nyregion/new-york-is-removing-over-400-children-from-2-homeless-shelters.html [perma.cc/TXN6-YHGQ]; Winnie Hu, "Review of New York Shelter System Finds Hundreds of Violations," NY Times (March 12, 2015), www.nytimes.com/2015/03/13/nyregion/new-york-homeless-shelter-system-violations-report.html [perma.cc/ELD2-MP9H].
93 Skolnik, "How and Why" at 317.
94 *Ibid.* at 313–19.
95 *Ibid.*
96 *Ibid.*
97 *Ibid.*

I.1.3 *Nonegalitarian Coercion and Punitive Entrenchment*

Why do others control unhoused persons' opportunities to obey laws that govern public property? Furthermore, why do these laws result in nonegalitarian sacrifices for people experiencing homelessness? This book argues that two interrelated realities explain why laws that regulate public property subject unhoused persons to double domination: nonegalitarian coercion and punitive entrenchment. Each are examined in turn.

I.1.3.1 Nonegalitarian Coercion

Nonegalitarian coercion implies that the State has a greater capacity to regulate and police unhoused persons compared to people with access to housing.[98] People experiencing homelessness are exposed to nonegalitarian coercion because the State has more power to prohibit need-alleviating acts that occur on public property than on private property. The distinct roles of private and public property account for this disparity.

Consider private property first. A private property right grants the rightsholder the power to determine who uses a thing and how they use it.[99] By conferring a power to exclude others, private property rights secure a sphere of individual freedom and autonomy.[100] These rights protect fundamental interests, such as privacy, security, liberty, and personhood.[101] A private property right secures these interests because it creates a barrier between the individual and the public sphere.[102] Private and public law confer legal rights that protect these fundamental interests. The tort of trespass prohibits individuals from entering others' land or interfering with their property.[103] Constitutional criminal procedure, for its part, generally requires police officers to obtain a warrant to enter or search a person's home.[104]

Public property – meaning open-access spaces that are managed by the State – fulfils a different role.[105] Parks, squares, streets, beaches, and sidewalks are examples of public property.[106] Various communal activities characteristically occur on public property: sports and recreation, spontaneous interactions between strangers,

98 *Ibid.*

99 Jeremy Waldron, *The Right to Private Property* (Oxford University Press, 1988) at 38–39.

100 Thomas W. Merrill, "Property and the Right to Exclude" (1998) 77:4 *Neb L Rev* 730 at 734–35; Morris Cohen, "Property and Sovereignty" (1927) 13:1 *Cornell L Rev* 8 at 12; Benjamin Barros, "Property and Freedom" (2009) 4:1 *NYU JL & Lib* 36 at 47.

101 Benjamin Barros, "Home as a Legal Concept" (2006) 46:2 *Santa Clara L Rev* 255 at 259–75.

102 Laura Underkuffler, "On Property: An Essay" (1990) 100 *Yale LJ* 127 at 132–33.

103 Barros, "Home as a Legal Concept" at 260–69.

104 *Ibid.*

105 Robertson, "Common Property *Redux*" at 608; Crawford Brough MacPherson, "The Meaning of Property" in Crawford Brough MacPherson (ed.), *Property: Mainstream and Critical Positions* (University of Toronto Press, 1978) at 5 (defining public property).

106 Waldron, "Homelessness and the Issue of Freedom" at 298.

commerce, democratic protest, travel, and more.[107] The State can regulate public property to protect its unique role and value within society.[108] Courts have recognized that cities can proscribe acts such as public defecation, urban camping, and sleeping on sidewalks for various reasons.[109] Justifications for regulating public property include public sanitation, efficiency, solving coordination problems, and promoting the aesthetic value of public space.[110]

The unique role of public property – and the justifications for regulating its use – underpin the three reasons why the State has more power to prohibit need-alleviating acts that occur in public than in private.[111] These same reasons, in turn, account for the State's greater power to regulate unhoused persons compared to people with access to housing.

First, some justifications for regulating public property cannot apply to private property.[112] The State may prohibit urban camping to solve coordination problems, promote the efficiency of public ways, and increase the aesthetic value of public spaces.[113] But these same rationales cannot justify a law that regulates how individuals shelter themselves or sleep within their homes.[114] The State cannot prohibit need-alleviating acts within one's home based on justifications that apply to public property but cannot apply to private property.[115] This partly explains why the State has more power to regulate how people sleep, shelter themselves, and alleviate their needs in public than in private.

Second, certain justifications for regulating need-alleviating acts on public property disappear when individuals alleviate their needs in private.[116] The State may prohibit acts such as public urination or public defecation because it is unsanitary and raises public health concerns.[117] But these concerns vanish when individuals do these acts in the bathrooms within their homes.[118] For this reason, the State can more justifiably prohibit need-alleviating acts that occur on public property versus on private property.

Third, a home's physical and legal protections limit the State's capacity to regulate how people alleviate their needs in private.[119] Constitutional norms bar

107 Carol Rose, "The Comedy of the Commons: Custom, Commerce, and Inherently Public Property" (1986) 53:3 *U Chi L Rev* 711 at 777–79.
108 Skolnik, "How and Why" at 313–19.
109 *Ibid.*
110 *Ibid.*
111 Skolnik, "Freedom and Access to Housing" at 239.
112 *Ibid.*
113 *Roulette* v. *City of Seattle*, 97 F (3d) 300 at 303–04 (9th Circ 1996); Nicholas Blomley, "How to Turn a Beggar into a Bus Stop: Law, Traffic and the 'Function of the Place'" (2007) 44:9 *Urb Stud* 1697 at 1700–02.
114 Skolnik, "How and Why" at 313–19.
115 *Ibid.*
116 *Ibid.*
117 *Davison* v. *City of Tucson*, 924 F Supp 989 at 991 (D Ariz 1996) at 991; *Aitken* v. *City of Aberdeen*, 393 F Supp (3d) 1075 - (Dist. Court, WD Washington 2019).
118 Skolnik, "How and Why" at 313–19.
119 *Ibid.*

officers from entering homes without a warrant to police how individuals sleep, rest, and perform their bodily functions.[120] Furthermore, even if a compelling State interest could justify such laws, it would be outweighed by individuals' interests in privacy, liberty, and dignity within their homes.[121] Together, these three reasons show why the State has more power to regulate need-alleviating acts that occur on public property than on private property, and to regulate unhoused persons more generally.

Police officers also enjoy more discretionary power to enforce laws that govern public property against unhoused persons. Compared to people with access to housing, unhoused persons are more vulnerable to police surveillance because they spend more time on public property.[122] Furthermore, although the police can lawfully patrol public property where unhoused persons tend to congregate, constitutional norms prohibit them from patrolling private property more intrusively, which explains why those with access to housing enjoy greater protection against police coercion.[123] And constitutional law recognizes that individuals' privacy is less protected on public property than on private property – a reality that skews against those who lack access to housing.[124] People experiencing homelessness are thus more vulnerable to routine exercises of police discretion; a type of vertical domination discussed in later chapters.[125]

I.1.3.2 Punitive Entrenchment

Punitive entrenchment also subjects unhoused persons to double domination. The term "punitive entrenchment" implies that the State enmeshes people in homelessness through harsh punishments and collateral consequences associated with laws that govern public property.[126] These punishments and consequences include incarceration, expensive fines, additional fees, and surcharges – all of which decrease unhoused persons' opportunities to access housing.[127] Financial penalties reduce their capacity to pay for their rent, utilities, medication, and other basic needs.[128]

The consequences of unpaid criminal justice debts exacerbate punitive entrenchment.[129] These consequences include a criminal record, driver's license

120 Barros, "Home as a Legal Concept" at 260–69; William Stuntz, "Privacy's Problem and the Law of Criminal Procedure" (1995) 93:5 *Mich L Rev* 1016 at 1024.

121 Skolnik, "How and Why" at 313–19.

122 Marie-Eve Sylvestre, "Disorder and Public Spaces in Montreal: Repression (and Resistance) Through Law, Politics, and Police Discretion" (2010) 31:6 *Urb Geo* 803 at 819.

123 Barros, "Home as a Legal Concept" at 260–69.

124 *See, e.g.*, William Stuntz, "Distribution of Fourth Amendment Privacy" (1999) 67:5 *Geo Wash L Rev* 1265 at 1270–71.

125 Eric Miller, "Challenging Police Discretion" (2015) 58:2 *Howard LJ* 521 at 540.

126 Terry Skolnik, "Rethinking Homeless People's Punishments" (2019) 22:1 *New Crim L Rev* 73 at 81–84.

127 *Ibid.*

128 *Ibid.*

129 *Ibid.*

suspension, civil asset forfeiture, adverse credit rating, social support ineligibility, and more.[130] The collateral consequences of unpaid criminal justice debt hinder access to housing in various ways. Landlords may refuse to lease apartments to individuals with a criminal record.[131] Driver's license suspensions bar various types of employment, such as operating a taxi, working as a delivery person, or participating in the gig economy.[132] These suspensions limit individuals' capacities to drive to work, especially in cities that lack adequate public transportation.[133] Banks are reluctant to offer loans or credit cards to individuals with bad credit ratings.[134] And individuals who live in extreme poverty may be forced to pay their criminal justice debts at the expense of their rent.

Punitive entrenchment is problematic for other reasons. People who are enmeshed in homelessness will continue to suffer nonegalitarian coercion from laws that govern public property; they will continue to experience domination.[135] Punitive entrenchment also creates a vicious cycle. Individuals who become enmeshed in homelessness are more likely to alleviate their needs on public property, violate laws that govern public property, and be punished in ways that limit their access to housing.[136]

I.1.4 *Republicanism and Fiduciary Theories of Legal Authority*

Republicanism is not only a theory of freedom; it is also a theory of government. The republican theory of freedom shows how unhoused persons suffer domination from laws that govern public property. It also demonstrates why nonegalitarian coercion and punitive entrenchment produce that domination. The republican theory of government, on the other hand, is a political theory positing that self-rule is necessary for political liberty.[137] Republican theorists draw analogies between the individual as a physical body and the State as a body politic comprised of its community members.[138] In the same way as an individual enjoys liberty only when they are free from domination, the polity is free only when its will is not subject to external control.[139] A free state implies that the population can participate in government,

130 *Ibid.*
131 Sara Rankin, "Punishing Homelessness" (2019) 22:1 *New Crim L Rev* 99 at 102, note 16 in the text; Kevin Lapp, "American Criminal Record Exceptionalism" (2016) 14:1 *Ohio St J Crim L* 303 at 311.
132 Beth Colgan, "Reviving the Excessive Fines Clause" (2014) 102:2 *Cal L Rev* 277 at 292.
133 *Ibid.*
134 Beth Colgan, "The Excessive Fines Clause: Challenging the Modern Debtors' Prison" (2018) 65:1 *UCLA L Rev* 2 at 65.
135 The relationship between nonegalitarian coercion and punitive entrenchment is discussed in Chapters 5 and 6 in this book.
136 Skolnik, "Rethinking Homeless People's Punishments" at 76, 81–82.
137 Quentin Skinner, "The Republican Ideal of Political Liberty" in Gisela Bock, Quentin Skinner, and Maurizio Viroli (eds.), *Machiavelli and Republicanism* (Cambridge University Press, 2011) at 301–02.
138 *Ibid.*
139 *Ibid.*

shape its laws, and control its actions, such that the will of the State reflects the will of the people.[140] Individual freedom is a precondition for political freedom, and vice versa.[141]

Yet even self-ruling polities can suffer vertical domination in various forms. Power can corrupt public officials.[142] They may exercise their discretion abusively or arbitrarily.[143] They may act in their own self-interest rather than for the common good of the community.[144] They may attempt to circumvent legal and political safeguards that protect individuals against abusive State action. Or the State may not provide such safeguards in the first place. There are other risks. A tyranny of the majority can occur within democracies, such that laws and policies which stem from majoritarian will disregard the rights and interests of the political minority. Majoritarian laws and policies may also authorize horizontal domination or fail to protect individuals against it. Even when individuals can vote and participate in public office, the State may subject them to these other forms of vertical domination.

One of republicanism's tenets is that the State and individuals are in a fiduciary relationship with one another – a bond that gives rise to the State's overarching fiduciary duty to counteract domination.[145] A fiduciary relationship involves two parties: the trustee (or fiduciary) and the beneficiary.[146] In these relationships, the trustee is unilaterally empowered to act on the beneficiary's behalf.[147] Trustees tend to have expertise, powers, skills, or capacities that beneficiaries lack.[148] Beneficiaries, for their part, are dependent upon trustees and their above-mentioned qualities.[149]

In fiduciary relationships, the beneficiary is unilaterally vulnerable to the trustee's power.[150] The trustee can exploit the beneficiary for private gain or for other opportunistic reasons. Beneficiaries are thus vulnerable to domination.[151] To counteract this domination, the law imposes a duty of loyalty on the fiduciary, who must act in the beneficiary's best interests.[152]

140 *See, e.g.*, Cécile Laborde and Miriam Ronzoni, "What Is a Free State? Republican Internationalism and Globalisation" (2016) 64:2 *Pol Stud* 279 at 288.

141 *Ibid.* at 287; Skinner, "The Republican Ideal of Political Liberty" at 301–02.

142 Mortimer Sellers, *The Sacred Fire of Liberty: Republicanism, Liberty & the Law* (London: Palgrave MacMillan, 1998) at 45, 48–50, 68.

143 Pettit, *On the People's Terms* at 176.

144 *Ibid.*

145 Evan Criddle, "Liberty in Loyalty: A Republican Theory of Fiduciary Law" (2017) 95:5 *Texas L Rev* 993 at 995–97.

146 Elizabeth Scott and Robert Scott, "Parents as Fiduciaries" (1995) 81:8 *Va L Rev* 2401 at 2419–24 (providing an overview of fiduciary relationships).

147 *Ibid.* at 2402.

148 Larry Ribstein, "Fencing Fiduciary Duties" (2011) 91:3 *BU L Rev* 899 at 907.

149 Matthew Bodie, "Employment as Fiduciary Relationship" (2017) 105:4 *Geo LJ* 819 at 858.

150 Scott and Scott, "Parents as Fiduciaries" at 2420, 2423; Criddle, "Liberty in Loyalty" at 999–1000.

151 Evan Fox-Decent and Evan Criddle, "The Fiduciary Constitution of Human Rights" (2009) 15 *Leg Theory* 301 at 311.

152 Evan Criddle, "Fiduciary Administration: Rethinking Popular Representation in Agency Rulemaking" (2009) 88:3 *Texas L Rev* 441 at 446–48.

Although some fiduciary relationships form through express or implied agreement, consent is not necessary to form them.[153] A fiduciary relationship can form given the beneficiary's unilateral vulnerability to the fiduciary's power.[154] For instance, doctors have a fiduciary duty to act in an unconscious patient's best interests, even though the patient could not validly consent to treatment given their incapacity.[155]

Fiduciary relationships also exist in various public law contexts. The Supreme Court of Canada has affirmed that the State is in a fiduciary relationship with Indigenous peoples.[156] The relationship arises *sui generis* due to colonialism and its legacy.[157] The State has a fiduciary duty to consult with Indigenous peoples and accommodate them in matters that affect their interests.[158] US public trust doctrine recognizes that the State holds certain natural resources – such as navigable waters, shorelines, and public lands – in trust for the public.[159] The doctrine prohibits the alienation and privatization of these forms of common property.[160] Canadian and US law acknowledge that the State holds public property in trust for the population – a duty that dates to the Roman republic.[161] As part of its duty, the State must maintain the shared value of spaces such as parks, streets, and squares for the general public.

Two characteristics underpin the public law fiduciary relationships described above – characteristics that also underpin the State's fiduciary duties related to homelessness and public property. First, the fiduciary relationship between the State and individuals is formed without consent.[162] Second, the State's fiduciary relationship with the polity exists to counteract both vertical and horizontal domination.[163] The State's fiduciary relationship with Indigenous persons in Canada aims to neutralize vertical domination, which flows from the State's unilateral discretionary control over their interests.[164] The public trust doctrine prevents horizontal domination. It bars individuals from amassing common property – such as waterbeds and shorelines – that would place others who wish to use that property

153 Evan Fox-Decent, *Sovereignty's Promise* (Oxford University Press, 2011) at 56, 67.

154 *Ibid.* at 89, 103.

155 *Ibid.* at 56, 67, 90, 92.

156 *Ibid.* at 59; *Guerin* v. *The Queen* [1984] 2 SCR 335 at 376 (per Dickson J); *R* v. *Sparrow* [1990] 1 SCR 1075 at 1108.

157 *Mitchell* v. *MNR*, 2001 SCC 33 at para. 9.

158 *Haida Nation* v. *British Columbia (Minister of Forests)* 2004 SCC 73 at paras. 16–20.

159 Richard Lazarus, "Changing Conceptions of Property and Sovereignty in Natural Resources: Questioning the Public Trust Doctrine" (1986) 71:3 *Iowa L Rev* 631 at 633–41.

160 Joseph Sax, "Liberating the Public Trust Doctrine from its Historical Shackles" (1980) 14:2 *UC Davis L Rev* 185 at 185–86.

161 *Hague* v. *Committee for Industrial Organization*, 307 US 496 (1939) at 515 (in the United States); *Committee for the Commonwealth of Canada* v. *Canada* [1991] 1 SCR 139 at 174 (in Canada).

162 Fox-Decent, *Sovereignty's Promise* at 56, 67.

163 *Ibid.* at 26, 38; Criddle, "Liberty in Loyalty" at 999–1000, 1006; Fox-Decent and Criddle, "The Fiduciary Constitution of Human Rights" at 310–11.

164 See, e.g., *Williams Lake Indian Band* v. *Canada (Aboriginal Affairs and Northern Development)*, 2018 SCC 4 at para. 44; *Haida Nation* v. *British Columbia (Minister of Forests)*, 2004 SCC 73 at para. 18.

in a state of dependency vis-à-vis the rightsholder.[165] The State's fiduciary guardianship over public property in Canada and the United States also neutralizes horizontal domination. The State controls and regulates public property so that people can freely travel and do things outside of their homes without being subject to others' power of exclusion.[166]

These three public law fiduciary duties discussed above flow from the fiduciary relationship between the State and individuals that is central to republicanism.[167] As part of that relationship, the State has an overarching fiduciary duty to counteract horizontal and vertical forms of domination, the fulfilment of which promotes political equality.[168]

The State's fiduciary relationship with the population is justified on two principal grounds. First, the Government and the people are in a fiduciary relationship because individuals are unilaterally vulnerable to State power.[169] Public officials can exercise public powers that individuals lack, such as powers of taxation, legislation, adjudication, criminalization, and punishment.[170] Individuals' vulnerability to these public powers – and their incapacity to exercise such powers reciprocally – renders them susceptible to domination by the State.[171] Furthermore, the exercise of such public powers can result in laws, policies, and decisions that produce or authorize horizontal domination.[172] These forms of vulnerability result in a fiduciary relationship between the Government and the people.[173] And this relationship gives rise to the State's overarching duty to counteract domination and exercise its public power in the people's best interests.[174]

Second, the fiduciary relationship between the Government and the people is justified by the fact that the State derives its power from individuals.[175] Individuals delegate power to public institutions and their officials through the democratic process.[176] Given this delegation of power, public officials must act in the people's best interests and counteract domination.[177] This account also explains why Indigenous persons are subject to a unique form of vertical domination, notably,

165 David Takacs, "The Public Trust Doctrine, Environmental Human Rights, and the Future of Private Property" (2008) 16:3 *NYU Env't LJ* 711 at 714–16.
166 Chapter 5 of this book.
167 Fox-Decent and Criddle, "The Fiduciary Constitution of Human Rights" at 311.
168 Criddle, "Liberty in Loyalty" at 999–1000, 1006; Fox-Decent, *Sovereignty's Promise* at 26, 38; Fox-Decent and Criddle, "The Fiduciary Constitution of Human Rights" at 310–11.
169 Fox-Decent, *Sovereignty's Promise* at 89, 103.
170 *Ibid.* at 29.
171 *Ibid.*
172 Pettit, *Just Freedom* at 5–7.
173 Fox-Decent, *Sovereignty's Promise* at 89, 103.
174 *Ibid.*
175 Theodore Rave, "Politicians as Fiduciaries" (2013) 126:3 *Harv L Rev* 671 at 708–11.
176 Criddle, "Liberty in Loyalty" at 1002; Pettit, *Republicanism* at 8.
177 Criddle, "Liberty in Loyalty" at 1002.

due to colonialism and the State depriving Indigenous peoples of their full power of self-government.

These three contexts in public law – the duty to consult and accommodate Indigenous peoples, the US public trust doctrine, and the State's guardianship of public property – flow from the State's fiduciary relationship with the people. Each of these contexts imposes distinct obligations on the State. But these are not the only duties in public law that flow from the State's fiduciary relationship with individuals. As discussed below, the State also has specific fiduciary obligations related to homelessness and public property.

I.1.5 *The State's Fiduciary Duties Related to Homelessness and Public Property*

The State's fiduciary relationship with the population – and its overarching fiduciary duty to counteract domination – gives rise to three interrelated fiduciary duties related to homelessness and public property. First, the State must end homelessness and ensure that individuals enjoy access to housing. Second, the State has a fiduciary duty to safeguard public property's shared value and secure liberty in the public sphere. Third, the State must legitimize coercion and punishment associated with laws that regulate public property. Such laws treat unhoused persons with greater concern and respect when the State increasingly fulfils its three fiduciary duties associated with homelessness and public property. These fiduciary duties stem from the State's failure to accommodate unhoused persons within two systems of mutual coercion that the State creates to secure liberty: the private property system and laws that govern public property. The State's fiduciary duties aim to counteract the domination that unhoused persons experience because they are not accommodated within these systems of mutual coercion.

The State's three fiduciary duties related to homelessness and public property can be described as follows. First, the State has a fiduciary duty to end homelessness and treat unhoused persons with equal respect, such that individuals enjoy access to housing. The justification for this duty can be summarized as follows. The State creates a system of private property rights to secure freedom between individuals and fulfil its overarching fiduciary duty to counteract domination.[178] But the State fails to accommodate unhoused persons within a market-based private property system, which subjects them to domination.[179] Without private property rights, unhoused persons are uniquely vulnerable to others' power of exclusion and to laws that govern public property.[180] The State's fiduciary duty to end homelessness and ensure access to housing aims to counteract these forms of domination.[181] And this first fiduciary duty provides a novel basis for a right to housing.

178 Essert, "Property and Homelessness" at 275–76.
179 *Ibid.*
180 Skolnik, "How and Why" at 313–19.
181 *See, e.g.*, Andy Yu, "Equity and Homelessness" (2020) 33:1 *Can JL & Jur* 245 at 250–51.

Second, the State has a fiduciary duty to protect public property's shared value and secure freedom in the public sphere, meaning outside of one's home. This duty is justified by the following considerations. The State provides a system of public property so that individuals can travel and do things outside of their homes without being subject to others' power of exclusion.[182]

The State regulates public property so that individuals can use public space on equal terms and respect each other's liberty in open-access spaces.[183] In the same way as the State establishes a private property system to secure freedom in the private sphere, it provides a public property system to secure freedom in the public sphere.[184] The State must fulfil this second fiduciary duty to counteract domination outside of one's home. However, the State fails to accommodate unhoused persons within its system of laws that govern public property, which results in domination.[185]

Third, the State has a fiduciary duty to legitimize coercion and punishment associated with laws that govern public property. The State must fulfil this third fiduciary duty to ensure that it regulates public property in a manner that does not constitute vertical domination and does not entrench individuals in homelessness. The State increasingly fulfils this duty when coercion and punishment associated with laws that govern public property are increasingly legitimate.

Coercion is more legitimate when individuals enjoy the undominated choice to obey these laws.[186] Freedom to comply with the law helps ensure that coercion respects human agency and that the duty to obey the law is imposed more fairly.[187] Punishment, for its part, is more legitimate when it is consistent with its two principal justifications: retributivism and consequentialism.[188] Beyond the freedom to obey the law, the State must satisfy two other requirements to legitimize the punishment associated with laws that govern public property: proportionality and instrumental rationality (the latter means that punishment is a logical means to achieve its end).[189] Together, these two constraints ensure that punishment neither entrenches individuals in homelessness nor subjects individuals to vertical domination.[190]

182 Arthur Ripstein, *Force and Freedom* (Cambridge: Harvard University Press, 2009) at 23–25, 238–39, 255–56.

183 Skolnik, "How and Why" at 313–19.

184 Terry Skolnik, "Homeless Encampments: A Philosophical Justification" (2023) 36 *JL & Soc Pol'y* 97 at 110.

185 *Ibid.*

186 Terry Skolnik, "Homelessness and the Impossibility to Obey the Law" (2016) 43 *Fordham Urb LJ* 741 at 745.

187 H. L. A. Hart and John Gardner, *Punishment and Responsibility* (Oxford University Press, 2008) at 22–23; George Klosko, *Political Obligations* (Oxford University Press, 2005) at 4–6, 115.

188 David Dolinko, "Punishment" in John Deigh and David Dolinko (eds.), *The Oxford Handbook on the Philosophy of the Criminal Law* (Oxford University Press, 2011) at 405–07.

189 Richard Frase, "Excessive Prison Sentences, Punishment Goals, and the Eighth Amendment: Proportionality Relative to What" (2005) 89:3 *Minn L Rev* 571 at 590; Colton Fehr, "General Deterrence and Instrumental Rationality" (2019) 57:1 *Alta L Rev* 53 at 61 (describing instrumental rationality).

190 Skolnik, "Rethinking Homeless People's Punishments" at 81–84.

The concluding parts of this book highlight the connection between the State's fulfilment of its three fiduciary duties. By ending homelessness and treating unhoused persons with equal respect, the State can better fulfil its other fiduciary duties. When individuals have access to housing, the State can regulate public property more effectively and protect its shared value because individuals have an alternative to alleviating their needs on public property. Furthermore, because individuals have such an alternative, coercion and punishment associated with laws that govern public property are more legitimate. The State better fulfils its fiduciary duty to end homelessness and safeguard public property's value when its punishments respect proportionality and instrumental rationality requirements, and ultimately, do not entrench individuals in homelessness. The State abdicates its overarching fiduciary duty to counteract domination when it does not fulfil one (or many) of these specific fiduciary duties related to homelessness and public property.

This book's final chapter provides a framework for how the State can better fulfil these fiduciary obligations. Building on existing empirical research, the final chapter offers a set of concrete proposals for how the State can attempt to end homelessness and treat unhoused persons with equal respect, maintain public property's shared value, and legitimize laws that govern public property.

I.2 SUMMARY OF CHAPTERS

The structure of this book is as follows. Chapter 1 sets out the historical and contemporary regulation of public property. It details the rise and fall of vagrancy statutes, and the increased use of municipal ordinances to regulate homelessness in Canadian and US cities. It provides an overview of the types of ordinances that govern individuals' need-alleviating acts, such as laws that proscribe urban camping, sleeping on public property, public urination, and more. This first chapter concludes with an overview of homelessness, including its risk factors, prevalence, and consequences, as well as the overrepresentation of individuals from certain communities within the unhoused population.

Chapter 2 explores the main constitutional challenges to laws that govern public property in Canada and the United States. These laws have been attacked on the grounds that they: (1) are unconstitutionally vague or overbroad, (2) violate the right to equal protection, (3) breach the fundamental right to travel, and (4) impose cruel and unusual punishments. This chapter analyzes the successes and failures of these claims. It also explores the reasons why courts have rejected a positive right to housing.

Chapter 3 examines the relationship between property and two conceptions of liberty: positive and negative. It canvasses the existing scholarship on how housing protects positive freedom (meaning liberty as self-actualization) and negative freedom (meaning liberty as noninterference). It shows how laws that govern public property undermine both forms of freedom.

Chapter 4 introduces the republican theory of liberty. It demonstrates why republicanism offers new insight into both homelessness and the regulation of public property in ways that positive and negative theories of freedom do not. It sets out why laws that govern public property subject unhoused persons to two forms of domination. Namely, others exert control over unhoused persons' opportunities to obey these laws, and unhoused persons must make nonegalitarian sacrifices to abide by them. This fourth chapter elucidates why unhoused persons lack liberty in all its forms: positive, negative, and republican. Its concluding parts highlight why unhoused persons' unfreedom undermines their political equality.

Chapter 5 argues that unhoused persons are vulnerable to nonegalitarian coercion, meaning that the State has greater power to regulate and police unhoused persons compared to people with access to housing. Its opening parts distinguish between the roles of private and public property. It then demonstrates why the State has more power to regulate and police need-alleviating conduct that occurs on public property than on private property. It explains how laws that govern public property operate differently for people with and without access to housing. Ultimately, this chapter shows why unhoused persons face domination that people with access to housing do not.

Chapter 6 discusses punitive entrenchment. It describes how fines, fees, surcharges, and incarceration enmesh individuals in the condition of homelessness, where they suffer nonegalitarian coercion. It explains how the consequences of criminal justice debt – such as criminal records and driver's license suspensions – worsen punitive entrenchment. It explores why punitive entrenchment is inconsistent with the two principal justifications for punishment: retributivism and consequentialism.

Chapter 7 discusses the State's overarching fiduciary duty to counteract domination, and its three specific fiduciary duties related to homelessness and public property. It begins by introducing the republican theory of government and shows why the State is in a fiduciary relationship with the population. It explains why the State has an overarching fiduciary obligation to secure liberty in the private and public spheres. It explores why the State creates a system of private property rights and regulates public property to achieve that end. Yet unhoused persons face domination because the State does not accommodate them within these systems of mutual coercion. This chapter demonstrates why the State has three fiduciary duties related to homelessness and public property which aim to counteract that domination. First, the State must end homelessness and treat unhoused persons with equal respect, which provides a novel justification for the right to housing. Second, the State must maintain public property's shared value and secure liberty in the public sphere. Third, the State must legitimize laws that govern public property.

Chapter 8 defends the State's three fiduciary duties related to homelessness and public property. It demonstrates why other ameliorative and coercive mechanisms that address homelessness either fail to reduce domination or exacerbate it.

These mechanisms include increased shelter spaces, zoning proposals, concentration strategies, and dispersal tactics. It also shows why encampments cannot constitute a complete justification, meaning that unhoused persons cannot permanently and unconditionally appropriate public property when they lack access to housing. However, in certain circumstances, encampments can be temporarily and partially justifiable where individuals lack access to housing and to other adequate alternatives and when the benefits of encampments outweigh their burdens. The fact that unhoused persons cannot justifiably establish permanent encampments to eliminate domination underpins a State duty to ensure access to housing.

Chapter 9 concludes this book. It offers concrete proposals for how the State may better fulfil its three fiduciary duties. It demonstrates how the State's duty to end homelessness is comprised of three elements: addressing the risk factors associated with homelessness, ensuring access to housing, and providing inclusive emergency and interim resources for individuals who become unhoused. It provides an overview of mechanisms that may help reduce homelessness and treat individuals with equal respect. Chapter 9 explores various mechanisms that may help prevent and rectify punitive entrenchment, such as avoiding incarceration, implementing graduated economic sanctions (or day fines), embracing collateral consequence minimalism, and ensuring criminal justice debt absolution.

Together, these chapters illuminate the important relationship between homelessness, liberty, and property. Republicanism is the thread that ties these different concepts together. It is the foundation of this book and its concrete proposals that aim to counteract domination, and ultimately, treat unhoused persons with greater concern and respect.

1

Homelessness, Vagrancy Laws, and Municipal Ordinances

This chapter begins with an overview of homelessness in the United States and in Canada. It discusses certain definitions of homelessness in both countries. It provides statistics regarding homelessness in these jurisdictions, including fluctuations in these unhoused populations over time. It also explains how certain individuals and groups are overrepresented in the unhoused population and explores the risk factors associated with homelessness.

The later parts of this chapter discuss the emergence and decline of vagrancy law, and the rise to prominence of municipal ordinances (or bylaws) that regulate public property in the United States and in Canada. These ordinances govern basic human acts that are done on public property, such as sleeping, sheltering oneself, sitting, urinating, and defecating. Its concluding parts offer an overview of studies that demonstrate how laws that govern public property impact unhoused persons disparately.

1.1 HOMELESSNESS IN CANADA AND THE UNITED STATES

1.1.1 *Estimates of the Number of Unhoused Persons in the United States and Canada*

The definition of homelessness varies between jurisdictions. The US Department of Housing and Urban Development (HUD) defines a person experiencing homelessness (or unhoused person, the terms are used interchangeably) as "a person who lacks a fixed, regular, and adequate nighttime residence."[1] The definition encompasses unsheltered persons who live in places that are not intended for human habitation (for instance, who sleep on the street or in a tent in a public park) as well as individuals who stay in shelters, transitional housing, or safe havens (meaning facilities that provide temporary services to individuals with severe mental illness).[2]

[1] US Department of Housing and Urban Development (HUD), *The 2022 Annual Homeless Assessment Report (AHAR) to Congress*, Part 1 (Washington: HUD, December 2022) at 4.

[2] *Ibid.* at 5.

According to the 2022 Homeless Point in Time count compiled by the HUD, roughly 582,500 people experienced homelessness on a single night in the United States during that year.[3] The HUD notes that the unhoused population increased by less than 1 percent between 2020 and 2022.[4] The figure is, however, a significant decrease from the 2006 statistics, where it was estimated that roughly 759,100 people experienced homelessness on a given night in the United States in January 2006.[5]

Certain US states have relatively high unhoused populations.[6] In 2022, the state of California's unhoused population was approximately 171,521 persons (or 30 percent of the total number of unhoused persons in the United States), while the state of New York was estimated to have an unhoused population of roughly 74,178 persons (or 13 percent of the total number of unhoused persons in the United States).[7] Furthermore, approximately half of unsheltered persons in the United States in 2022 were in the state of California.[8] In 2022, roughly 67 percent of unhoused persons in California were unsheltered, whereas over 95 percent of unhoused persons in Vermont, Maine, and New York were sheltered.[9] Other states have high proportions of unsheltered people experiencing homelessness. In 2022, unsheltered persons constituted between 50 and 65 percent of the unhoused population in Mississippi, Hawaii, Oregon, Arizona, Tennessee, Georgia, and Washington.[10]

The Government of Canada, for its part, employs the following definition of homelessness that is adapted from the Canadian Observatory on Homelessness (COH):

> Homelessness is the situation of an individual or family who does not have a permanent address or residence; the living situation of an individual or family who does not have stable, permanent, appropriate housing, or the immediate prospect, means and ability of acquiring it. It is often the result of what are known as systemic or societal barriers, including a lack of affordable and appropriate housing, the individual/household's financial, mental, cognitive, behavioural or physical challenges, and/or racism and discrimination.[11]

3 *Ibid.* at 2.

4 *Ibid.*

5 US Department of Housing and Urban Development (HUD), *The Second Annual Homeless Assessment Report to Congress* (Washington: HUD, March 2008) at ii.

6 HUD, *The 2022 Annual Homeless Assessment Report (AHAR) to Congress* at 16.

7 *Ibid.*

8 *Ibid.*

9 *Ibid.*

10 *Ibid.*

11 Government of Canada, "Reaching Home: Canada's Homelessness Strategy Directives" (Infrastructure Canada, 2022), www.infrastructure.gc.ca/homelessness-sans-abri/directives-eng.html#fn1. As the Government of Canada notes in that publication, the definition was "adapted from the Canadian Definition of Homelessness developed by the Canadian Observatory of Homelessness." *See* Canadian Observatory on Homelessness, "Canadian Definition of Homelessness" (2012), http://homelesshub.ca/sites/default/files/COHhomelessdefinition.pdf.

The most recent national statistics compiled by the COH estimate that approximately 235,000 people experienced homelessness in Canada in 2016.[12] Furthermore, the COH estimates that roughly 35,000 individuals experienced homelessness on a given night during that year.[13] According to the 2018 Canadian Housing Survey (CHS), "3% of Canadians responsible for housing decisions within their household reported experiencing unsheltered homelessness at some point in their lives."[14]

The number of unhoused persons in the United States and Canada may be significantly higher due to the reality of hidden homelessness.[15] The term "hidden homelessness" refers to unhoused persons who may not be identified in official Point-In-Time counts because they are staying with friends or family, in their cars, in hospitals, or in other provisional accommodation.[16]

Homelessness tends to be classified into three principal typologies: transitional, episodic, and chronic.[17] Transitional (or temporary) homelessness refers to one-off situations where individuals are unhoused for a short period of time as they transition to more stable forms of housing.[18] Episodic homelessness connotes that individuals are periodically unhoused and experience repeated short-term cycles of homelessness.[19] Chronic homelessness refers to individuals who experience long-term homelessness that lasts months or years.[20] Research demonstrates that most unhoused persons experience transitory or periodic homelessness rather than chronic homelessness.[21]

12 Stephen Gaetz, Erin Dej, Tim Richter et al., *The State of Homelessness in Canada 2016* (Toronto: Canadian Observatory on Homelessness Press, 2016) at 5.

13 *Ibid.*

14 Sharanjit Uppal, *A Portrait of Canadians Who Have Been Homeless* (Ottawa: Statistics Canada, 2022) at 3, www150.statcan.gc.ca/n1/en/pub/75-006-x/2022001/article/00002-eng.pdf?st=XaxOj47U.

15 Samantha Rodrigue, *Hidden Homelessness in Canada* (Ottawa: Statistics Canada, 2016) at 2 (describing hidden homelessness).

16 *See, e.g.*, Josie Watson, Jamie Crawley, and Deborah Kane, "Social Exclusion, Health and Hidden Homelessness" (2016) 139 *Pub Health* 96 at 97 (defining hidden homelessness as individuals who stay with friends or family); Havi Echenberg and Laura Munn-Rivard, *Defining and Enumerating Homelessness in Canada* (Ottawa: Parliamentary Information and Research Service, 2020) at i, 2 (defining hidden homelessness as individuals without a home of their own who live in car, with family or friends, or in a long-term institution); Jamie Crawley, Deborah Kane, L. Atkinson-Plato et al., "Needs of the Hidden Homeless Are No Longer Hidden: A Pilot Study" (2013) 127 *Pub Health* 674 at 674–75.

17 *See, e.g.*, Randall Kuhn and Dennis Culhane, "Applying Cluster Analysis to Test a Typology of Homelessness by Pattern of Shelter Utilization: Results from the Analysis of Administrative Data" (1998) 26:2 *Am J Cmty Psych* 207 at 210–12; Barrett Lee, Kimberly Tyler, and James Wright, "The New Homelessness Revisited" (2010) 36 *Ann Rev Socio* 501 at 503.

18 Lee, Tyler, and Wright, "The New Homelessness Revisited" at 503.

19 *Ibid.*

20 *Ibid.*

21 C. James Frankish, Stephen Hwang, and Darryl Quantz, "Homelessness and Health in Canada: Research Lessons and Priorities" (2005) 96 *Can J Pub Health* S23 at S24; Lee, Tyler, and Wright, "The New Homelessness Revisited" at 503.

1.1.2 *The Overrepresentation of Certain Groups in the Unhoused Population*

Certain individuals and groups are more likely to experience homelessness compared to the general population. Indigenous persons are overrepresented in the Canadian unhoused population,[22] and Native Americans are overrepresented in the US unhoused population.[23] For instance, Indigenous persons represented 2.5 percent of the city of Toronto's population in 2021 but comprised 15 percent of the total number of unhoused persons in the city.[24] Similarly, Indigenous persons represented approximately 0.6 percent of Montreal's population in 2018 yet comprised roughly 16 percent of the total number of unhoused persons.[25]

Racialized persons – meaning individuals who are nonwhite and non-Indigenous – are also overrepresented in the US and Canadian unhoused population.[26] Racialized persons comprised roughly 23 percent of Canada's population in 2016 yet represented 28.2 percent of individuals who experienced homelessness within the country.[27] In the city of Toronto in 2021, nearly 60 percent of people experiencing homelessness identified as racialized persons, 31 percent of whom identified as Black persons.[28] In the United States in 2022, Black persons represented 12 percent of the country's population yet made up 37 percent of the total number of unhoused persons.[29]

Individuals who identify as members of the lesbian, gay, bisexual, transgender, and queer (LGBTQ) community are more likely to experience homelessness compared to individuals who do not.[30] Transgender persons face especially high rates of homelessness. Some studies estimate that transgender adults constituted roughly 0.39 percent of the US population in 2016.[31] Yet the 2015 US Transgender Survey indicates that 30 percent of transgender persons reported that they experienced

[22] Caryl Patrick, *Aboriginal Homelessness in Canada: A Literature Review* (Toronto: Canadian Homelessness Research Network Press, 2014) at 19.

[23] Wilder Research, *Homelessness in Minnesota: Findings from the 2015 Minnesota Homeless Study* (Saint Paul: Wilder Research, November 2016) at 16.

[24] City of Toronto, *Street Needs Assessment Report 2021* (Toronto: City of Toronto, 2021) at 6, www.toronto.ca/legdocs/mmis/2021/ec/bgrd/backgroundfile-171729.pdf.

[25] Eric Latimer and François Bordeleau, *Dénombrement des personnes en situation d'itinérance sur l'île de Montréal le 24 avril 2018* (Montreal, March 2019) at ix, 19–21.

[26] Canadian Observatory on Homelessness (COH), "Racialized Communities" (2021), www.homeleshub.ca/about-homelessness/population-specific/racialized-communities; HUD, *The 2022 Annual Homeless Assessment Report (AHAR)* at 1.

[27] COH, "Racialized Communities"; Kaitlin Schwan, *Too Little, Too Late: Reimagining Our Response to Youth Homelessness in Canada* (Toronto: Canadian Observatory on Homelessness, 2016).

[28] City of Toronto, *Street Needs Assessment Report 2021* at 6.

[29] HUD, *The 2022 Annual Homeless Assessment Report (AHAR)* at 2.

[30] *See, e.g.*, Emmett Henderson, Jennifer Jabson, Jennifer Russomanno et al., "Housing and Food Stress among Transgender Adults in the United States" (2019) 38 *Ann Epidemiol* 42 at 42; Uppal, "A Portrait of Canadians who Have Been Homeless" at 3; Institute of Medicine, *The Health of Lesbian, Gay, Bisexual, and Transgender People: Building a Foundation for Better Understanding* (Washington: National Academies Press, 2011) at 161–62.

[31] Esther Meerwijk and Jae Sevelius, "Transgender Population Size in the United States: A Meta-Regression of Population-Based Probability Samples" (2017) 107:2 *Am J Pub Health* e1 at e5.

homelessness at some point of their lives, while 12 percent experienced homelessness in the year prior to the survey.[32]

Survivors of domestic violence (DV) are also overrepresented in the unhoused population.[33] Domestic violence is an important cause of homelessness for women.[34] Dessie Lee Clark, Leila Wood, and Cris Sullivan note that "One in four homeless women have cited DV as being a major contributor to their current homelessness" and "DV survivors are four times more likely than other women to experience housing instability."[35] Unhoused women are disproportionately subject to physical and sexual violence compared to women with access to housing.[36] Moreover, some studies demonstrate that women who experience homelessness are more likely to be victims of violence compared to unhoused men.[37]

Veterans, for their part, are also overrepresented in the unhoused population.[38] The HUD reports that in 2022, roughly 20 per 10,000 veterans experienced homelessness compared to 18 per 10,000 civilians.[39] The number of unhoused veterans in the United States has continued to decline steadily since 2010.[40] While approximately 74,087

32 Sandy James, Jody Herman, Susan Rankin et al., *The Report of the 2015 U.S. Transgender Survey* (Washington: National Center for Transgender Equality, 2015) at 5.

33 HUD, *2022 Continuum of Care Homeless Assistance Programs Homeless Populations and Subpopulations* (Washington: HUD, 2022) at 2.

34 *See, e.g.*, Alexa Yakubovich and Krys Maki, "Preventing Gender-Based Homelessness in Canada During the COVID-19 Pandemic and Beyond: The Need to Account for Violence Against Women" (2022) 28:10 *Violence Against Women* 2587 at 2588; Emo Zhao, "The Key Factors Contributing to the Persistence of Homelessness" (2023) 30:1 *Int'l J Sustainable Dev & World Ecology* 1 at 2; Kaitlin Schwan, Alicia Versteegh, Melissa Perri et al., *The State of Women's Housing Need & Homelessness in Canada: A Literature Review* (Toronto: Canadian Observatory on Homelessness Press, 2020) at 121.

35 Dessie Lee Clark, Leila Wood, and Cris Sullivan, "Examining the Needs and Experiences of Domestic Violence Survivors in Transitional Housing" (2019) 34 *J Fam Violence* 275 at 275, citing Joane Pavao, Jennifer Alvarez, Nikki Baumrind, et al., "Intimate Partner Violence and Housing Instability" (2007) 32:2 *Am J Preventive Med* 143 at 145 and Wilder Research, *Overview of Homelessness in Minnesota 2006: Key Facts from the Statewide Survey* (St. Paul: Wilder Research, 2007) at 2 (noting that roughly 32 percent of women reported domestic violence as a contributing factor to homelessness).

36 *See, e.g.*, Joshua Ellsworth, "Street Crime Victimization among Homeless Adults: A Review of the Literature" (2019) 14:1 *Victims Offenders* 96 at 112.

37 Ann Elizabeth Montgomery, Dorota Szymkowiak, and Dennis Culhane, "Gender Differences in Factors Associated with Unsheltered Status and Increased Risk of Premature Mortality among Individuals Experiencing Homelessness" (2017) 27:3 *Women's Health Issues* 256 at 261–62; Sara Rodriguez-Moreno, José J. Vázquez, Pablo Roca et al., "Differences in Stressful Life Events between Men and Women Experiencing Homelessness" (2021) 49 *J Cmty Psych* 375 at 383.

38 Jack Tsai and Robert Rosenheck, "Risk Factors for Homelessness among US Veterans" (2015) 37:1 *Epidemiologic Rev* 177 at 177; Carol Canton, Carol Wilkins, Jacquelyn Anderson et al., "People Who Experience Long-Term Homelessness: Characteristics and Interventions" in Deborah Dennis, Gretchen Locke, and Jill Khadduri (eds.), *Toward Understanding Homelessness: The 2007 Symposium on Homelessness Research* (Washington, U.S. Department of Health and Human Services and U.S. Department of Housing and Urban Development, 2007) at 4–4 (describing overrepresentation of veterans amongst individuals experiencing homelessness).

39 HUD, *The 2022 Annual Homeless Assessment Report (AHAR)* at 60.

40 *Ibid.*

veterans experienced homelessness in 2010, roughly 33,129 veterans were unhoused in 2022.[41]

Certain youth populations are overrepresented in the total number of unhoused persons. In Canada, Indigenous youth are more likely to experience homelessness than non-Indigenous youth.[42] In the United States, Black youth experience higher rates of homelessness compared to white persons and compared to members of other racialized communities.[43] Young persons who self-identify as members of the LGBTQ community are also more likely to experience homelessness than the general youth population.[44] As John Ecker, Tim Aubry, and John Sylvestre note, studies suggest that between 15–30 percent of unhoused youth identify as members of the LGBTQ community.[45]

1.1.3 *Risk Factors and Consequences Associated with Homelessness*

The risk factors associated with homelessness are generally divided into two categories, both of which can overlap and are not mutually exclusive: individual (or micro) and structural (or macro).[46] Individual risk factors include mental illness, substance use disorder, poverty, self-identification as a member of the LGBTQ community, prior experience in foster care, having a criminal record, and a history of physical and/or sexual violence.[47] Various studies highlight how certain individual risk factors are associated with homelessness. For instance, individuals who suffer from mental illness or substance use disorder are overrepresented in the unhoused population.[48] Some

41 *Ibid.*

42 Patrick, *Aboriginal Homelessness in Canada: A Literature Review* at 32. Cited in Sean. A. Kidd, Jesse Thistle, Teresa Beaulieu et al., "A National Study of Indigenous Youth Homelessness in Canada" (2019) 176 *Pub Health* 163 at 164.

43 Jeffrey Olivet, Catriona Wilkey, Molly Richard et al., "Racial Inequity and Homelessness: Findings from the SPARC Study" (2021) 693 *Annals AAPSS* 82 at 96.

44 Alex Abramovich, *LGBTQS2 Homelessness in Canada* (Toronto: The 519, 2015); John Ecker, Tim Aubry, and John Sylvestre, "A Review of the Literature on LGBTQ Adults Who Experience Homelessness" (2019) 66:3 *J Homosexuality* 297 at 297.

45 Ecker, Aubry, and Sylvestre, "A Review of the Literature on LGBTQ Adults Who Experience Homelessness" at 297. Ecker and colleagues' exact quote is: "Although determining the number of LGBTQ youth who experience homelessness is difficult, studies have reported anywhere from 15% to 30% of youth experiencing homelessness may identify as LGBTQ" (*ibid.*).

46 *See, e.g.*, Myra Piat, Lauren Polvere, Maritt Kirst et al., "Pathways into Homelessness: Understanding How Both Individual and Structural Factors Contribute to and Sustain Homelessness in Canada" (2015) 52:13 *Urb Stud* 2366 at 2367–69; Patrick Fowler, Peter Hovmand, Katherine Marcal et al., "Solving Homelessness from a Complex Systems Perspective: Insights for Prevention Responses" (2019) 40 *Ann Rev Pub Health* 465 at 467; Stephen Gaetz, Tanya Gulliver, and Tim Richter, *The State of Homelessness in Canada 2014* (Toronto: Homeless Hub Press, 2014) at 37–38; NLCHP, *Homelessness in America: Overview of Data and Causes* (Washington, National Law Center on Homelessness and Poverty, January 2015).

47 *See, e.g.*, Fowler, Hovmand, Marcal et al., "Solving Homelessness from a Complex Systems Perspective" at 467; Lee, Tyler, and Wright, "The New Homelessness Revisited" at 509–10.

48 Carol Caton, Boanerges Dominguez, Bella Schanzer et al., "Risk Factors for Long-Term Homelessness: Findings from a Longitudinal Study of First-Time Homeless Single Adults" (2005) 95:10 *Am J Pub Health* 1753 at 1753; Stefan Gutwisnki, Stefanie Schreiter, Karl Deutscher et al., "The

studies suggest that unhoused persons are roughly ten times more likely to have an alcohol-related or drug-related substance use disorder compared to the general population.[49] Other research notes that individuals who have suffered physical or sexual violence are more likely to experience homelessness compared to individuals who have not.[50] Placement in foster care is also a risk factor associated with an increased likelihood of homelessness, especially at the time when individuals transition out of foster care.[51]

Structural risk factors associated with homelessness, for their part, include increased cost of living, lack of access to affordable housing, unemployment, and housing and employment discrimination, amongst others.[52] Scholars note that lack of access to affordable housing is one of the principal causes of homelessness – one that partly explains regional variations in the per capita homelessness rate between cities.[53] Furthermore, as Thomas Byrne and colleagues observe, various studies indicate that high costs of rent and low vacancy rates are associated with a higher rate of homelessness in cities.[54] Housing discrimination, unemployment, and criminal justice system involvement also contribute to homelessness.[55] Racialized participants of interview studies report that they were subject to racial discrimination in these areas, and moreover, that they experienced discrimination when using homelessness-related services.[56]

Unhoused persons face worse health disparities and outcomes compared to individuals with access to housing.[57] The mortality rate for people experiencing

Prevalence of Mental Disorders among Homeless People in High-Income Countries: An Updated Systematic Review and Meta-Regression Analysis" (2021) 18:8 *PLoS* 1 at 12–14.

49 Gutwisnki, Schreiter, Deutscher et al., "The Prevalence of Mental Disorders among Homeless People in High-Income Countries" at 12.

50 *See, e.g.*, Michelle Tong, Lauren Kaplan, David Guzman et al., "Persistent Homelessness and Violent Victimization Among Older Adults in the HOPE HOME Study" (2021) 36:17–18 *J Interpers Violence* 8519 at 8520; Ahyoung Song, Suzanne Wenzel, and Yusun Cho, "Child Abuse Victimization, Depression, and Substance Use among Homeless Women: Application of General Strain Theory" (2021) 36 *J Interpers Violence* 8852 at 8855.

51 *See, e.g.*, Amy Dworsky, Laura Napolitano, and Mark Courtney, "Homelessness during the Transition from Foster Care to Adulthood" (2013) 103:S2 *Am J Pub Health* S318 at S318, S320; Kimberly Bender, Jessica Yang, Kristin Ferguson et al., "Experiences and Needs of Homeless Youth with a History of Foster Care" (2015) 55 *Children and Youth Services Rev* 222 at 222–23; Nicholas Forge, Robin Hartinger-Saunders, Eric Wright et al., "Out of the System and onto the Streets" (2018) 96:2 *Child Welfare* 47 at 49.

52 *See, e.g.*, Fowler, Hovmand, Marcal et al., "Solving Homelessness from a Complex Systems Perspective" at 467; Lee, Tyler, and Wright, "The New Homelessness Revisited" at 509–10.

53 *See, e.g.*, Gregg Colburn and Clayton Page Aldern, *Homelessness Is a Housing Problem* (Oakland: University of California Press, 2022) at 121–23, 127–44, 159.

54 Thomas Byrne, Ellen Munley, Jamison Fargo et al., "New Perspectives on Community-Level Determinants of Homelessness" (2013) 35:5 *J Urb Aff* 607 at 609.

55 Olivet, Wilkey, Richard et al., "Racial Inequity and Homelessness" at 84.

56 *Ibid.* at 93.

57 *See, e.g.*, Brendan Clifford, Andrew Wilson, and Patrick Harris, "Homelessness, Health and the Policy Process: A Literature Review" (2019) 123 *Health Pol'y* 1125 at 1125.

homelessness is roughly three to four times higher than the general population.[58] Unhoused persons have high rates of chronic pain.[59] They also suffer from high rates of short-term and long-term health problems.[60] Unhoused persons are also more likely to contract certain infectious diseases, such as tuberculosis.[61] Compared to the general population, people experiencing homelessness tend to have a lower life expectancy and worse quality of life.[62] They are also disproportionately likely to experience physical and sexual violence.[63] Unhoused youth faced particularly adverse health outcomes. Elise Roy and colleagues' research compared the mortality rates of unhoused youth in Montreal with those of the general youth population.[64] Their study suggests that the mortality rates for unhoused youth was eleven times higher than the general youth population.[65]

1.2 THE RISE AND FALL OF VAGRANCY LAW

Historically, vagrancy laws regulated people experiencing homelessness.[66] These laws are traced back to England's Statute of Labourers 1351.[67] The Statute was passed after the bubonic plague swept through the country and killed a significant portion of the country's working population.[68] This led to severe labor shortages, especially in agriculture and manual labor.[69] As feudalism broke down and the working class experienced new freedom and possibilities, people wandered the country seeking better employment and higher wages.[70] As a response to that phenomenon, the Statute of Labourers was passed in 1351, primarily for economic

58 James O'Connell, *Premature Mortality in Homeless Populations: A Review of the Literature* (Nashville, TN: National Health Care for the Homeless Council, 2005) at 13.

59 Amy Funk, R. Neil Greene, Kate Dill et al., "The Impact of Homelessness on Mortality of Individuals Living in the United States: A Systematic Review of the Literature" (2022) 33:1 *J Health Care for the Poor and Underserved* 457 at 458.

60 Roger Nooe and David Patterson, "The Ecology of Homelessness" (2010) 20:2 *J Hum Behav in the Soc Env't* 105 at 121 (noting: "chronic and acute health problems are frequent among the homeless").

61 Frankish, Hwang, and Quantz, "Homelessness and Health in Canada" at S25.

62 *Ibid.* at S25; Stephen Hwang, "Homelessness and Health" (2001) 164 *CMAJ* 229 at 229–31.

63 Dallas Augustine and Margot Kushel, "Community Supervision, Housing Insecurity, and Homelessness" (2022) 701 *Annals AAPSS* 152 at 156; Ellsworth, "Street Crime Victimization among Homeless Adults" at 107–08.

64 Elise Roy, Nancy Haley, Pascale Leclerc et al., "Mortality in a Cohort of Street Youth in Montreal" (2004) 292 *JAMA* 569 at 571–72.

65 *Ibid.* at 572.

66 Harry Simon, "Towns without Pity: A Constitutional and Historical Analysis of Official Efforts to Drive Homeless Persons from American Cities" (1992) 66:4 *Tulane L Rev* 631 at 635–40.

67 Statute of Labourers (1351) 25 Edward III, stat. 1. William Chambliss, "A Sociological Analysis of the Law of Vagrancy" (1964–65) 12:1 *Soc Probs* 67 at 68; Audrey Eccles, *Vagrancy in Law and Practice under the Old Poor Law* (Farnham: Ashgate Publishing Ltd., 2012) at 1; Bertha Haven Putnam, *The Enforcement of the Statute of Labourers in the First Century after the Black Death 1349–1359* (Brooklyn, NY: AMS Press, 1908) at 2–3.

68 Putnam, *The Enforcement of the Statute of Labourers* at 1–3.

69 *Ibid.* at 2.

70 Caleb Foote, "Vagrancy-Type Law and Its Administration" (1955–56) 104 *U Pa L Rev* 603 at 615–16.

reasons.[71] The Statute fixed wages, regulated begging, and prevented workers from roaming throughout the country to seek better remuneration.[72]

The scope of vagrancy law shifted towards the end of the fifteenth century and beginning of the sixteenth century. Vagrancy statutes became "the criminal aspect of the poor laws."[73] Since these laws were vague, the State had broad discretion to control different types of conduct, and regulate individuals and groups that were considered to be socially undesirable.[74] Throughout history, vagrancy laws regulated labor, migration, immigration, poverty, morality, sexuality, prostitution, and criminality.[75] These laws were thus employed as a form of social control.[76] Vagrancy statutes classified vagrants into different categories – rogues, vagabonds, and idle and disorderly persons – based on their way of life, occupation, or conduct.[77] These statutes regulated unhoused persons' condition and need-alleviating conduct. For instance, vagrancy laws prohibited conduct related to sleeping, wandering, loitering, and being unemployed.[78]

Vagrancy statutes were imported from English law into the United States and Canada and prohibited a variety of acts. In the 1950s, every American state had its own vagrancy statutes.[79] State laws criminalized acts such as sleeping on public property without permission, loitering, and wandering at night without providing an adequate account of oneself.[80] Some US courts defined a common law vagrant as an idle person who wandered without visible means of support and refused to work when able.[81] In Canada, vagrancy statutes were already in force prior to Confederation in 1867.[82] Before

71 Putnam, *The Enforcement of the Statute of Labourers* at 3; Robert Humphreys, *No Fixed Abode: A History of Responses to the Roofless and the Rootless in Britain* (New York: Palgrave MacMillan, 1999) at 22–23.

72 Putnam, *The Enforcement of the Statute of Labourers* at 3.

73 James Fitzjames Stephen, *History of the Criminal Law England*, Vol. III (London: MacMillan, 1883) at 266.

74 Risa Goluboff, *Vagrant Nation: Police Power, Constitutional Change, and the Making of the 1960s* (Oxford: Oxford University Press, 2016) at 2.

75 Prashan Ranasinghe, "Vagrancy as a Penal Problem: The Logistics of Administering Punishment in Late-Nineteenth-Century Canada" (2012) 25 *J Hist Socio* 531 at 531.

76 Risa Goluboff, "Dispatch from the Supreme Court Archives: Vagrancy, Abortion, and What the Links Between Them Reveal About the History of Fundamental Rights" (2010) 62 *Stan L Rev* 1361 at 1371.

77 Nicholas Rogers, "Policing the Poor in Eighteenth-Century London: The Vagrancy Laws and Their Administration" (1991) 24 *Soc Hist* 127 at 131; Prashan Ranasinghe, "Reconceptualizing Vagrancy and Reconstructing the Vagrant: A Socio-Legal Analysis of Criminal Law Reform in Canada, 1953–1972" (2010) 48:1 *Osgoode Hall LJ* 55 at 58.

78 Ranasinghe, "Reconceptualizing Vagrancy" at 58, 69–70.

79 Forrest Lacey, "Vagrancy and Other Crimes of Personal Condition" (1952–53) 66:7 *Harv L Rev* 1203 at 1207; Gary Dubin and Richard Robinson, "The Vagrancy Concept Reconsidered: Problems and Abuses of Status Criminality" (1962) 37:1 *NYU L Rev* 102 at 108.

80 Dubin and Robinson, "The Vagrancy Concept Reconsidered" at 109–11.

81 Lacey, "Vagrancy and Other Crimes of Personal Condition" at 1207. For instance, in West Virginia, the common law definition of vagrancy is provided in *City of Huntington* v. *Salyer*, 63 SE (2d) 575 at 577–78 (W Va Sup Ct App 1951).

82 Ranasinghe, "Reconceptualizing Vagrancy" at 60–62, citing Constance Backhouse, "Nineteenth Century Canadian Prostitution Law: Reflection of a Discriminatory Society" (1985) 18 *Soc Hist* 387 at 389, fn. 3 in the text.

the 1930s, it was a criminal offense in Canada to wander or lodge on public property without providing an adequate account of oneself.[83] It was also a crime for a person to be unemployed while lacking the visible means to support themselves.[84]

Vagrancy laws declined in the United States following the 1972 US Supreme Court decision *Papachristou* v. *City of Jacksonville*.[85] In *Papachristou*, several defendants challenged the constitutionality of a Jacksonville vagrancy ordinance that prohibited a litany of acts associated with incivility, immorality, or disorder.[86] The ordinance proscribed such a sweeping array of conduct that individuals would eventually violate it.[87] The ordinance stated:

> Rogues and vagabonds, or dissolute persons who go about begging, common gamblers, persons who use juggling or unlawful games or plays, common drunkards, common night walkers, thieves, pilferers or pickpockets, traders in stolen property, lewd, wanton and lascivious persons, keepers of gambling places, common railers and brawlers, persons wandering or strolling around from place to place without any lawful purpose or object, habitual loafers, disorderly persons, persons neglecting all lawful business and habitually spending their time by frequenting houses of ill fame, gaming houses, or places where alcoholic beverages are sold or served, persons able to work but habitually living upon the earnings of their wives or minor children shall be deemed vagrants and, upon conviction in the Municipal Court shall be punished as provided for Class D offenses.[88]

The Court unanimously struck down the Jacksonville vagrancy ordinance on the grounds that it was void for vagueness.[89] The law failed to provide fair warning as to which conduct was illegal and conferred too much discretion to police officers.[90] The judges were concerned that the law prohibited harmless and innocent acts: going for a walk, relaxing in a park, or simply doing nothing at all.[91] They worried that the law disproportionately impacted impecunious persons and other marginalized individuals.[92] The statute placed tremendous power in the hands of law enforcement, who decided whether individuals received full respect for their social condition and lifestyle.[93]

83 Criminal Code, RSC 1927, 14–15 George V, c. 36, s. 238(a). Cited in Ranasinghe, "Reconceptualizing Vagrancy" at 69.
84 Ranasinghe, "Reconceptualizing Vagrancy" at 69–70.
85 405 US 156 (1972).
86 Tammy Sun, "Equality by Other Means: The Substantive Foundations of the Vagueness Doctrine" (2011) 46:1 *Harv CR-CLL Rev* 149 at 155.
87 *See, e.g.*, Emily Snoddon, "Clarifying Vagueness: Rethinking the Supreme Court's Vagueness Doctrine" (2019) 86:8 *U Chi L Rev* 2301 at 2309.
88 Jacksonville, Fla Ordinance Code § 26–57 (1965). Cited in *Papachristou* v. *City of Jacksonville*, 405 US 156 (1972), note 1 in the decision.
89 *City of Jacksonville*, 405 US 156 at 162 (1972).
90 *Ibid.* at 163.
91 *Ibid.*
92 *Ibid.* at 170.
93 *Ibid.*

The void for vagueness doctrine was later used to strike down loitering laws. The 1983 US Supreme Court decision *Kolender* v. *Lawson* is an example.[94] In *Kolender*, the impugned law required individuals who wander or loiter to give an account of themselves and provide identification to police officers.[95] The Court reasoned that the law failed to adequately inform individuals about how they could comply with the law, and encouraged arbitrary enforcement by the police.[96] Officers had the authority to interpret terms such as wandering and loitering, and to assess the reliability of an individual's identification.[97] For similar reasons, in the 1999 decision *Chicago* v. *Morales*, the US Supreme Court decided that a law was unconstitutionally vague because it criminalized gang members who remained "in any one place with no apparent purpose."[98]

1.3 THE BROKEN WINDOWS THEORY AND MUNICIPAL ORDINANCES

1.3.1 *The Broken Windows Theory*

Municipal ordinances rose to prominence following the decline of vagrancy laws.[99] The increased enforcement of these ordinances is typically associated with the Broken Windows Theory advanced by James Wilson and George Kelling.[100] Their theory built on an earlier study conducted by the psychologist Philip Zimbardo.[101] As part of his experiment, Zimbardo placed a car with its hood up in the Bronx in New York, and a similar car in Palo Alto, California.[102] The car in the Bronx was burglarized within ten minutes of its abandonment.[103] The other components of the car were stolen within twenty-four hours.[104] The rest of the car was then vandalized

94 *Kolender* v. *Lawson*, 461 US 352 at 353–54 (1983).

95 *Ibid.*; Cal Penal Code Ann. § 647(e) (West 1970).

96 *Kolender* v. *Lawson*, 461 US 352 at 357–58 (1983).

97 *Ibid.* at 360–1.

98 *Chicago* v. *Morales*, 527 US 41 (1999); Chicago, IL, Mun Code, § 8–4–015 (1992).

99 Katherine Beckett and Steve Herbert, "Managing the Neo-Liberal City: 'Quality of Life' Policing in the Twenty-First Century" in Stephen Haymes, Maria Vidal de Haymes, and Reuben Miller (eds.), *The Routledge Handbook of Poverty in the United States* (New York: Routledge, 2015) at 350–1; Jeffrey Fagan and Garth Davies, "Street Stops and Broken Windows: Terry, Race, and Disorder in New York City" (2000) 28:2 *Fordham Urb LJ* 457 at 467.

100 James Wilson and George Kelling, "Broken Windows: The Police and Neighborhood Safety," The Atlantic (March 1982), www.theatlantic.com/magazine/archive/1982/03/broken-windows/304465/ [perma.cc/MM5T-W4XZ]. For an overview of the Broken Window Theory, see Bernard Harcourt, "Reflecting on the Subject: A Critique of the Social Influence Conception of Deterrence, the Broken Windows Theory, and Order-Maintenance Policing New York Style" (1998) 97:2 *Mich L Rev* 291 at 291–92, 301–02; Bernard Harcourt, *Illusion of Order: The False Promise of Broken Windows Policing* (Cambridge: Harvard University Press, 2001) at 23–27.

101 Wilson and Kelling, "Broken Windows" at 31. Note that the description and results of the experiment are taken from Wilson and Kelling, *ibid.*

102 *Ibid.*

103 *Ibid.*

104 *Ibid.*

and destroyed.[105] The car in Palo Alto, on the other hand, sat undamaged for a week until Zimbardo broke one of its windows.[106] It was then destroyed and flipped upside down within the span of several hours.[107] Wilson and Kelling posited that the first broken window triggered a cascade of increasingly serious property offenses involving the car.[108]

According to Wilson and Kelling, untended low-level incivilities – much like a broken window – invite more serious crimes.[109] Such incivilities signal breakdowns of social control within the community.[110] Individuals may change their behavior as a response to these signals.[111] They may fear that they will become victims of crime and avoid public spaces.[112] Eventually, they may not call the police when they witness crimes or are victimized because they believe that law enforcement is ineffective.[113] Criminals, for their part, will commit more crimes because signs of incivility telegraph that the police do not enforce the law.[114] And criminals prefer to commit crimes in neighborhoods where their chances of being caught are lower rather than higher.[115] Like a self-fulfilling prophecy, the appearance of crime and disorder was said to result in greater crime and disorder.[116]

Wilson and Kelling explained that, historically, vagrancy laws controlled public property's use and helped maintain order in public spaces.[117] They argued that vagrancy statutes provided the police with crucial legal tools to control crime and incivilities when other informal methods of social control failed.[118] To be clear, Wilson and Kelling also recognized that vagrancy statutes raised legitimate concerns about discriminatory enforcement practices.[119] They observed that vagrancy was a charge "with scarcely any legal meaning."[120] When they considered how best to prevent discriminatory enforcement, they argued that better police selection, training, and supervision would be effective, even though they conceded that those

105 *Ibid.*
106 *Ibid.*
107 *Ibid.*
108 *Ibid.*
109 *Ibid.* at 31.
110 *Ibid.*
111 *Ibid.* at 32.
112 *Ibid.*
113 *Ibid.* at 33.
114 *Ibid.*
115 *Ibid.* at 32, 34.
116 *Ibid. See, e.g.*, Adam Samaha, "Regulation for the Sake of Appearance" (2012) 125:7 *Harv L Rev* 1563 at 1621; David Garland, *The Culture of Control: Crime and Social Order in Contemporary Society* (University of Chicago Press, 2001) at 181; Robert Ellickson, "Controlling Chronic Misconduct in City Spaces: Of Panhandlers, Skid Rows, and Public-Space Zoning" (1996) 105:5 *Yale LJ* 1165 at 1177–78; Bernard Harcourt, "The Collapse of the Harm Principle" (1999) 90 *J Crim L & Criminology* 109 at 110–11.
117 Wilson and Kelling, "Broken Windows" at 35.
118 *Ibid.*
119 *Ibid.*
120 *Ibid.*

solutions were not satisfactory.[121] Although they recognized how vagrancy laws impact civil liberties, they posited that many discounted the criminogenic effects of compounding incivilities over time.[122]

The Broken Windows Theory signaled a major shift in policing and in the regulation of public property.[123] US cities enacted and enforced narrowly tailored municipal ordinances that prohibited much of what vagrancy law once proscribed.[124] Some Canadian cities, such as Montreal, did not enact new ordinances, but changed the classification of certain spaces to impose curfews more easily.[125] Unlike vagrancy laws, municipal ordinances generally withstood vagueness challenges because they were narrow and precise.[126] These ordinances prohibited a wide range of conduct, such as panhandling, public urination or defecation, sleeping on public property, urban camping, sitting or lying down on streets or sidewalks, littering, graffiti, excessive noise, and more.[127]

Wilson and Kelling's theory ushered in a new era of policing.[128] When Rudy Giuliani became New York City's mayor in 1994, the city adopted a zero-tolerance enforcement policy for low-level incivilities.[129] The city's crime rate dropped a reported 40 percent in the four years after the strategy was adopted.[130] Other US cities – such as Chicago, Los Angeles, and San Francisco – also adopted a Broken Windows policing strategy.[131] Some Canadian cities adopted a similar approach.[132]

121 *Ibid.*

122 *Ibid.*

123 Andrew Ingram, "Breaking Laws to Fix Broken Windows: A Revisionist Take on Order Maintenance Policing" (2014) 19:2 *Berkeley J Crim L* 113 at 127–39; Bernard Harcourt and Jens Ludwig, "Broken Windows: New Evidence from New York City and a Five-City Social Experiment" (2006) 73:1 *U Chi L Rev* 271 at 272.

124 Debra Livingston, "Police Discretion and the Quality of Life in Public Places: Courts, Communities, and the New Policing" (1997) 97:3 *Colum L Rev* 551 at 608–09.

125 Marie-Eve Sylvestre and Céline Bellot, "Challenging Discriminatory and Punitive Responses to Homelessness in Canada" in Bruce Jackman and Martha Porter (eds.), *Advancing Social Rights in Canada* (Markham: Irwin Law, 2014) at 168–69.

126 Donald Baker, "'Anti-Homeless' Legislation: Unconstitutional Efforts to Punish the Homeless" (1990) 45:2–3 *U Miami L Rev* 417 at 430–31.

127 *Ibid.*; Harcourt, "Reflecting on the Subject" at 301.

128 Harcourt, *Illusion of Order* at 2–5.

129 Peter Barta, "Note: Giuliani, Broken Windows, and the Right to Beg" (1999) 6:2 *Geo J Poverty L & Pol'y* 165 at 166.

130 *Ibid.*

131 Harcourt and Ludwig, "Broken Windows: New Evidence" at 272; Laura Huey, *Negotiating Demands: The Politics of Skid Row Policing in Edinburgh, San Francisco, and Vancouver* (University of Toronto Press, 2007) at 104.

132 Walter DeKeseredy, "Canadian Crime Control in the New Millennium: The Influence of Neo-Conservative US Policies and Practices" (2009) 10:4 *Police Prac & Rsch* 305 at 308; Marie-Eve Sylvestre, "Disorder and Public Spaces in Montreal: Repression (and Resistance) through Law, Politics, and Police Discretion" (2010) 31:6 *Urb Geo* 803 at 806–07; Sylvestre and Bellot, "Challenging Discriminatory Responses" at 167.

The Broken Windows Theory has been criticized heavily on various grounds.[133] First, scholars argue that Broken Windows policing did not cause crime rates to decrease.[134] Some observe that other factors were responsible for lower crime rates during the era of Broken Windows policing, such as the decline of crack cocaine's popularity, increased police surveillance, favorable economic conditions, and the increased incarceration of violent offenders.[135] Second, some contend that the crime rate in New York City – the most notable example of Broken Windows policing – was already in decline before the strategy was implemented.[136] Third, as John Eck and Edward McGuire remark, crime rates dropped in cities that did not adopt Broken Windows policing strategies, such as Boston and San Diego.[137] Fourth, Broken Windows policing disproportionately impacted racialized and socioeconomically disadvantaged persons, and resulted in increased surveillance, discrimination, and harassment.[138] Broken Windows policing imposes important costs on individuals and communities. Proactive police encounters can be humiliating and traumatizing.[139] They may result in physical or psychological harm, violate privacy, and demean human dignity.[140] Aggressive policing tactics can also decrease individuals' trust in law enforcement.[141] The police require individuals' cooperation to prevent and solve crimes.[142] However, individuals who distrust the police may be reluctant to report crimes, collaborate with law enforcement, or testify in trials.[143]

[133] *See, e.g.*, Harcourt and Ludwig, "Broken Windows: New Evidence" at 286–88; John Eck and Edward McGuire, "Have Changes in Policing Reduced Violent Crime? An Assessment of the Evidence?" in Alfred Blumstein and Joel Wallman (eds.), *The Crime Drop in America* (Cambridge University Press, 2005) at 226–28 (providing an overview of critiques of the Broken Windows Theory).

[134] Harcourt, *Illusion of Order*, ch. 3; Harcourt and Ludwig, "Broken Windows: New Evidence" at 272–73, 277; Ralph Taylor, *Breaking Away from Broken Windows: Baltimore Neighborhoods and the Nationwide Fight against Crime, Grime, Fear, and Decline* (Boulder: Westview Press, 2001).

[135] Harcourt, "Reflecting on the Subject" at 332 (providing an overview of these contentions).

[136] *See, e.g.*, Eck and McGuire, "Have Changes in Policing Reduced Violent Crime?" at 226 (providing an overview of these studies and critiques of Broken Windows policing).

[137] *Ibid.*; DeKeseredy, "Canadian Crime Control in the New Millennium" at 308; Bill O'Grady, Stephen Gaetz, and Kristy Buccieri, *Can I See Your ID? The Policing of Youth Homelessness in Toronto* (Toronto: JFCY & Homeless Hub, 2011) at 25.

[138] Fagan and Davies, "Street Stops and Broken Windows" at 462–63; Babe Howell, "The Costs of Broken Windows Policing: Twenty Years and Counting" (2016) 37:3 *Cardozo L Rev* 1059 at 1068–69.

[139] *See, e.g.*, Jeffrey Fagan, Anthony Braga, Rod Brunson et al., "Stops and Stares: Street Stops, Surveillance, and Race in the New Policing" (2016) 43 *Fordham Urb LJ* 539 at 559; Susan Bandes, Marie Prior, Erin M. Kerrison et al., "The Mismeasure of Terry Stops: Assessing the Psychological and Emotional Harms of Stop and Frisk to Individuals and Communities" (2019) 37:2 *Behav Sci L* 176 at 180.

[140] *See, e.g.*, Jeffrey Fagan, "Terry's Original Sin" [2016] *U Chicago Leg F* 43 at 90, citing William Stuntz, "Terry's Impossibility" (1998) 72:3–4 *St John's L Rev* 1213 at 1218.

[141] John MacDonald and Robert Stokes, "Race, Social Capital, and Trust in the Police" (2006) 41:3 *Urb Aff Rev* 358 at 361.

[142] Tom Tyler and Jeffrey Fagan, "Legitimacy and Cooperation: Why Do People Help the Police Fight Crime in Their Communities" (2008) 6:1 *Ohio St J Crim L* 231 at 233 at 233.

[143] Tom Tyler, "From Harm Reduction to Community Engagement: Redefining the Goals of American Policing in the Twenty-First Century" (2017) 111 *Nw U L Rev* 1537 at 1543.

1.3.2 *An Overview of Municipal Ordinances*

Today, municipal ordinances are ubiquitous in US and Canadian cities.[144] Some of these ordinances govern basic human acts that everyone must do – such as sleeping, urinating, defecating, and sitting – and that take place on public property.[145] Certain ordinances categorically prohibit certain need-alleviating acts on public property, such as laws that proscribe public urination and defecation.[146] Cities such as Dallas, Texas, Atlantic City, and New Jersey prohibit sleeping on public property, including in parks, parking lots, streets, alleys, and on sidewalks.[147]

Other municipal ordinances do not comprehensively prohibit certain acts, but instead impose time, place, and manner restrictions.[148] Some cities – such as Virginia Beach – prohibit people from sleeping on public property between specific hours.[149] A San Francisco ordinance proscribes sitting or lying on the city's streets or sidewalks.[150] A Toronto bylaw prohibits individuals from lying down on any bench, seat, or floor on property owned by the Toronto Transportation Commission, such as subway and bus stations.[151]

Since 2006, the National Homelessness Law Center (or NHLC) – formerly the National Law Center on Homelessness and Poverty – tracks and analyzes municipal ordinances in 187 American cities.[152] Their research details the extent to which cities completely or partially ban certain need-alleviating conduct. According to the NHLC's most recent report on the criminalization of homelessness published in

144 Marie-Eve Sylvestre and Céline Bellot, "Challenging Discriminatory and Punitive Responses to Homelessness in Canada" in Bruce Jackman and Martha Porter (eds.), *Advancing Social Rights in Canada* (Markham: Irwin Law, 2014) at 166–69; Hannah Kieschnick, "A Cruel and Unusual Way to Regulate the Homeless: Extending the Status Crimes Doctrine to Anti-Homeless Ordinances" (2018) 70:5 *Stan L Rev* 1569 at 1571.

145 Terry Skolnik, "How and Why Homeless People Are Regulated Differently" (2018) 43 *Queen's LJ* 297 at 306.

146 *See, e.g.*, LA, Cal, Mun. Code, § 41.472.2.

147 Dall, TX, Mun. Code, § 31–13. The provision was upheld by the Court of Appeals for the Fifth Circuit in *Johnson* v. *City of Dallas* 61 F (3d) 442 (5th Circ 1995); Atlantic City, NJ, Mun. Code, § 204–29.

148 *See, e.g.*, Christine Bella and David Lopez, "Quality of Life – At What Price: Constitutional Challenges to Laws Adversely Impacting the Homeless" (1994) 10:1 *St John's J Leg Comment* 89 at 100 (describing a panhandling ordinance that imposes a time, place, or manner restriction); Elizabeth O'Connor, "The Cruel and Unusual Criminalization of Homelessness: Factoring Individual Accountability into the Proportionality Principle" (2007) 12:2 *Tex J CL & CR* 233, note 78 in the text. For examples of such laws, see NLCHP, "Housing Not Handcuffs: State Law Supplement" (2021) at 9–10, 12, https://homelesslaw.org/wp-content/uploads/2021/11/2021-HNH-State-Crim-Supplement.pdf [perma.cc/QN3A-DC3H].

149 Virginia Beach, Va, Mun. Code, § 23–55.

150 SF, Cal, Police Code, § 168.

151 Toronto, By-law No. 1, Regulates the use of the TTC local passenger transportation system (January 21, 2009), s. 3.19(b).

152 NLCHP, "Housing Not Handcuffs: Ending the Criminalization of Homelessness in U.S. Cities" (2019) at 12, https://homelesslaw.org/wp-content/uploads/2019/12/HOUSING-NOT-HANDCUFFS-2019-FINAL.pdf [perma.cc/QZD6-7K7E].

2019, roughly 21 percent of the American cities they surveyed imposed citywide bans against sleeping on public property, while 37 percent of those cities imposed citywide bans against camping on public property.[153] The NHLC notes that citywide bans against sleeping on public property increased by roughly 50 percent since 2006, while citywide bans against camping on public property increased by approximately 92 percent since 2006.[154]

With respect to loitering offenses, this same report states that roughly 35 percent of cities they track imposed citywide bans on "loitering, loafing, and/or vagrancy," whereas approximately 60 percent banned those acts in specific public places.[155] The NHLC further notes that the number of municipal ordinances that imposed citywide bans on loitering increased by roughly 103 percent since 2006, and that there was a 28 percent increase in ordinances that prohibited loitering in certain public spaces.[156] These figures represent an increase since the NHLC's previous annual report in 2016.[157]

Studies demonstrate how municipal ordinances disproportionately impact people experiencing homelessness. A survey study – which combined the results of a 2013 statewide Colorado study and a 2014 local Denver study – explored the extent to which unhoused persons were contacted, cited, or arrested by the police for municipal ordinances.[158] The study comprised a total of roughly 950 unhoused persons who participated in the statewide and local surveys.[159] Results indicated that roughly 70 percent of respondents were contacted, cited, or arrested for sleeping in public, 64 percent were subject to such encounters for sitting or lying down on public property, and 50 percent were subject to such encounters for loitering.[160] Approximately 70 percent of respondents reported that they were ticketed for violating a municipal ordinance, while 36 percent reported that they were incarcerated for doing so.[161] Roughly 60 percent of respondents who were ticketed were subsequently jailed because they could not pay their fine or failed to appear in court.[162]

A 2015 study in San Francisco surveyed 351 unhoused respondents and analyzed court data regarding municipal ordinance citations.[163] Although the city issued over 27,000 citations that year, 14,000 of those citations involved laws that govern public

153 *Ibid.*

154 *Ibid.*

155 *Ibid.* at 13.

156 *Ibid.*

157 *Ibid.* at 10.

158 Tony Robinson, "No Right to Rest: Police Enforcement Patterns and Quality of Life Consequences of the Criminalization of Homelessness" (2019) 55:1 *Urb Aff* 41.

159 *Ibid.* at 53.

160 *Ibid.* at 53, 56.

161 *Ibid.* at 55.

162 *Ibid.*

163 Chris Herring, Dilara Yarbrough, and Lisa Marie Alatorre, "Pervasive Penality: How the Criminalization of Poverty Perpetuates Homelessness" (2020) 67:1 *Soc Probs* 131 at 134–37.

property and homelessness.[164] Approximately 11,900 of the 14,000 citations were issued for sleeping or sitting on public property, unlawful lodging, or obstructing the sidewalk.[165] Roughly 22 percent of respondents received five or more citations.[166]

Some scholars have conducted empirical studies that examine the rates at which unhoused persons receive municipal ordinance citations. Researchers Céline Bellot and Marie-Eve Sylvestre scrutinized municipal court data from the years 1994–2010 in the city of Montreal.[167] Their study examined how municipal ordinances and transportation bylaws were enforced against unhoused persons during those years.[168] Their research showed that the number of fines issued per year in Montreal increased by six-and-a-half times between 1994 and 2010, from 1,054 to 6,562.[169] Of the total number of citations, unhoused persons were most commonly fined for using public transport without payment (33.7 percent), public intoxication (31.5 percent), consuming alcohol on public property (29.6 percent), sleeping or lying down in a subway station or train (23.3 percent), smoking inside transportation authority facilities (14.6 percent), and loitering (11.8 percent).[170] Their study also assessed the number of fines issued to each unhoused person within their study between 2006 and 2010.[171] Although 42.6 percent of unhoused persons received only one fine during that period, 30.6 percent received between two and five fines, while 12 percent received between ten and twenty-five fines.[172] Approximately 6 percent of unhoused persons in the study received more than twenty-five fines during that period.[173]

1.4 CONCLUSION

This chapter provided a historical overview of vagrancy law and the rise to prominence of municipal ordinances in Canada and in the United States. It offered examples of ordinances that are in force within these jurisdictions. Its concluding parts described the prevalence of homelessness in these countries, the personal and structural factors that contribute to it, and certain characteristics that are more common amongst unhoused persons compared to the general population. The next chapter explains how US and Canadian constitutional law have approached homelessness and laws that govern public property. It highlights how constitutional safeguards have largely failed to protect unhoused persons against laws that govern public property and their associated consequences.

164 *Ibid.* at 137.
165 *Ibid.*
166 *Ibid.*
167 Céline Bellot and Marie-Eve Sylvestre, "La Judiciarisation de l'itinérance à Montréal: les dérives sécuritaires de la gestion pénale de la pauvreté" (2017) 47: *Hors Série Rev Gen* 11 at 13.
168 *Ibid.* at 18.
169 *Ibid.* at 20.
170 *Ibid.* at 23.
171 *Ibid.* at 29.
172 *Ibid.*
173 *Ibid.*

2

Homelessness and the Constitution

Following the Broken Windows Theory's emergence, courts and scholars devoted greater attention to how the regulation of public property impacted people experiencing homelessness. Beginning in the 1980s, scholars, public interest groups, and civil libertarians increasingly argued that laws that regulate public property violated unhoused persons' constitutional rights and criminalized the condition of homelessness.[1] Others disagreed. Certain cities and local governments claimed that civil libertarians ignored the need to regulate public property to maintain its communal purpose and foster its aesthetic value.[2] Courts sought to balance unhoused persons' fundamental rights with cities' need to regulate public property.[3]

This chapter provides an overview of how US and Canadian constitutional law approach homelessness and the regulation of public property. It explores the limited success of constitutional rights and doctrines that are invoked to challenge laws that govern public property and to protect unhoused persons' fundamental interests. These constitutional rights and doctrines are: (1) the void for vagueness doctrine, (2) the overbreadth doctrine, (3) the fundamental right to travel, (4) the equal

1 *See, e.g.*, Gregg Barak and Robert Bohm, "The Crimes of the Homeless or the Crime of Homelessness? On the Dialectics of Criminalization, Decriminalization, and Victimization" (1989) 13:3 *Contemp Crises* 275 at 278–79; Judy Aulette and Albert Aulette, "Police Harassment of the Homeless: The Political Purpose of the Criminalization of Homelessness" (1987) 11 *Human and Soc'y* 244 at 246–47 (cited in Barak and Bohm, "The Crimes of the Homeless or the Crime of Homelessness?"); Maria Foscarinis, "Downward Spiral: Homelessness and Its Criminalization" (1996) 14:1 *Yale L & Pol'y Rev* 1 at 25; Donald Baker, "'Anti-Homeless' Legislation: Unconstitutional Efforts to Punish the Homeless" (1990) 45:2–3 *U Miami L Rev* 417 at 424; Don Mitchell, "Anti-Homeless Laws and Public Space II: Further Constitutional Issues" (1998) 19:2 *Urb Geo* 98 at 103.

2 Robert Teir, "Restoring Order in Urban Public Spaces" (1998) 2 *Tex Rev L & Pol* 255 at 257; Robert Ellickson, "Controlling Chronic Misconduct in City Spaces: Of Panhandlers, Skid Rows, and Public-Space Zoning" (1996) 105:5 *Yale LJ* 1165 at 1170–71, 1173–74; James Wilson and George Kelling, "Broken Windows: The Police and Neighborhood Safety," The Atlantic (March 1982), www.theatlantic.com/magazine/archive/1982/03/broken-windows/304465 [perma.cc/MM5T-W4XZ].

3 *See, e.g.*, *Pottinger* v. *City of Miami*, 810 F Supp 1551 at 1554 (SD Fla 1992), noting: "In essence, this litigation results from an inevitable conflict between the need of homeless individuals to perform essential, life-sustaining acts in public and the responsibility of the government to maintain orderly, aesthetically pleasing public parks and streets."

protection clause, and (5) the right to be free from cruel and unusual punishments.[4] This chapter highlights how these doctrines fail to protect unhoused persons against various forms of actual and potential interference, such as displacement, fines, arrests, and imprisonment. It also discusses how US and Canadian courts have rejected a positive right to housing, which would better safeguard unhoused persons' basic interests (more on this point in the next chapter).[5] By exploring the limitations of these constitutional rights and doctrines, this chapter lays the groundwork for later parts of the book that show why unhoused persons tend to lack liberty and political equality.

2.1 VOID FOR VAGUENESS

The void for vagueness doctrine prohibits unconstitutionally vague or ambiguously worded penal statutes.[6] There are three justifications for the void for vagueness doctrine.[7] First, the doctrine promotes fair notice and helps prevent unfair surprises.[8] Individuals can obey the law and plan their lives more easily when statutes are clearer and more precise.[9] Second, the void for vagueness doctrine helps deter arbitrary and discriminatory enforcement because it constrains police discretion.[10] Officers enjoy greater police discretion to interpret and enforce vague penal statutes. By limiting police discretion, the void for vagueness doctrine promotes the rule of law and political equality.[11] Third, the doctrine encourages respect for the separation of powers.[12] Ambiguous laws require judges to determine which conduct is illegal, which delegates lawmaking authority from legislators to judges.[13]

4 Kathryn Hansel, "Constitutional Othering: Citizenship and the Insufficiency of Negative Rights-Based Challenges to Anti-Homeless Systems" (2011) 6:2 *Nw JL & Soc Pol'y* 445 at 448–61; Foscarinis, "Downward Spiral" at 26–49.

5 Chester Hartman, "The Case for a Right to Housing" (1998) 9:2 *Hous Pol'y Debate* 223 at 229–30; Curtis Berger, "Beyond Homelessness: An Entitlement to Housing" (1991) 45:2–3 *U Miami L Rev* 315 at 324–25; Shelby Green, "Imagining a Right to Housing, Lying in the Interstices" (2012) 19:3 *Geo J Poverty L & Pol'y* 393 at 396–97; Martha Jackman and Bruce Porter, "Rights-Based Strategies to Address Homelessness and Poverty in Canada" in Martha Jackman and Bruce Porter (eds.), *Advancing Social Rights in Canada* (Toronto: Irwin Law, 2014) at 101.

6 *See, e.g.*, Peter Low and Joel Johnson, "Changing the Vocabulary of the Vagueness Doctrine" (2015) 101:8 *Va L Rev* 2051 at 2052, citing *Kolender* v. *Lawson*, 461 US 352 (1983).

7 *See, e.g.*, Andrew Goldsmith, "The Void-for-Vagueness Doctrine in the Supreme Court, Revisited" (2003) 30:2 *Am J Crim L* 279 at 283–93.

8 Marc Ribeiro, *Limiting Arbitrary Power: The Vagueness Doctrine in Canadian Constitutional Law* (Vancouver: UBC Press, 2004) at 1.

9 *Reference re ss. 193 and 195.1(1)(c) of the Criminal Code (Man.)* [1990] 1 SCR 1123 at 1150–52; *Papachristou* v. *Jacksonville*, 405 US 156 at 162 (1972), citing *United States* v. *Harriss*, 347 US 612 at 617 (1954).

10 *Kolender* v. *Lawson*, 461 US 352 at 357.

11 John Calvin Jeffries Jr., "Legality, Vagueness, and the Construction of Penal Statutes" (1985) 71:2 *Va L Rev* 189 at 212; *R* v. *Levkovic*, 2013 SCC 25 at para. 32.

12 Goldsmith, "The Void-for-Vagueness Doctrine in the Supreme Court, Revisited" at 284–86.

13 *Ibid.* at 284–85.

Precise statutory language can reduce the risk that judges usurp the legislature's role.[14]

Penal laws must be adequately precise to withstand constitutional scrutiny. The US Supreme Court stated in *Kolender* v. *Lawson* that penal statutes must be defined with "sufficient definiteness that ordinary people can understand what conduct is prohibited and in a manner that does not encourage arbitrary and discriminatory enforcement."[15] The Supreme Court of Canada, for its part, stated in *R* v. *Levkovic* that "the essential elements of the crime must be ascertainable in advance."[16] In Canada, a law is unconstitutionally vague where it fails to give "sufficient guidance for legal debate."[17] Furthermore, a Canadian court can conclude that a law fails to meet that requirement only when it has exhausted all of its interpretive function yet still cannot ascertain the statute's scope or meaning.[18]

Following US Supreme Court decisions such as *Papachristou*, *Morales*, and *Kolender* discussed in the previous chapter, civil libertarians argued that some laws that govern public property were unconstitutionally vague.[19] They argued that statutory terms such as "camping," "loitering," and "vagrancy" were unconstitutionally vague and empowered police officers to selectively enforce municipal ordinances against unhoused persons.

In some cases, the arguments succeeded. For example, in the 2007 Supreme Court of Hawaii decision *State* v. *Beltran*, a Honolulu ordinance prohibited "what reasonably appears to constitute camping" in a public area "regardless of the intent of the participants or the nature of any other activities in which they may also be engaging."[20] The court held that the ordinance was void for vagueness. In their view, the ordinance vested the police with virtually unlimited enforcement discretion because officers could disregard both the participants' intent and any activities suggesting that the person was not camping.[21]

The Ninth Circuit Court of Appeals arrived at a similar conclusion in the 2014 decision *Desertrain* v. *City of Los Angeles*.[22] In that case, the court struck down a law that prohibited using a car "as a living quarters either overnight, day-by-day, or

14 Larry Alexander and Emily Sherwin, *Demystifying Legal Reasoning* (Cambridge University Press, 2008) at 14. Their original quote is: "The interpreter then becomes a rule maker in its own right" (*ibid.*). *See, e.g.*, *James* v. *US*, 550 US 192 at 1609 (2007).

15 *Kolender* v. *Lawson*, 461 US 352 at 357. *See also Chicago* v. *Morales*, 527 US 41 at 56–57 (1999).

16 *R* v. *Levkovic*, 2013 SCC 25 at para. 34.

17 *Ontario* v. *Canadian Pacific Ltd.* [1995] 2 SCR 1031 at para. 2.

18 *R.* v. *Levkovic* [2013] 2 SCR 204, 2013 SCC 25 at para. 34.

19 *See, e.g.*, John Ammann, "Addressing Quality-of-life Crimes in Our Cities: Criminalization, Community Courts and Community Compassion" (2000) 44 *St Louis U LJ* 811 at 814; Jamie Michael Charles, "'America's Lost Cause': The Unconstitutionality of Criminalizing Our Country's Homeless Population" (2009) 18 *Pub Int LJ* 315 at 321.

20 *State* v. *Beltran*, 172 P (3d) 458 at 465–67 (Haw Sup Ct 2007).

21 *Ibid.* at 466.

22 *Desertrain* v. *City of Los Angeles*, 754 F (3d) 1147 (9th Circ 2014).

otherwise" because it was unconstitutionally vague.[23] The court decided that although the ordinance was sufficiently vague to apply to any driver who kept food, clothing, or other belongings in their car, it appeared to be enforced exclusively against unhoused persons.[24] In the court's view, the statute conferred too much police discretion and failed to provide fair warning as to the prohibited conduct.[25]

But void for vagueness challenges tend to fail when lawmakers employ precise language in penal statutes.[26] Legislators responded to the void for vagueness doctrine's emergence by enacting a greater number of narrowly tailored ordinances that used precise language.[27] Cities replaced vague loitering laws and urban camping bans with precise legislation that targeted conduct such as staying in a park past its closing hours or sleeping on a subway bench.[28]

Many of these more narrowly tailored laws withstood constitutional scrutiny. For instance, in the Eleventh Circuit Court of Appeals decision *Joel* v. *City of Orlando* decided in 2000, the claimant brought a void for vagueness challenge against an ordinance that prohibited camping on public property.[29] Joel argued that the ordinance was unconstitutionally vague because it did not define the term "camping" with sufficient precision.[30] The court rejected that argument. The appeal justices noted that the statute defined camping as "Sleeping or otherwise being in a temporary shelter out-of-doors" or "Sleeping out-of-doors."[31] The court also observed that the Most Used City Ordinance Book (MUCOB) – a handbook that governs the enforcement of ordinances – provided additional statutory precision.[32] The MUCOB stated that a person did not necessarily camp if they fell asleep on public property.[33] Other indications of camping were required, including whether the individual slept in a tent or sleeping bag, or was covered by materials such as bedrolls.[34] The court concluded that Joel's conduct fell within that description.[35] They also explained that the combination of definitions provided in the ordinance and MUCOB adequately limited police discretion and risks of arbitrary enforcement.[36]

23 *Ibid.* at 1149, 1157.
24 *Ibid.* at 1156.
25 *Ibid.* at 1155–56.
26 *See, e.g.*, Foscarinis, "Downward Spiral" at 34; Hansel, "Constitutional Othering" at 449.
27 Baker, "'Anti-Homeless' Legislation" at 429–32.
28 *Ibid.*
29 *Joel* v. *City of Orlando*, 232 F (3d) 1353 (11th Circ 2000).
30 *Ibid.* at 1359–60.
31 Orlando, Fla, Code of Ordinances, ch. 43, § 43.52 (2000).
32 *Joel* v. *City of Orlando*, 232 F (3d) 1353 (11th Circ 2000) at 1356.
33 *Ibid.*
34 *Ibid.*
35 *Ibid.* at 1360.
36 *Ibid.*

The justices arrived at a similar conclusion in the 2015 California Court of Appeals decision *Allen* v. *Sacramento*.[37] The unhoused plaintiffs challenged the constitutionality of an urban camping ban.[38] They argued that the ordinance was unconstitutionally vague and permitted arbitrary enforcement by the police.[39] The justices remarked that the ordinance defined various terms, such as "camp," "camp facilities," and "public property."[40] Furthermore the court observed that the plaintiffs' conduct clearly violated the ordinance.[41] The justices rejected the plaintiffs' void for vagueness challenge.

Courts have rejected void for vagueness arguments in other cases that involve narrowly tailored laws that employ precise language or define key terms within the statute.[42] Although the void for vagueness doctrine successfully struck down ambiguous statutes, its usefulness has been constrained by narrowly tailored ordinances that target specific acts, and that can result in displacement, fines, arrests, and imprisonment.

2.2 OVERBREADTH

Second, the overbreadth doctrine has also been invoked to strike down some laws that regulate public property. Although overbreadth claims generally fail in the United States, they have been one of the most successful types of constitutional challenges to laws that regulate public property in Canada. In the United States, the overbreadth doctrine is used to attack the facial constitutionality of a law that violates a person's right to free speech.[43] The doctrine applies in contexts where a law regulates "too much speech that is protected."[44] A law in the United States will be unconstitutionally overbroad where its overbreadth is substantial "not only in an absolute sense, but also relative to the statute's plainly legitimate sweep."[45] Overbreadth doctrine protects individuals against broad laws that chill speech and promote self-censorship.[46]

37 *Allen* v. *City of Sacramento*, 234 Cal App (4th) 41 (App Ct 2015)
38 *Ibid.* at 48–49.
39 *Ibid.* at 55.
40 *Ibid.*
41 *Ibid.*
42 *See, e.g.*, *People* v. *Diaz* (Cal Sup Ct 2018); *Catron* v. *City of St. Petersburg* (MD Fla 2009); *McArdle* v. *City of Ocala*, FL, 519 F Supp (3d) 1045 at 1052–53 (MD Fla 2021); *Davidovich* v. *City of San Diego* (SD Cal 2011).
43 *See, e.g.*, Richard H. Fallon Jr., "Making Sense of Overbreadth" (1991) 100:4 *Yale LJ* 853 at 863; Brandice Canes-Wrone and Michael C. Dorf, "Measuring the Chilling Effect" (2015) 90:4 *NYU L Rev* 1095 at 1096; Henry Paul Monaghan, "Overbreadth" [1981] Sup Ct Rev 1 at 3; *Osborne* v. *Ohio*, 495 US 103 at 112 (1990).
44 Kent Greenawalt, "Free Speech in the United States and Canada" (1992) 55:1 *Law & Contemp Probs* 5 at 16; *US* v. *Williams*, 553 US 285 at 1838 (2008).
45 *US* v. *Williams*, 553 US 285 at 1838 (2008).
46 *Virginia* v. *Hicks*, 539 US 113 at 119 (2003).

In the United States, overbreadth challenges to laws that prohibit sleeping, camping, or urinating on public property generally fail.[47] The main problem is that the statute must limit some form of expression for overbreadth doctrine to succeed. Although certain acts or conduct (such as flag burning) are sufficiently expressive to be protected by the First Amendment, the relevant act must intend "to convey a particularized message" and there must be great likelihood "that the message would be understood by those who viewed it."[48] In US contexts, those requirements create a major obstacle for claimants who invoke the overbreadth doctrine to challenge laws that regulate public property. Notably, the claimants must pigeon-hole their interest in sleeping or lying down into a First Amendment claim; they must argue that sleeping, pitching a tent, or sitting on public property are expressive acts.[49] Yet courts tend to reject these claims for two reasons.

First, some courts conclude that sitting or sleeping do not constitute expressive conduct. For instance, in the Ninth Circuit Court of Appeals decision *Roulette* v. *City of Seattle*, the claimants challenged an ordinance that prohibited sitting and lying on the city's sidewalks.[50] They argued that such acts conveyed a message of passivity to pedestrians to whom they were panhandling.[51] In the claimants' view, the statute was unconstitutionally overbroad because it limited that form of expression.[52] The majority of the court rejected that argument and concluded that sitting and lying down are not "integral to, or commonly associated with, expression."[53]

Second, even when courts have recognized that sleeping or camping are expressive – for instance, as a form of protest – courts uphold the law when it is narrowly tailored to achieve a compelling State interest.[54] The US Supreme Court decision *Clark* v. *Community for Creative Non-Violence (CCNV)* illustrates this point.[55] The claimants organized a protest where people camped overnight in Lafayette park in Washington, DC to draw attention to the plight of people experiencing homelessness.[56] They violated a regulation that prohibited camping in certain parks without a permit.[57]

While the Court accepted the premise that the conduct was expressive in the circumstances, it rejected the claimants' overbreadth argument. The majority noted that the State had a substantial interest to maintain the condition of public parks for

47 Hansel, "Constitutional Othering" at 450.

48 *Spence* v. *Washington*, 418 US 405 at 410–11 (1974); *Texas* v. *Johnson*, 491 US 397 at 404 (1989). See a summary of these requirements in Robert Post, "Recuperating First Amendment Doctrine" (1995) 47:7 *Stan L Rev* 1249 at 1251–52.

49 Hansel, "Constitutional Othering" at 451.

50 *Roulette* v. *City of Seattle*, 97 F (3d) 300 at 303–04 (9th Circ 1996).

51 *Ibid.* at 303.

52 *Ibid.* at 303–04.

53 *Ibid.*

54 *Clark* v. *Community for Creative Non-Violence*, 468 US 288 at 293 (1984).

55 *Ibid.*

56 *Ibid.* at 289.

57 *Ibid.* at 290–91.

the population's use and enjoyment.[58] The Court also concluded that the law was narrowly tailored to achieve the State's objective, and that the State can legitimately restrict the time, place, and manner of certain forms of expression.[59]

The overbreadth doctrine plays a different role in Canada. Canadian case law recognizes the principle of fundamental justice that laws cannot be overbroad in a way that deprives a person of their right to life, liberty, or security of the person.[60] Compared to US overbreadth doctrine, Canadian overbreadth doctrine is more expansive because it applies in contexts other than freedom of speech. An overbroad law regulates conduct that the State did not intend to control.[61] In Canada, laws are unconstitutionally overbroad when they violate individuals' right to life, liberty, or security of the person for no reason.[62] Overbreadth claims have succeeded in certain contexts when unhoused persons challenged the constitutionality of laws that govern public property.[63] The British Columbia (BC) judicial decisions *Victoria (City)* v. *Adams* and *Abbotsford (City)* v. *Shantz* illustrate this point.[64]

First, in the 2009 BC Court of Appeal decision *Victoria (City)* v. *Adams*, municipal ordinances comprehensively prohibited individuals from erecting temporary shelters on public property despite the lack of available shelter spaces in the city.[65] At the time of the litigation, there were over 1,000 people experiencing homelessness in the city of Victoria, and 141 permanent shelter beds in the city which expanded to 326 during extreme weather conditions.[66]

The court observed that homelessness was an involuntary condition for most unhoused persons in Victoria, and stemmed from a confluence of economic, structural, and individual factors.[67] The evidence showed that the temporary shelter ban prevented unhoused persons from protecting themselves against the elements, which subjected them to risks of physical and psychological harm.[68] The medical

58 *Ibid.* at 299.

59 *Ibid.* at 295–96, 298–99.

60 Canadian Charter of Rights and Freedoms, s. 7, Part I of the Constitution Act, 1982, being Schedule B to the Canada Act 1982 (UK), 1982, c. 11; *Canada (Attorney General)* v. *Bedford*, 2013 SCC 72 at para. 105; Colton Fehr, "The Individualistic Approach to Arbitrariness, Overbreadth, and Gross Disproportionality" (2018) 51:1 *UBC L Rev* 55 at 59–60.

61 *Bedford* at para. 101. *See, e.g.*, Wayne Renke, "Bedford, Substantive Rationality, and Participatory Democracy" (2015) 20:1 *Rev Const Stud* 30 at 60–61 (noting that an overbroad law is partly arbitrary because it regulates conduct that exceeds its intended scope).

62 Hamish Stewart, "*Bedford* and the Structure of Section 7" (2015) 60:3 *McGill LJ* 575 at 584, 586; *Bedford* at paras. 108–09.

63 *See, e.g.*, Terry Skolnik, "Homelessness and the Impossibility to Obey the Law" (2016) 43:3 *Fordham Urb LJ* 741 at 756–59.

64 Terry Skolnik, "Homelessness and Unconstitutional Discrimination" (2019) 15 *JL & Equal* 69 at 81 (providing an overview of these decisions).

65 *Victoria (City)* v. *Adams*, 2009 BCCA 563 at paras. 21–24, 28.

66 *Ibid.* at para. 28.

67 *Ibid.* at paras. 104–11; *Victoria (City)* v. *Adams*, 2008 BCSC 1363 at paras. 59–66.

68 *Victoria (City)* BCCA at paras. 103–10.

experts noted that people experiencing homelessness were vulnerable to frostbite and hypothermia during the winter months.[69]

The BC Court of Appeal concluded that the ordinance violated the claimants' constitutional right to life, liberty, and security of the person and that it was unconstitutionally overbroad.[70] In their view, the ordinance was unconstitutional because it prohibited individuals from erecting temporary shelters at all times while there was insufficient shelter space to accommodate the city's unhoused population.[71] In the court's view, the ordinance was overbroad because it was unnecessary for the city to comprehensively forbid individuals from erecting temporary shelters to promote the shared use of public spaces.[72] Although the purpose of the ordinance was to maintain the environmental, recreational, and social benefits of parks, the court concluded that those objectives could be achieved without endangering unhoused persons' physical and psychological integrity.[73] In the court's view, the ordinance would be constitutional if it proscribed temporary shelters at nighttime and required them to be taken down during the day – an approach that sought to balance the interests of unhoused persons' and the city.[74]

The BC Supreme Court reached a similar conclusion in the 2015 decision *Abbotsford (City)* v. *Shantz*.[75] In *Shantz*, city ordinances prohibited individuals from erecting temporary shelters on public property without a permit despite insufficient shelter spaces for the city's unhoused population.[76] Individuals were required to obtain a camping permit using a credit card and pay $15/hour.[77] The city's decision to grant a permit was discretionary – the city could refuse a permit if an individual's proposed use of the park could damage the grounds.[78] Like in Adams, the court struck down the ordinance and permit requirement because they violated the claimants' section 7 Charter interests and were both unconstitutionally overbroad and grossly disproportionate.[79]

2.3 THE FUNDAMENTAL RIGHT TO TRAVEL

The third type of constitutional challenge to laws that govern public property applies only in the United States. Some courts have decided that laws governing public

69 *Ibid.* at para. 28.
70 *Ibid.* at paras. 110, 116.
71 *Ibid.* at para. 116.
72 *Ibid.*
73 *Ibid.* at paras. 116, 122.
74 *Ibid.* at paras. 122, 166.
75 *Abbotsford (City)* v. *Shantz*, 2015 BCSC 1909.
76 *Ibid.* at paras. 17–25, 82.
77 *Ibid.* at para. 22.
78 *Ibid.*
79 *Ibid.* at paras. 6, 203, 224.

property can violate unhoused persons' fundamental right to travel.[80] This right protects people's ability to move between states and within one's own state without being subject to punishment or loss of entitlements.[81]

The fundamental right to travel is justified on various grounds.[82] For one, interstate travel facilitates federalism.[83] More specifically, federalism would be hindered if protectionist policies by one state resulted in retaliatory measures by another.[84] The right to travel thus promotes interstate cooperation.[85] Second, the right protects individual autonomy and promotes self-actualization.[86] The right to travel allows individuals to move between states in search of better employment, to be with their romantic partners who live in other states, to pursue better educational opportunities that exist outside of one's state, or to receive better medical care.[87] Third, the right to travel protects against discrimination because it helps prevent the government from penalizing certain groups from traveling between states.[88] For instance, this right allows individuals to escape state laws that they view to be discriminatory or that limit human flourishing.[89] The right to travel also prevents states from adopting policies that curb the influx of immigration of marginalized groups from other states, and conversely, allows marginalized groups to leave their home state if they construe its laws or policies to be oppressive.[90] Some US Supreme Court justices have connected the right to travel to the notion of political equality

80 *Pottinger* v. *City of Miami*, 810 F Supp 1551 at 1579–83 (SD Fla, 1992). *See also*, Farida Ali, "Limiting the Poor's Right to Public Space: Criminalizing Homelessness in California" (2014) 21:2 *Geo J Poverty L & Pol'y* 197 at 222; Christine Bella and David Lopez, "Quality-of-life – At What Price? Constitutional Challenges to Laws Adversely Impacting the Homeless" (1994) 10 *J CR & Econ Dev* 89 at 106.

81 *See, e.g.*, Andrew Porter, "Toward a Constitutional Analysis of the Right to Intrastate Travel" (1991–1992) 86:3 *Nw U L Rev* 820 at 824–25; Paul Ades, "The Unconstitutionality of Antihomeless Laws: Ordinances Prohibiting Sleeping in Outdoor Public Areas as a Violation of the Right to Travel" (1989) 77:3 *Cal L Rev* 595 at 605–13 (providing an overview of the fundamental right to travel); Karthryn Wilhelm, "Freedom of Movement at a Standstill – Toward the Establishment of a Fundamental Right to Intrastate Travel" (2010) 90:6 *BU L Rev* 2461 at 2466.

82 Patrick Garry, *An Entrenched Legacy: How the New Deal Constitutional Revolution Continues to Shape the Role of the Supreme Court* (University Park: Penn State University Press, 2010) at 125–26.

83 Mark Strasser, "The Privileges of National Citizenship: On *Saenz*, Same-Sex Couples, and the Right to Travel" (2000) 52:2 *Rutgers L Rev* 553 at 568.

84 *Ibid.* at 568–70.

85 *Ibid.*; Seth Kreimer, "The Law of Choice and Choice of Law: Abortion, the Right to Travel, and Extraterritorial Regulation in American Federalism" (1992) 67:3 *NYU L Rev* 451 at 500; Seth Kreimer, "But Whoever Treasures Freedom: The Right to Travel and Extraterritorial Abortions" (1993) 91:5 *Mich L Rev* 907 at 918–19.

86 R. Linus Chan, "The Right to Travel: Breaking Down the Thousand Petty Fortresses of State Self-Deportation Laws" (2014) 34:2 *Pace L Rev* 814 at 852.

87 *Saenz* v. *Roe*, 526 US 489 at 502 (1999); Leonard Boudin, "The Constitutional Right to Travel" (1956) 56:1 *Colum L Rev* 47 at 49.

88 *See, e.g.*, Stewart Baker, "A Strict Scrutiny of the Right to Travel" (1975) 22:5 *UCLA L Rev* 1129 at 1135–36.

89 Garry, *An Entrenched Legacy* at 125–26.

90 *Ibid.*

because economically disadvantaged persons can seek better economic opportunities in other states, which reduces the likelihood of social hierarchies.[91]

In rare cases, courts have accepted that laws that regulate public property undermined the right to travel. In the 1992 decision *Pottinger* v. *Miami* discussed more below, municipal ordinances prohibited sleeping on public property even though there was only enough shelter spaces for 700 of the city's 6,000 unhoused persons.[92] Shortly after the trial and before the court rendered its decision, Hurricane Andrew struck southern Florida.[93] The consequences were devastating: the storm's aftermath left roughly 200,000 additional people without housing.[94] The court concluded that the ordinances violated the right to travel for various reasons. The laws expelled people experiencing homelessness from the city and forced them to travel somewhere else to comply with the laws.[95] Additionally, the law deterred unhoused people from other cities from moving to Miami.[96]

Since *Pottinger*, courts overwhelmingly reject the claim that laws that regulate public property violate the right to travel.[97] Some courts have concluded that the *Pottinger* decision was wrong because it misapplied a heightened standard of strict scrutiny to a law that was facially neutral.[98] Such decisions viewed *Pottinger* as bad precedent and reasoned that the decision departed significantly from prior Supreme Court case law.[99] Other courts decided that laws that prohibit camping on public property do not violate the right to travel directly, but instead, impact it incidentally.[100] According to this view, the right is violated only when a law directly penalizes travel and impacts mobility, or, denies entitlements or necessities because one travels.[101] Some justices have ruled that camping ordinances do not violate the right to travel because those who camp on public property do not seek to travel but to remain in one place.[102] For these reasons, laws that govern public property are rarely struck down on the basis that they violate the fundamental right to travel.

91 *Saenz*, 526 US 489 at 506–07.

92 *Pottinger* v. *City of Miami*, 810 F Supp 1551 at 1564 (SD Fla 1992).

93 *Ibid.* at 1558–59.

94 *Ibid.*

95 *Ibid.* at 1581.

96 *Ibid.*

97 Hansel, "Constitutional Othering" at 452–53; *Sanchez* v. *City of Fresno*, 914 F Supp (2d) 1079 at 1111 (ED Cal 2012); *Davison* v. *City of Tucson*, 924 F Supp 989 at 993–94 (D Ariz 1996); *Allen* v. *City of Sacramento*, 234 Cal App (4th) 41 at 62 (App Ct 2015); *Tobe* v. *City of Santa Ana*, 892 P (2d) 1145 at 1100–04 (Cal Sup Ct 1995); *Joyce* v. *City and County of San Francisco*, 846 F Supp 843 at 861 (ND Cal 1994).

98 *Joyce*, 846 F Supp 843 at 860–61 (ND Cal 1994).

99 *Ibid.*

100 *Tobe* v. *City of Santa Ana*, 892 P (2d) 1145 at 1100–04 (Cal Sup Ct 1995).

101 *Ibid.* at 1101–04; *Sanchez*, 914 F Supp (2d) 1079 at 1109 (ED Cal 2012).

102 *Davison*, 924 F Supp 989 at 993–94 (D Ariz 1996).

2.4 DISCRIMINATION AND EQUAL PROTECTION

Fourth, some argue that laws that govern public property are unconstitutional because they discriminate against unhoused persons.[103] Generally speaking, unconstitutional discrimination implies that the State imposes disadvantages or denies benefits to groups based on their immutable or constructively immutable personal characteristics.[104] Immutable characteristics imply traits that individuals did not choose and generally cannot change, such as race or age.[105] In contrast, constructively immutable traits are associated with an individual's personhood and can be changed only at great personal cost, such as religion, marital status, or citizenship.[106] Courts and scholars generally distinguish between two forms of discrimination: direct and indirect.[107] Direct discrimination (or disparate treatment) implies that the State singles out certain groups for adverse treatment.[108] Indirect discrimination (or disparate impact) implies that the State's neutrally worded laws adversely impact certain groups.[109] Equal protection claims have been the least successful type of constitutional challenge to laws that govern public property in the United States and in Canada.

In the United States, the Fourteenth Amendment's Equal Protection Clause safeguards individuals against unconstitutional discrimination.[110] The judiciary accords the highest level of judicial scrutiny – strict scrutiny – to legislation that discriminates against a constitutionally protected class (or suspect class).[111] Notably, the law must pursue a sufficiently important State objective and employ means that are sufficiently narrowly tailored to achieve that end.[112] To date, the US Supreme Court has recognized five suspect classifications that are subject to some form of heightened scrutiny: race, national origin, alienage, sex, and nonmarital parentage.[113] Suspect classification extends to historically marginalized

103 *See, e.g.*, Jennifer Watson, "When No Place Is Home: Why the Homeless Deserve Suspect Classification" (2002) 88:2 *Iowa L Rev* 501 at 512–13; Sarah Finnane Hanafin, "Legal Shelter: A Case for Homelessness as a Protected Status under Hate Crime Law and Enhanced Equal Protection Scrutiny" (2011) 40:2 *Stetson L Rev* 435 at 456; Jason Leckerman, "City of Brotherly Love? Using the Fourteenth Amendment to Strike Down an Anti-Homeless Ordinance in Philadelphia" (2001) 3:1 *U Pa J Const L* 540 at 561–62; Greg Vamos, "*Kreimer* v. *Bureau of Police*: Are the Homeless Ready for Suspect Classification" (1993) 14 *Whittier L Rev* 731.

104 *See, e.g.*, *Andrews* v. *Law Society of British Columbia* [1989] 1 SCR 143 at 174–75.

105 Jessica Clarke, "Against Immutability" (2015) 125:2 *Yale LJ* 2 at 14–15.

106 *Ibid.* at 24–25; *Gosselin* v. *Quebec (Attorney General)*, 2002 SCC 84 at para. 105.

107 Oran Doyle, "Direct Discrimination, Indirect Discrimination and Autonomy" (2007) 27:3 *Oxford J Leg Stud* 537 at 537–38.

108 Sophia Moreau, "What Is Discrimination?" (2010) 38 *Phil & Pub Aff* 143 at 154.

109 *Ibid.*

110 US Const amend XIV, § 1.

111 Roy Spece Jr. and David Yokum, "Scrutinizing Strict Scrutiny" (2015) 40:2 *Vt L Rev* 285 at 292.

112 *Wygant* v. *Jackson Bd. of Ed.*, 476 US 267 at 274 (1986); Spece Jr. and Yokum, "Scrutinizing Strict Scrutiny" at 295.

113 Kenji Yoshino, "The New Equal Protection" (2011) 124:3 *Harv L Rev* 747 at 756. Yoshino's exact quote is: "The Supreme Court has formally accorded heightened scrutiny to classifications based on five characteristics: race, national origin, alienage, sex, and nonmarital parentage." Internal citations omitted.

groups that have lacked political power, such that they require additional protection against the majoritarian political process.[114] US courts apply a rational basis standard when individuals who do not fall within a suspect classification claim that they suffered unconstitutional discrimination.[115] Rational basis review is satisfied where the disputed law is "rationally related to a legitimate governmental interest."[116] Statutes that are subject to rational basis review tend to withstand constitutional scrutiny.[117]

US courts have rejected poverty and homelessness as suspect classes.[118] In the 1973 US Supreme Court decision *San Antonio Independent School District* v. *Rodriguez*, the Court decided that wealth was not a suspect classification because it lacked the classic indicia of protected classes – such as political powerlessness and a history of unequal treatment – and because its definition was too amorphous.[119] Some US courts have rejected homelessness as a suspect classification on similar grounds,[120] while others have rejected homelessness as a suspect classification without providing reasons for that conclusion.[121] Absent evidence of discriminatory legislative intent – which is rarely established – facially neutral laws tend to withstand equal protection challenges even when they disparately impact unhoused persons.

The 1971 Supreme Court of California decision *Parr* v. *Municipal Court* remains one of the few instances where such a claim succeeded.[122] In *Parr*, the city of Carmel-by-the-Sea enacted an ordinance that prohibited a range of conduct on public property, including loitering, sitting or lying on steps or lawns, and erecting temporary structures.[123] The city also issued a Declaration of Urgency that was discriminatory on its face against hippies.[124] The court struck down the ordinance.[125] The

114 Watson, "When No Place Is Home" at 509, citing *San Antonio Independent School Dist.* v. *Rodriguez*, 411 US 1 at 28 (1973).

115 Yoshino, "The New Equal Protection" at 756.

116 Thomas Nachbar, "The Rationality of Rational Basis Review" (2016) 102:7 *Va L Rev* 1627 at 1629.

117 Yoshino, "The New Equal Protection" at 755–56; Katie Eyer, "The Canon of Rational Basis Review" (2018) 93:3 *Notre Dame L Rev* 1317 at 1318–19.

118 *San Antonio Independent School Dist.* v. *Rodriguez*, 411 US 1 at 32–33; *Lindsey* v. *Normet*, 405 US 56 at 74 (1972); Danieli Evans Peterman, "Socioeconomic Status Discrimination" (2018) 104:7 *Va L Rev* 1283 at 1290–91.

119 *San Antonio Independent School Dist.* v. *Rodriguez*, 411 US 1 at 19–20, 28–29 (1973); Bertrall Ross II and Su Li, "Measuring Political Power: Suspect Class Determinations and the Poor" (2016) 104:2 *Cal L Rev* 323 at 343.

120 *See, e.g.*, *Joyce* v. *City and County of San Francisco*, 846 F Supp 843 at 859–61 (ND Cal 1994).

121 *D'Aguanno* v. *Gallagher*, 50 F (3d) 877 (11th Circ 1995), fn. 2 in that decision; *Kreimer* v. *Bureau of Police for Town of Morristown*, 958 F (2d) 1242 (3rd Circ 1992), fn. 32 in the decision.

122 *Parr* v. *Municipal Court*, 3 Cal App (3d) 861 (App Ct 1971).

123 *Ibid.* at 862–63; Carmel-by-the-Sea, Cal, Ordinance 697.02 (1968).

124 *Parr* v. *Municipal Court*, 3 Cal App (3d) 861 (App Ct 1971) at 863. The Declaration of Emergency stated: "The City Council of Carmel-by-the-Sea has observed an extraordinary influx of undesirable and unsanitary visitors to the City, sometimes known as 'hippies,' and finds that unless proper regulations are adopted immediately the use and enjoyment of public property will be jeopardized if not entirely eliminated; the public parks and beaches are, in many cases, rendered unfit for normal public use by the unregulated and uncontrolled conduct of the new transients."

125 *Ibid.* at 865–66.

court observed that the provision and its accompanying declaration were directly discriminatory because they singled out people experiencing homelessness and used pejorative terms such as "undesirable" and "unsanitary."[126] Although the targets of the law were not a suspect class, the court nonetheless struck down the law because its purpose was impermissible and expressed hostility and animus, which violated the right to equal protection.[127]

Canadian courts have also rejected poverty and homelessness as constitutionally protected classes.[128] In Canada, section 15 of the Charter prohibits direct and indirect discrimination on the basis of enumerated and analogous grounds.[129] Enumerated grounds of discrimination are expressly mentioned in section 15's wording and include personal characteristics such as race, age, color, gender, religion, national or ethnic origin, and disability.[130] Analogous grounds of discrimination are not expressly mentioned in section 15 of the Charter's wording yet have been identified by courts as prohibited grounds of discrimination, such as citizenship, marital status, and sexual orientation.[131] Courts recognize new analogous grounds of discrimination based on a group's immutable or constructively immutable personal traits, and factors such as a group's historical disadvantage and lack of political power.[132]

The 2007 Ontario Court of Appeal decision *R* v. *Banks* rejected poverty as a constitutionally protected class.[133] In that decision, a group of impecunious and unhoused persons challenged the constitutionality of a provincial law that prohibited individuals from soliciting money from drivers.[134] They argued that the provisions discriminated against panhandlers.[135] The court rejected that argument. The justices observed that panhandling is an activity rather than a constitutionally protected characteristic, and that impecunious persons are an amorphous group that are not akin to other grounds of discrimination.[136]

Later, in the 2013 Superior Court of Ontario decision *Tanudjaja* v. *Canada (Attorney General) (Application)*, the Superior Court of Ontario rejected homelessness as an analogous ground of discrimination.[137] In *Tanudjaja*, the applicants alleged that the federal and provincial governments made certain decisions in the

126 *Ibid.* at 867–68.
127 *Ibid.* at 864–67.
128 Skolnik, "Homelessness and Unconstitutional Discrimination" at 70; Jessica Eisen, "On Shaky Grounds: Poverty and Analogous Grounds under the *Charter*" (2013) 2 *Can J Poverty L* 1 at 19–20.
129 *Quebec (Attorney General)* v. A [2013] 1 SCR 61, [2013] SCC 5.
130 Canadian Charter, s. 15.
131 *Andrews* v. *Law Society of British Columbia* [1989] 1 SCR 143 [citizenship]; *Miron* v. *Trudel* [1995] 2 SCR 418 [marital status]; *Vriend* v. *Alberta* [1998] 1 SCR 493 [sexual orientation].
132 *Corbiere* v. *Canada (Minister of Indian and Northern Affairs)* [1999] 2 SCR 203 at paras. 13, 60.
133 *R* v. *Banks* [2007] ONCA 19.
134 *Ibid.* at paras. 1–10; Safe Streets Act, 1999, SO 1999, c. 8.
135 *R* v. *Banks* 2007 ONCA 19 at para. 7.
136 *Ibid.* at paras. 98–99, 104.
137 *Tanudjaja* v. *Attorney General (Canada) (Application)*, 2013 ONSC 5410.

1990s that decreased access to housing which adversely impacted unhoused persons' fundamental interests.[138] One of the applicants was living on public property and in the shelter system.[139] The other three applicants were living in unaffordable and inadequate housing.[140] The claimants sought remedies that would require the provincial and federal governments to implement strategies and programs that reduce homelessness and improve access to housing.[141] They claimed that courts should exercise their supervisory jurisdiction to ensure that the governments fulfil such positive obligations.[142]

The court rejected their section 15 Charter argument and concluded that homelessness was not an analogous ground of discrimination for several reasons.[143] First, the court concluded that it was not possible to determine objectively who fell within the definition of "homelessness" for the purposes of the application.[144] The court noted that some of the applicants were unsheltered while others were living in inadequate or unaffordable housing.[145] Second, the court concluded that homelessness was not an immutable or constructively immutable personal characteristic akin to age, ethnicity, or gender, that could be determined by objective criteria.[146]

2.5 CRUEL AND UNUSUAL PUNISHMENTS

Fifth, some contend that laws that regulate public property violate the Eighth Amendment because they impose cruel and unusual punishment on people experiencing homelessness.[147] In the United States, Eighth Amendment claims have been the most successful constitutional challenge to laws that govern public property. The Eighth Amendment limits the State's criminal law power in three ways.[148] Notably, the cruel and unusual punishments clause limits the kinds of punishments that the State can impose, prohibits grossly disproportionate punishments, and imposes substantive limits on criminalization and punishment.[149] Most Eighth Amendment challenges to laws that govern public property fall into this third category. Some

138 *Ibid.* at para. 2.
139 *Ibid.* at para. 13.
140 *Ibid.* at paras. 12–14.
141 *Ibid.* at paras. 2, 110.
142 *Ibid.*
143 *See* Skolnik, "Homelessness and Unconstitutional Discrimination" at 70.
144 *Tanudjaja* v. *Attorney General (Canada) (Application)*, 2013 ONSC 5410 at para. 129.
145 *Ibid.*
146 *Ibid.* at para. 130; Eisen, "On Shaky Grounds" at 20.
147 Harry Simon, "Towns without Pity: A Constitutional and Historical Analysis of Official Efforts to Drive Homeless Persons from American Cities" (1992) 66:4 *Tul L Rev* 631 at 634; Juliette Smith, "Arresting the Homeless for Sleeping in Public: A Paradigm for Expanding the Robinson Doctrine" (1996) 29:2 *Colum JL & Soc Probs* 293 at 293–94; Edward Walters, "No Way Out: Eighth Amendment Protection for Do-or-Die Acts of the Homeless" (1995) 62:4 *U Chi L Rev* 1619 at 1641–42.
148 *Ingraham* v. *Wright*, 430 US 651 at 667 (1977).
149 *Ibid.*; Hannah Kieschnick, "A Cruel and Unusual Way to Regulate the Homeless: Extending the Status Crimes Doctrine to Anti-homeless Ordinances" (2018) 70:5 *Stan L Rev* 1569 at 1578–79.

courts have decided that the State violates the Eighth Amendment when it punishes unhoused persons' involuntary need-alleviating acts that stem from their involuntary condition of homelessness.[150]

In the 1992 District Court decision *Pottinger* v. *Miami* discussed above, the court concluded that the State imposed a cruel and unusual punishment when it prohibited sleeping in public despite the lack of sufficient shelter spaces for the city's unhoused population.[151] The court first concluded that homelessness was an involuntarily acquired condition due to factors such as lack of access to housing, financial hardship, and illness.[152] The court noted that unhoused persons had to sleep somewhere but did so on public property involuntarily because they lacked alternatives – involuntary conduct that was inseparable from their involuntary condition.[153] In the court's view, the punishment was cruel and unusual because unhoused persons had no choice but to sleep on public property, violate the law, and face punishment.[154]

The Court of Appeals for the Ninth Circuit arrived at a similar conclusion in *Jones* v. *City of Los Angeles*, where a municipal ordinance prohibited sleeping on the city's streets, sidewalks, and public ways.[155] The offense was punishable by a $1,000 fine and/or six months' imprisonment.[156] At the time, there were roughly 11,000–12,000 unhoused persons in Skid Row, Los Angeles, yet only 9,000–10,000 available spaces to accommodate the city's unhoused population.[157] The court concluded that the ordinance violated the Eighth Amendment.[158] The majority observed that the defendants did not choose to live on the streets.[159] The evidentiary record showed that individuals experience homelessness due to a range of individual and structural factors as well as the lack of affordable housing in Los Angeles.[160] In the court's view, the ordinance violated the Eighth Amendment because homelessness and the act of sleeping in public were both involuntary and inseparable from one another.[161] The holding in *Jones* was, however, vacated when the city reached a settlement with the defendants in 2007.[162]

Lastly, in the 2018 Ninth Circuit Court of Appeals decision *Martin* v. *City of Boise*, the majority of the court applied the principles set out in *Pottinger* and *Jones* to enjoin the city from enforcing an ordinance that prohibited camping on public

150 *See, e.g.*, Kieschnick, "A Cruel and Unusual Way to Regulate the Homeless" at 1618.
151 *Pottinger* v. *City of Miami*, 810 F Supp 1551 at 1564 (SD Fla 1992).
152 *Ibid.* at 1559, 1563–64.
153 *Ibid.* at 1564–65.
154 *Ibid.*
155 *Jones* v. *City of Los Angeles*, 444 F (3d) 1118 (9th Circ 2006).
156 *Ibid.* at 1123.
157 *Ibid.* at 1122.
158 *Ibid.* at 1136.
159 *Ibid.* at 1137–38.
160 *Ibid.* at 1123.
161 *Ibid.* at 1136.
162 *Jones* v. *City of Los Angeles*, 505 F (3d) 1006 (9th Circ 2007).

property.[163] The court concluded that the ordinance violated the Eighth Amendment. Point-in-time counts showed that there were over 850 homeless people in Boise, yet roughly 350 homeless shelter spaces and an additional 92 overflow mats.[164] The majority of the court decided that the State cannot criminalize and punish unhoused persons who sleep, sit, or shelter themselves on public property when there are insufficient shelter spaces to accommodate them.[165] Other courts have arrived at similar conclusions in similar circumstances.[166]

Despite these successes, courts may reject unhoused persons' Eighth Amendment claims in other contexts. Eighth Amendment claims may not succeed when defendants challenge a law that comprehensively bans urban camping or sleeping on public property, yet they fail to establish a lack of available shelter space for the unhoused population.[167] In other cases, courts have rejected similar claims when the defendants did not prove that they applied for social or public assistance that could have secured access to housing.[168] Eighth Amendment claims may also fail when a municipal ordinance prohibits need-alleviating conduct through a time, place, or manner restriction rather than a comprehensive prohibition.[169]

More recently, defendants have invoked the Eighth Amendment's Excessive Fines Clause to challenge the severity of fines associated with laws that govern public property.[170] The clause "limits the government's power to extract payments, whether in cash or in kind, as punishment for some offense."[171] The Excessive Fines Clause was incorporated into the states via the Fourteenth Amendment in the 2019 US Supreme Court decision *Timbs* v. *Indiana*.[172]

Some of these challenges have succeeded. In the 2021 decision *City of Seattle* v. *Long*, the defendant was living in his truck, which he parked illegally.[173] The city impounded the vehicle, issued a $44 ticket, and charged him roughly $950 in impoundment fees.[174] The Washington Supreme Court decided that the seizure of the truck and the impoundment fee constituted an excessive fine that violated the Eighth Amendment.[175] Similarly, in the 2020 District Court decision *Blake* v. *City of*

163 *Martin* v. *City of Boise*, 902 F (3d) 1031 at 1046–50 (9th Circ 2018). Motion for rehearing denied in *Martin* v. *City of Boise*, 920 F (3d) 584 (9th Circ 2019).

164 *Ibid.* at 1035–38.

165 *Ibid.* at 1048–49.

166 *Johnson* v. *City of Grants Pass*, 50 F (4th) 787 (9th Circ 2022).

167 *See, e.g.*, *Joel* v. *City of Orlando*, 232 F (3d) 1353 at 1362 (11th Circ 2000).

168 *Tobe* v. *City of Santa Ana*, 892 P (2d) 1145 at 1088–89 (Cal Sup Ct 1995)

169 *See, e.g.*, *Gomes* v. *County of Kauai*, 481 F Supp 3d 1104 at 1108–09 (Dist Court D Hawaii 2020).

170 *See, e.g.*, *Blake* v. *City of Grants Pass* (D Or 2020); *McArdle* v. *City of Ocala*, 519 F Supp (3d) 1045 (MD Fla 2021).

171 *Timbs* v. *Indiana*, 139 US 682 (2019) at 687, citing *United States* v. *Bajakajian*, 524 US 321 (1998) at 327–28.

172 *Timbs* v. *Indiana*, 139 US 682 (2019); "Fourteenth Amendment – Due Process Clause – Incorporation Doctrine – *Timbs* v. *Indiana*" (2019) 133:1 *Harv L Rev* 342 at 344.

173 *City of Seattle* v. *Long*, 493 P (3d) at 97 (Wash Sup Ct 2021).

174 *Ibid.*

175 *Ibid.*

Grants Pass, a group of unhoused persons argued that an urban camping ban violated the Excessive Fines Clause.[176] The ordinances were punishable by a mandatory fine of $295 for urban camping, which increased to $537.60 if the fine was unpaid.[177] The court decided that the ordinances violated the Excessive Fines Clause because the financial penalty was grossly disproportionate to the gravity of the offense.[178] Although the Excessive Fines Clause is still in its early stages, it may play a greater role in invalidating unhoused persons' excessive fines in the future.[179]

In Canada, the constitutional right to be free from cruel and unusual punishments has played virtually no role in striking down the financial penalties associated with laws that govern public property. Section 12 of the Canadian Charter prohibits cruel and unusual punishments.[180] In Canadian law, a punishment is cruel and unusual "if it is grossly disproportionate to the punishment that is appropriate, having regard to the nature of the offence and the circumstances of the offender … or if the law's reasonably foreseeable applications will impose grossly disproportionate sentences on others."[181] This latter portion of the test permits a law to be struck down if, according to a reasonable hypothetical, it would impose a cruel and unusual punishment on a hypothetical offender.[182] As the court explained in *R* v. *Lloyd*, gross disproportionality implies that "the punishment prescribed is so excessive as to outrage standards of decency" and is "abhorrent and intolerable."[183]

The Supreme Court of Canada has concluded that mandatory victim surcharges impose a cruel and unusual punishment that violates section 12 of the Charter.[184] Prior to the 2018 *R* v. *Boudreault* decision, individuals convicted of crimes were required to pay these surcharges, which funded services for victims of crime.[185] The victim surcharge was $100 for summary conviction offenses (the equivalent of misdemeanor offenses), and $200 for indictable offenses (the equivalent of felony offenses).[186] Due to the statutory scheme, judges could not modify or waive the quantum of the surcharge.[187]

176 *Blake* v. *City of Grants Pass* (D Or 2020).
177 *Ibid.*
178 *Ibid.*
179 *See, e.g.*, Raul Aguilar, "Unconstitutionally Fining: Fining People Experiencing Homelessness in the Era of *Timbs*" (2021) 53:3 UIC L Rev 587 at 603–05; Siobhan Allen, "The Role of the Excessive Fines Clause in Ending the Criminalization of Homelessness" (2022) 55: 4 Colum JL & Soc Probs 499 at 502–03, 533–38.
180 Canadian Charter, s. 12.
181 *R* v. *Lloyd*, 2016 SCC 13, [2016] 1 SCR 130 at para. 22; *R* v. *Nur*, 2015 SCC 15, [2015] 1 SCR 773 at para. 39.
182 *R* v. *Lloyd*, 2016 SCC 13, [2016] 1 SCR 130 at para. 25.
183 *Ibid.* at para. 24; *R* v. *Smith* [1987] 1 SCR 1045 at para. 54.
184 *R* v. *Boudreault*, 2018 SCC 58; Terry Skolnik, "Beyond Boudreault: Challenging Choice, Culpability, Punishment" (2019) 50 *CR* (7th) 283 at 283, 287–88.
185 *R* v. *Boudreault*, 2018 SCC 58 at para. 62.
186 *Ibid.*; Criminal Code, RSC 1985, c. C-46, s. 737.
187 *R* v. *Boudreault*, 2018 SCC 58 at para. 2.

The Court struck down the mandatory surcharge for several reasons. The financial penalties ignored the defendant's ability to pay, their level of culpability, and the potentially harmless nature of the offense that gave rise to a surcharge, such as breaching a probation order.[188] In the majority's view, the surcharge imposed the equivalent of indeterminate sentences on impecunious individuals who could not afford to pay the fines.[189] Defendants who failed to pay the fine were also subject to civil collection efforts.[190] The justices also determined that the threat of detention and imprisonment loomed over those who could not afford to pay the surcharge.[191] Notably, police officers could detain individuals prior to committal hearings, which assessed their capacity to pay their fines.[192] For these reasons, the mandatory surcharge constituted a cruel and unusual punishment.

The Supreme Court of Canada recognizes that punishments tend to respect the right to be free from cruel and unusual punishments when judges have the discretion to mitigate their severity.[193] Whereas mandatory minimum penalties result in excessive punishments, judicial discretion permits a judge to impose a proportionate penalty that respects section 12 of the Charter.[194] In *Boudreault*, the mandatory nature of the victim surcharge – and the lack of judicial discretion to mitigate or waive it – underpinned its cruel and unusual character.[195] In contrast, some provinces permit judges to waive or decrease the quantum of a fine – a safety valve that largely insulates financial penalties against successful section 12 Charter challenges.[196] For these reasons, section 12 Charter claims may also fail to protect unhoused persons against financial penalties that can be waived or reduced by judges.

The financial penalty scheme in other provinces may be vulnerable to section 12 Charter claims. Some provinces authorize judges to reduce the quantum of a fine to the minimum amount prescribed by law.[197] However, the minimum fine may still be excessive given a defendant's financial capacities. Furthermore, even when judges have discretion to waive or decrease the quantum of a fine, unhoused persons

188 *Ibid.* at para. 68.

189 *Ibid.* at paras. 76–79.

190 *Ibid.* at para. 74; Catherine Chesnay, Céline Bellot, and Marie-Eve Sylvestre, "Taming Disorderly People One Ticket at a Time: The Penalization of Homelessness in Ontario and British Columbia" (2013) 55:2 *Can J Corr* 161 at 176. *See* Offence Act, RSBC 1996, c. 338, s. 82(6)–(8).

191 R v. *Boudreault*, 2018 SCC 58 at paras. 69–73.

192 *Ibid.*

193 R v. *Lloyd*, 2016 SCC 13, [2016] 1 SCR 130 at para. 36; Debra Parkes, "Punishment and Its Limits" (2019) 88 *Sup Ct L Rev* 351 at 361; Sarah Chaster, "Cruel, Unusual, and Constitutionally Infirm: Mandatory Minimum Sentences in Canada" (2018) 23 *Appeal: Rev Current L & L Reform* 89 at 105, 107–08; Lauren Witten, "Proportionality as a Moral Process: Reconceiving Judicial Discretion and Mandatory Minimum Penalties" (2016) 48:1 *Ottawa L Rev* 81 at 130.

194 David Paciocco, "The Law of Minimum Sentences: Judicial Responses and Responsibility" (2015) 19:2 *CCLR* 173 at 173–74.

195 R v. *Boudreault*, 2018 SCC 58 at paras. 2, 56, 66.

196 Provincial Offences Act, RSO 1990, c. P33, s. 69(15) (permitting waiver or reduction of a fine).

197 Offence Act, RSBC 1996, c. 338, s. 88; Arts. 180.1, 218.6 CPP.

may not contest them due to personal factors such as mental illness, substance use disorder, or unfamiliarity with the justice system.[198] They may still accumulate significant criminal justice debt from unpaid fines.[199]

2.6 THE POSITIVE RIGHT TO HOUSING

Lastly, some have argued that the Constitution provides a positive right to housing.[200] US and Canadian courts have rejected this claim.[201] The US Supreme Court expressly rejected a positive right to housing in the 1972 decision *Lindsey* v. *Normet.*[202] In *Lindsey*, the claimants were renting a single family residence in Portland, Oregon, on a month-to-month basis.[203] The city declared their property unfit for habitation as a result of substandard living conditions.[204] The claimants then requested that the landlord make certain repairs to the property.[205] The landlord responded by making some of the requested repairs but not others.[206] The claimants subsequently refused to pay the next month's rent until the landlord made the remaining repairs.[207]

The landlord sought a court order to evict the tenant in accordance with Oregon's Forcible Entry and Wrongful Detainer Act.[208] Before the order was executed, the claimants challenged the statute's constitutionality. They argued that it violated the Due Process Clause and the Equal Protection Clause and sought to enjoin the eviction order from being executed.[209] The claimants contended that the "need for decent shelter" and "the right to retain peaceful possession of one's home" were fundamental rights.[210] They argued that the State could only limit those rights if

198 Terry Skolnik, "The Punitive Impact of Physical Distancing Laws on Homeless People" in Colleen Flood, Vanessa MacDonnell, Jane Philipott et al. (eds.), *The Law, Policy, and Ethics of COVID-19* (University of Ottawa Press, 2020) at 293.

199 Emily Knox, "Poverty Is Not a Crime – So Why Is Montreal Still Ticketing the Unhoused?" CBC News (October 28, 2021), www.cbc.ca/news/canada/montreal/first-person-bylaw-infraction-unhoused-poverty-tickets-1.6221531 [perma.cc/2RVP-G5Y].

200 *See, e.g.*, Shelby Green, "Imagining a Right to Housing, Lying in the Interstices" (2012) 19:3 Geo J Poverty L & Pol'y 393 at 396; Tracy Heffernan, Fay Faraday, and Peter Rosenthal, "Fighting for the Right to Housing in Canada" (2015) 24 JL & Soc Pol'y 10 at 11.

201 *See, e.g., Lindsey* v. *Normet*, 405 US 56 (1972); Maria Massimo, "Housing as a Right in the United States: Mitigating the Affordable Housing Crisis Using an International Human Rights Law Approach" (2021) 62:1 *BC L Rev* 273 at 287; *Tanudjaja* v. *Canada (Attorney General)*, 2014 ONCA 852 at para. 30; Sarah Hamill, "Caught between Deference and Indifference: The Right to Housing in Canada" (2018) 7 *Can J Hum Rts* 67 at 70; Casey Dawkins. "The Right to Housing in an Ownership Society" (2020) 47:2 *Hous & Soc'y* 81 at 82–83.

202 *Lindsey* v. *Normet*, 405 US 56 (1972) at 74; Maria Foscarinis, "The Growth of a Movement for a Human Right to Housing in the United States" (2007) 20 *Harv Hum Rts J* 35 at 37.

203 *Lindsey* v. *Normet*, 405 US 56 (1972) at 74.

204 *Ibid.* at 58–59.

205 *Ibid.*

206 *Ibid.*

207 *Ibid.*

208 *Ibid.*

209 *Ibid.* at 59–64.

210 *Ibid.* at 74. Quotation marks in original decision.

justified by a compelling interest and narrowly tailored means to achieve the State's objective.[211] The majority of the Court disagreed.[212] Although the Court recognized the importance of housing, they concluded that the Constitution's wording provided no affirmative right to housing.[213]

The 2014 Ontario Court of Appeal decision *Tanudjaja* v. *Canada (Attorney General)* declined to recognize a positive right to housing.[214] The majority of the justices cited Supreme Court of Canada precedent that rejected a freestanding right to healthcare.[215] They noted that existing Supreme Court of Canada decisions have not affirmed a positive State duty to ensure that individuals enjoy the section 7 Canadian Charter right to life, liberty, and security of the person.[216] They also observed that the court would usurp the legislator's function if it judicially reviewed the government's public policy approach to homelessness without a constitutional challenge to a particular law or policy.[217]

To be clear, positive economic and social rights have not been foreclosed entirely in Canada.[218] The Supreme Court of Canada noted that the State may have some positive duties to allocate resources or entitlements in certain contexts, even though such contexts have not yet been recognized.[219] Similarly, in the Ontario Court of Appeal's decision in *Tanudjaja*, the majority of the court noted that the Supreme Court of Canada left open the possibility that the State may have positive duties to remedy Charter rights violations in certain contexts.[220]

There are different reasons why courts are reticent to constitutionalize a right to housing that is not provided expressly in the Constitution. First, some courts worry that the recognition of justiciable positive rights erodes the separation of powers.[221] According to this argument, courts would usurp the functions of other branches of government by second-guessing their priorities and public policy

211 *Ibid.*

212 *Ibid.*

213 *Ibid.*

214 *Tanudjaja* v. *Canada (Attorney General)*, 2014 ONCA 852 at paras. 30–32.

215 *Ibid.*, citing *Chaoulli* v. *Quebec (Attorney General)*, 2005 SCC 35 at para. 104.

216 *Gosselin* v. *Quebec (Attorney General)*, 2002 SCC 84 at para. 81. *See also*, *Auton (Guardian ad litem of)* v. *British Columbia (Attorney General)*, 2004 SCC 78 at para. 41.

217 *Tanudjaja* v. *Canada (Attorney General)*, 2014 ONCA 852 at paras. 33–34.

218 *See, e.g.*, Miriam Cohen and Martin-Olivier Dagenais, "The Implementation of Economic, Social and Cultural Rights in Canada: Between Utopia and Reality" (2021) 7:1 *Const Rev* 26 at 40; Martha Jackman, "One Step Forward and Two Steps Back: Poverty, the Charter and the Legacy of *Gosselin*" (2019) 39:1 *NJCL* 85 at 100–01.

219 *Gosselin* v. *Quebec (Attorney General)*, 2002 SCC 84 at para. 82, noting: "One day s. 7 [of the Canadian Charter] may be interpreted to include positive obligations." Words in brackets mine.

220 *Tanudjaja* v. *Canada (Attorney General)*, 2014 ONCA 852 at para. 37.

221 *Tanudjaja* v. *Attorney General (Canada) (Application)*, 2013 ONSC 5410 at paras. 140–43; Katharine Young, "The Minimum Core of Economic and Social Rights: A Concept in Search of Content" (2008) 33 *Yale J Int'l L* 113 at 159 (describing this argument); Herman Schwartz, "Do Economic and Social Rights Belong in a Constitution" (1995) 10:3 *Am U J Intl L & Pol'y* 1233 at 1237–38.

decisions.[222] Furthermore, some scholars note that the recognition of positive rights raises democratic legitimacy concerns.[223] Namely, few unelected justices can override the complex public policy decisions made by many democratically elected lawmakers.[224] Some note that this is problematic because lawmakers are more representative of the population's diversity compared to judges.[225] Second, some courts observe that the judiciary lacks the institutional competence to implement or supervise redistributive schemes that involve complex public policy concerns.[226] Courts lack the information-gathering capacities that other branches of government have.[227] They also lack the expertise to devise or enforce complicated schemes whose implementation affects other public policy areas.[228] Finally, courts are concerned that they cannot devise a concrete threshold for what constitutes "adequate" housing and ensure that the government respects that standard.[229] For these types of reasons, courts have rejected a positive right to housing in the United States and Canada.

2.7 CONCLUSION

This chapter provided an overview of how US and Canadian constitutional law approach homelessness and the regulation of public property. It analyzed the principal constitutional challenges to municipal ordinances that govern need-alleviating conduct and highlighted their limitations. It demonstrated how constitutional claims fail to protect unhoused persons against various forms of actual and threatened interference associated with these laws, such as displacement, fines, arrests, and imprisonment. This chapter also explained how US and Canadian courts have thus far rejected a positive right to housing that would safeguard individuals against such forms of actual and threatened interference.

222 *Tanudjaja* v. *Canada (Attorney General)*, 2014 ONCA 852 at para. 33; Malcolm Langford "The Justiciability of Social Rights: From Practice to Theory" in Malcolm Langford (ed.), *Social Rights Jurisprudence: Emerging Trends in International and Comparative Law* (Cambridge University Press, 2008) at 31 (describing this argument).

223 Frank Cross, "The Error of Positive Rights" (2000) 48 *UCLA L Rev* 857 at 890, 914.

224 *Ibid.*

225 *Ibid.*

226 *Tanudjaja* v. *Attorney General (Canada) (Application)*, 2013 ONSC 5410 at paras. 33–34; *Chaoulli* v. *Quebec (Attorney General)*, 2005 SCC 35 at para. 164; Mitra Ebadolahi, "Using Structural Interdicts and the South African Human Rights Commission to Achieve Judicial Enforcement of Economic and Social Rights in South Africa" (2008) 83:5 *NYU L Rev* 1565 at 1567 (providing an overview of this argument); Helen Hershkoff, "Positive Rights and State Constitutions: The Limits of Federal Rationality Review" (1999) 112:6 *Harv L Rev* 1131 at 1175 (summarizing this argument).

227 Cass Sunstein, "The Most Knowledgeable Branch" (2016) 164 *U Pa L Rev* 1607 at 1613–15.

228 *Tanudjaja* v. *Canada (Attorney General)*, 2014 ONCA 852 at para. 34. *See, e.g.*, Wayne McCormack, "Property and Liberty – Institutional Competence and the Functions of Rights" (1994) 51:1 *Wash & Lee L Rev* 1 at 55–57.

229 *Tanudjaja* v. *Canada (Attorney General)*, 2014 ONCA 852 at paras. 34–35; Hershkoff, "Positive Rights and State Constitutions" at 1179 (summarizing this argument).

The next chapter explores how legal theorists have analyzed the relationship between homelessness, liberty, and property from the standpoint of two theories of freedom: positive and negative. Subsequent parts of this book highlight how these theories provide an important – but limited – understanding of this relationship, and overlook how unhoused persons face different forms of domination that undermine their freedom and equality.

3

Homelessness, Liberty, and Property

The previous chapter provided an overview of the main constitutional challenges related to homelessness and laws that govern public property in Canada and the United States. It showed how constitutional law does not provide a positive right to housing, and it demonstrated how existing interpretations of constitutional rights fail to protect unhoused persons against different threats of governmental interference.

This chapter explores how legal theorists have examined the relationship between homelessness, property, and two forms of liberty: negative liberty as noninterference, and positive liberty as self-actualization.[1] These conceptions of liberty (or freedom) deepen our understanding of homelessness.

The present chapter shows why positive and negative conceptions of liberty provide an incomplete understanding of the relationship between homelessness, liberty, and property. Subsequent parts of the book show why we gain a more complete understanding of this relationship when also consider how unhoused persons lack a third form of liberty: republican liberty as nondomination.[2] The term "domination" implies that individuals are vulnerable to the threat of unilateral interference by others.[3] Together, this chapter and the following ones illustrate how

[1] Isaiah Berlin, "Two Concepts of Liberty" in Henry Hardy (ed.), *Liberty* (Oxford University Press, 2002) at 169–70 (distinguishing positive and negative liberty). For examples of scholars who have examined the connection between homelessness, property, and positive and negative liberty, see Jeremy Waldron, "Homelessness and Community" (2000) 50:4 *U Toronto LJ* 371; Jeremy Waldron, "Community and Property – For Those Who Have Neither" (2008) 10:1 *Theor Inq L* 161; Jeremy Waldron, "Homelessness and the Issue of Freedom" (1991) 39 *UCLA L Rev* 295; Nicholas Blomley, "Homelessness, Rights, and the Delusions of Property" (2009) 30:6 *Urb Geo* 577; Jane Baron, "Property and No Property" (2006) 42:5 *Hous L Rev* 1425; Jane Baron, "Homelessness as a Property Problem" (2004) 36 *Urb Law* 273; Jane Baron, "Rescuing the Bundle-of-Rights Metaphor in Property Law" (2013) 82:1 *U Cin L Rev* 57; Ben McJunkin, "The Negative Right to Shelter" (2023) 111 Cal L Rev 127.

[2] Christopher Essert, "Property and Homelessness" (2016) 44 *Phil & Pub Aff* 266 at 266.

[3] Philip Pettit, *On the People's Terms: A Republican Theory and Model of Democracy* (Cambridge University Press, 2012) at 7; Philip Pettit, *Republicanism: A Theory of Freedom and Government* (Oxford University Press, 1999) at 22–23.

unhoused persons lack political equality because their positive, negative, and republican freedom are all limited in ways that do not affect people with access to housing.[4]

3.1 PRIVATE PROPERTY AND POSITIVE FREEDOM

3.1.1 *An Overview of Positive Freedom*

Isaiah Berlin famously distinguished between two conceptions of liberty: positive and negative. Positive freedom implies liberty as a form of self-mastery, self-actualization, or self-government.[5] The positive conception of liberty seeks to answer basic questions such as "who governs me?" and "by whom am I ruled?"[6] It is closely related to values such as autonomy and self-government.[7] Berlin argued that the positive conception of freedom distinguishes between one's higher and lower selves.[8] The higher self is self-actualized, rational, self-controlling, and concerned with one's long-term interests.[9] The lower self is the opposite: irrational, impulsive, and driven by impulses and short-term interests.[10] Berlin contended that positive liberty is central to certain religious and philosophical traditions, such as Ascetism, Quietism, Stoicism, and Buddhism.[11]

Positive liberty acknowledges that structural factors can influence the availability of opportunities that promote self-actualization.[12] For instance, poverty and lack of access to resources can hinder individuals' liberty to achieve certain goals, pursue certain plans, or make certain decisions.[13] Matthew Kramer notes that positive freedom emphasizes the availability of resources and opportunities, and individuals' actual use of such resources and opportunities to achieve their own authentic

4 Terry Skolnik, "Freedom and Access to Housing: Three Conceptions" (2018) 35 *Windsor YB Access Just* 226 at 242.

5 Berlin, "Two Concepts of Liberty" at 178. *See also* Matthew Kramer, *The Quality of Freedom* (Oxford University Press, 2003) at 96. Kramer points out that the concept of positive liberty is often associated with other terms that resemble self-mastery and self-actualization, such as autonomy, self-government, and self-determination. *See also* John Christman, "Liberalism and Individual Positive Freedom" (1991) 101 *Ethics* 343 at 344.

6 Berlin, "Two Concepts of Liberty" at 177; Lester Crocker, "Rousseau's Soi-Disant Liberty" in Robert Wokler (ed.), *Rousseau and Liberty* (Manchester University Press, 1995) at 244.

7 *See, e.g.*, Deborah Hellman, "Resurrecting the Neglected Liberty of Self-Government" (2015–16) 164 *U Pa L Rev Online* 233 at 233; Kai Möller, "Two Conceptions of Positive Liberty: Towards an Autonomy-Based Theory of Constitutional Rights" (2009) 29:4 *Oxford J Leg Stud* 757 at 757–58.

8 Berlin, "Two Concepts of Liberty" at 179.

9 *Ibid.*

10 *Ibid.*

11 *Ibid.* at 182; Charles Taylor, *Sources of the Self: The Making of Modern Identity* (Cambridge University Press, 1989) at 115; Richard Sorabji, "Freedom and Will: Greco-Roman Origins" in Richard Seaford, John Wilkins, and Matthew Wright (eds.), *Selfhood and the Soul: Essays on Ancient Thought and Literature in Honour of Christopher Gill* (Oxford University Press, 2017) at 49–50.

12 Lawrence Crocker, *Positive Liberty: An Essay in Normative Political Philosophy* (The Hague: Martinus Nijhoff, 1980) at 2.

13 *Ibid.*

ends.[14] In his view, positive liberty emphasizes the accomplishment of objectives rather than whether others physically hinder an individual's actions or plans.[15] In contrast to the negative theory of liberty – which construes freedom as noninterference – positive liberty is less concerned with coercion and concrete obstructions that restrict with one's movement or actions.[16]

Berlin was preoccupied by how the positive conception of liberty was incorporated within political theory and ideology.[17] He argued that authoritarian and totalitarian regimes emphasized positive liberty to justify tyranny.[18] In his view, these regimes employed coercion under the guise of necessity for individual and collective self-actualization.[19] He objected that totalitarian regimes portrayed coercion as a form of liberation rather than a hinderance to freedom.[20] Despite these concerns, Berlin also recognized that positive freedom is an essential component of liberty and that it is a "valid universal goal."[21]

Scholars argue that the positive conception of liberty is valuable for various reasons. First, in contrast to negative liberty theory, the positive conception of freedom more heavily emphasizes how access to opportunities and resources are necessary for self-actualization.[22] Impecunious persons may lack the financial resources to travel, access education, or enjoy a basic standard of living – all of which endow greater positive liberty to pursue their authentic interests and shape the course of their lives.[23] This explains why positive liberty is associated with the welfare State, resource redistribution, and structural forces within society that influence individuals' opportunities.[24]

14 Matthew Kramer, "Freedom and the Rule of Law" (2010) 61:4 *Ala L Rev* 827 at 830.

15 *Ibid.*

16 *See, e.g.*, Steven Heyman, "Positive and Negative Liberty" (1992) 68:1 *Chi-Kent L Rev* 81 at 81; Ernest van den Haag, "Liberty: Negative or Positive" (1978) 1 *Harv JL & Pub Pol'y* 63 at 63–64.

17 Berlin, "Two Concepts of Liberty" at 179; Isaiah Berlin, "Introduction" in Henry Hardy (ed.), *Liberty* (Oxford University Press, 2002) at 37; Maria Dimova-Cookson, "Defending Isaiah Berlin's Distinctions between Positive and Negative Freedoms" in Maria Dimova-Cookson (ed.), *Isaiah Berlin and the Politics of Freedom* (New York: Routledge, 2013) at 79; Ian Shapiro and Alicia Steinmetz, "Negative Liberty and the Cold War" in Steven Cherniss and Joshua Smith (eds.), *The Cambridge Companion to Isaiah Berlin* (Cambridge University Press, 2018) at 208.

18 Berlin, "Two Concepts of Liberty" at 179–81, 197–99; Gina Gustavsson, "The Psychological Dangers of Positive Liberty: Reconstructing a Neglected Undercurrent in Isaiah Berlin's 'Two Concepts of Liberty'" (2014) 76:2 *Rev Pol* 267 at 268 (summarizing how some scholars have interpreted Berlin's conception of positive liberty).

19 Berlin, "Two Concepts of Liberty" at 179–81, 197–99.

20 *Ibid.* at 179–81, 197–99. *See also* Gustavsson, "The Psychological Dangers of Positive Liberty" at 269, 272–73.

21 Berlin, "Two Concepts of Liberty" at 192–93; quoted portion in Berlin, "Introduction" in Hardy (ed.), *Liberty* at 39.

22 Crocker, *Positive Liberty* at 2. Note that Crocker disagrees with Berlin's conception of positive freedom as self-mastery (*ibid.* at 4).

23 *Ibid.* at 2–7.

24 *See, e.g.*, Robert Goodin, "Freedom and the Welfare State: Theoretical Foundations" (1982) 11:2 *J Soc Pol'y* 149 at 151–52; Partha Dasgupta, "Positive Freedom, Markets, and the Welfare State" (1986) 2:2 *Oxford Rev Econ Pol'y* 25 at 26; Crocker, *Positive Liberty* at 2; Jason Brennan and John Tomasi,

Second, the positive conception of liberty elucidates the comparative or relative social dimension of freedom.[25] All individuals may enjoy the same negative rights, meaning rights that protect against State interference. Yet positive liberty underscores how impecunious persons enjoy less positive freedom compared to affluent ones, even if the former experience no concrete interference.[26] Positive liberty thus acknowledges how individuals may enjoy different degrees of freedom based on the resources and opportunities that are available to them.

Third, positive freedom is concerned with the authenticity of human agency.[27] It accords importance to the ways in which values and preferences are shaped, and the ways in which individuals maintain control over the formation of their values and preferences.[28] For instance, individuals enjoy less positive freedom when their preferences and choices are conditioned by external influence, brainwashing, or manipulation.[29] Positive liberty thus connotes that individuals act consistently with reasons and values that they themselves shaped.[30]

Fourth, positive freedom is associated with the protection of basic capabilities that are necessary to live a dignified life.[31] Scholars such as Amartya Sen and Martha Nussbaum have advanced the Capabilities Approach, which posits that a central set of capabilities – or freedoms – must be protected so that individuals can live a meaningful life.[32] Central capabilities include, for instance, being able to live a normal-length life, enjoy bodily health and integrity, have control over one's environment, and affiliate with others.[33] Factors such as poverty, lack of educational resources, and diminished opportunities all influence the degree to which individuals enjoy such basic capabilities and can live a meaningful life.[34] The Capabilities Approach also recognizes that the State must provide access to resources that protect the basic capabilities and allow for human flourishing.[35]

"Classical Liberalism" in David Estlund (ed.), *The Oxford Handbook of Political Philosophy* (Oxford University Press, 2020) at 120.

25 Crocker, *Positive Liberty* at 7.

26 *Ibid.* at 2.

27 John Christman, "Freedom in Times of Struggle: Positive Liberty, Again" (2015) 37:1–2 *Analyse & Kritik* 171 at 177.

28 Christman, "Liberalism and Individual Positive Freedom" at 344–46.

29 *Ibid.* at 345–46; George Crowder, "Why We Need Positive Liberty" (2015) 77 *Rev Pol* 271 at 277.

30 Christman, "Liberalism and Individual Positive Freedom" at 345–46.

31 Christman, "Freedom in Times of Struggle" at 177–79. *See, e.g.*, Martha Nussbaum, *Creating Capabilities: The Human Development Approach* (Cambridge: Harvard University Press, 2011) at 17–21 (on the Capabilities Approach).

32 *See, e.g.*, Nussbaum, *Creating Capabilities* at 18–20; Amartya Sen, *Development as Freedom* (Oxford University Press, 2001) at 18, 24–25.

33 Nussbaum, *Creating Capabilities* at 33–34.

34 Sen, *Development as Freedom* at 87–88.

35 Martha Nussbaum, "Foreword: The Constitution and Capabilities: 'Perception' against Lofty Formalism" (2007) 121 *Harv L Rev* 4 at 11–13.

The distinction between positive and negative liberty is not neat. Some posit that positive and negative freedom are inseparable from one another.[36] They suggest that the negative conception of liberty as noninterference is valuable because it secures positive freedom and individual autonomy.[37] According to this view, negative freedom is thus a precondition for positive liberty.[38] In other words, "freedom is always *both* freedom from something and freedom to do or become something."[39]

3.1.2 *Property Rights, Positive Freedom, and Homelessness*

Property promotes positive liberty in various ways. First, a private property right allows a person to secure autonomy through means other than their physical bodies.[40] Individuals use property – such as structures, objects, and things – to pursue their authentic goals and purposes.[41] The ways in which property resolves allocation problems fosters autonomy in a consistent and predictable manner. The property law regime solves issues regarding the allocation, control, and use of things.[42] A private property scheme settles competing claims about who is entitled to use or enjoy a given thing.[43] In doing so, it protects expectations, ensures predictability, and promotes stability in how individuals can use objects to self-actualize.[44] Individuals can better plan their lives and coordinate with others knowing that they can use property to further their interests.[45]

Second, property protects the central capabilities, and safeguards interests that are central to self-actualization, such as liberty, privacy, well-being, and security.[46] A home characteristically safeguards these interests and can promote an individual's sense of belonging.[47] Within the home, individuals can privately pursue certain

36 *See, e.g.*, Maeve Cooke, "A Space of One's Own: Autonomy, Privacy, Liberty" (1999) 25:1 *Phil & Soc Criticism* 25:1 at 39.

37 *Ibid.*

38 *Ibid.* at 32.

39 Gerald McCallum Jr., "Negative and Positive Freedom" in David Miller (ed.), *Liberty Reader* (New York: Routledge, 2017) at 102, 107 (quoted portion at 107, emphasis in original).

40 Arthur Ripstein, *Force and Freedom: Kant's Legal and Political Philosophy* (Cambridge: Harvard University Press, 2009) at 88.

41 *Ibid.*

42 Jeremy Waldron, "What Is Private Property" (1985) 5:3 *Oxford J Leg Stud* 313 at 318. Private property rights also help ensure stability because they solve allocation problems within society. Namely, a private property scheme settles competing claims about who is entitled to use or enjoy a given thing.

43 *Ibid.*

44 Nestor Davidson, "Property's Morale" (2011) 110:3 *Mich L Rev* 437 at 439; Gregory Alexander, "Property, Dignity, and Human Flourishing" (2019) 104:4 *Cornell L Rev* 991 at 1045–46 (describing how property promotes self-authorship).

45 Henry Smith, "Mind the Gap: The Indirect Relation between Ends and Means in American Property Law" (2009) 94:4 *Cornell L Rev* 959 at 970.

46 Margaret Jane Radin, "Property and Personhood" (1982) 34:5 *Stan L Rev* 957; Gregory Alexander, *Property and Human Flourishing* (Oxford University Press, 2018) at 200.

47 Benjamin Barros, "The Home as a Legal Concept" (2006) 46:2 *Santa Clara L Rev* 255 at 259; Alexander, "Property, Dignity, and Human Flourishing" at 1045.

aims free from scorn, judgment, or ridicule by others.[48] Similarly, a home's privacy allows for intimate acts or deep discussions that may be less appropriate or candid in public.[49] Housing fosters self-authorship because an individual controls access to a place that safeguards their interests without the need to rely on others.[50]

Third, certain types of property – such as a wedding ring or a home – are bound up with an individual's personhood and are central to their past, present, and future.[51] The home is often the locus of family life, intimacy, holidays, friendships, and gatherings.[52] Children are often raised within their homes. And certain monumental life events – such as moving to a different city to pursue education or employment – are marked by one's departure from their home. The notion that something "feels like home" exemplifies a sense of comfort, belonging, and familiarity that highlights the relationship between property and personhood.

Fourth, private property rights structure legal relationships in a manner that promotes autonomy.[53] Private property confers normative powers – such as the power to exclude others – which individuals exercise to secure their privacy, security, and liberty.[54] In this way, the right to enjoy property constitutes a form of "keystone right" that secures other rights, interests, and ultimately, individual autonomy.[55]

To be clear, distinct types of private property – such as homes, condominium units, apartments, trailers, and so on – foster positive freedom to different extents. Moreover, each of these types of private property also vary in terms of their size, location, quality, and degree of governmental regulation, which affects the rightsholder's autonomy and self-actualization. A rightsholder's status can also shape the degree of positive freedom they enjoy. For instance, individuals who own a detached home may enjoy the greatest privacy and liberty to undertake certain activities that are associated with self-actualization. In contrast, tenants may not engage in autonomy-promoting activities – especially those that result in greater noise or movement within the dwelling – because it may lead to conflicts with neighbors, noise complaints, or eviction. Tenants also enjoy less positive freedom in contexts where landlords fail to maintain a dwelling's quality, such that the tenant is exposed to danger, unsanitary living conditions, or excessive noise.

The fact that unhoused persons lack private property rights explains why they enjoy less positive freedom than others. Those who must live on public property lack the security and privacy that others enjoy.[56] They may suffer physical and

48 Benjamin Barros, "Property and Freedom" (2009) 36:4 *NYU JL & Lib* 36 at 47.

49 Emily Stolzenberg, "Properties of Intimacy" (2021) 80:3 *Md L Rev* 627 at 666–67 (noting the relationship between property and intimacy).

50 Alexander, "Property, Dignity, and Human Flourishing" at 1045.

51 Radin, "Property and Personhood" at 959, 991–92.

52 *Ibid.* at 1013.

53 Hanoch Dagan, *A Liberal Theory of Property* (Cambridge University Press, 2021) at 41–49.

54 Jeremy Waldron, *The Right to Private Property* (Oxford University Press, 1990) at 294–96.

55 *Ibid.*; Carol Rose, "Property as the Keystone Right?" (1996) 71:3 *Notre Dame L Rev* 329 at 362.

56 Terry Skolnik, "Freedom and Access to Housing" at 232.

psychological harm because they lack protection against the elements, and against threats of interference by other individuals.[57] As discussed in previous chapters, unhoused persons have a lower life expectancy compared to the general population.[58] They may be less able to plan their lives because they lack the stability and predictability that housing affords.[59] Furthermore, without access to housing, they may be unable to accumulate or store a significant amount of property that individuals normally keep within their homes.[60] They may not have access to basic sanitation infrastructure that helps them live a meaningfully dignified life, such as a bathroom or shower.[61] And without access to housing, they may lack free access to the place that typically anchors family life, belongingness, and continuity with the community.

The lack of a judicially enforceable right to housing in Canada and the United States contributes to unhoused persons' lack of positive freedom. Courts in Canada and the United States have not yet recognized a positive constitutional right to housing, which would protect individuals against the condition of homelessness, and safeguard their most basic capabilities and interests.[62] Without the judicial acknowledgment of such a right, the State has no constitutional duty to secure one of the most fundamental resources to promote self-actualization and human flourishing: access to housing.

3.2 PRIVATE PROPERTY AND NEGATIVE FREEDOM

3.2.1 *An Overview of Negative Freedom*

Isaiah Berlin's second conception of freedom is negative liberty, which construes freedom as noninterference.[63] Individuals are negatively free to the extent that they do not experience concrete interference by others.[64] The fewer externally imposed constraints, the greater an individual's freedom.[65] Negative liberty is fundamentally

57 Terry Skolnik, "Homeless Encampments: A Philosophical Justification" (2023) 36 *JL & Soc Pol'y* 97 at 100.

58 *See, e.g.*, C. James Frankish, Stephen Hwang, and Darryl Quantz, "Homelessness and Health in Canada: Research Lessons and Priorities" (2005) 96:2 *Can J Pub Health* S23 at S24; Stephen Hwang, "Homelessness and Health" (2001) 164:1 *CMAJ* 229 at 230–31; James O'Connell, *Premature Mortality in Homeless Populations: A Review of the Literature* (Nashville: National Health Care for the Homeless Council, 2005) at 13; Elise Roy, Nancy Haley, Pascale Leclerc et al., "Mortality in a Cohort of Street Youth in Montreal" (2004) 292:5 *JAMA* 569 at 569–70.

59 Alexander, "Property, Dignity, and Human Flourishing" at 1045.

60 Kevin Bundy, "Officer, Where's My Stuff? The Constitutional Implications of a *De Facto* Property Disability for Homeless People" (2003) 1 *Hastings Race & Poverty LJ* 57 at 67.

61 *See, e.g.*, Taunya Lovell Banks, "The Disappearing Public Toilet" (2020) 50:4 *Seton Hall L Rev* 1061 at 1080; Ron Hochbaum, "Bathrooms as a Homeless Rights Issue" (2020) 98:2 *NC L Rev* 205 at 208.

62 *See* Chapter 2 of this book.

63 Berlin, "Two Concepts of Liberty" at 169.

64 *Ibid.*

65 *Ibid.* at 170.

concerned with coercion, which Berlin described as "deliberate interference of other human beings within the area in which I could otherwise act."[66] The negative theory of freedom seeks to answer basic questions such as "how far does government interfere with me?" or "how much am I governed?"[67] As Philip Pettit notes, various influential political theorists described liberty in negative terms, including Thomas Hobbes,[68] William Paley,[69] and Jeremy Bentham.[70]

The negative conception of liberty posits that actual interference is necessary to restrict freedom.[71] According to this view, individuals enjoy freedom unless others concretely hinder their actions, movement, or choices.[72] Negative freedom theory underpins the ways in which constitutional law primarily protects negative rights, which safeguard individuals against concrete governmental interference.[73] Doctrines such as standing – which requires an individual's rights to be infringed to bring a constitutional claim – and the cases and controversies requirement in the United States – which authorizes courts only to hear cases between parties and forbids judicial advisory opinions – exemplify the role of negative rights and actual interference within constitutional law.[74]

Private property rights safeguard negative freedom in various ways. First, the physical structure of a home protects individuals and their property against attacks, trespasses, and intrusions by others.[75] It also shields individuals against

66 *Ibid.*

67 *Ibid.* at 178. The latter question is asked in Oren Ben-Dor, *Constitutional Limits and the Public Sphere: A Critical Study of Bentham's Constitutionalism* (London: Hart, 2000) at 254.

68 Pettit, *Republicanism* at 41, citing Thomas Hobbes, *Leviathan* (New York: Barnes and Nobel, 2004) at 158–59.

69 Pettit, *Republicanism* at 46, citing William Paley, *The Principles of Moral and Political Philosophy*, Vol. I (New York: B&S Collins, 1835) at 74.

70 Pettit, *Republicanism* at 44, citing Letter from Jeremy Bentham to John Lind (March 27–28–April 1, 1776) in Timothy Sprigge (ed.), *Correspondence of Jeremy Bentham*, Vol. I: *1752–1776* (London: UCL Press, 2017) at 310–11.

71 Philip Pettit, *On the People's Terms: A Republican Theory and Model of Democracy* (Cambridge University Press, 2012) at 9; Charles Larmore, "Liberal and Republican Conceptions of Freedom" in Daniel Weinstock and Christian Nadeau (eds.), *Republicanism: History, Theory, and Practice* (London: Frank Cass, 2004) at 92.

72 Larmore, "Liberal and Republican Conceptions of Freedom" at 84–85. As Larmore explains, though, Berlin also observed that threats or penalties undermine negative liberty because they make actions more costly. *See* Charles Larmore, *The Autonomy of Morality* (Cambridge University Press, 2008) at 171.

73 *See, e.g.*, Eoin Daly, "Freedom as Non-Domination in the Jurisprudence of Constitutional Rights" (2015) 28:2 *Can JL & Jur* 289 at 308; David Currie, "Positive and Negative Constitutional Rights" (1986) 53:3 *U Chi L Rev* 864 at 864, 886 (providing an overview of how the Bill of Rights primarily protects negative liberties).

74 *See, e.g.*, Eugene Kontorovich, "What Standing Is Good For" (2007) 93:7 *Va L Rev* 1663 at 1670–71. Note that the doctrines of third-party standing in the United States and public interest standing in Canada also exist. However, these doctrines apply exceptionally. *See, e.g.*, Brian Charles Lea, "The Merits of Third-Party Standing" (2015) 24:2 *Wm & Mary Bill Rts J* 277 at 278–79; Jane Bailey, "Reopening Law's Gate: Public Interest Standing and Access to Justice" (2011) 44:2 *UBC L Rev* 255 at 259–62.

75 Barros, "The Home as a Legal Concept" at 260–63.

surveillance.[76] Actual or suspected surveillance alters how an individual experiences a situation.[77] Surveillance unwillingly turns authentic participants of an unfiltered experience into guarded observers of their own actions.[78] A person may watch themselves, change their behavior, or self-censor because they are concerned with how they appear to outsiders – all of which undermine autonomy and authenticity.[79] Private property rights are valuable because they enhance authenticity by shielding individuals against surveillance. Private property rights also confer private law protections that safeguard individuals against interference by others.[80] Statutes and the common law prohibit individuals from trespassing onto others' private property.[81] The police are empowered to remove trespassers from an individual's property.[82] Private property rights also safeguard individuals' land against encroachments, which also constitute a form of trespass.[83] For instance, individuals cannot lawfully place fences or billboards on another's property without permission.[84]

Second, private property rights protect individuals against governmental interference.[85] The home attracts one of the strongest expectations of privacy in search and seizure law.[86] Leaving aside exigent circumstances, officers generally require a warrant to search a person's home.[87] They also tend to require a warrant to arrest someone within their home.[88] The State is also prohibited from using various forms of warrantless surveillance within a person's home, such as wiretaps or surreptitious video recordings.[89] The areas surrounding a person's home – such as their yard and the home's perimeter – also enjoy protection against trespassing and police surveillance.[90]

Third, private property rights protect negative liberty because they reallocate power away from the State and towards individuals.[91] Property rights trace

76 Robert Gerstein, "Intimacy and Privacy" (1978) 89 *Ethics* 76 at 79–80.
77 *Ibid.* at 77, 79.
78 *Ibid.*
79 *Ibid.*
80 *Ibid.* at 263–69.
81 James Penner, "The 'Bundle of Rights' Picture of Property" (1996) 43:3 *UCLA L Rev* 711 at 743.
82 Waldron, "Homelessness and the Issue of Freedom" at 300.
83 Gideon Parchomovsky and Alex Stein, "Reconceptualizing Trespass" (2009) 103:4 *Nw U L Rev* 1823 at 1857 (describing trespass and encroachments).
84 *Ibid.*
85 Barros, "The Home as a Legal Concept" at 263–70.
86 *Ibid.*; Stephanie Stern, "The Inviolate Home: Housing Exceptionalism in the Fourth Amendment" (2010) 95:5 *Cornell L Rev* 905 at 912–13.
87 Barros, "Home as a Legal Concept" at 267–68.
88 *Ibid.* at 268.
89 *Ibid.* at 269. In Canada, *see R* v. *Wong* [1990] 3 SCR 36 and Criminal Code, RSC 1985, c. C-46, s. 487.01 (video surveillance within a dwelling home requires a general warrant); ss. 185–86 (setting out the requirements for judicial authorization of wiretaps); *R* v. *Duarte* [1990] 1 SCR 30.
90 Anna Lvovsky, "Fourth Amendment Moralism" (2018) 116:5 *U Pa L Rev* 1189 at 1211.
91 Benjamin Barros, "Property and Freedom" (2009) 4:1 *NYU JL & Lib* 36 at 47; Robert Ellickson, "Property in Land" (1993) 102 *Yale LJ* 315 at 1352–54; Jennifer Nedelsky, "Reconceiving Autonomy:

a boundary between the individual and the State.[92] Private property imposes limits on the State's authority over certain matters, activities, and conduct that take place in the private sphere – a sphere where individual liberty takes precedence over State regulation or intrusion.[93] Given the vast array of authority that the State exercises over individuals, private property shifts some of that power back to the individual and allows them to be the master of their own lives within a certain space.[94] To the extent that a person's lawful conduct on private property defies majoritarian preferences, the sanctity of private property protects that individual's lifestyle against majoritarian will.[95] Conversely, without private property rights, the State has greater power over the individual and the latter is subject to a greater degree of majoritarian will.[96]

Fourth, private property rights help secure negative freedom because they grant a power to exclude others.[97] Individuals preserve their negative liberty by excluding others from their homes.[98] Conversely, a home maximizes freedom as noninterference because it protects individuals against others' power of exclusion.[99] This power of exclusion protects an individual's agenda-setting authority, meaning that they can determine who can access their private property and what they can do in that space.[100] Agenda-setting authority enables a person to control and enjoy property by simultaneously denying that same control and enjoyment to others.[101]

Fifth, private property rights protect third parties' negative freedom and other interests. These rights ensure that an individual can privately engage in conduct in a manner that does not affect others.[102] Rightsholders can engage in personal or intimate acts in the privacy of their homes without turning others into unwilling spectators.[103] In this way, an individual's private property rights promote others' sovereignty and autonomy.[104] Individuals who engage in private conduct within their homes respect others' choices not to witness conduct that may be personal, inappropriate, or offensive.[105]

Sources, Thoughts and Possibilities" (1989) 1 *Yale JL & Feminism* 7 at 17, cited in Laura Underkuffler, "On Property: An Essay" (1990) 100:1 *Yale LJ* 127 at 132–33.

92 Charles Reich, "The New Property" (1964) 73 *Yale LJ* 733 at 733, 771.

93 *Ibid.* at 771; Helen Nissenbaum, "Privacy as Contextual Integrity" (2004) 79 *Wash L Rev* 119 at 125.

94 Reich, 'The New Property" at 771.

95 *Ibid.*

96 Charles Reich, "The Liberty Impact of the New Property" (1990) 31:2 *Wm & Mary L Rev* 295 at 304–05.

97 Waldron, "Homelessness and the Issue of Freedom" at 305; Skolnik, "Freedom and Access to Housing" at 233.

98 Skolnik, "Freedom and Access to Housing" at 233.

99 Skolnik, "Homeless Encampments" at 99.

100 Larissa Katz, "Exclusion and Exclusivity in Property Law" (2008) 58:3 *U Toronto LJ* 275 at 277–78.

101 Laura Underkuffler, "Property: A Special Right" (1996) 71:5 *Notre Dame L Rev* 1033 at 1039.

102 Andrew Simester and Andrew von Hirsch, "Rethinking the Offense Principle" (2002) 8:3 *Leg Theory* 269 at 275–76.

103 *Ibid.*

104 Joel Feinberg, *Offense to Others* (Oxford University Press, 1985) at 24.

105 *Ibid.*

Several caveats are necessary. For one, private property can also negatively impact an individual's liberty, security, and autonomy.[106] The home may be a place where a person is subject to violence, abuse, and neglect – acts that are hidden from others' view because they take place within the home.[107] Although private property rights can promote a range of fundamental interests, a home's physical barriers can also conceal particularly egregious forms of wrongdoing.

Furthermore, an individual's degree of negative freedom also varies according to their type of private property right. Different types of private property may be subject to varying degrees of governmental regulation and interference. For instance, police officers typically require a warrant (or judicial authorization) to enter a private home or its periphery to conduct a search.[108] Yet individuals who reside in public housing may be subject to more surveillance, inspections, and other forms of interference that restrict the degree of their liberty.[109]

Lastly, the extent of a rightsholder's reasonable expectation of privacy also varies according to their type of private property.[110] Individuals who own a detached home may enjoy greater protection against governmental surveillance compared to tenants who reside in an apartment building.[111] Police officers cannot lawfully trespass onto the perimeter of a detached home to look through its windows, or to attempt to listen to conversations that take place within the home.[112] In contrast, individuals who reside in an apartment enjoy less privacy. Police officers can freely enter common areas in an apartment building, such as entrances and hallways.[113] Like everyone else, they may be able to hear conversations or smell substances that emanate from a particular apartment without having to obtain a warrant.[114] The scope of a rightsholder's negative freedom thus varies according to their type of private

106 Catherine MacKinnon, *Towards a Feminist Theory of the State* (Cambridge: Harvard University Press, 1989) at 186–91; Ruth Gavison, "Feminism and the Public/Private Distinction" (1992) 45:1 *Stan L Rev* 1 at 24, 35–37.

107 *See, e.g.*, Catherine MacKinnon, "Privacy v. Equality: Beyond *Roe* v. *Wade* in Catherine Mackinnon (ed.), *Feminism Unmodified: Discourses on Life and Law* (Cambridge: Harvard University Press, 1988) at 96–97.

108 William Stuntz, "Privacy's Problem and the Law of Criminal Procedure" (1995) 93:5 *Mich L Rev* 1016 at 1024, 1029–30.

109 *See, e.g.*, Priscilla Ocen, "The New Racially Restrictive Covenant: Race, Welfare, and the Policing of Black Women in Subsidized Housing" (2012) 59:6 *UCLA L Rev* 1540 at 1566–67; Erin Murphy, "The Politics of Privacy in the Criminal Justice System: Information Disclosure, the Fourth Amendment, and Statutory Law Enforcement Exemptions" (2013) 111:4 *Mich L Rev* 485 at 509–10; Alexis Karteron, "When Stop and Frisk Comes Home: Policing Public and Patrolled Housing" (2019) 69:3 *Case W Res L Rev* 669 at 682–83.

110 William Stuntz, "Distribution of Fourth Amendment Privacy" (1999) 67:5 *Geo Wash L Rev* 1265 at 1270, 1272.

111 *Ibid.*

112 In Canada, *see, e.g.*, *R* v. *Grant* [1993] 3 SCR 223.

113 *See, e.g.*, Jackie McCaffrey, "Fourth Amendment Protections in Common Areas of Apartment Buildings: How the Whitaker Holding Contributes to the Circuit Split" (2018) 2018:3 *U Ill L Rev* 1147 at 1148–49.

114 Stuntz, "Distribution of Fourth Amendment Privacy" at 1270, 1272.

property. And as discussed in the next subsection, unhoused persons tend to enjoy the least negative freedom because they have no private property rights.

3.2.2 *Property Rights, Negative Freedom, and Homelessness*

Compared to people with access to housing, unhoused persons enjoy less negative freedom because they lack private property rights and the physical and legal protections that these rights secure. Without access to housing, unhoused persons do not have physical protection against violence, threats, and theft.[115] Research indicates that compared to individuals with access to housing, unhoused persons are roughly ten times more likely to be victims of assault.[116] Studies also show that people experiencing homelessness are more likely to be victims of theft compared to the general population.[117] Unhoused persons also lack various legal protections that safeguard negative liberty. Some courts decide that unhoused persons have no right to store their belongings on public property.[118] Others conclude that the police do not require a warrant to search an unhoused person's tent because they have no right to erect one on public property.[119] Furthermore, people experiencing homelessness are more vulnerable to police surveillance because they spend much of their time in public space.[120]

Jeremy Waldron argues that unhoused persons are negatively unfree because of the cumulative effects of two forces: laws that regulate public property and others' private power of exclusion.[121] The starting point of Waldron's argument is that "[e]verything that is done has to be done somewhere," meaning on public property or on private property.[122] As part of the human experience, everyone must sleep, eat, urinate, defecate, sit, and so on.[123] Individuals cannot refrain from these acts without experiencing harm.[124] Most individuals alleviate their

115 Amanda Eisenmann and Francis Origanti, "Homeless Rights: A Call for Change" (2021) 30:1 *J Soc Distress & Homelessness* 90 at 92.

116 Joshua Ellsworth, "Street Crime Victimization Among Homeless Adults: A Review of the Literature" (2019) 14:1 *Victims & Offenders* 96 at 96–97, 112.

117 *Ibid.* at 112.

118 *Church* v. *City of Huntsville*, 30 F (3d) 1332 at 1335 (11th Circ 1994).

119 *Ibid.*; Lindsay Gus, "The Forgotten Residents: Defining the Fourth Amendment House to the Detriment of the Homeless" [2016] *U Chi Leg F* 769 at 784; Evanie Parr, "When a Tent Is Your Castle: Constitutional Protection against Unreasonable Searches of Makeshift Dwellings of Unhoused Persons" (2019) 42:2 *Seattle U L Rev* 993 at 1007, citing *State* v. *Cleator*, 857 P (2d) 306 (Wash Ct App 1993); *United States* v. *Ruckman*, 806 F (2d) 1471 (10th Circ 1986). *See also* R v. *Picard*, 2018 BCPC 344 at paras. 39–41; Sarah Ferencz et al., "Are Tents a 'Home'? Extending Section 8 Privacy Rights for the Precariously Housed" (2022) 67:4 *McGill LJ* 369 at 371.

120 *See, e.g.*, Don Mitchell and Nik Heynen, "The Geography of Survival and the Right to the City: Speculations on Surveillance, Legal Innovation, and the Criminalization of Intervention" (2009) 30:6 *Urb Geo* 611 at 619–20.

121 Waldron, "Homelessness and the Issue of Freedom" at 315.

122 *Ibid.* at 296.

123 *Ibid.* at 321.

124 *Ibid.*

basic needs within their homes.[125] But the situation is different for unhoused persons. Since they lack private property rights, they have no default private place where they can freely alleviate their basic needs without interference.[126]

The problem is that the law prohibits unhoused persons from alleviating their needs on public property and on others' private property.[127] As discussed in the Introduction, municipal ordinances proscribe sleeping, erecting shelters, urinating, and defecating on public property.[128] However, unhoused persons require permission to do these acts on others' private property.[129] People experiencing homelessness commit a trespass if they attempt to access others' private property or alleviate their needs on others' land without permission.[130] This explains why there is no public or private place where unhoused persons can freely and consistently alleviate their needs without interference; it is as if the law comprehensively prohibits them from alleviating their needs.[131] For this reason, Waldron concludes that "homelessness *consists* in unfreedom."[132]

Waldron's Complementarity Thesis offers an account of why laws that govern public property are objectionable in how they apply to unhoused persons.[133] The Complementarity Thesis evaluates whether individuals do acts on public property *as a complement* to what they could have done on private property.[134] When all individuals have access to housing or shelter, they have a private place to alleviate their needs, and enjoy complementarity between public and private property.[135] Laws that govern public property are more legitimate in such contexts because individuals can obey them freely. In contrast, unhoused persons lack such complementarity.[136] Laws that regulate public property are objectionable in such contexts because unhoused persons lack reasonable alternatives to violating these laws. Ultimately, municipal ordinances are problematic because they presume that unhoused persons enjoy complementarity between public and private property that they in fact lack.[137]

Other scholars highlight that unhoused persons lack negative freedom because of how the private property regime disparately allocates rights, duties, liabilities, and powers within society – an argument that is based on Wesley Hohfeld's concept of

125 *Ibid.* at 311.
126 *Ibid.*
127 *Ibid.* at 304, 315.
128 *Ibid.*
129 *Ibid.*
130 *Ibid.* at 297.
131 *Ibid.* at 302, 310.
132 *Ibid.* at 306. Italics in original text.
133 *Ibid.* at 301, 310.
134 Waldron, "Homelessness and Community" at 374, 394–95.
135 *Ibid.*
136 *Ibid.*
137 *Ibid.*

jural correlatives.[138] Hohfeld famously argued that the jural correlative of a right is a duty and that the jural correlative of a power is a liability.[139] When an individual has a real private property right, others have a duty not to interfere with that right.[140] The rightsholder also has a private power to exclude others from that property, while others are liable to that power of exclusion.[141]

Jeremy Waldron and Jane Baron note that the private property regime disproportionately burdens unhoused persons with duties and liabilities yet confers them none of its rights and powers.[142] Unhoused persons have a duty not to interfere with everyone else's private property rights.[143] They are liable to civil trespass or criminal liability if they do not fulfil that duty.[144] Yet they have no correlative power to exclude others because they lack private property rights.[145] Conversely, others have no duty to respect unhoused persons' private property rights because they have no such rights.[146] This explains why people experiencing homelessness enjoy less negative liberty than people with access to housing. To paraphrase Jeremy Waldron, unhoused persons bear all the burdens of the private property regime that constrain their negative liberty yet enjoy few of its benefits that would expand their negative freedom.[147] This unequal allocation of benefits and burdens results in rightsholders exercising their power of exclusion simultaneously and collectively against unhoused persons.[148] People experiencing homelessness are constantly at the receiving end of interference, with none of the rights or powers that can protect them against it.

3.3 CONCLUSION

This chapter provided an overview of two main conceptions of freedom: positive liberty as self-actualization and negative liberty as noninterference. It showed how private property rights promote both forms of freedom. It demonstrated how the extent of a rightsholder's positive and negative freedom vary according to their type

138 Baron, "Homelessness as a Property Problem" at 287; Waldron, "Community and Property" at 164–67; Terry Skolnik, "Homelessness and Unconstitutional Discrimination" (2019) 15 *JL & Equal* 69 at 91; Walter Wheeler Cook, "Hohfeld's Contributions to the Science of Law" (1918–19) 28:8 *Yale LJ* 721 at 723 (describing Hohfeld's concept of jural correlatives).

139 Wesley Hohfeld, "Fundamental Legal Conceptions as Applied in Judicial Reasoning" (1916–17) 26:8 *Yale LJ* 710 at 710.

140 *Ibid.*

141 *Ibid.*

142 Baron, "Property and No Property" at 1427–29; Waldron, "Community and Property" at 164–67.

143 Baron, "Property and 'No Property'" at 1427–29.

144 *Ibid.*

145 *Ibid.* at 1427, 1429.

146 *Ibid.*

147 Waldron, "Community and Property" at 171. Waldron's exact quote: "[The poverty stricken and the homeless] are people who bear all of the restraints, but enjoy none of the benefits, that accrue from the rights distributed in a property regime."

148 *Ibid.* at 164–67.

of private property right. And it explained why unhoused persons enjoy less positive and negative liberty because they lack private property rights.

The next chapter introduces a third conception of liberty: republican freedom as nondomination.[149] It argues that republican freedom offers new insight into the importance of private property rights, the nature of homelessness, and the impact of laws that govern public property. Together, this chapter and the next show how unhoused persons lack political equality because they lack freedom in all its forms: positive, negative, and republican.[150]

149 Pettit, *Republicanism* at 22–23.
150 Skolnik, "Freedom and Access to Housing" at 242; Skolnik, "Homelessness and Unconstitutional Discrimination" at 94.

4

Homelessness and the Insights of Republicanism

The republican theory of freedom (or republicanism) offers new insight into the importance of private property rights, the nature of homelessness, and the impact of laws that govern public property. In contrast to the negative conception of liberty as noninterference, republicanism provides a broader conception of liberty as non-domination, meaning freedom from the unilateral threat of interference by others.[1] Republican liberty acknowledges that the threat of interference undermines freedom even when individuals do not experience actual interference, and that individuals suffer domination when they are unilaterally vulnerable to others' power.[2] Individuals enjoy republican liberty when they are protected against domination.[3]

Domination exists in various forms, which can overlap and are not necessarily mutually exclusive.[4] Individuals suffer horizontal domination when they are vulnerable to the prospect of interference by others.[5] They experience vertical domination when they are unilaterally subject to risks of governmental interference.[6] And they face double domination when they are subject to both horizontal and vertical domination that may mutually reinforce one another.[7]

1 Philip Pettit, *Republicanism: A Theory of Freedom and Government* (Oxford University Press, 1999) at 22–23, 85–90.

2 *Ibid.* at 63–65; Cécile Laborde, "Republicanism" in Michael Freeden, Lyman Tower Sargent, and Marc Stears (eds.), *The Oxford Handbook of Political Ideologies* (Oxford University Press, 2013) at 519.

3 Matthew Kramer, "Liberty and Domination" in Cécile Laborde and John Maynor (eds.), *Republicanism and Political Theory* (Oxford: Blackwell, 2008) at 32.

4 *See, e.g.*, David Casassas and Jurgen De Wispelaere, "Republicanism and the Political Economy of Democracy" (2016) 19:2 *Eur J Soc Theory* 283 at 285; Marie Garrau and Cécile Laborde, "Relational Equality, Non-Domination, and Vulnerability" in Carina Fourie, Fabian Schuppert, and Ivo Wallimann-Helmer (eds.), *Social Equality: On What It Means to Be Equals* (Oxford University Press, 2015) at 51; Philip Pettit, *Just Freedom: A Moral Compass for a Complex World* (New York: Norton and Co., 2014) at 5–7.

5 Pettit, *Just Freedom.*

6 *Ibid.*

7 *See, e.g.*, Cécile Laborde, *Critical Republicanism: The Hijab Controversy and Political Philosophy* (Oxford University Press, 2008) at 151; this definition of double domination builds on Laborde's recognition that domination can be both public and private (at 169).

This chapter shows how laws that govern public property subject unhoused persons to double domination for two reasons.[8] First, others exert control over unhoused persons' opportunities to obey laws that govern public property.[9] Second, unhoused persons must make nonegalitarian sacrifices of their basic interests to obey these laws.[10] These two forms of domination – others' control over law-abidingness and nonegalitarian trade-offs – are aggravated by unhoused persons' lack of political and legal power. Subsequent chapters then demonstrate why the State has a greater capacity to regulate and police unhoused persons compared to people with access to housing, and to entrench them in homelessness.

4.1 THE REPUBLICAN THEORY OF FREEDOM

The republican theory of freedom emerged during the Roman republic.[11] It was revived during the Renaissance period and was invoked by neorepublican scholars such as Niccolò Machiavelli, James Harrington, and Montesquieu.[12] Whereas negative liberty theory construes freedom as noninterference, the republican theory of liberty construes freedom as nondomination.[13] Domination implies that others have a unilateral power to interfere with an individual's actions, movement, or choices.[14] Individuals who suffer domination are dependent upon others' goodwill to avoid interference.[15] Republican scholars associate domination with the notion of arbitrary (or uncontrolled) interference.[16] In the republican tradition, arbitrariness connotes that the dominated party cannot control whether they experience interference.[17] The dominating party thus dictates whether the dominated party suffers a hinderance to their action, movement, or choices.[18]

Unlike negative liberty theory, republicanism accepts that a person is unfree when they experience domination without interference.[19] The prospect of such

8 This argument was first advanced in Terry Skolnik, "How and Why Homeless People Are Regulated Differently" (2018) 43 *Queen's LJ* 297.

9 *Ibid.* at 309.

10 *Ibid.* at 316–17.

11 Quentin Skinner, *Liberty before Liberalism* (Cambridge University Press, 1998) at 84; Mortimer Sellers, *The Sacred Fire of Liberty: Republicanism, Liberalism, and the Law* (London: Palgrave Macmillan, 1998) at 7.

12 Pettit, *Republicanism* at 19; Sharon Krause, "Beyond Non-Domination: Agency, Inequality and the Meaning of Freedom" (2013) 39 *Phil & Soc Criticism* 187 at 188.

13 Pettit, *Republicanism* at 22–23.

14 *Ibid.*

15 Philip Pettit, *On the People's Terms: A Republican Theory and Model of Democracy* (Cambridge University Press, 2013) at 7–8, 61–62.

16 *Ibid.* at 58.

17 *Ibid.*

18 *Ibid.*

19 Pettit, *Republicanism* at 63–65. Steven Wall, "Freedom, Interference, and Domination" (2001) 49 *Pol Stud* 216 at 216–20; Frank Lovett, "Non-Domination" in David Schmidtz and Carmen Pavel (eds.), *The Oxford Handbook of Freedom* (Oxford University Press, 2018) at 107, 110–11.

hinderances is thus sufficient to restrict liberty.[20] Domination without interference is problematic because an individual may limit their own freedom as a coping mechanism to avoid interference.[21] The individual may ingratiate others or act deferentially towards them so that others do not hinder the individual's movement or choices.[22] The individual may adapt their preferences to those of the dominating party so that the latter does not block the individual's choices or thwart their plans.[23] Or, the individual may abandon their authentic choices or pursuits to escape concrete obstructions by others.[24] Dominated individuals are unfree in such contexts because they depend on others' goodwill or benevolence to avert such hinderances.[25]

Historically, in the republican tradition, domination was exemplified by the relationship between master and slave, where the master holds a unilateral power to interfere with the slave's actions, choices, and movements.[26] Negative liberty theory may construe a slave as free so long as the master does not concretely obstruct the slave's movement or choices.[27] In contrast, republicanism acknowledges that the master's power to interfere with the slave undermines the latter's freedom, irrespective of whether actual interference occurs.[28]

Philip Pettit notes that domination is present in a range of relationships that involve asymmetric power dynamics.[29] An abusive spouse may unilaterally interfere with their partner's actions and plans.[30] A tyrannical parent may thwart their children's choices.[31] And police officers have the authority to pull over drivers and question pedestrians at will.[32] Drivers and pedestrians, for their part, may comply with the police because they fear arrest, criminal charges, or physical harm.[33]

Domination is different than interference in important ways.[34] First, compared to negative liberty as noninterference, republican liberty as nondomination places

20 Philip Pettit, "Freedom as Anti-Power" (1996) 106 *Ethics* 576 at 600.
21 Pettit, *On the People's Terms* at 64.
22 *Ibid.*
23 *Ibid.*
24 *Ibid.*
25 *Ibid.*; Matthew Kramer, *The Quality of Freedom* (Oxford University Press, 2005) at 125.
26 Pettit, *Republicanism* at 22; Fabian Wendt, "Slaves, Prisoners, and Republican Freedom" (2011) 17:2 *Res Publica* 175 at 179–82.
27 Pettit, *Republicanism* at 22.
28 Pettit, *On the People's Terms* at 64; Jed Atkins, *Roman Political Thought* (Cambridge University Press, 2018) at 39; Charles Larmore, "Liberal and Republican Conceptions of Freedom" in Daniel Weinstock and Christian Nadeau (eds.), *Republicanism: History, Theory, and Practice* (London: Frank Cass, 2004) at 84.
29 Pettit, *Republicanism* at 57.
30 *Ibid.*
31 *Ibid.* This example provided in Skinner, *Liberty before Liberalism* at 41.
32 Eric Miller, "Challenging Police Discretion" (2015) 58:2 *Howard LJ* 521 at 540–41.
33 Terry Skolnik, "Policing in the Shadow of Legality: Pretext, Leveraging, and Investigation Cascades" (2023) 60 Osgoode Hall LJ 505 at 525.
34 Pettit, *Republicanism* at 85.

greater emphasis on the psychological costs of unfreedom.[35] Domination generates uncertainty as to when interference will occur, which can instill a sense of anxiety and fear in the dominated party.[36] They may become hyper-vigilant to better anticipate and avoid interference.[37] Or, they may debase themselves as a coping mechanism because they have internalized domination.[38]

Second, in contrast to negative liberty, republican freedom incorporates a commitment to political equality.[39] Domination involves subjective, intersubjective, and objective components that exemplify subordination and rank-ordering.[40] Subjectively, the dominated party is aware that they are vulnerable to someone else's power, while the dominating party is conscious that they wield that power.[41] Intersubjectively, both parties are aware of the asymmetric power dynamic inherent to their relationship, which influences how their view themselves and interact with one another.[42] Objectively, it is a matter of common knowledge within society that the dominating party wields unilateral power over the dominated party.[43] Philip Pettit remarks that in the republican tradition, free persons can pass a metaphorical "eyeball test," meaning they can "walk tall amongst others and look any in the eye without reason for fear or deference."[44] Individuals satisfy this test when they can live their lives and interact with one another aware that they are in "positions of relatively equal strength."[45]

Third, while negative freedom can be construed as a binary concept characterized by the presence or absence of interference, republican freedom acknowledges that domination can exist across a spectrum.[46] Republicanism affirms that different factors shape the extent of one's liberty. Philip Pettit points out that domination can vary in intensity, frequency, and consistency.[47] For instance, a person can be

35 *See, e.g.*, Tom O'Shea, "A Civic Republican Analysis of Mental Capacity Law" (2018) 38:1 *Leg Stud* 147 at 152; Philip Pettit, "Discourse Theory and Republican Freedom" in Daniel Weinstock and Christian Nadeau (eds.), *Republicanism: History, Theory, and Practice* (London: Frank Cass, 2004) at 77.

36 Philip Pettit, "On the People's Terms: A Reply to Five Critiques" (2015) 18 *Critical Rev Int'l Soc & Pol Phil* 687 at 693.

37 *Ibid.*

38 Frank Lovett, A *General Theory of Domination and Justice* (Oxford University Press, 2010) at 133.

39 *See, e.g.*, Pettit, *Republicanism* at 63–64; Kyle Swan, "Republican Equality" (2012) 38:3 *Soc Theory & Prac* 432 at 434–35; Fabian Schuppert, "Non-Domination, Non-Alienation and Social Equality: Towards a Republican Understanding of Equality" (2015) 18 *Critical Rev of Int'l Soc & Pol Phil* 440 at 441–42; Laborde, "Republicanism" at 525; Garrau and Laborde, "Relational Equality, Non-Domination, and Vulnerability" at 50–53.

40 Pettit, *Republicanism* at 60–61.

41 *Ibid.*

42 *Ibid.*

43 *Ibid. See also*, Catherine MacKinnon, "Substantive Equality: A Perspective" (2011) 96 *Minn L Rev* 1 at 11.

44 Pettit, *On the People's Terms* at 8, 84. Quoted portion at 8.

45 *Ibid.* at 82.

46 Pettit, *Republicanism* at 58.

47 *Ibid.*

subject to domination by some individuals but not others, or can experience it in some places but not others.[48] Furthermore, the threat of interference can constrain one's freedom to act to greater or lesser extents.[49] Rather than classify one's action as free or unfree, republicanism adopts a more holistic approach that recognizes how domination renders one's actions increasingly or decreasingly free.[50]

Individuals can experience different forms of domination: horizontal, vertical, and double.[51] Horizontal (or private) domination implies that a person is unilaterally vulnerable to another individual's private power.[52] Examples of horizontal domination include the employer's power to fire their employee at will, and a dominating spouse's tyrannical control in an abusive relationship.[53]

Vertical (or public) domination refers to domination by the State.[54] Republican theorists have described various forms of vertical domination. Some republican theorists associate vertical domination with individuals' lack of a self-governing power.[55] According to this view, individuals face vertical domination when they could not vote to elect a representative government, participate in political office to shape the laws that governed them, or were ruled by an alien will (such as a dictatorial or colonial power).[56] Others observe that vertical domination arises from State power that is unconstrained by the rule of law, exercised arbitrarily, or subject to insufficient checks and balances.[57] Similarly, some suggest that individuals must have the capacity to challenge exercises of State power to enjoy republican liberty.[58] Finally, some observe that laws result in domination when the State enacts

48 *Ibid.*

49 *Ibid.*

50 *Ibid.*

51 Pettit, *Just Freedom* at 5–7; Laborde, *Critical Republicanism* at 151; Casassas and De Wispelaere, "Republicanism and the Political Economy of Democracy"; Christina Bambrick, "Horizontal Rights: A Republican Vein in Liberal Constitutionalism" (2020) 52:3 *Polity* 401 at 407, 418; Matthew Hoye and Jeffrey Monaghan, "Surveillance, Freedom and the Republic" (2018) 17: 3 *Eur J Pol Theory* 343 at 349; Henry Richardson, "Republicanism and Democratic Injustice" (2006) 5:2 *Pol, Phil & Econ* 175 at 176.

52 Pettit, *Just Freedom* at 5–6; Garrau and Laborde, "Relational Equality, Non-Domination, and Vulnerability" at 51.

53 *See, e.g.*, Pettit, *Republicanism* at 61.

54 Garrau and Laborde, "Relational Equality, Non-Domination, and Vulnerability" at 51.

55 *See, e.g.*, Skinner, *Liberty before Liberalism* at 23–26.

56 Philip Pettit, "Law and Liberty" in Samantha Besson and José Luis Martí (eds.), *Legal Republicanism: National and International Perspectives* (Oxford University Press, 2009) at 53. Pettit refers specifically to "colonial or dictatorial forms of government" (*ibid.*).

57 *See, e.g.*, Quentin Skinner, "Classical Liberty and the Coming of the English Civil War" in Van Gelderen (ed.), *Republicanism*, Vol. II: *The Value of Republicanism in Early Modern Europe* (Cambridge University Press, 2002) at 12–13; Assaf Sharon, "Domination and the Rule of Law" in David Sobel, Peter Vallentyne, and Steven Wall (eds.), *Oxford Studies in Political Philosophy* (Oxford University Press, 2016) at 128–29; Philip Pettit, "The General Will, the Common Good, and the Democracy of Standards" in Yiftah Elazar and Genevieve Rosselière (eds.), *Republicanism and the Future of Democracy* (Cambridge University Press, 2019) at 36–37.

58 Jacob Weinrib, *Dimensions of Dignity: The Theory and Practice of Modern Constitutional Law* (Cambridge University Press, 2016) at 159.

laws or implements policies that fail to track individuals' common interests.[59]

Lastly, individuals can experience *double* domination, meaning that they are subject to both horizontal and vertical domination that may mutually reinforce one another.[60] For instance, religious or cultural minority groups – especially minorities *within* minority groups – may be subject to unique threats of interference from the State and from other private individuals.[61] Cécile Laborde observes that double domination can arise in different relationships and contexts: inter- and intra-group, public and private, formal and informal, secular and religious, and more.[62] Individuals who suffer double domination may be unable to rely on the State to protect them against threats of private interference and may be unable to turn to other individuals to escape risks of governmental interference. Together, the combined effects of horizontal and vertical domination may cement an individual's subordinated position in the public and private spheres.

4.2 HOMELESSNESS AND DOMINATION

4.2.1 *Homelessness, Private Property Rights, and Horizontal Domination*

Republicanism demonstrates why unhoused persons lack liberty in ways that negative and positive theories of freedom overlook. Some scholars have explored the relationship between homelessness and republican liberty.[63] Christopher Essert contends that homelessness is a legal condition where individuals are subject to horizontal domination because they lack private property rights.[64] Without private property rights, unhoused persons constantly rely on others' permission to access private property.[65] Yet access to private property is a precondition to lawfully engage in any conduct in that location.[66] For this reason, people experiencing homelessness suffer domination because they depend on others to access their private property and do any act within that space.[67]

59 *See, e.g.*, Christian List, "Republican Freedom and the Rule of Law" (2006) 5:2 *Pol, Phil & Econ* 201 at 201–02; Philip Pettit, "The Common Good" in Keith Dowding, Robert Goodin and Carole Patemen (eds.), *Justice and Democracy: Essays for Brian Barry* (Cambridge University Press, 2004) at 151; Pettit, *Republicanism* at 287.

60 Laborde, *Critical Republicanism* at 151

61 *Ibid.*; David Watkins, "Institutionalizing Freedom as Non-Domination: Democracy and the Role of the State" (2015) 47:4 *Polity* 508 at 519.

62 Laborde, *Critical Republicanism* at 151, 169–70.

63 Note that some scholars such as Christopher Essert expressly refer to republicanism, while other scholars such as Jane Baron do not refer directly to the republican theory of liberty but allude to its core concerns.

64 Christopher Essert, "Property and Homelessness" (2016) 44:4 *Phil & Pub Aff* 266 at 266.

65 *Ibid.* at 276–77.

66 *Ibid.* at 275–77.

67 *Ibid.*

Similarly, Jane Baron argues that unhoused persons are in a position of social and legal vulnerability because they disproportionately bear duties and liabilities associated with private property.[68] They are frequently vulnerable to others' power of exclusion yet lack a comparable power to exclude others.[69] The private property system's disparate allocation of powers and liabilities results in an asymmetric power dynamic, such that unhoused persons are in a condition of dependency vis-à-vis rightsholders.[70]

These accounts elucidate how private property allocates power – and protects individuals against others' power – in a manner that structures social relations.[71] Individuals must have some authority to dictate what others can and cannot do to secure their liberty.[72] A private property right provides such authority because it confers a power to exclude others and to insulate oneself against others' power of exclusion.[73] Unhoused persons suffer horizontal domination because they lack private property rights that allocate the power to secure their freedom through means other than their physical bodies.[74]

Essert and Baron's scholarship deepen our comprehension of why unhoused persons experience horizontal domination because they lack private property rights. However, their contributions focus primarily on how people experiencing homelessness are uniquely vulnerable to others' private power. We gain a more complete understanding of unhoused persons' double domination when we consider the combined effects of their lack of private property rights and their vulnerability to laws that govern public property. Notably, laws that govern public property subject unhoused persons to two unique forms of double domination that further restricts their republican liberty, each of which are discussed next.[75]

4.2.2 *Homelessness and Dependence on Others to Obey the Law*

First, people experiencing homelessness face double domination because others exert meaningful control over their ability to obey laws that govern public

68 Jane Baron, "Homelessness as a Property Problem" (2004) 36:2 *Urb Law* 273 at 287; Jane Baron, "Property and 'No Property'" (2006) 42 *Hous L Rev* 1425 at 1427 (describing homelessness as a condition of legal and social vulnerability). *See also* Kevin Bundy, "Officer, Where's My Stuff? The Constitutional Implications of a De Facto Property Disability for Homeless People" (2003) 1 *Hastings Race & Poverty LJ* 57 at 81–82 (describing homelessness as a form of property disability).

69 Baron, "Property and 'No Property'" at 1427.

70 *Ibid.*

71 For a summary of scholars' views on that position, see Jane Baron, "The Contested Commitments of Property" (2010) 61:4 *Hastings LJ* 917 at 928; Gregory Alexander, "The Complex Core of Property" (2009) 94:4 *Cornell L Rev* 1063 at 1066; Nestor Davidson, "Property and Relative Status" (2009) 107:5 *Mich L Rev* 757 at 771–74.

72 Morris Cohen, "Property and Sovereignty" (1927) 13 *Cornell LQ* 8 at 12.

73 *Ibid.*

74 Arthur Ripstein, *Force and Freedom: Kant's Legal and Political Philosophy* (Cambridge: Harvard University Press, 2009) at 88.

75 Skolnik, "How and Why" at 309, 317.

property.[76] Unhoused persons experience this form of double domination due to the combined effects of municipal ordinances and individuals' private power of exclusion.[77]

Municipal ordinances prohibit unhoused persons from sleeping, sheltering themselves, urinating, or defecating on public property.[78] Individuals must engage in these biologically necessary acts as part of their daily existence.[79] Unhoused persons are vulnerable to different threats of governmental interference if they alleviate their needs on public property: displacement, tickets, arrests, and incarceration.[80] They are more vulnerable to these risks of State interference because they lack private property rights, and thus a default private place where they can freely alleviate their needs and obey laws that govern public property.[81]

But unhoused persons require permission from others – homeless shelter staff, restaurant or café employees, or acquaintances – to access their private property, alleviate their needs lawfully, and escape governmental coercion.[82] For these reasons, unhoused persons routinely depend on others to obey laws that regulate public property in ways that do not affect people with access to housing.[83]

The upshot is that others exert control over unhoused persons' opportunities to comply with these laws.[84] Rightsholders decide whether they grant or deny permission to access their private property.[85] Furthermore, rightsholders enjoy a broad power of exclusion that is generally insulated against judicial and constitutional review, which highlights the uncontrolled nature of interference in unhoused persons' lives.[86] Since permission to access private property is a precondition to lawfully doing any act in that space – including need-alleviating acts – rightsholders exercise control over whether unhoused persons access private property, alleviate their needs, and obey laws that govern public property.[87]

This explains why unhoused persons suffer double domination when others exert control over their opportunities to obey these laws. They experience horizontal

76 *Ibid.* at 309.

77 *Ibid.* at 309–10.

78 Terry Skolnik, "Homelessness and Unconstitutional Discrimination" (2019) 15 *JL & Equal* 69 at 80.

79 Jeremy Waldron, "Homelessness and the Issue of Freedom" (1991) 39 *UCLA L Rev* 295.

80 NLCHP, "Housing Not Handcuffs: Ending the Criminalization of Homelessness in U.S. Cities" (2019) *Homeless Law at* 8, 37, https://homelesslaw.org/wp-content/uploads/2019/12/HOUSING-NOT-HANDCUFFS-2019-FINAL.pdf [perma.cc/E8NZ-Y5H4].

81 Chapters 4 and 5 of this book provide a thorough overview of why unhoused persons are more vulnerable to coercion from laws that govern public property.

82 Waldron, "Homelessness and the Issue of Freedom" at 297, 304 (describing the relationship between the power to exclude others and permission to access another's private property). *See, e.g.*, Skolnik, "How and Why" at 309–10.

83 Skolnik, "How and Why" at 309–10.

84 *Ibid.*

85 *Ibid.*; Waldron, "Homelessness and the Issue of Freedom" at 297, 304.

86 Skolnik, "How and Why" at 310.

87 *Ibid.*; Essert, "Property and Homelessness" at 275–77 (noting that permission to access private property is a precondition to doing any act in that space).

domination because they depend on others to access private property and escape governmental coercion associated with laws that regulate public property.[88] They experience vertical domination because the State enacts and enforces laws that fail to track the shared interests of people experiencing homelessness. Notably, these laws overlook unhoused persons' common interests in being able to control their law-abidingness, and ultimately, avoid displacement, fines, arrests, and incarceration on equal terms with others.

Coercion and punishment are objectionable when individuals lack the undominated choice to obey the law.[89] Such punishments disingenuously treat legal transgressions as the product of a free and rational choice rather than acknowledge others' control over that choice.[90] Rather than punish individuals because they freely and unreasonably rejected available alternatives to violating the law, the State may coerce and punish individuals because they lacked such alternatives in the first place.[91] The lack of control over one's opportunity to obey the law delegitimizes convictions and punishment, both of which are generally premised on the notion of free choice to obey the law and the availability of alternatives to lawbreaking.[92] Furthermore, the State cannot deter individuals from violating the law when others' exerted – and continue to exert – control over their law-abidingness.[93] Since only the individual will face coercion and punishment for their legal transgressions, they alone should control their opportunities to obey the law.

Certain examples illustrate how unhoused persons experience double domination when their law-abidingness is subject to others' control.[94] A person experiencing homelessness may attempt to access a coffee shop or restaurant to obey laws that

88 Essert, "Property and Homelessness" at 266, 277.

89 H. L. A. Hart and John Gardner, *Punishment and Responsibility* (Oxford University Press, 2008) at 152.

90 *See, e.g.*, Terry Skolnik, "Three Problems with Duress and Moral Involuntariness" (2016) 63 *Crim LQ* 124 at 144; Terry Skolnik, "Homelessness and the Impossibility to Obey the Law" (2016) 43 *Fordham Urb LJ* 741 at 745.

91 For a similar argument, see, for instance, Andrew Simester, "A Disintegrated Theory of Culpability" in Dennis Baker and Jeremy Horder (eds.), *The Sanctity of Life and the Criminal Law: The Legacy of Glanville Williams* (Cambridge University Press, 2013) at 184. Simester's original quote is: "*Prima facie*, we ought to blame people for unreasonably deploying the intelligence they have, not for failing to be reasonably intelligent." Similarly, we should blame people because they unreasonably rejected available opportunities and not because they lacked such opportunities.

92 *See, e.g.*, Antony Duff, "Choice, Character, and Criminal Liability" (1993) 12:4 *L & Phil* 345 at 346–51 (describing the relationship between choice and culpability); Terry Skolnik, "Beyond *Boudreault*: Challenging Choice, Culpability, Punishment" (2019) 50 *CR* (7th) 283 at 284–85 (same); Skolnik, "Homelessness and the Impossibility to Obey the Law" at 742; Terry Skolnik, "Socially Deprived Offenders" in Jesper Ryberg (ed.), *The Oxford Handbook of Punishment Theory and Philosophy* (Oxford University Press, 2024) (forthcoming). Draft on file with author.

93 *See, e.g.*, Maria Foscarinis, "Downward Spiral: Homelessness and Its Criminalization" (1996) 14:1 *Yale L & Pol'y Rev* 1 at 58.

94 These examples are mentioned in Terry Skolnik, "Freedom and Access to Housing: Three Conceptions" (2018) 35 *Windsor YB Access Just* 226 at 240.

prohibit public urination because there are few if any public washrooms in a city.[95] Yet the establishment's employees may state that washrooms are for customers only, require individuals to make a purchase to use the washroom, or deny entry for some other reason.[96] Employees or rightsholders of other establishments may exercise their power of exclusion similarly.[97] The unhoused persons' opportunity to access these private spaces, obey the law, and avoid police coercion are subject to others' control. Or consider how an unhoused person must stay in a shelter to comply with laws that prohibit sleeping or camping on public property.[98] However, shelter staff may deny entry to individuals for various reasons. They may limit the length of one's stay, impose sobriety or curfew requirements, or deny entry for other reasons.[99] The rules that govern homeless shelters – and the discretionary decisions of their employees – influence whether unhoused persons can freely obey laws that prohibit sleeping or camping on public property.[100]

Admittedly, rightsholders may exercise their power of exclusion benevolently and grant unhoused persons access to use their private property, such that they can obey these laws.[101] Yet domination without interference persists in such contexts.[102] Unhoused persons still rely on others' permission to use private property and escape interference from laws that govern public property, and others continue to exert control over unhoused persons' law-abidingness.[103]

4.2.3 *Laws that Govern Public Property and Nonegalitarian Trade-Offs*

Second, unhoused persons face double domination when they must make nonegalitarian trade-offs (or sacrifices) to obey laws that regulate public property.[104] A nonegalitarian trade-off implies that only certain individuals must risk their health, safety, property, or other interests to comply with the law.[105] Individuals

95 *Ibid.*; Skolnik, "How and Why" at 309–10.

96 Waldron, "Homelessness and the Issue of Freedom" at 311; Harvey Moloch, "Learning from the Loo" in Harvey Moloch and Laura Noren (eds.), *Toilet: Public Restrooms and the Politics of Sharing* (New York University Press, 2010) at 3.

97 *See, e.g.*, Jeremy Waldron, "Community and Property – For Those Who Have Neither" (2008) 10:1 *Theor Inq L* 161 at 165–56 (discussing the cumulative effects of various rightsholders' power of exclusion).

98 Skolnik, "Freedom and Access to Housing" at 240.

99 *See, e.g., Abbotsford (City)* v. *Shantz*, 2015 BCSC 1909 at paras. 53–55; Suzanne Skinner and Sara Rankin, "Shut Out: How Barriers Often Prevent Meaningful Access to Emergency Shelter" (May 2016) at 19, 26, Homeless Rights Advocacy Project, https://digitalcommons.law.seattleu.edu/cgi/viewcontent.cgi?article=1004&context=hrap [perma.cc/LW3T-HHNV]; John Calterone Williams, *A Roof Over My Head: Homeless Women and the Shelter Industry* (Boulder: Colorado University Press, 2016) at 91.

100 Skolnik, "Freedom and Access to Housing" at 240.

101 *See, e.g.*, Skolnik, "How and Why" at 315.

102 *Ibid.*

103 *Ibid.*

104 Skolnik, "How and Why" at 316–17.

105 *Ibid.* (providing an overview of types of nonegalitarian trade-offs); Skolnik, "Freedom and Access to Housing" at 241.

who refuse to make those sacrifices and who violate the law face a different threat of interference: coercion and punishment.

The law imposes nonegalitarian trade-offs on unhoused persons in various contexts. They may be required to stay in a shelter that is dangerous, unsanitary, or overcrowded to obey laws that ban sleeping or camping on public property.[106] They may be victims of property crime or violent crime during their stay at a shelter.[107] Certain shelters have rodent and insect infestations, while others have communicable disease outbreaks, such as staph infections and tuberculosis.[108] Some shelters are overcrowded, which creates risks of communicable disease transmission.[109] Unhoused persons may also sleep in a secluded and more dangerous area because they do not want to be caught violating laws that govern public property.[110]

The nonegalitarian trade-offs imposed by such laws subject unhoused persons to double domination for the following reasons. They may be required to submit to various threats of horizontal interference – such as violence, theft, and overcrowding in shelters – to escape governmental interference from laws that govern public property.[111] Yet they face potential displacement, fines, arrests, and incarceration if they refuse to submit themselves to horizontal domination within shelters and violate municipal ordinances.[112] Unhoused persons are subject to vertical domination from nonegalitarian trade-offs because the law fails to track their common

106 *See, e.g.*, Sara Rankin, "Hiding Homelessness: The Transcarceration of Homelessness" (2021) 109:2 *Cal L Rev* 559 at 585; Caryl Patrick, "Aboriginal Homelessness in Canada: A Literature Review" (2014) Homeless Hub at 54, www.homelesshub.ca/sites/default/files/AboriginalLiteratureReview.pdf [perma.cc/8DXH-5MQM].

107 *See, e.g.*, Abby O'Brien, "'Like a Rat Cage': Toronto's Homeless Describe Packed Shelters, Surge in Violence and Death," CTV News (June 15, 2021), https://toronto.ctvnews.ca/like-a-rat-cage-toronto-s-homeless-describe-packed-shelters-surge-in-violence-and-death-1.5471155 [perma.cc/WRV5-B2C6]; David Bartelt, Karin Eyrich-Garg, and Brian Lockwood, "The Relationships between Community Context and Entry into a Homeless Shelter System" (2017) 39:5 *J Urb Aff* 675 at 686.

108 Nick Falvo, "Homelessness in Yellowknife: An Emerging Social Challenge" (2011) Homeless Hub at 16, www.homelesshub.ca/sites/default/files/Falvo_Homelessness_Policy_Report_finalMAY25.pdf [perma.cc/27NN-RRKK]; Andrea Elliot and Rebecca Ruiz, "New York Is Removing Over 400 Children from 2 Homeless Shelters," NY Times (February 21, 2014), www.nytimes.com/2014/02/21/nyregion/new-york-is-removing-over-400-children-from-2-homeless-shelters.html [perma.cc/WJ5M-BZHY]; Winnie Hu, "Review of New York Shelter System Finds Hundreds of Violations," NY Times (March 12, 2015), www.nytimes.com/2015/03/13/nyregion/new-york-homeless-shelter-system-violations-report.html [perma.cc/J2XG-VAQT].

109 Michelle Moffa, Ryan Cronk, and Donald Fejfar et al., "A Systematic Scoping Review of Environmental Health Conditions and Hygiene Behaviors in Homeless Shelters" (2019) 222:3 *Int'l J Hygiene & Env't Health* 335 at 345.

110 *See, e.g.*, *Abbotsford (City)* v. *Shantz*, 2015 BCSC 1909 at para. 213; Tony Robinson, "No Right to Rest: Police Enforcement Patterns and Quality of Life Consequences of the Criminalization of Homelessness" (2019) 55:1 *Urb Aff Rev* 41 at 64.

111 *See, e.g.*, Sara Rankin, "Punishing Homelessness" (2019) 22:1 *New Crim L Rev* 99 at 117 (noting how shortages in shelter spaces may result in overcrowding, violence, and unsanitary conditions).

112 *See, e.g.*, Jamie Michael Charles, "America's Lost Cause: The Unconstitutionality of Criminalizing Our Country's Homeless Population" (2009) 18:2 *BU Pub Int LJ* 315 at 336–37 (noting how unhoused persons may face the choice to either stay in a shelter with unacceptable conditions, leave the jurisdiction, or face governmental coercion).

interests in security, autonomy, and physical and mental well-being.[113] Laws that impose nonegalitarian trade-offs treat certain individuals' interests as less worthy of equal concern and respect.[114]

The State may require individuals to sacrifice interests of varying degrees of importance. Scholars recognize the primacy of interests related to survival and physical integrity – such as health and security – compared to other interests.[115] For instance, Abraham Maslow's hierarchy of human needs places survival and safety-related interests above those related to esteem or the desire for knowledge.[116] The latter cannot be satisfied if the former are not protected.[117] Similarly, Andrew von Hirsch and Nils Jareborg argue that crimes that endanger survival or physical integrity are more serious than crimes that merely decrease one's well-being.[118] They note that survival must be safeguarded to improve one's quality of life.[119] These theorists do not disregard the importance of interests other than survival, security, or well-being. They simply recognize that the threat to certain interests is comparatively more serious than the threat to other interests.

The republican theory of freedom captures how laws can impose nonegalitarian trade-offs that result in different degrees of domination. Recall how domination can occur across a spectrum of intensity, frequency, or consistency.[120] Republicanism acknowledges why the threat of interference to some interests is worse than the threat of interference to others. Laws that govern public property produce greater and more egregious domination when individuals must sacrifice their most fundamental interests – survival, security, physical integrity, and mental well-being – to obey them. Conversely, laws that impose nonegalitarian sacrifices to interests such as companionship or privacy are still morally objectionable and result in domination, yet to a lesser extent than laws that endanger one's survival or physical integrity. For instance, although an unhoused person may have a significant other, they may sleep in a shelter that does not admit couples to obey an urban camping ban – a nonegalitarian sacrifice that other individuals are not required to make. Such nonegalitarian trade-offs still constitute a form of domination, although one that is less severe than other nonegalitarian sacrifices.

113 Skolnik, "Homelessness and Unconstitutional Discrimination" at 82.

114 *Ibid.* at 82. On the relationship between equality and equal concern, consideration, and respect, see Ronald Dworkin, *Taking Rights Seriously* (Cambridge: Harvard University Press, 1977) at 272–73, cited in *Quebec (Attorney General)* v. A, 2013 SCC 5 at para. 136.

115 *See, e.g.*, Tony Honore, *Responsibility and Fault* (London: Bloomsbury, 1999) at 63 (noting the primacy of survival-related interests).

116 Abraham Maslow, "A Theory of Human Motivation" (1943) 50 *Psych Rev* 370 at 372–73.

117 *Ibid.*

118 Andrew von Hirsch and Nils Jareborg, "Gauging Harm: A Living Standards Analysis" (1991) 11 *Oxford J Leg Stud* 1 at 17.

119 *Ibid.*

120 Pettit, *Republicanism* at 58.

4.3 HOMELESSNESS, DOMINATION, AND UNCONTROLLED INTERFERENCE

These two forms of domination – others' control over law-abidingness and nonegalitarian trade-offs – are exacerbated by unhoused persons' lack of political and legal power to control the interference they face. People experiencing homelessness generally lack the political power – and financial resources – to lobby governmental officials so that they enact laws or policies that improve access to housing or reduce domination.[121] Furthermore, unhoused persons are rarely elected as lawmakers or participate in governmental decision-making bodies.[122] Some jurisdictions impose a requirement that lawmakers own real property or have a certain value of assets, which further precludes impecunious persons from participating in political office.[123] Unhoused persons may be unable to vote because they lack a fixed address or governmental identification.[124] For these reasons, they may not enjoy the participatory power to shape housing policy or influence the enactment of laws that regulate homelessness and public property.[125]

Discrimination – and the contempt or hostility that others have for unhoused persons – also contributes to their political powerlessness.[126] Groups, such as impecunious persons and unhoused persons, may be highly stigmatized and politically unpopular.[127] Individuals living in poverty also tend to be blamed for their plight.[128] Research demonstrates that they are generally viewed unfavorably by a significant portion of the population.[129] Furthermore, poverty and homelessness are associated with negative feelings and stereotypes.[130] These considerations explain why groups that enjoy greater political clout may be reluctant to assist unhoused persons or advocate for them.[131]

Unhoused persons also lack the legal power to control interference to which they are subject. Like other police interventions, the discretionary enforcement of laws that govern public property tends to be low-visibility and is not subject to meaningful

121 *See, e.g.*, Jennifer Watson, "When No Place Is Home: Why the Homeless Deserve Suspect Classification" (2003) 88:2 *Iowa L Rev* 501 at 517–23.

122 Bertrall II Ross and Su Li, "Measuring Political Power: Suspect Class Determinations and the Poor" (2016) 104:2 *Cal L Rev* 323 at 344.

123 *See, e.g.*, Constitution Act, 1867 (UK), 30 and 31 Victoria, c. 3, s. 23(3) and (4); Christopher Cornell, "*Reference re Senate Reform* and the Supreme Court of Canada's Clarification of the Constitutional Procedure for Reforming the Canadian Parliament's Upper House" (2014) 20:3 *L & Bus Rev Am* 451 at 453.

124 Watson, "When No Place Is Home" at 522.

125 *Ibid.*

126 Ross and Li, "Measuring Political Power" at 343–44; Watson, "When No Place Is Home" at 518–23.

127 *See, e.g.*, John Belcher and Bruce DeForge, "Social Stigma and Homelessness: The Limits of Social Change" (2012) 22:8 *J Hum Behav in the Soc Env't* 929 at 931–32; David Fathi, "The Challenge of Prison Oversight" (2010) 47:4 *Am Crim L Rev* 1453 at 1453.

128 Belcher and DeForge, "Social Stigma and Homelessness" at 931–32.

129 Danieli Evans Peterman, "Socioeconomic Status Discrimination" (2018) 104:7 *Va L Rev* 1283 at 1310.

130 *Ibid.*

131 Fathi, "The Challenge of Prison Oversight" at 1453.

judicial scrutiny (more on this point in the next chapter).[132] Police encounters that result in unhoused persons being displaced, fined, or arrested will not be subject to oversight by the legal system – a form of insufficiently controlled interference that exemplifies domination.[133] Unhoused persons may be unable to afford to pay for legal representation to defend their rights in various contexts, such as civil damage claims for unlawful police conduct, eviction protection in housing court, or human rights tribunal complaints related to housing or employment discrimination.[134] Unhoused persons' legal and political powerlessness worsen the domination that they experience, and aggravate the uncontrolled nature of that interference.

4.4 CONCLUSION

This chapter introduced the republican conception of freedom. It demonstrated why unhoused persons lack this third form of freedom that is distinct from negative and positive conceptions of liberty. It explained why laws that govern public property subject unhoused persons to two forms of double domination. Namely, unhoused persons depend on others to obey laws that govern public property, and they must make nonegalitarian sacrifices to comply with these laws. Unhoused persons' legal and political powerlessness worsens these forms of domination. Together, the previous chapter and this chapter illustrate why people experiencing homelessness enjoy less positive, negative, and republican liberty than others.

But why does the State have the power to subject unhoused persons to double domination? The next chapters explain why the State has a greater power to regulate and to police unhoused persons' need-alleviating acts compared to people with access to housing, and to entrench them in the condition of homelessness.

132 Joseph Goldstein, "Police Discretion Not to Invoke the Criminal Process; Low-Visibility Decisions in the Administration of Justice" (1960) 69:4 *Yale LJ* 543 at 543.

133 Frank Lovett, "Non-Domination" in David Schmidtz and Carmen Pavel (eds.), *The Oxford Handbook of Freedom* (Oxford University Press, 2016) at 109.

134 *See, e.g.*, Matthew Desmond and Monica Bell, "Housing, Poverty, and the Law" (2015) 11 *Ann Rev L Soc Sci* 15 at 26 (describing the lack of legal representation in housing court).

5

Nonegalitarian Coercion

The previous chapter showed how laws that govern public property subject unhoused persons to two unique forms of double domination. First, others exert control over unhoused persons' opportunities to obey these laws. Second, people experiencing homelessness must make nonegalitarian trade-offs to comply with laws that regulate public property.

This chapter explains why unhoused persons suffer these forms of domination. It demonstrates why the State has more power to regulate and police unhoused persons compared to people with access to housing, which will be referred to as "nonegalitarian coercion."[1] This disparity exists because the State can more justifiably prohibit and police need-alleviating conduct that occurs on public property than on private property.[2]

Nonegalitarian coercion constitutes a form of domination that shapes how laws that govern public property operate differently for unhoused persons. For people with access to housing, these laws function more like typical crimes that proscribe positive acts and that limit freedom minimally. In contrast, for unhoused persons, laws that govern public property operate more like crimes of omission that impose affirmative duties to act and that restrict liberty significantly.[3] Unhoused persons have a positive duty to secure access to a private place to alleviate their needs lawfully.[4] They suffer domination because others exert control over whether they fulfil that duty and avoid coercion, and because they must make nonegalitarian trade-offs to obey the law.[5] This chapter's concluding parts elucidate why the State can more easily regulate and police unhoused persons than people with access to housing and explain why it constitutes a form of vertical domination.

1 This argument was first advanced in Terry Skolnik, "How and Why Homeless People Are Regulated Differently" (2018) 43:2 *Queen's LJ* 297 at 319–23.

2 *Ibid.*

3 *Ibid.* at 307–10.

4 *Ibid.*

5 *Ibid.* at 309–10.

5.1 THE ROLE OF PUBLIC PROPERTY

Public property's role and the justifications for protecting it help explain why the State has more power to regulate and police unhoused persons compared to people with access to housing. Although there are many descriptions of "public property," this chapter adopts Michael Robertson's definition.[6] According to Robertson:

> Public property is a type of common property that is owned by the State, but to which the general public has a broad right of access. The strong right to exclude non-owners, which the State enjoys with respect to state property (private property owned by the State), does not exist with public property, although the State, as owner, can still make rules to manage the public access efficiently, equitably, and safely.[7]

Public property has two notable characteristics. First, individuals lack a private power to exclude others on public property.[8] Second, individuals have a general right of access to public property, subject to regulations that govern its use.[9] Jeremy Waldron observes that public property encompasses places that are "fairly accessible to everyone" and "where anyone may be," such as streets, sidewalks, parks, public squares, and beaches.[10] For public property to operate as a truly open-access space, all community members must be able to share its use.

Public property fulfils several fundamental roles within society. First, it serves an important communal and social function.[11] Public places such as parks, streets, and beaches allow for commerce, the free exchange of ideas, recreation, social gatherings, and relaxation.[12] Carol Rose explains that public property's value stems from the fact that each individual's presence can reinforce a sense of community, solidarity, and togetherness.[13] There is also a connection between the role of public property and the instilment of civic virtue.[14] Public property's communal nature incentivizes individuals to learn to live together despite their conflicting interests and expectations.[15]

6 Michael Robertson, "Common Property *Redux*" (2016) 49:2 *UBC L Rev* 563 at 608.

7 *Ibid.*

8 *Ibid. See also* Crawford Brough MacPherson, "The Meaning of Property" in Crawford Brough MacPherson (ed.), *Property: Mainstream and Critical Positions* (University of Toronto Press, 1978) at 5.

9 Sarah Hamill, "Private Rights to Public Property: The Evolution of Public Property in Canada" (2012) 58:2 *McGill LJ* 365 at 400–01.

10 Robertson, "Common Property *Redux*" at 608. Quoted portions in Jeremy Waldron, "Homelessness and the Issue of Freedom" (1991–92) 39 *UCLA L Rev* 295 at 298. The list of places that fall within the definition of public property are cited in Robertson, "Common Property *Redux*."

11 Carol Rose, "The Comedy of the Commons: Custom, Commerce, and Inherently Public Property" (1986) 53:3 *U Chi L Rev* 711 at 777–78.

12 *Ibid.* at 778–79.

13 *Ibid.*

14 Carol Rose, "Romans, Roads, and Romantic Creators: Traditions of Public Property in the Information Age" (2003) 66 *L & Contemp Prob* 89 at 98–99.

15 Rose, "The Comedy of the Commons" at 775–78.

Second, public property furthers certain democratic values.[16] Free access to public property allows for organized demonstrations against the State and other entities, promotes freedom of speech, and fosters freedom of association.[17] The US and Canadian supreme courts have also recognized that public property advances these types of values that are important for a democracy.[18]

Third, public property safeguards liberty outside of one's home. It ensures that individuals can use open-access spaces without being subject to others' exclusionary power or agenda-setting authority.[19] Public property helps guarantee that persons can freely travel between locations and engage in certain conduct in the public sphere without the risk of interference by others.[20] Individuals would constantly be subject to others' power of exclusion if all land were privatized.[21] Rightsholders could refuse to let others pass through their land.[22] Without public property, individuals who attempt to leave their private property would face horizontal domination as they could constantly be excluded from others' land.[23] Public property thus promotes liberty in the public sphere because it neutralizes the horizontal domination that would exist if all land were privatized.[24]

5.2 JUSTIFICATIONS FOR REGULATING PUBLIC PROPERTY

5.2.1 *General Justifications for Regulating Public Property*

The open-access nature of areas such as parks, streets, public squares, and beaches generates certain risks related to public property's communal value. Individuals share similar goals and desires when using these spaces.[25] But they also have opposing expectations about how public property can and should be used.[26] Each

16 *Ibid.* at 777–79; Anna di Robilant, "Common Ownership and Equality of Autonomy" (2012) 58 *McGill LJ* 263 at 274–75; Robert Ellickson, "Controlling Chronic Misconduct in City Spaces: Of Panhandlers, Skid Rows, and Public-Space Zoning" (1996) 105 *Yale LJ* 1165 at 1173; Margaret Kohn, *Brave New Neighbourhoods: The Privatization of Public Space* (New York: Routledge, 2004) at 2–3.

17 Rose, "The Comedy of the Commons" at 778–79.

18 In the United States, *see Hague* v. *Committee for Industrial Organization*, 307 US 496 (1939); *International Soc. for Krishna Consciousness, Inc.* v. *Lee*, 505 US 672 at 679 (1992); *Frisby* v. *Schultz*, 487 US 474 at 488–89 (1988); Stacey Schesser, "A New Domain for Public Speech: Opening Public Spaces Online" (2006) 94:6 *Cal L Rev* 1791 at 1807. In Canada, *see Committee for the Commonwealth of Canada* v. *Canada* [1991] 1 SCR 139 at 167–68; *Montréal (City)* v. *2952–1366 Québec Inc.*, 2005 SCC 62 at para. 68, cited in Sarah Hamill, "Private Rights to Public Property: The Evolution of Common Property in Canada" (2012) 58 *McGill LJ* 365 at 395.

19 MacPherson, "The Meaning of Property" at 5.

20 Arthur Ripstein, *Force and Freedom: Kant's Legal and Political Philosophy* (Cambridge: Harvard University Press, 2009) at 238–39, 255–56.

21 *Ibid.*

22 *Ibid.*

23 *Ibid.*

24 *Ibid.*

25 Skolnik, "How and Why" at 303.

26 *Ibid.*

person's rational attempt to derive the greatest benefit from public property can lead to collectively irrational outcomes; namely, the decline of public property's shared value for all.[27]

Garrett Hardin famously referred to this collective action problem as a "tragedy of the commons."[28] Hardin summarized: "Ruin is the destination toward which all men rush, each pursuing his own best interest in a society that believes in the freedom of the commons. Freedom in a commons brings ruin to all."[29] Hardin argued that different forms of mutual coercion are necessary to prevent a tragedy of the commons.[30] These include a private property scheme, taxation, and laws that govern public property.[31] These forms of mutual coercion help prevent congestion, overexploitation, rivalry between users, and usages of public property that decrease its shared value or limit others' liberty to use these spaces on equal terms.[32]

Some contend that the State must regulate public property to prevent a tragedy of the urban commons.[33] Robert Ellickson and Robert Teir argue that laws that govern public property promote individual freedom because they allow people with opposing expectations to use public space on equal terms.[34] They suggest that when the State does not enforce such laws, public property's value will decline, which discourages individuals from using it.[35]

Sheila Foster contends that a tragedy of the urban commons can occur from regulatory slippage.[36] The term "regulatory slippage" implies that local governments underenforce laws that regulate public property, or increasingly tolerate acts that undermine its collective value.[37] Lax enforcement standards can lead to public property's congestion and overexploitation.[38] Congestion and overexploitation can

27 *Ibid.* at 304; Elinor Ostrom, *Governing the Commons* (Cambridge University Press, 1990) at 5. Ostrom's original quote is: "individually rational strategies lead to collectively irrational outcomes" (*ibid.*).

28 Skolnik, "How and Why" at 304; Garrett Hardin, "The Tragedy of the Commons" (1968) 162 *Science* 1243 at 1244.

29 Hardin, "The Tragedy of the Commons" at 1244.

30 *Ibid.* at 1247–48.

31 *Ibid.* at 1247.

32 Sheila Foster and Christian Iaione, "The City as a Commons" (2016) 34:2 *Yale L & Pol'y Rev* 281 at 288; Brett Frischmann, "An Economic Theory of Infrastructure and Commons Management" (2005) 89:4 *Minn L Rev* 917 at 984.

33 Sheila Foster, "Urban Informality as a Commons Dilemma" (2009) 40:2 *U Miami Inter-Am L Rev* 261 at 267–71.

34 Ellickson, "Controlling Chronic Misconduct" at 1174; Robert Teir, "Restoring Order in Urban Public Spaces" (1997–98) 2 *Tex Rev L & Pol* 255 at 288–89.

35 Ellickson, "Controlling Chronic Misconduct" at 1174.

36 Sheila Foster, "Collective Action and the Urban Commons" (2011) 87:1 *Notre Dame L Rev* 57 at 59–61. *See also* Abraham Bell and Gideon Parchomovsky, "Of Property and Antiproperty" (2003) 102:1 *Mich L Rev* 1 at 8–9; Lee Anne Fennell, "Agglomerama" (2014) 2014:6 *BYU L Rev* 1373 at 1380–81.

37 Foster, "Collective Action and the Urban Commons" at 67; Foster and Iaione, "The City as a Commons" at 298–99.

38 Foster and Iaione, "The City as a Commons" at 298–99.

produce rivalry between users, and may lead some persons to avoid public property.[39]

Similarly, George Kelling and Catherine Coles posit that underenforcement can result in a tragedy of the urban commons.[40] In their view, enforcement failure leads to a rise of suboptimal norms on public property that prevent or discourage others from using it.[41] A tragedy of the commons occurs when underenforcement allows suboptimal norms to displace optimal ones, such that public property's shared value declines.[42]

5.2.2 *Specific Justifications for Regulating Public Property*

These accounts highlight that public property's shared value will deteriorate when "anything goes" in these spaces.[43] These same accounts illustrate how the State must regulate public property to safeguard its collective worth and ensure that all persons can enjoy its use on equal terms. Canadian and US courts have decided that the State (including local governments) can justifiably regulate public property for these reasons.[44] Judicial decisions affirm that there are several justifications for laws that govern public property.

First, courts acknowledge that the State can regulate public property to promote sanitation and safety.[45] For example, in *Abbotsford (City)* v. *Shantz*, the British Columbia (BC) Supreme Court recognized that a homeless encampment created certain public health and safety risks due to violence and the accumulation of garbage and human waste.[46] In the Supreme Court of California decision

39 *See, e.g.*, Foster, "Collective Action and the Urban Commons" at 68; Teir, "Restoring Order in Urban Public Spaces" at 274 (describing how some individuals avoided Thompkins Square Park when there was a tent encampment).

40 George Kelling and Catherine Coles, *Fixing Broken Windows: Restoring Order and Reducing Crime in Our Communities* (New York: Touchstone, 1996) at 19–22.

41 *Ibid.*

42 *Ibid.*

43 Rose, "Romans, Roads, and Romantic Creators" at 99.

44 Andrew Liese, "We Can Do Better: Anti-Homeless Ordinances as Violations of State Substantive Due Process Law" (2006) 59:4 *Vand L Rev* 1413 at 1421; Maria Foscarinis, Kelly Cunningham-Bowers, and Kristen Brown, "Out of Sight – Out of Mind: The Continuing Trend toward the Criminalization of Homelessness" (1999) 6:2 *Geo J Poverty L & Pol'y* 145 at 152–56.

45 *See, e.g., Davison* v. *City of Tucson*, 924 F Supp 989 at 991 (D Ariz 1996); *Aitken* v. *City of Aberdeen* (WD Wash 2019); *Sanchez* v. *City of Fresno*, 914 F Supp (2d) 1079 at 1113 (ED Cal 2012); Nicholas May, "Fourth Amendment Challenges to Camping Ordinances: The Government Acquiescence Doctrine as a Legal Strategy to Force Legislative Solutions to Homelessness" (2008) 8:1 *Conn Pub Int LJ* 113 at 115.

46 *Abbotsford (City)* v. *Shantz*, 2015 BCSC 1909 at paras. 19, 274. On sanitation problems in certain homeless encampments, *see, e.g.*, Alene Tchekmedyian, "Blaze at Homeless Encampment in San Diego County May Have Exposed Firefighters to Hepatitis A," LA Times (September 25, 2017), www.latimes.com/local/lanow/la-me-ln-hepatitis-firefighters-20170925-story.html [perma.cc/Q9RZ-TG5G]; Lizzie Johnson, "Complaints of Syringes and Feces Rise Dramatically in SF," SF Gate (November 2, 2016), www.sfgate.com/bayarea/article/Complaints-of-syringes-human-waste-rise-10459969.php [perma.cc/F99J-QSRN].

Tobe v. *City of Santa Ana*, the court observed that the city could prohibit camping on public property to promote sanitation and public health.[47] The court explained: "Adoption of the ordinance was clearly within the police power of the city, which may 'make and enforce within its limits all local, police, sanitary, and other ordinances and regulations not in conflict with general laws'."[48] Other US courts agree on these points.[49]

Second, courts acknowledge that cities can regulate public property to protect its aesthetic quality, foster its attractiveness, and promote the city's economic vitality.[50] In the *Adams* decision, the BC Court of Appeal concluded that the city can prohibit camping on public property to maintain "the environmental, recreational and social benefits of urban parks" and protect "the economic viability of adjacent areas."[51] The Court remarked that the city of Victoria "bears the responsibility to the public to preserve public places for the use of all."[52] In the US Supreme Court decision *Clark* v. *CCNV*, the Court upheld the constitutionality of a federal law that banned camping in national parks not designated for that purpose for similar reasons.[53] The majority concluded that certain acts that occur on public property discourage others from using it.[54] In *Joyce* v. *City and County of San Francisco*, the court affirmed that the State can enact laws that protect public property to promote economic vitality.[55] In that case, the city estimated that homelessness resulted in an estimated loss of $173 million in sales.[56] The court recognized that the city had constitutional authority to regulate public property and to prohibit acts such as camping, urinating, and defecating.[57]

Third, the State can regulate public property to solve coordination problems and promote efficiency.[58] Courts uphold laws that prohibit individuals from obstructing streets and sidewalks so that pedestrians and goods can move efficiently between

47 *Tobe* v. *City of Santa Ana*, 9 Cal (4th) 1069 at 1109 (Sup Ct 1995).

48 *Ibid.*

49 *Joel* v. *City of Orlando*, 232 F (3d) 1353 at 1358–59 (11th Circ 2000); *Joyce* v. *City and County of San Francisco*, 846 F Supp 843 at 860 (ND Cal 1994).

50 *Joyce* v. *City and County of San Francisco*, 846 F Supp 843 at 860 (ND Cal 1994); *Members of City Council of Los Angeles* v. *Taxpayers for Vincent*, 466 US 789 at 805 (1984).

51 *Victoria (City)* v. *Adams*, 2009 BCCA 563 at paras. 119–21. The laws were ultimately struck down as unconstitutional due to overbreadth, but the justification for regulating public property was accepted in rejecting arbitrariness arguments.

52 *Ibid.* at para. 4.

53 *Clark* v. *Community for Creative Non-Violence*, 468 US 288 at 296 (1984).

54 *Ibid.*

55 *Joyce* v. *City and County of San Francisco*, 846 F Supp 843 at 846 (ND Cal 1994).

56 *Ibid.*

57 *Ibid.* at 860.

58 See Blomley's analysis in Nicholas Blomley, "How to Turn a Beggar into a Bus Stop: Law, Traffic and the 'Function of the Place'" (2007) 44 *Urb Stud* 1697 at 1700–02. On coordination problems, see Joseph Raz, "Justification and Authority" (1985) 14 *Phil & Pub Aff* 1 at 17.

places.[59] These laws are also upheld because they minimize congestion and optimize the flow of traffic on public ways.[60]

5.3 NONEGALITARIAN COERCION

The State has more power to regulate and to police unhoused persons compared to people with access to housing. This disparity exists for the following reasons. The justifications for regulating need-alleviating conduct on public property either do not apply to private property or are outweighed by the protection of individual interests within the home.[61] Housing safeguards individuals against laws that regulate their most basic human acts.[62] People experiencing homelessness lack that protection. For this reason, the State has more power to regulate and police their basic human acts.

Nonegalitarian coercion is comprised of two components: nonegalitarian regulation and nonegalitarian enforcement. Nonegalitarian regulation refers to how the State can enact laws that govern unhoused persons disparately because they lack private property rights.[63] Nonegalitarian enforcement, on the other hand, implies that law enforcement has more power to police unhoused persons for that same reason.

5.4 NONEGALITARIAN REGULATION

5.4.1 *The State's Greater Capacity to Regulate Unhoused Persons*

Nonegalitarian regulation occurs because the same act affects interests differently when done on public property as opposed to private property. This distinction is exemplified by how the law prohibits some conduct in public spaces yet permits it in private.[64] Nearly every city prohibits defecation on public property yet allows individuals to defecate at home in their bathroom. The State forbids sexual activity on public property yet permits it on private

59 Christine Bella and David Lopez, "Quality-of-life – At What Price? Constitutional Challenges to Laws Adversely Impacting the Homeless" (1994) 10 *J Civ R and Econ Dev* 89 at 111–12; *International Soc. for Krishna Consciousness, Inc.* v. *Lee*, 505 US 672 at 682–83 (1992); *Roulette* v. *City of Seattle*, 97 F (3d) 300 at 302 (9th Circ 1996); *Justin* v. *City of Los Angeles* (CD Cal 2000) 2000 WL 1808426. This last decision cited in Farida Ali, "Limiting the Poor's Right to Public Space: Criminalizing Homelessness in California" (2014) 21:2 *Geo J Poverty L & Pol'y* 197 at 225.

60 *One World One Family* v. *City and County of Honolulu*, 76 F (3d) 1009 at 1014 (9th Circ 1996); *White* v. *City of Laguna Beach*, 679 F Supp (2d) 1143 at 1152–54 (CD Cal 2010); *Roulette* v. *City of Seattle*, 97 F (3d) 300 at 308 (9th Circ 1996).

61 Skolnik, "How and Why" at 319–23.

62 *Ibid.*

63 *Ibid.*

64 Joel Feinberg, *Offense to Others* (Oxford University Press, 1985) at 39–40.

property.[65] Many cities ban camping on public property, but individuals can lawfully erect tents in their living rooms.[66]

The State can justifiably prohibit certain acts that take place on public property to preserve its collective value and to safeguard liberty outside of one's home. In contrast, private property's role and value are different. Unlike public property, private property is not an open-access space. It does not allow for large-scale interaction between strangers with shared and conflicting interests.[67] Nor does private property aim to promote certain democratic, communal, and civic values that are integral to the open-access nature of public property.[68]

Private property fulfils a different role. By insulating individuals from public life and forced interactions with others, it protects interests such as liberty, autonomy, privacy, and personhood.[69] In many senses, private property is a refuge from public property and the public sphere. Public property and private property's distinct roles – and the different interests that they foster – explain why the State can justifiably prohibit certain acts on public property but not on private property.[70] There are three reasons for this.

First, certain justifications for prohibiting an act on public property cannot apply to private property.[71] The State regulates public property to solve coordination problems and increase the efficiency of public ways.[72] Such justifications underpin laws that prohibit individuals from sitting or camping on sidewalks.[73] These same justifications could not support a law that regulates how individuals sit or camp within their homes because it is not an open-access space that requires efficiency and cooperation between persons. Instead, rightsholders set the agenda of their private property and can exclude others from it. This preempts coordination problems and mitigates efficiency concerns that justify the prohibition of certain acts of public property.[74] These examples show how some justifications for proscribing a particular act on public property cannot be transposed to justify proscribing that same act on private property.[75]

Second, the justifications for prohibiting some act on public property diminish or disappear when that same act is done on private property.[76] The State can regulate sexual acts, defecation, and nudity on public property because it offends others and

65 Richard Posner and Katharine Silbaugh, *A Guide to America's Sex Laws* (University of Chicago Press, 1996) at ch. 6.
66 Skolnik, "How and Why" at 321.
67 *Ibid.* at 320.
68 *Ibid.* at 321.
69 Margaret Jane Radin, "Property and Personhood" (1982) 34:5 *Stan L Rev* 957 at 968.
70 Skolnik, "How and Why" at 320.
71 *Ibid.* at 321.
72 *Ibid.* at 322.
73 See Section 5.2.2.
74 Skolnik, "How and Why" at 321–22.
75 *Ibid.* at 321.
76 *Ibid.*

breaches "norms about public behavior."[77] When individuals do these acts in a park, they may force unwilling observers to enter into their private domain.[78] However, these concerns largely disappear when individuals do these acts in the privacy of their homes.[79] The same is true for sanitation and public health justifications that underpin municipal ordinances. Cities prohibit public defecation.[80] Yet individuals can lawfully defecate in bathrooms within their homes – a private space that reduces sanitation concerns and mitigates public health risks. This explains why the State can justifiably prohibit public defecation and urination but can less justifiably proscribe these acts when they are done within one's home.

Two caveats are necessary here. First, to some extent, the State can justifiably regulate how people alleviate their needs within their homes. To ensure that dwellings are fit for habitation, the State can prohibit defecating and urinating in places within one's home that are not intended for that purpose.[81] The State can declare private property unfit for human habitation when it poses a significant health risk to the occupants or to others.[82] Second, the State may regulate or police certain forms of housing more than others. Public housing, for instance, may be subject to more invasive regulation and policing compared to private housing.[83] Furthermore, individuals may face more police scrutiny or enjoy less privacy in these spaces.[84] Leaving aside these circumstances, the justifications for prohibiting certain acts on public property tend to diminish or disappear when people do these same acts on private property.[85]

There is a third reason why the State can more justifiably regulate certain acts that occur on public property versus on private property. On public property, the State's interests may outweigh individual rights.[86] Yet on private property, the individual's

77 *Ibid.*; Larry Alexander, "Harm, Offense, and Morality" (1994) 7:2 *Can JL & Jur* 199 at 211.

78 Dennis Baker, *The Right Not to Be Criminalized: Demarcating Criminal Law's Authority* (London: Routledge, 2011) at 248. This sentence paraphrased from Baker, who explains: "Exhibitionism is a wrong not because of the natural content of the exhibit, but because *x*'s nudity forces *y* to enter *x*'s private domain . . . ."

79 Skolnik, "How and Why" at 321.

80 Donald Saelinger, "Nowhere to Go: The Impacts of City Ordinances Criminalizing Homelessness" (2006) 13:3 *Geo J Poverty L & Pol'y* 545 at 551.

81 Skolnik, "How and Why" at 321.

82 *Ibid.*; *Mchanga* v. *Huang*, 2005 CanLII 2089 (QC CQ).

83 Skolnik, "How and Why" at 321; Jeffrey Fagan, Garth Davies, and Adam Carlis, "Race and Selective Enforcement in Public Housing" (2012) 9:4 *J Empirical Leg Stud* 697 at 699–701.

84 *See, e.g.*, William Stuntz, "Distribution of Fourth Amendment Privacy" (1999) 67:5 *Geo Wash L Rev* 1265 at 1270, 1272.

85 Skolnik, "How and Why" at 321.

86 *See, e.g.*, Charles Reich, "The New Property" (1964) 73:5 *Yale LJ* 733 at 771 (advancing a similar argument). Reich notes at 771: "Property draws a circle around the activities of each private individual or organization. Within that circle, the owner has a greater degree of freedom than without. Outside, he must justify or explain his actions, and show his authority. Within, he is master, and the state must explain and justify any interference. It is as if property shifted the burden of proof; outside, the individual has the burden; inside, the burden is on government to demonstrate that something the owner wishes to do should not be done."

rights tend to outweigh the State's interests.[87] There may be compelling justifications to prohibit and police some act on private property. However, the individual's fundamental interests in dignity, privacy, and liberty may take precedence over the State's interests in prohibiting some conduct that is done on private property.[88] Recall how private property rights strongly protect certain individual interests and confer one of the highest expectations of privacy.[89] If the State attempts to police how individuals alleviate their needs within their homes, the State will unjustifiably impact these interests. Private property rights limit the State's power to prohibit and police need-alleviating acts that are done within one's home.[90]

Nonegalitarian regulation constitutes a form of domination for various reasons. For one, the State enjoys a unilateral and largely uncontrolled power to enact laws that interfere with unhoused persons' most basic interests in ways that do not affect others. Furthermore, the nonegalitarian regulation of unhoused persons subjects them to the two types of domination discussed in the previous chapter: others' control over unhoused persons' law-abidingness and nonegalitarian trade-offs. And as discussed further in Section 5.5, nonegalitarian regulation results in disparate enforcement actions against unhoused persons that exemplify domination, and that can entrench individuals in the condition of homelessness.

5.4.2 *Privacy-Dependent Laws and Homelessness*

Nonegalitarian regulation shapes how laws that govern public property operate differently for unhoused persons. Many municipal ordinances operate like typical criminal law prohibitions for people with access to housing, but they impose the equivalent of affirmative duties to act on people experiencing homelessness.[91] Although unhoused persons have a positive duty to secure access to a private place to alleviate their needs, others exert control over whether unhoused persons can fulfil that duty – a form of domination introduced in the previous chapter.[92] In contrast, people with private property rights have free access to a default private place where they can engage in their most basic human acts. They generally do not have an affirmative duty to secure access to a private place where they can do these acts and obey laws that govern public property.[93] Instead, they must abstain from alleviating their needs in public property because they have free access to a lawful alternative.[94]

87 *Ibid.*
88 *Ibid.*
89 *R* v. *Tessling*, 2004 SCC 67 at para. 22.
90 Skolnik, "How and Why" at 322.
91 *Ibid.* at 307–08.
92 *Ibid.*
93 *Ibid.*
94 *Ibid.*; Jeremy Waldron, "Homelessness and Community" (2000) 50:4 *U Toronto LJ* 371 at 373–74 (discussing the complementarity principle, whereby laws that govern public property function differently for individuals who enjoy complementarity between public and private property).

To illustrate this point, notice how some municipal ordinances operate differently than typical crimes. Laws that govern public property constitute privacy-dependent laws. The term "privacy-dependent law" implies that a statute proscribes a particular act on public property but permits that same act when it is done in private. Examples of privacy-dependent laws include statutes that prohibit urban camping, public urination, and loitering.

Privacy-dependent laws result in nonegalitarian regulation because they operate more like crimes of omission for unhoused persons and as crimes of commission for people with access to housing.[95] The distinction between these two categories of crimes is as follows. Crimes of commission are committed by positive acts.[96] The term "positive act" refers to actions, interventions, or affirmative conduct that worsens another's situation or sets back their interests.[97] The majority of crimes are crimes of commission. Typical examples include proscriptions against acts such as assault, theft, fraud, murder, arson, mischief, and so on. Individuals obey these laws when they abstain from the unlawful positive act.[98] Admittedly, it may be difficult for some people to refrain from certain conduct, especially where the conduct is compelled by addiction or irresistible impulses.[99] Most people, however, can abstain from committing the proscribed act to obey the law.

Laws that criminalize omissions are different. The term "omission" implies that an individual fails to fulfil an affirmative duty to act that is imposed by the law.[100] In the context of omissions liability, an individual is culpable because they failed to do a certain act that was required by law; their nonintervention is what makes their conduct morally blameworthy. Examples of affirmative duties to act include parents' positive obligations to feed and clothe their children, the affirmative duty to file a tax return, and the affirmative duty to stop at the scene of an accident that one causes.[101]

Crimes of omission tend to limit freedom more considerably than crimes of commission.[102] Crimes of omission require the individual to fulfil an affirmative

95 On the distinction between crimes of commission versus crimes of omission, see Michael Corrado, "Is There an Act Requirement in the Criminal Law?" (1994) 142:5 *U Pa L Rev* 1529 at 1537.

96 Andrew Ashworth, "The Scope of Criminal Liability for Omissions" (1989) 105 *LQ Rev* 424 at 424; Andrew Ashworth and Eva Steiner, "Criminal Omissions and Public Duties: The French Experience" (1990) 10 *LS* 153 at 154.

97 *See, e.g.*, Tony Honoré, *Responsibility and Fault* (Oxford: Hart, 1999) at 53, 64.

98 Randolph Clarke, *Omissions, Metaphysics, Agency, and Responsibility* (Oxford University Press, 2014) at 91–93; Graham Hughes, "Criminal Omissions" (1958) 67 *Yale LJ* 590 at 590.

99 Deborah Denno, "Crime and Consciousness: Science and Involuntary Acts" (2002) 87 *Minn L Rev* 269 at 313; Stephen Garvey, "Dealing with Wayward Desire" (2009) 3 *Crim L & Phil* 1 at 1; Richard Boldt, "The Construction of Responsibility in the Criminal Law" (1992) 140 *U Pa L Rev* 2245 at 2248.

100 Arthur Leavens, "A Causation Approach to Criminal Omissions" (1988) 76 *Cal L Rev* 546 at 547.

101 Paul Robinson, "Criminal Liability for Omissions: A Brief Summary and Critique of the Law in the United States" (1984) 29 *NY L Sch L Rev* 101 at 103.

102 Ashworth, "The Scope of Criminal Liability for Omissions" at 427–28.

duty to act but prohibit all other conduct, whereas crimes of commission proscribe a single act but permit the individual to engage in other actions.[103]

The combination of two factors explain why laws that regulate public property impose the equivalent of affirmative duties to act on unhoused persons but not on people with access to housing.[104] First, like in the context of omissions liability, individuals who must alleviate their needs cannot engage in alternate courses of action.[105] As part of the human experience, everyone must sleep, urinate, defecate, and so on.[106] When an individual must alleviate their needs as a matter of biological necessity – for instance, when they must sleep or defecate – they must do so to the exclusion of all other acts.

Second, since laws that regulate public property require individuals to alleviate their needs in private, individuals have a positive duty to secure access to a private space to obey these laws.[107] While the biological requirement to alleviate one's needs limits the range of alternate courses of action, the prohibition against alleviating one's needs on public property imposes a positive duty to secure access to a private space to comply with the law.[108]

Some privacy-dependent laws limit freedom more than others. Consider the difference between indecency laws that prohibit sexual activity on public property versus laws that proscribe sleeping or urination on public property. Indecency laws require individuals to engage in sexual activity in private. Since individuals retain the choice of whether to engage in sexual activity, they maintain the freedom to comply with indecency laws through abstention.

Statutes that proscribe sleeping or urinating on public property restrict liberty and free choice more severely. Unlike other criminal laws, a person's opportunity to obey privacy-dependent laws hinges on their opportunity to access a private space to alleviate their biologically necessary needs.[109] Since others exert control over unhoused persons' access to private property, others also exert control over whether they fulfil their positive duty to alleviate their needs in private and, ultimately, obey the law.[110]

In contrast, for people with access to housing, privacy-dependent laws function more like typical crimes of commission that proscribe positive acts. Although biological necessity requires people with access to housing to alleviate their needs to the exclusion of all other acts, they have free access to a default private place where they can shelter themselves, sleep, and urinate.[111] Access to housing helps

[103] *Ibid.*

[104] Skolnik, "How and Why" at 306–08.

[105] *Ibid.*

[106] *Ibid.*; Waldron, "Homelessness and the Issue of Freedom" at 321.

[107] Skolnik, "How and Why" at 306–08.

[108] *Ibid.*

[109] Terry Skolnik, "Homelessness and the Impossibility to Obey the Law" (2016) 43 *Fordham Urb LJ* 741 at 746–50.

[110] Skolnik, "How and Why" at 306–08.

[111] Jeremy Waldron, "Property and Community: For Those Who Have Neither" (2009) 10:1 *Theor Inq L* 161 at 175–77.

ensure that individuals are not constantly burdened with an affirmative duty to secure access to a private place to obey laws that govern public property. This explains why these laws subject unhoused persons to affirmative duties to act more frequently than people with access to housing.

To be clear, this does not mean that people with access to housing are never subject to the affirmative duty to act described above. Individuals who leave their homes must urinate, defecate, or rest, and they must still obtain permission to enter a private place to do so. Yet in comparison to unhoused persons, people with access to housing are imposed this duty far less regularly and consistently. This is especially true with respect to certain need-alleviating conduct that people with access to housing routinely do without having to secure access to a private space, such as sleeping and sheltering themselves.

Private property rights – and one's freedom to access private property – thus shape whether laws that govern public property operate more like crimes of omission versus crimes of commission. Access to housing influences whether laws that govern public property constantly subject individuals to affirmative duties to act, and whether others exert control over whether they fulfil that duty.

5.5 NONEGALITARIAN ENFORCEMENT

The second aspect of nonegalitarian coercion is nonegalitarian enforcement, meaning that officers have more discretionary power to police unhoused persons than people with access to housing – a form of vertical domination. Police discretion can result in domination for several reasons. Police discretion can be exercised arbitrarily and without adequate checks and balances.[112] Law enforcement interactions tend to be low-visibility, and many exercises of police discretion are never reviewed by courts.[113] Officers may also single out marginalized persons who lack sufficient political power, legal knowledge, or finances to contest such mistreatment.[114] There may be so many applicable laws that individuals will inevitably violate one of them, such that officers enjoy vast enforcement discretion.[115] Officers, in turn, enjoy the power to unilaterally interfere at will with individuals who break these laws. Officers may also abuse their authority and denigrate or humiliate members of the public.[116]

112 Eric Miller, "Challenging Police Discretion" (2015) 58:2 *Howard LJ* 521 at 540.

113 Terry Skolnik, "Racial Profiling and the Perils of Ancillary Police Powers" (2021) 99:2 *Can Bar Rev* 429 at 435; Joseph Goldstein, "Police Discretion Not to Invoke the Criminal Process; Low-Visibility Decisions in the Administration of Justice" (1960) 69:4 *Yale LJ* 543 at 580–81.

114 Josh Bowers, "Probable Cause, Constitutional Reasonableness, and the Unrecognized Point of a Pointless Indignity" (2014) 66:5 *Stan L Rev* 987 at 1038, fn. 261; Debra Livingston "Police Discretion and the Quality of Life in Public Places: Courts, Communities, and the New Policing" (1997) 97 *Colum L Rev* 551 at 592.

115 Kim Forde-Mazrui, "Ruling Out the Rule of Law" (2007) 60 *Vand L Rev* 1495 at 1513–14.

116 Vincent Chiao, "Discretion and Domination in Criminal Procedure: Reflections on Pettit" (2016) 15:1 *Pol, Phil & Econ* 92 at 105–06.

Police discretion has various other characteristics that are associated with domination. Police officers and individuals are in an asymmetrical power dynamic vis-à-vis one another; a dynamic that is known to officers and individuals, and that shapes how law enforcement encounters unfold.[117] Furthermore, officers can exercise public powers that private individuals lack. The police have the power to issue fines, confiscate property, incarcerate persons, arrest people in contexts where individuals have no such authority, and charge persons with crimes and regulatory offenses.[118]

Nonegalitarian enforcement subjects people experiencing homelessness to vertical domination for three principal reasons. First, since unhoused persons must spend much of their time on public property where privacy-dependent laws are enforced, they are frequently subject to uncontrolled police discretion associated with these laws.[119] Without access to housing, unhoused persons are constantly at risk of violating laws that govern public property and facing coercion and punishment by the police.[120] People with access to housing, on the other hand, can freely alleviate their needs within their homes – the very spaces where privacy-dependent laws do not apply and are not enforced by the police.[121] Housing shields individuals against the discretionary enforcement of laws that govern public property.[122]

Second, unhoused persons are vulnerable to vertical domination because they lack physical and legal protection against police discretion. The police cannot freely access an individual's home because of the significant legal protections that private property rights afford against State intrusion.[123] Save for exigent circumstances, officers require warrants to enter someone's home or access its perimeter.[124] People experiencing homelessness lack this protection.[125] The police patrol public places, which is where unhoused persons tend to spend their time and alleviate their needs when they lack alternatives. As a result, people experiencing homelessness are vulnerable to disproportionate levels of surveillance, law enforcement encounters, and police discretion.[126]

117 Ekow Yankah, "Pretext and Justification: Republicanism, Policing, and Race" (2019) 40 *Cardozo L Rev* 1543 at 1572–73, 1619–22.

118 Malcolm Thorburn, "Policing and Public Office" (2020) 70:2 *U Toronto LJ* 248 at 248–49.

119 Terry Skolnik, "Freedom and Access to Housing: Three Conceptions" (2018) 35 *Windsor YB* Access Just 226 at 240; Marie-Eve Sylvestre, "Disorder and Public Spaces in Montreal: Repression (and Resistance) Through Law, Politics, and Police Discretion" (2010) 31:6 *Urb Geo* 803 at 819; Tony Sparks, "Broke Not Broken: Rights, Privacy, and Homelessness in Seattle" (2010) 31:6 *Urb Geo* 842 at 847–48.

120 Skolnik, "Homelessness and the Impossibility to Obey the Law" at 745, 750, 786.

121 Skolnik, "How and Why" at 322.

122 Skolnik, "Freedom and Access to Housing" at 240.

123 Benjamin Barros, "The Home as a Legal Concept" (2006) 46:2 *Santa Clara L Rev* 255 at 263–70.

124 *Ibid.* at 267–68.

125 Kevin Fitzpatrick and Brad Myrstol, "The Jailing of America's Homeless: Evaluating the Rabble Management Thesis" (2011) 57:2 *Crime & Delinquency* 271 at 275.

126 Sylvestre, "Disorder and Public Spaces in Montreal" at 819.

Third, police officers may exercise their discretion abusively and arbitrarily against unhoused persons. In survey studies, people experiencing homelessness report that they have been fined, arrested, or harassed by the police even though they did not violate any laws. For instance, in 2009, Bill O'Grady and colleagues conducted an empirical study comprised of survey questions and semi-structured interviews that involved 244 unhoused youth aged 16–24 in the city of Toronto.[127] One-third of the respondents who received a fine contended that they had committed no offense and that the sanction was unfair.[128] The National Law Center on Homelessness and Poverty conducted a similar survey that involved ninety unhoused adults in New York City.[129] Roughly 60 percent of the participants indicated that they experienced harassment by the police.[130] A 2014 survey study questioned 441 people experiencing homelessness in Colorado.[131] Approximately 76 percent of respondents indicated that they were harassed by the police despite having done nothing wrong.[132] Beyond harassment, citations, and arrests, many unhoused persons report that police officers confiscate or destroy their property without legal authorization or prior warning.[133] Certain judicial decisions support these findings.[134]

Furthermore, in certain studies, unhoused persons report that they were singled-out by the police because they were experiencing homelessness. In the Colorado study discussed above, nearly 86 percent of respondents stated that the police targeted them for that reason.[135] In O'Grady and colleagues' study of unhoused youth in Toronto, many respondents reported that they were fined for an offense that the police do not enforce against others, such as jaywalking.[136] A study conducted by

[127] Bill O'Grady, Stephen Gaetz, and Kristy Buccieri, "Policing Street Youth in Toronto" in Stephen Gaetz, Bill O'Grady, Kristy Buccieri et al. (eds.), *Youth Homelessness in Canada: Implications for Policy and Practice* (Toronto: Canadian Homeless Research Network, 2013) at 339–40; Bill O'Grady, Stephen Gaetz, and Kristy Buccieri, "Can I See Your ID? The Policing of Youth Homelessness in Toronto" (2011) Homeless Hub at 44, https://homelesshub.ca/sites/default/files/CanISeeYourID_nov9.pdf [perma.cc/2QWT-Q3S2].

[128] O'Grady, Gaetz, and Buccieri, "Policing Street Youth" at 345.

[129] National Law Center on Homelessness and Poverty, "Serving and Protecting? Survey Results on Homeless New Yorkers' Experience with Law Enforcement" (November 2018), https://homelesslaw.org/wp-content/uploads/2019/02/serveandprotect2018.pdf [perma.cc/M9BN-H7C8].

[130] *Ibid.* at 5.

[131] Tony Robinson and Allison Sickels, "No Right to Rest: Criminalizing Homelessness in Colorado" (April 2015) at 33, https://wp-cpr.s3.amazonaws.com/uploads/2019/06/homelessness-study.pdf [perma.cc/8T9E-AK5A].

[132] *Ibid.* at 9.

[133] *Ibid.* at 44; Coalition on Homelessness, "Punishing the Poorest: How the Criminalization of Homelessness. Perpetuates Poverty in San Francisco" (June 2015) at 2, www.cohsf.org/Punishing.pdf [perma.cc/NM26-9F68].

[134] *See, e.g.*, *Lehr* v. *City of Sacramento*, 624 F Supp (2d) 1218 (ED Cal 2009); *Lavan* v. *City of Los Angeles*, 797 F Supp (2d) 1005 (CD Cal 2011); *Sanchez* v. *City of Fresno*, 914 F Supp (2d) 1079 at 1111 (ED Cal 2012); *Pottinger* v. *City of Miami*, 810 F Supp 1551 at 1555–56 (SD Fla 1992); *Tobe* v. *City of Santa Ana*, 9 Cal (4th) 1069 at 1122 (Sup Ct 1995).

[135] Robinson and Sickels, "No Right to Rest" at 9.

[136] O'Grady, Gaetz, and Buccieri, "Policing Street Youth" at 345.

the Quebec Human Rights Commission concluded that unhoused persons are socially profiled and frequently receive fines for committing offenses that were rarely enforced against others, such as lying across a park bench rather than sitting at it.[137] These examples illustrate how unhoused persons are vulnerable to the prospect of unilateral interference by the police, and to the nonegalitarian enforcement of laws that govern public property.

5.6 CONCLUSION

This chapter demonstrated why the State has more power to regulate and police unhoused persons compared to people with access to housing. It showed why the State can more justifiably regulate and control certain acts that occur on public property than on private property. It explained why unhoused persons experience two forms of nonegalitarian coercion that produce domination: nonegalitarian regulation and nonegalitarian enforcement. And it elucidated how nonegalitarian coercion constitutes a unique form of domination that affects people experiencing homelessness. More specifically, nonegalitarian coercion subjects unhoused persons' law abidingness to others' control, requires them to make nonegalitarian trade-offs to obey the law, and contributes to discriminatory policing practices. The next chapter explores the notion of punitive entrenchment. It elucidates how and why the State can entrench individuals in the condition of homelessness, such that they experience nonegalitarian coercion and its accompanying forms of domination.

137 Commission des droits de la personne et des droits de la jeunesse (CDPDJ), "The Judiciarization of Homelessness in Montreal: A Case of Social Profiling" (November 6, 2009) at 3, www.cdpdj.qc.ca/storage/app/media/publications/Homeless_Summary.pdf [perma.cc/D5LN-VYVE]; Justin Douglas, "The Criminalization of Poverty: Montreal's Policy of Ticketing Homeless Youth for Municipal and Transportation By-Law Infractions" (2011) 16:1 *Appeal* 49 at 58.

6

Punitive Entrenchment

The State not only has greater power to regulate and to police unhoused persons compared to people with access to housing. This chapter argues that the State also has the power to entrench people in the condition of homelessness.[1] Individuals who are entrenched in homelessness continue to experience the forms of double domination described in Chapter 4. Notably, they depend on others to obey laws that govern public property, and they must make nonegalitarian sacrifices to comply with these laws.[2]

This chapter begins with an overview of punitive entrenchment and the main mechanisms that enmesh individuals in poverty and homelessness: fines, fees, surcharges, and collateral consequences of punishment.[3] The chapter then discusses the traditional objections to the punishments imposed on unhoused persons who violate laws that regulate public property, namely that these sanctions are difficult to justify according to retributivist and consequentialist theories of punishment.[4] This chapter's concluding parts demonstrate that the punishments associated with these laws are objectionable because they cement unhoused persons in the condition of homelessness where they are subject to double domination.

6.1 PUNITIVE ENTRENCHMENT

Unhoused persons who violate laws that govern public property can be subject to fines, fees, surcharges, penalties, and collateral consequences, all of which can

[1] Terry Skolnik, "Rethinking Homeless People's Punishments" (2019) 22:1 *New Crim L Rev* 73 at 81–84.

[2] Terry Skolnik, "How and Why Homeless People Are Regulated Differently" (2018) 43 *Queen's LJ* 297 at 309, 316–19.

[3] *See, e.g.*, Neil Sobol, "Fighting Fines & Fees: Borrowing from Consumer Law to Combat Criminal Justice Debt Abuses" (2017) 88:4 *U Colo L Rev* 841 at 850, 874; Tia Lee Kerkhof, "Small Fines and Fees, Large Impacts: Ability-to-Pay Hearings" (2021) 95:2 *S Cal L Rev* 447 at 452–53.

[4] David Dolinko, "Retributivism, Consequentialism, and the Intrinsic Goodness of Punishment" (1997) 16:5 *Law & Phil* 507 at 507–08 (describing retributivism); David Dolinko, "Punishment" in John Deigh and David Dolinko (eds.), *The Oxford Handbook on the Philosophy of the Criminal Law* (Oxford University Press, 2011) at 405–07 (describing consequentialism).

entrench them in the condition of homelessness.[5] These punishments result in poverty penalties for unhoused persons who face harsher financial sanctions because they cannot afford to pay their initial fine.[6] The cumulative effect of these penalties results in a vicious cycle for impecunious and unhoused persons.[7] The direct and collateral consequences of punishment prevent unhoused persons from obtaining private property rights, enjoying all forms of liberty, and escaping double domination.[8]

6.1.1 *Fines*

Punitive entrenchment begins when an unhoused person receives a fine because they violated a law that governs public property.[9] For some individuals, expensive fines can be very difficult if not impossible to pay.[10] In the Ninth Circuit Court of Appeals decision Jones v. City of Los Angeles, the claimants sought an injunction that would preclude the police from enforcing a law that prohibited sitting, lying down, or sleeping on the city's sidewalks.[11] The offense was punishable by up to six months' imprisonment and/or a $1,000 fine – the same maximum penalty that was imposed for assault or drunk driving.[12] At the time when the claimants brought the injunction, there were roughly 1,000 more homeless people than available shelter spaces in Skid

5 *See, e.g.*, Skolnik, "Rethinking Homeless People's Punishments" at 80–84; Lisa Foster, "The Price of Justice: Fines, Fees and the Criminalization of Poverty in the United States" (2020) 11:1 *U Miami Race & Soc Just L Rev* 1 at 3, 6, 8, 15.

6 Beth Colgan, "The Excessive Fines Clause: Challenging the Modern Debtors' Prison" (2018) 65:1 *UCLA L Rev* 2 at 7, 9, 48 (describing poverty penalties).

7 *See, e.g.*, Alicia Bannon, Mitali Nagrecha, and Rebekah Diller, "Criminal Justice Debt: A Barrier to Reentry" (2010) at 13, Brennan Center for Justice, www.brennancenter.org/sites/default/files/legacy/Fees%20and%20Fines%20FINAL.pdf [perma.cc/6UWJ-NC9A]; Justin Jouvenal, "Homeless Say Booming Cities Have Outlawed Their Right to Sleep, Beg and Even Sit," Washington Post (June 2, 2016) at 10, www.washingtonpost.com/local/public-safety/homeless-say-booming-cities-have-outlawed-their-right-to-sleep-beg-and-even-sit/2016/06/02/7dde62ea-21e3-11e6-aa84-42391ba52c91_story.html [perma.cc/7RYT-VU4W]; Bill O'Grady, Stephen Gaetz, and Kristy Buccieri "Can I See Your ID? The Policing of Youth Homelessness in Toronto" (2011) at 81, https://homelesshub.ca/sites/default/files/CanISeeYourID_nov9.pdf [perma.cc/3HV8-3RCU]; NLCHP, "Housing Not Handcuffs: Ending the Criminalization of Homelessness in U.S. Cities" (2016) at 7, 23, https://homelesslaw.org/wp-content/uploads/2019/12/HOUSING-NOT-HANDCUFFS-2019-FINAL.pdf [perma.cc/QZD6-7K7E]; Marianne Quirouette, Tyler Frederick, Jean Hughes et al., "'Conflict with the Law': Regulation & Homeless Youth Trajectories toward Stability" (2016) 31 CJLS 383 at 386; Coalition on Homelessness, "Punishing the Poorest: How the Criminalization of Homelessness. Perpetuates Poverty in San Francisco" (June 2015) at 38–39, www.cohsf.org/Punishing.pdf [perma.cc/NM26-9F68].

8 *See, e.g.*, Skolnik, "Rethinking Homeless People's Punishments" at 82; Beth Colgan, "Fines, Fees, and Forfeiture" (2017) 18:3 *Criminology, Crim J L & Soc'y* 22 at 24–25.

9 Skolnik, "Rethinking Homeless People's Punishments" at 82.

10 *Ibid.* at 78. *See also* Terry Skolnik, "The Punitive Impact of Physical Distancing Laws on Homeless People" in Colleen Flood, Vanessa MacDonnell, and Jane Philpott et al. (eds.), *Vulnerable: The Law, Policy, and Ethics of COVID-19* (University of Ottawa Press, 2020) at 291–92; Stephanie Ben-Ishai and Arash Nayerahmadi, "Over-Indebted Criminals in Canada" (2019) 42:4 *Man LJ* 207 at 208.

11 *Jones* v. *City of Los Angeles*, 444 F (3d) 1118 at 1120 (9th Circ 2006).

12 *Ibid.*; Skolnik, "Rethinking Homeless People's Punishments" at 85, citing Cal Penal Code, § 241 and Cal Vehicle Code, §§ 23152 and 23636.

Row.[13] The maximum fine imposed for violating the law amounted to roughly four and half months' worth of welfare payments.[14] The quantum of the fine was the financial equivalent of approximately three months of rent in a single rate occupancy hotel (SRO) – the city's cheapest rental accommodation.[15]

Other cities impose expensive fines for violating laws that regulate public property. In the city of Montreal, sleeping or lying down on a subway bench is punishable by a fine between $75 and $500 prior to applicable administrative fees and penalties.[16] The California Penal Code prohibits individuals from lodging on public property and imposes a minimum fine of $275, a maximum fine of $500, and/or six months' imprisonment.[17] Boulder, Colorado, prohibits camping or lodging on public property without consent, which is punishable by a fine of up to $1,000.[18]

Research demonstrates that most unhoused persons do not pay the fines that they receive for violating laws that govern public property. Marie-Eve Sylvestre and colleagues conducted an empirical study that examined the payment rate of fines issued to people experiencing homelessness in Toronto and Ottawa between the years 2000 and 2006.[19] Their research showed that less than 1 percent of unhoused persons paid the fines that they received when they violated a municipal ordinance.[20] San Francisco's Coalition for the Homeless conducted a similar study between 2007 and 2013.[21] The study concluded that fewer than 10 percent of homeless people paid the fines that they received for violating laws that govern public property.[22]

13 *Jones* v. *City of Los Angeles*, 444 F (3d) 1118 at 1122 (9th Circ 2006).

14 *Ibid.* at 1122–23.

15 *Ibid.*

16 City of Montréal, revised by-law R-036, By-law on the Standards of Safety and Conduct to be Observed by Persons in the Rolling Stock and Buildings Operated by or for the Société de Transport de Montréal, s. 4(c).

17 Berkeley Law Policy Advocacy Clinic, "California's New Vagrancy Laws: The Growing Enactment and Enforcement of Anti-Homeless Laws in the Golden State" (2015) at 25–26, https://dx.doi.org/10.2139/ssrn.2558944 [perma.cc/3W7P-8HXB]; Cal Penal Code, § 647(e).

18 Boulder, Colo, Mun. Code, §§ 5–6–10 and 5–2–4; Rachel Adcock et al., "Too High a Price: What Criminalizing Homelessness Costs Colorado" (2016) at 19–20, www.law.du.edu/documents/homeless-advocacy-policy-project/2–16–16-Final-Report.pdf [perma.cc/9LLH-SJPW].

19 Marie-Eve Sylvestre, Céline Bellot, Philippe Antoine Couture Ménard et al., "Le Droit est aussi une question de visibilité: l'occupation des éspaces publics et les parcours judiciaires des personnes itinérantes à Montréal et à Ottawa" (2011) 26:3 *CJLS* 531 at 550; Marie-Eve Sylvestre and Céline Bellot, "Challenging Discriminatory and Punitive Responses to Homelessness in Canada" in Bruce Porter and Martha Jackman (eds.), *Advancing Social Rights in Canada* (Markham: Irwin Law, 2013) at 181.

20 *Ibid.*

21 Coalition for the Homeless, "Punishing the Poorest: How the Criminalization of Homelessness Perpetuates Poverty in San Francisco" (June 2015) at 37, Coalition on Homelessness, San Francisco, www.cohsf.org/Punishing.pdf [perma.cc/NM26-9F68].

22 *Ibid.*

6.1.2 *Administrative Fees, Surcharges, and Penalties*

Unpaid criminal justice debts can result in additional surcharges, fees, and penalties.[23] The State can attach different types of surcharges to fines.[24] Certain jurisdictions impose administrative surcharges for certain types of offenses, such as traffic offenses or municipal ordinance violations.[25] The revenue from surcharges funds state-related compensation schemes – such as services for victims of crime – or supports certain governmental programs – such as legal aid.[26]

Beth Colgan notes that various forms of surcharges exist. First, the State can impose a fixed surcharge amount irrespective of the quantum of the fine.[27] For instance, in Minnesota, each traffic offense includes a $75 surcharge.[28] Second, the quantum of the surcharge may increase for fines between certain amounts.[29] For example, in the province of Ontario, fines between $101 and $150 incur a $25 surcharge, whereas fines between $301 and $350 incur a $75 surcharge.[30] Third, the surcharge may be proportional to the quantum of the penalty.[31] California imposes a State surcharge that represents 20 percent of the amount of a traffic fine.[32]

The State can also attach administrative fees to fines.[33] Administrative fees recover the cost of investigating, recouping, and adjudicating fines.[34] For instance, fees subsidize court costs, pay for public defenders, and recoup post-conviction costs.[35]

23 Christopher Hampson, "The New American Debtors' Prisons" (2016) 44:1 *Am J Crim L* 1 at 3–4; Beth Colgan, "Addressing Modern Debtors' Prisons with Graduated Economic Sanctions that Depend on Ability to Pay" (2019) at 6–7, Hamilton Project, www.hamiltonproject.org/assets/files/Colgan_PP_201903014.pdf [perma.cc/BF37-QP96].

24 Colgan, "The Excessive Fines Clause" at 32–33.

25 *Ibid.*

26 *Ibid.* at 32–34; Criminal Justice Policy Program (CJPP), "Confronting Criminal Justice Debt: A Guide for Policy Reform" (2016) at 6, www.nclc.org/wp-content/uploads/2022/10/confronting-criminal-justice-debt-3.pdf [perma.cc/A7Y5-PYFA]; Karen Martin, Bryan Sykes, Sarah Shannon et al., "Monetary Sanctions: Legal Financial Obligations in U.S. Systems of Justice" (2018) 1 *Annual Rev Criminology* 471 at 473.

27 Colgan, "The Excessive Fines Clause" at 32–33. *See, e.g.*, Karin Martin, Kimberly Spencer-Suarez, and Gabriela Kirk, "Pay or Display: Monetary Sanctions and the Performance of Accountability and Procedural Integrity in New York and Illinois Courts" (2022) 8:1 *Russell Sage Foundation J Soc Sci* 128 at 136.

28 *See, e.g.*, Martin, Sykes, Shannon et al., "Monetary Sanctions: Legal Financial Obligations in US Systems of Justice" at 474 (citing Minnesota as an example). *See* Minn. Stat. 2022, § 357.021(6)(a) (2022) (surcharges on criminal and traffic offenders).

29 Colgan, "The Excessive Fines Clause" at 32–33.

30 O Reg 161/00, s. 1.

31 Colgan, "The Excessive Fines Clause" at 32–33.

32 Min Su, "Taxation by Citation? Exploring Local Governments' Revenue Motive for Traffic Fines" (2019) 80:1 *Pub Admin Rev* 36 at 37; Cal Penal Code, § 1465.7.

33 Colgan, "The Excessive Fines Clause" at 35.

34 *Ibid.*

35 Eisha Jain, "Capitalizing on Criminal Justice" (2018) 67:7 *Duke LJ* 1381 at 1404–05.

Some jurisdictions impose fees even when the prosecution drops the charges against the defendant, or they are acquitted.[36]

Penalties, for their part, are imposed when defendants do not pay the total amount of their fine.[37] There are various types of penalties: late-payment fees, interest charges, collection costs, and charges to enter into installment plans.[38] Penalties result in more expensive fines for impecunious persons because they cannot afford to pay their initial fines.[39] For this reason, some scholars refer to these supplemental charges as "poverty penalties."[40] In certain cases, the total amount of fees and surcharges can exceed the quantum of the initial fine.[41]

Although an unhoused person may be unable to pay a single expensive fine, research shows that many people experiencing homelessness receive multiple citations that lead to additional fees, surcharges, and penalties, and result in significant criminal justice debt.[42] Marie-Eve Sylvestre and Céline Bellot's research highlights how a 52-year-old unhoused man in Montreal received roughly $89,000 worth of fines that he could not afford to pay.[43] Another person experiencing homelessness in Montreal was fined so many times that he owed roughly $44,000 worth of criminal justice debts.[44] In 2015, a social worker at Montreal's "Droit Devant" organization – an alternative justice organization that helps absolve unhoused persons' criminal justice debts – explained that she frequently encounters people experiencing homelessness who owe over $10,000 in unpaid fines.[45]

36 Policy Advocacy Clinic, "Making Families Pay: The Harmful, Unlawful, and Costly Practice of Charging Juvenile Administrative Fees in California" (March 2017) at 3, 14, www.law.berkeley.edu/wp-content/uploads/2015/12/Making-Families-Pay.pdf [perma.cc/8DXG-Q2B7].

37 CJPP, "Confronting Criminal Justice Debt" at 15.

38 *Ibid.*

39 *Ibid.*; Colgan, "The Excessive Fines Clause" at 32–33.

40 CJPP, "Confronting Criminal Justice Debt" at 15; Beth Colgan, "Wealth-Based Penal Disenfranchisement" (2019) 72:1 *Vand L Rev* 55 at 62; Ronald Mendoza, "Why Do the Poor Pay More? Exploring the Poverty Penalty Concept" (2008) 23 *J Int'l Dev* 1 at 2.

41 Beth Colgan, "Reviving the Excessive Fines Clause" (2014) 102:2 *Cal L Rev* 277 at 286.

42 *See, e.g.*, Céline Bellot and Marie-Eve Sylvestre, "La Judiciarisation de l'itinérance à Montréal: les dérives sécuritaires de la gestion pénale de la pauvreté" (2017) 47 *RGD* 11 at 31–35.

43 *Ibid.* at 33–35.

44 *Ibid.*

45 "Homeless man's $110K in fines sign of 'systemic' issue with police, advocate says," CBC News (March 15, 2016), www.cbc.ca/news/canada/montreal/montreal-homeless-man-100k-fines-1.3473707 [perma.cc/P7LV-DDFT]. *See also* "Montreal Homeless Facing up to $110,000 in Fines," CTV News (March 3, 2016), www.ctvnews.ca/canada/montreal-homeless-facing-up-to-110–000-in-fines-1.2802694 [perma.cc/8E7T-B7LQ]. *See also* Christopher Curtis, "She's Got $25,000 in Fines and Was Homeless: How Will She Clear the Slate?" Montreal Gazette (June 1, 2018), https://montrealgazette.com/news/local-news/fined-for-being-homeless [perma.cc/ZN9K-94GE].

6.1.3 *Criminal and Civil Collateral Consequences of Punishment*

Unpaid criminal justice debts result in significant consequences. First, courts may issue bench warrants that result in incarceration.[46] In *Bearden* v. *Georgia*, the US Supreme Court decided that the Fourteenth Amendment prohibits the State from imprisoning defendants because they cannot afford to pay their criminal justice debts.[47] The Court decided that judges must hold a *Bearden* hearing to assess a defendant's ability to pay their fines.[48] These hearings assess, for instance, a defendant's employment history and their available assets.[49]

However, the *Bearden* decision held that indigent defendants may still be imprisoned for unpaid criminal justice debts in two circumstances.[50] First, when they did not make *bona fide* efforts to pay their fines, such as seeking employment or borrowing money.[51] Second, even if the defendant made such efforts, they may be incarcerated if alternate forms of punishment are inadequate in the circumstances.[52] The American Civil Liberties Union (ACLU) has demonstrated that many courts do not conduct *Bearden* hearings to evaluate defendants' financial capacities before incarcerating them.[53] Other research confirms the ACLU's findings.[54]

Canadian case law and legislation also prohibit the State from incarcerating individuals because they cannot afford to pay their criminal justice debts. In *R* v. *Wu*, the Supreme Court of Canada stated that "[g]enuine inability to pay a fine is

46 Matthew Menendez, Michael Crowley, and Lauren-Brooke Eise et al., *The Steep Costs of Criminal Justice Fees and Fines: A Fiscal Analysis of Three States and Ten Counties* (New York: New York University School of Law, 2019) at 20; Sarah Morgan, "Civil Rights/Constitutional Law – Indebted to the State: How the Thirteenth Amendment's Promise of Abolition Holds Protections against the Modern Debtors' Prisons" (2017) 39:2 *W New Eng L Rev* 327 at 332.

47 *Bearden* v. *Georgia*, 461 US 660 at 664–67 (1983).

48 *Ibid.*; Torie Atkinson, "A Fine Scheme: How Municipal Fines Become Crushing Debt in the Shadow of the New Debtors' Prison" (2016) 51 *Harv CR-CLL Rev* 189 at 235.

49 *Bearden* v. *Georgia*, 461 US 660 (1983).

50 *Ibid.*

51 *Ibid.* at 665–73.

52 *Ibid.*

53 ACLU Colorado, "Justice Derailed: A Case Study of Abusive and Unconstitutional Practices in Colorado City Courts" (October 5, 2017) at 4, 8–10, www.aclu-co.org/sites/default/files/JUSTICE-DERAILED-web.pdf [perma.cc/MZS6-QGM4]; ACLU Ohio, "The Outskirts of Hope: How Ohio's Debtors' Prisons Are Ruining Lives and Costing Communities" (April 2013) at 9, 12, 14, www.acluohio.org/sites/default/files/TheOutskirtsOfHope2013_04.pdf [perma.cc/LNE2-MQQW]; ACLU Louisiana, "Louisiana's Debtor Prisons: An Appeal to Justice" (2015) at 19–21, www.laaclu.org/en/publications/louisianas-debtors-prisons-appeal-justice [perma.cc/427Z-77GK]; ACLU Washington, "Modern Day Debtors' Prisons: The Ways Court-Imposed Debts Punish People for Being Poor" (2014), www.aclu-wa.org/docs/modern-day-debtors-prisons-washington [perma.cc/7WMW-S88U].

54 *See, e.g.*, Menendez, Crowley, Eise et al., "The Steep Costs of Criminal Justice Fees and Fines" at 11. See a useful summary of that research in Martin et al., "Monetary Sanctions: Legal Financial Obligations in US Systems of Justice" at 476; Jack Furness, "Willful Blindness: Challenging Inadequate Ability to Pay Hearings through Strategic Litigation and Legislative Reforms" (2021) 52:2 *Colum Hum Rts L Rev* 957 at 984–88.

not a proper basis for imprisonment."[55] Imprisonment for debt is permissible only where other alternatives are inappropriate and the defendant refuses to pay their fine without reasonable excuse.[56] Like in the United States, Canadian courts must assess the defendant's ability to pay prior to incarcerating them for unpaid criminal justice debts.[57] For instance, the province of Ontario requires judges to gauge a defendant's ability to pay a criminal justice debt before they can be imprisoned.[58] A defendant who cannot afford to pay their fines may also request that the court expunge their fine.[59]

However, in other Canadian jurisdictions, impecunious defendants who cannot afford to pay their fines have been incarcerated. Montreal ended the practice in 2004.[60] In contrast, in 2017, the city of Val d'Or imposed a moratorium on the incarceration of impecunious persons who could not afford to pay their fines.[61] Research demonstrated that 100 percent of individuals who were incarcerated for failing to pay their criminal justice debts were Indigenous.[62] Quebec City ceased incarcerating impecunious persons for unpaid fines in 2018.[63]

Unpaid fines lead to other consequences. They may constitute a breach of one's parole or probation conditions and result in imprisonment.[64] Individuals who are incarcerated for criminal justice debts are unable to work and may lose their jobs, which undermines their ability to support themselves and their families.[65] They are

55 *R* v. *Wu* 2003 SCC 73 at paras. 3, 60–66.

56 *Ibid.* at para. 47; Ben-Ishai and Nayerahmadi, "Over-Indebted Criminals in Canada" at 213.

57 *R* v. *Wu* 2003 SCC 73 at para. 47; *R* v. *Franc*, 2020 ABPC 156 at para. 74; *R* v. *Schultz (No.3)*, 2019 ABPC 97 at para. 76.

58 Provincial Offences Act, RSO 1990, c. P33, s. 69(9).

59 *Ibid.* s. 69(15)(c).

60 Véronique Fortin and Isabelle Raffestin, "Le Programme d'Accompagnement Justice-Itinérance à la Cour Municipale de Montréal (PAJIC): un tribunal spécialisé ancré dans le communautaire" (2017) 47 RGD 177 at 180–81.

61 *See, e.g.*, Public Inquiry Commission on Relations between Indigenous Peoples and Certain Public Services in Québec, *Listening, Reconciliation, and Progress: Final Report* (Quebec: Government of Quebec, 2019) at 318, www.cerp.gouv.qc.ca/fileadmin/Fichiers_clients/Rapport/Final_report.pdf [perma.cc/ZMA6-LSG5]; Marilyn Coupienne and Édith Perrault, "De la rue à la prison et de la prison à la rue: une analyse du caractère cruel et inusité de l'emprisonnement pour non-paiement d'amendes des personnes en situation d'itinérance" (2020) 50:1 *RGD* 285 at 288.

62 Coupienne and Perrault, "De la rue à la prison et de la prison à la rue" at 288, citing Public Inquiry Commission on Relations between Indigenous Peoples and Certain Public Services in Québec, *Listening, Reconciliation, and Progress* at 317.

63 Jean Luc-Lavallée, "Amendes impayées: fini la prison à Québec pour les itinerants," Le Journal de Québec (November 7, 2018), www.journaldequebec.com/2018/11/07/amendes-impayees–fini-la-prison-a-quebec-pour-les-itinerants [perma.cc/FLA2-P4XS]. *But see* Marc Allard, "Encore la prison pour des amendes impayées," Le Soleil (January 16, 2020), www.lesoleil.com/2020/01/16/encore-la-prison-pour-des-amendes-impayees-081314dc29795282760de780a340269d [perma.cc/WP72-962D] (the article notes that precariously housed individuals could still be imprisoned for unpaid fines, as well as individuals experiencing hidden homelessness who stay with acquaintances).

64 Katherine Beckett and Alexes Harris, "On Cash and Convictions: Monetary Sanctions as Misguided Policy" (2011) 10 *Criminology & Pub Pol'y* 509 at 524.

65 Menendez et al., "The Steep Costs of Criminal Justice Fees and Fines" at 6.

also exposed to various harms and risks during imprisonment, such as violence and psychological abuse.[66]

Criminal justice debt can also result in civil consequences that more deeply entrench individuals in homelessness. Various US states suspend an individual's driver's license if they do not pay their fines.[67] Some forms of employment – such as being a taxi driver, bus driver, long-haul trucker, or delivery person – require a driver's license.[68] An individual may lose their job because their profession required a driver's license.[69] Or, they may lose their job because their city lacks adequate public transportation infrastructure and they cannot commute to work.[70] Many individuals who lose their job due to a driver's license suspension receive a lower salary in their subsequent employment.[71] Driver license suspensions also tend to disproportionately impact racialized and socioeconomically disadvantaged persons.[72] Despite these drawbacks, many US states continue to suspend driver's licenses for unpaid criminal justice debt.[73]

Some jurisdictions convert unpaid criminal justice debts into default civil judgments.[74] Cities may contract out unpaid fines to debt-collection agencies.[75] Criminal justice debt can also be disclosed to consumer reporting companies.[76] Unpaid fines can negatively impact a person's credit rating, which can make it more

66 *See, e.g.*, Benjamin Hattem, "Carceral Trauma and Disability Law" (2020) 72 *Stan L Rev* 995 at 997–98; The Correctional Investigator of Canada, "Annual Report: Office of the Correctional Investigator, 2019–2020" (Ottawa, 2020) at 23–25 (describing sexual coercion in prisons); Terry Skolnik, "Use of Force and Criminalization" (2021) 85:3 *Alb L Rev* 663 at 675.

67 Atkinson, "A Fine Scheme" at 218–19; ACLU, "Reckless Lawmaking: How Debt-Based Driver's License Suspension Laws Impose Harm and Waste Resources" (2021) at 5, www.aclu.org/wp-content/uploads/legal-documents/reckless_lawmaking_aclu_final_4.19.21.pdf [perma.cc/X3PE-5827]; Joni Hirsch and Priya Sarathy Jones, "Driver's License Suspension for Unpaid Fines and Fees: The Movement for Reform" (2021) 54:4 *U Mich JL Reform* 875 at 876. *Ibid.* at fn. 1, citing Free to Drive, "Existing Laws for Failure to Pay," www.freetodrive.org/maps/#page-content [perma.cc/8ZDA-FAVZ]. The website provides a map of states that continue to suspend driver's licenses for criminal justice debt.

68 William Crozier and Brandon Garrett, "Driven to Failure: An Empirical Analysis of Driver's License Suspension in North Carolina" (2020) 69:7 *Duke LJ* 1585 at 1599.

69 *Ibid. See, e.g.*, Elizabeth Forester, "Impact of Criminal Justice Debt on Indigent Defendants in Tennessee" (2020) 61 *Wash U JL & Pol'y* 253 at 263.

70 Crozier and Garrett, "Driven to Failure" at 1599–600.

71 *See, e.g.*, Alan Voorhees and Edward Bloustein, "Motor Vehicle Affordability and Fairness Taskforce" (2006) at XII, www.state.nj.us/mvc/pdf/about/AFTF_final_02.pdf [perma.cc/9LRY-74ZL].

72 *See, e.g.*, Mario Salas and Angela Ciolfi, "Driven by Dollars: A State-By-State Analysis of Driver's License Suspensions for Failure to Pay Court Debt" (2017) at 4, www.justice4all.org/wp-content/uploads/2017/09/Driven-by-Dollars.pdf [perma.cc/W4YP-GAXG]; Melissa Toback Levin, "Driver's License Suspensions for Nonpayments: A Discriminatory and Counterproductive Policy" (2020) 48:1 *Hastings Const LQ* 73 at 76–78.

73 Free to Drive, "Existing Laws for Failure to Pay."

74 *See, e.g.*, Ilya Slavinski and Kimberly Spencer-Suarez, "The Price of Poverty: Policy Implications of the Unequal Effects of Monetary Sanctions on the Poor" (2021) 37:1 *J Contemp Crim Just* 45 at 49; Bannon, Nagrecha, and Diller, "Criminal Justice Debt: A Barrier to Reentry."

75 Justin Olson and Scott Macdonald, "Washington's War on the Visibly Poor: A Survey of Criminalizing Ordinances and Their Enforcement" (2015) at 16, fn. 64, https://digitalcommons.law.seattleu.edu/cgi/viewcontent.cgi?article=1001&context=hrap [perma.cc/Z6MJ-NZY4].

76 Bannon, Nagrecha, and Diller, "Criminal Justice Debt: A Barrier to Reentry" at 27.

difficult to rent an apartment and register for utilities.[77] A bad credit rating also decreases one's ability to obtain loans, receive credit cards, or open bank accounts.[78] Empirical research also indicates that unhoused persons who accumulate greater criminal justice debts tend to experience homelessness for longer periods.[79] Together, the cumulative effects of fines, fees, surcharges, penalties, and the collateral consequences of criminal justice debt entrench individuals in the condition of homelessness.

6.2 DISPROPORTIONALITY AND PUNITIVE ENTRENCHMENT

Laws that govern public property may impose disproportionate punishments on unhoused persons.[80] Proportionality implies that a punishment is commensurate with the offense's severity and the defendant's blameworthiness.[81] In terms of offense severity, conduct that harms others or violates their physical integrity are punished more serious than those that do not.[82] Crimes that are committed intentionally are punished more harshly than those that are committed as a result of recklessness or negligence.[83]

Proportionality comprises two elements: cardinal proportionality and ordinal proportionality.[84] Cardinal (or absolute) proportionality refers to the proportionate punishment for a certain crime without having to compare it to other offenses in the criminal justice system.[85] The notion of cardinal proportionality suggests that certain punishments are inherently appropriate for certain crimes.[86] Ordinal proportionality, on the other hand, determines the punishments for different offenses

77 Catherine Chesnay, Céline Bellot, and Marie-Eve Sylvestre, "Taming Disorderly People One Ticket at a Time: The Penalization of Homelessness in Ontario and British Columbia" (2013) 55:2 *Can J Corr* 161 at 178; Sylvestre and Bellot, "Challenging Discriminatory and Punitive Responses to Homelessness in Canada" at 183.

78 Atkinson, "A Fine Scheme" at 220.

79 Jessica Mogk, Valerie Shmigol, Marvin Futrell et al., "Court-Imposed Fines as a Feature of the Homelessness- Incarceration Nexus: A Cross-Sectional Study of the Relationship between Legal Debt and Duration of Homelessness in Seattle, Washington, USA" (2019) 42:2 *J Pub Health* at 5.

80 This Section's arguments were first advanced in Skolnik, "Rethinking Homeless People's Punishments" at 84–88.

81 *See, e.g., R* v. *M(CA)* [1996] 1SRC 500 at paras. 39–40; Adam Kolber, "The Subjective Experience of Punishment" (2009) 109 *Colum L Rev* 182 at 199.

82 Andrew von Hirsch, *Deserved Criminal Sentences: An Overview* (Oxford: Hart, 2017) at 65–69.

83 *Ibid.* at 64.

84 Andrew von Hirsch, *Censure and Sanctions* (Oxford University Press, 1991) at 17–18; Andrew von Hirsch, "Proportionality in the Philosophy of Punishment" (1992) 16 *Crime & Just* 55 at 75–79. Note that other scholars refer to cardinal proportionality as "absolute" proportionality" and ordinal proportionality as "comparative proportionality." *See, e.g.*, Göran Duus-Otterström, "Weighing Relative and Absolute Proportionality in Punishment" in Michael Tonry (ed.) *Of One-Eyed and Toothless Miscreants: Making the Punishment Fit the Crime?* (Oxford University Press, 2019) at 33–34.

85 *See, e.g.*, Vincent Chiao, "Proportionality and its Discontents" (2022) 41 *L & Phil* 193 at 195.

86 *Ibid.*; Nicola Lacey and Hannah Packard, "The Chimera of Proportionality: Institutionalising Limits on Punishment in Contemporary Social and Political Systems" (2015) 78:2 *Mod L Rev* 216 at 227.

based on their comparative gravity.[87] The concept of ordinal proportionality contains three principles. *Parity* entails that comparably serious offenses should result in similar punishments.[88] *Rank ordering* implies that more serious crimes should receive harsher punishments than less serious crimes.[89] *Spacing* implies that that punishments for more and less serious crimes should vary sufficiently to reflect their relative gravity.[90]

Unhoused persons' punishments for violating laws that govern public property can raise three types of proportionality concerns.[91] First, the quantum of a fine may be disproportional to the offense's gravity, such that it violates both cardinal and ordinal proportionality constraints.[92] Recall that in *Jones* v. *City of Los Angeles*, discussed in Section 6.1.1, unhoused persons who slept on a sidewalk could be fined up to $1,000 fine and/or receive a six-month prison sentence.[93] This same punishment is imposed for assault or drinking and driving, even though sleeping on a sidewalk neither harms others nor endangers others' well-being.[94] By treating sleeping on a sidewalk as if it were as harmful as assaulting others or driving while intoxicated, the punishment contravenes rank ordering, spacing, and absolute proportionality requirements.[95]

Second, unhoused persons' punishments can be excessive because the law ignores their personal circumstances, which results in harsher sanctions for certain individuals.[96] This second form of disproportionate punishment violates the parity principle because it results in additional poverty penalties for unhoused persons.[97] All other things equal, even though unhoused persons committed the same offense, they are punished more harshly than people with access to housing because they cannot afford to pay their fines.[98] For instance, people experiencing homelessness accumulate additional fees, surcharges, and penalties that people with access to housing will not incur.[99] In some cases, the quantum of the fine becomes so high that it is virtually impossible for an unhoused person to pay it. For this reason, the Supreme Court of Canada decided that mandatory minimum financial penalties

87 Von Hirsch, *Censure and Sanctions* at 18–19.
88 *Ibid.*
89 *Ibid.*
90 *Ibid.*
91 Skolnik, "Rethinking Homeless People's Punishments" at 84–88.
92 *Ibid.* at 84.
93 *Ibid.*; Cal Penal Code, §§240 and 241 (assault) and Cal Vehicle Code §§ 23152 and 23536 (driving while intoxicated). Cited in Skolnik, "Rethinking Homeless People's Punishments."
94 Skolnik, "Rethinking Homeless People's Punishments" at 84.
95 *Ibid.*
96 *Ibid.* at 88; Colgan, "The Excessive Fines Clause" at 48–51.
97 Colgan, "The Excessive Fines Clause" at 48–51 (describing how such fines violate equality in sentencing).
98 *See, e.g.*, April Fernandes, "Monetary Sanctions: A Review of Revenue Generation, Legal Challenges, and Reform" (2019) 15 *Ann Rev L & Soc Sci* 397 at 404.
99 Colgan, "The Excessive Fines Clause" at 48–51.

can constitute a cruel and unusual punishment because they result in de facto indeterminate sentences for unhoused persons.[100] Unhoused persons' punishments can violate the parity principle in other ways. Due to extreme poverty, people experiencing homelessness may also be incarcerated for unpaid criminal justice debts, while those who can afford to pay their fines will not.

Third, unhoused persons punishments are excessive when they ignore the extent of the defendant's culpability given the circumstances.[101] Many laws that govern public property are strict liability offenses that impose a fixed fine on offenders irrespective of their moral blameworthiness.[102] Because these laws do not generally impose a *mens rea* requirement, the punishments do not generally distinguish between intentional legal transgressions versus negligent or unintentional ones. If an unhoused person takes reasonable precautions to obey a law that governs public property yet violates it, they risk being punished as harshly as someone who intentionally transgresses the law.[103] Such penalties ignore the defendant's degree of culpability, which in addition to the severity of the offense, is the other crucial factor when determining the proportionality of an individual's punishment.[104] Such punishments are objectionable because they communicate that the defendant is more blameworthy than they are.[105]

6.3 RETRIBUTIVISM, CONSEQUENTIALISM, AND LAWS THAT GOVERN PUBLIC PROPERTY

The sanctions associated with laws that govern public property can be difficult to justify according to retributivist and consequentialist theories of punishment. Retribution is a backwards-looking punishment theory.[106] It holds that offenders deserve punishment because of their culpable wrongdoing.[107] As a backward-looking theory, retributivists value punishment irrespective of whether it produces

100 *R* v. *Boudreault*, 2018 SCC 58 at paras. 3, 64 (striking down the mandatory victim surcharge for that reason); Terry Skolnik, "Beyond *Boudreault*: Challenging Choice, Culpability, and Punishment" (2019) 50 *CR* (7th) 283 at 283.

101 Skolnik, "Rethinking Homeless People's Punishments" at 85–87.

102 David Smith, "A Theoretical and Legal Challenge to Homeless Criminalization as Public Policy" (1994) 12:2 *Yale L & Pol'y Rev* 487 at 494; Donald Baker, "Anti-Homeless' Legislation: Unconstitutional Efforts to Punish the Homeless" (1991) 45 *U Miami L Rev* 417 at 450–51.

103 Skolnik, "Rethinking Homeless People's Punishments" at 85–87.

104 *See, e.g.*, Richard Frase, "Excessive Prison Sentences, Punishment Goals, and the Eighth Amendment: Proportionality Relative to What" (2005) 89:3 *Minn L Rev* 571 at 590.

105 Antony Duff, *Trials and Punishments* (Cambridge University Press, 1991) at 155, cited in Skolnik, "Rethinking Homeless People's Punishments" at 86; *R* v. *M (CA)* [1996] 1 SCR 500.

106 Leo Zaibert, *Punishment and Retribution* (New York: Routledge, 2006) at 35, 135; Ted Honderich, *Punishment: The Supposed Justifications Revisited*, 5th ed. (Ann Arbor: Pluto, 2006) at 17–19.

107 John Kleinig, "What Does Wrongdoing Deserve?" in Michael Tonry (ed.), *Retributivism Has A Past: Has It A Future?* (Oxford University Press, 2011) at 54–55.

prospective benefits.[108] Proportionality is central to retributivism.[109] The defendant's desert is calculated according to the crime's severity and the offender's level of moral blameworthiness.[110] Excessive punishments are objectionable because defendants are punished more harshly than they deserve.

Retributive theories of punishment recognize that individuals deserve punishment only when they had the free choice to obey the law.[111] For instance, H. L. A. Hart famously argued that individuals can be punished only when they had the capacity and fair opportunity to comply with the law.[112] These requirements aim to recognize the importance of human agency and rationality.[113] The law instrumentalizes individuals, treats them as scapegoats, and disregards their human agency when they are punished for violating laws that they could not obey even if they tried.[114]

The importance of free choice to obey the law underpins excusatory defenses such as duress and necessity.[115] Individuals are acquitted when threats, violence, or perilous circumstances undermined their freedom to comply with the law.[116] In such contexts, law-abidingness is not a reasonable alternative to breaking the law.[117] For this reason, individuals do not deserve punishment when they lacked a free choice – and thus a fair opportunity – to obey the law.[118]

108 Michael Moore, *Placing Blame: A Theory of the Criminal Law* (Oxford University Press, 2010) at 153–54; Russell Christopher, "Deterring Retributivism: The Injustice of 'Just' Punishment" (2002) 96:3 *Nw U L Rev* 843 at 847–48.

109 *See, e.g.*, William W. Berry II, "Promulgating Proportionality" (2011) 46:1 *Ga L Rev* 69 at 92–93; Thom Brooks, "Retribution" in Thom Brooks (ed.), *Retribution* (London: Routledge, 2019) at 83.

110 Andrew von Hirsch, "Proportionality in the Philosophy of Punishment: From 'Why Punish' to 'How Much'" (1990) 1 *Crim LF* 259 at 262; Douglas Husak, "Why Punish the Deserving?" (1992) 26 *Nous* 447 at 462.

111 *See, e.g.*, Michael Moore, "Choice, Character, and Excuse" (1990) 7 *Soc Phil & Pol'y* 29 at 31–35; Herbert Morris, "Persons and Punishment" (1968) 52:4 *Monist* 475 at 485; Samuel Pillsbury, "The Meaning of Deserved Punishment: An Essay on Choice, Character, and Responsibility" (1992) 67:3 *Ind LJ* 719 at 722; Antony Duff, "Choice, Character, and Criminal Liability" (1993) 12:4 *L & Phil* 345 at 346–55.

112 H. L. A. Hart and John Gardner, *Punishment and Responsibility* (Oxford University Press, 2008) at 22–23, 153. It is important to note that Hart advanced a mixed theory of punishment.

113 Peter Aranella, "Convicting the Morally Blameless: Reassessing the Relationship between Legal and Moral Accountability" (1992) 39:6 *UCLA L Rev* 1511 at 1532–33, 1534–35.

114 Antony Duff, "Penal Communications: Recent Work in the Philosophy of Punishment" (1996) 20 *Crime & Just* 1 at 10; Terry Skolnik, "Homelessness and the Impossibility to Obey the Law" (2016) 43:3 *Fordham Urb LJ* 741 at 745.

115 Moore, "Choice, Character, and Excuse" at 29.

116 *See, e.g.*, Terry Skolnik, "Three Problems with Duress and Moral Involuntariness" (2016) 63:1 *Crim LQ* 124 at 127–28.

117 *See, e.g.*, Benjamin Berger, "Emotions and the Veil of Voluntarism: The Loss of Judgment in Canadian Criminal Defences" (2005) 51:1 *McGill LJ* 99 at 107–08.

118 Moore, "Choice, Character, and Excuse" at 29; Joshua Dressler, "Reflections on Excusing Wrongdoers: Moral Theory, New Excuses and the Model Penal Code" (1988) 19:3 *Rutgers LJ* 671 at 674–75, 701–02.

Scholars contend that retribution cannot justify the punishment of unhoused persons who violate laws that govern public property in two contexts. First, some argue that unhoused persons do not deserve punishment when they lacked a fair opportunity to obey laws that govern public property, especially when laws prohibit urban camping or sleeping in public despite insufficient shelter space to accommodate the city's unhoused population.[119] Notably, the lack of shelter space undermines unhoused persons' fair opportunity to obey these laws.[120] Second, some argue that unhoused persons' punishments violate retributivism's proportionality constraint.[121] Unhoused persons' sanctions can be excessive for various reasons.[122] As discussed in Section 6.2, punishments can be disproportionate with respect to the nature of the offense, individuals' personal circumstances, and their level of moral blameworthiness.[123] Retributivism's core tenets are violated in these contexts because unhoused persons do not deserve punishment or are punished more harshly than they deserve.

Others argue that unhoused persons' punishments cannot be justified by consequentialist theories of punishment in certain contexts.[124] Consequentialism is a forward-looking punishment theory.[125] It posits that punishment is justified because of its future benefits – namely, that it prevents the offender and others from committing crimes.[126] Like retributivism, consequentialism also appeals to the offender's rationality, agency, and freedom of choice.[127] The threat of punishment incentivizes individuals to comply with the law.[128] The prospect of punishment appeals to individuals' self-interest to maximize their freedom and avoid coercion.[129]

119 Skolnik, "Homelessness and the Impossibility to Obey the Law" at 749.

120 *See, e.g., ibid.*; Smith, "A Theoretical and Legal Challenge to Homeless Criminalization as Public Policy" at 488, 498–99; Sara Rankin, "Punishing Homelessness" (2019) 22:1 *New Crim L Rev* 99 at 116–17; Sara Rankin, "Hiding Homelessness: The Transcarceration of Homelessness" (2021) 109:2 *Cal L Rev* 559 at 571; Edward Walters, "No Way Out: Eighth Amendment Protection for Do-Or-Die Acts of the Homeless" (1995) 62:4 *U Chi L Rev* 1619 at 1641.

121 Skolnik, "Rethinking Homeless People's Punishments" at 84–88. *See also* Siobhan Allen, "The Role of the Excessive Fines Clause in Ending the Criminalization of Homelessness" (2022) 55:4 *Colum JL & Soc Probs* 499 at 526–30; Sara Rankin, "Civilly Criminalizing Homelessness" (2021) 56:2 *Harv CR-CL L Rev* 367 at 385–87.

122 *Ibid.*

123 Section 6.2.

124 Skolnik, "Homelessness and the Impossibility to Obey the Law" at 749.

125 Dolinko, "Punishment" at 405.

126 *Ibid.*

127 Ronald Akers, "Rational Choice, Deterrence, and Social Learning Theory in Criminology: The Path Not Taken" (1990) 81:3 *J Crim L & Criminology* 653 at 654; Terry Skolnik, "Socially Deprived Offenders" in Jesper Ryberg (ed.), *The Oxford Handbook of Punishment Theory and Philosophy* (Oxford University Press, 2024) (forthcoming). Draft on file with author.

128 Von Hirsch, *Censure and Sanctions* at 13.

129 *See, e.g.*, Alan Brudner, *Punishment and Freedom: A Liberal Theory of Penal Justice* (Oxford University Press, 2009) at 47–48.

Some note that punishments cannot prevent unhoused persons from alleviating their needs on public property when they lack reasonable alternatives.[130] According to this argument, since individuals without access to property must alleviate their needs, access to private property – rather than punishment – is necessary to ensure compliance.[131] The brunt of this argument is that punishment is not an instrumentally rational means to deter unhoused persons from alleviating their needs on public property when they lack other reasonable options.[132]

6.4 COUNTERPRODUCTIVITY, PUNITIVE ENTRENCHMENT, AND DOMINATION

The punishments imposed on unhoused persons for violating laws that govern public property are objectionable for another reason: these punishments are counterproductive. Harsh punishments increase the risk that individuals will become entrenched in homelessness, continue to alleviate their needs on public property, and repeatedly violate laws that govern public property.[133] Punitive entrenchment prolongs and aggravates the double domination that unhoused persons experience.

The relationship between need-alleviating conduct, negative externalities, and punishment highlights the self-defeating nature of unhoused persons' harsh penalties for violating laws that regulate public property. Need-alleviating conduct that occurs on public property generates negative externalities.[134] The term "negative externalities" implies "acts that impose unaccounted-for costs on others."[135] The previous chapter demonstrated how individuals who alleviate their needs on public property may create public health concerns, decrease the aesthetic value of public space, reduce the efficiency of public ways, deprive others from using certain spaces, and more.[136] These acts can diffuse negative externalities (or unaccounted-for costs) amongst many individuals who use public property simultaneously.[137]

130 Maria Foscarinis, "Downward Spiral: Homelessness and its Criminalization" (1996) 14 *Yale L & Pol'y Rev* 1 at 58.

131 *Ibid.*; Jane Baron, "Homelessness as a Property Problem" (2004) 36:2 *Urb Law* 273 at 287.

132 Colton Fehr, "Instrumental Rationality and General Deterrence" (2019) 57:1 *Alta L Rev* 53 at 61 (describing the relationship between deterrence and instrumental rationality; although Fehr focuses primarily on the relationship between punishment and general deterrence, similar arguments apply to the relationship between punishment and specific deterrence).

133 Terry Skolnik, "Freedom and Access to Housing: Three Conceptions" (2018) 35 *Windsor YB Access Just* 226 at 240; Skolnik, "Rethinking Homeless People's Punishments" at 82.

134 *See, e.g.*, Robert Ellickson, "Controlling Chronic Misconduct in City Spaces: Of Panhandlers, Skid Rows, and Public-Space Zoning" (1996) 105:5 *Yale LJ* 1165 at 1172.

135 Gideon Parchomovsky and Peter Siegelman, "Cities, Property, and Positive Externalities" (2012) 54:1 *Wm & Mary L Rev* 211 at 214.

136 *See* Chapter 5 of this book; Skolnik, "Freedom and Access to Housing" at 240.

137 Ellickson, "Controlling Chronic Misconduct in City Spaces" at 1177.

Private property is valuable because it internalizes unaccounted-for costs that would otherwise occur on public property.[138] Individuals who can freely access private property can alleviate their needs without creating negative externalities that undermine others' use and enjoyment of public space. In contrast, individuals who lack access to private property may generate such unaccounted-for costs because they have no alternative but to alleviate their needs on public property.[139] Since individuals cannot abstain from alleviating their needs, they must access a private place that absorbs these unaccounted-for costs.[140]

Access to housing endows individuals with the greatest liberty to access private property, alleviate their needs in private, and generate fewer negative externalities on public property. Conversely, individuals without access to housing will continue to alleviate their needs in public and generate these unaccounted-for costs.[141]

This explains why punitive entrenchment is morally objectionable for various reasons. First, harsh punishments and their collateral consequences may not only decrease access to housing for unhoused persons, but may also increase the likelihood that they will consistently alleviate their needs on public property.[142] These punishments can be more than ineffective from the standpoint of deterrence; they can be counterproductive.[143] Second, punitive entrenchment can cement individuals in the condition of homelessness where they will continue to experience nonegalitarian coercion.[144] So long as individuals remain entrenched in homelessness, the State will have greater power to regulate and police their basic needs compared to people with access to housing.[145] Third, individuals who are entrenched in homelessness will persistently suffer double domination, as described in earlier chapters. Notably, others will control their opportunities to obey laws that govern public property, and they will be forced to make nonegalitarian sacrifices to comply with these laws.[146] Ultimately, punitive entrenchment leads to nonegalitarian coercion and double domination.

6.5 CONCLUSION

This chapter demonstrated why the punishments associated with laws that govern public property entrench individuals in homelessness. It highlighted why unhoused persons' punishments can be excessive and violate basic proportionality constraints.

138 *See generally* Harold Damsetz, "A Theory of Property Rights" (1967) 57:2 *Am Econ Rev* 347 at 348 (noting that private property internalizes externalities).

139 *See, e.g.*, Skolnik, "Freedom and Access to Housing: Three Conceptions" at 240.

140 Jeremy Waldron, "Homelessness and the Issue of Freedom" (1991) 39:1 *UCLA L Rev* 295 at 321 (describing how unhoused persons must alleviate their needs).

141 *Ibid.*

142 Skolnik, "Rethinking Homeless People's Punishments" at 82.

143 *Ibid.* at 83.

144 Skolnik, "Freedom and Access to Housing" at 240–41.

145 Skolnik, "How and Why" at 323.

146 Skolnik, "Freedom and Access to Housing: Three Conceptions" at 240–41.

It demonstrated why some of these punishments and their collateral consequences cannot be justified by retributive and consequentialist theories of punishment. Its concluding parts explained why these punishments can be counterproductive. The next chapter explains how the State has an overarching fiduciary duty to counteract domination, and three specific fiduciary duties related to homelessness and public property.

7

Homelessness, Public Property, and the State's Fiduciary Duties

Republicanism is a theory of both freedom and government.[1] Previous chapters focused primarily on the republican theory of freedom as nondomination. These chapters explained why the State has more power to regulate and police unhoused persons than people with access to housing. They demonstrated why laws that govern public property subject unhoused persons to unique forms of domination. The republican theory of government, on the other hand, is a political theory that is more concerned with vertical domination.[2] It offers an account of when political authority is increasingly legitimate because individuals are free from domination by the State. The republican theory of government also justifies the State's duties to neutralize domination.

Unifying republican theories of freedom and government, this chapter shows why the State and the people are in a fiduciary relationship, which results in certain fiduciary duties related to homelessness and public property.[3] A fiduciary relationship arises where one party – the fiduciary (or trustee) – unilaterally wields power over the other party – the beneficiary.[4] Although the fiduciary is empowered to act on the beneficiary's behalf, the fiduciary can exercise that power abusively or exploitatively.[5] To counteract this form of domination, the law imposes fiduciary duties on the trustee; they owe a duty of loyalty to the beneficiary and must act in their best interests.[6]

1 Philip Pettit, *Republicanism: A Theory of Freedom and Government* (Oxford University Press, 1999) at 37.

2 Philip Pettit, *On the People's Terms: A Republican Theory and Model of Democracy* (Cambridge University Press, 2012) at 152; Frank Michelman, "Law's Republic" (1988) 97:8 *Yale LJ* 1493 at 1499–501; Frank Michelman, Foreword, "Traces of Self-Government" (1986) 100:1 *Harv L Rev* 4 at 24–28; Ekow Yankah, "The Sovereign and the Republic: A Republican View of Political Obligation" in Jack Knight and Melissa Schwartzberg (eds.), *NOMOS, LXI: Political Legitimacy* (New York University Press, 2019) at 102–03.

3 Evan Fox-Decent, *Sovereignty's Promise* (Oxford University Press, 2011) at 104.

4 Paul Miller and Andrew Gold, "Fiduciary Governance" (2015) 57:2 *Wm & Mary L Rev* 513 at 542–44; Ernest Weinrib, "The Fiduciary Obligation" (1975) 25:1 *U Toronto LJ* 1 at 4.

5 Evan Fox-Decent and Evan Criddle, "The Fiduciary Constitution of Human Rights" (2009) 15 *Leg Theory* 301 at 320–23.

6 Evan Criddle, "Liberty in Loyalty: A Republican Theory of Fiduciary Law" (2017) 95:5 *Tex L Rev* 993 at 999–1000, 1006.

This chapter explains why the State has three fiduciary duties related to homelessness and public property – duties that flow from the State's overarching fiduciary obligation to counteract domination. First, the State has a fiduciary duty to end homelessness and treat unhoused persons with equal concern and respect. As part of this fiduciary obligation, the State must address the underlying factors that contribute to homelessness and ensure access to housing. Second, the State has a fiduciary obligation to protect public property's shared value and secure freedom in the public sphere. Third, the State must legitimize the coercion and punishment associated with laws that govern public property.

These fiduciary duties counteract domination that stems from two systems of mutual coercion that the State creates and enforces to secure liberty: the private property system and laws that govern public property. But the State's failure to accommodate unhoused persons within these systems of mutual coercion results in domination. The State's fiduciary duties related to homelessness and public property aim to neutralize this domination. The concluding parts of this chapter highlight the interrelationship between these duties. Namely, the State must fulfil its fiduciary duty to end homelessness to counteract private domination, safeguard public property's shared value to neutralize public domination, and legitimize laws that govern public property to impose coercion and punishment in a justifiable manner.

7.1 FIDUCIARY RELATIONSHIPS AND FIDUCIARY DUTIES

The State's duties related to homelessness and public property stem from its fiduciary relationship with individuals – a unique relationship that results in distinct duties that aim to counteract domination. To illustrate this point, it is necessary to first explain the nature of fiduciary relationships, their sources, and their application to public law.

Fiduciary relationships involve two parties: the fiduciary (or the trustee) and the beneficiary.[7] The fiduciary is authorized to act on the beneficiary's behalf and unilaterally wields power over them.[8] Typically, fiduciaries have powers, expertise, or capacities that beneficiaries lack.[9] Conversely, beneficiaries are dependent on fiduciaries and their above-mentioned qualities.[10] For instance, in a fiduciary relationship between attorney and client, the attorney has legal expertise that the client does not. In a fiduciary relationship between a physician and a patient, the physician has medical expertise and knowledge that the patient lacks.

Fiduciary relationships are characterized by an asymmetric power dynamic between the parties.[11] Beneficiaries are vulnerable to domination because the

7 Elizabeth Scott and Robert Scott, "Parents as Fiduciaries" (1995) 81:8 *Va L Rev* 2401 at 2419–24.

8 *Ibid.* at 2401–02.

9 Larry Ribstein, "Fencing Fiduciary Duties" (2011) 91:3 *BU L Rev* 899 at 907; Criddle, "Liberty in Loyalty" at 1026–29.

10 Matthew Bodie, "Employment as Fiduciary Relationship" (2017) 105:4 *Geo LJ* 819 at 858.

11 Fox-Decent and Criddle, "The Fiduciary Constitution of Human Rights" at 321–23; Evan Criddle and Evan Fox-Decent, "Keeping the Promise of Public Fiduciary Theory: A Reply to Leib and Galoob" (2016) 126 *Yale LJ* F 192 at 199.

fiduciary can unilaterally interfere with their interests.[12] The fiduciary can exploit the beneficiary for private gain or for other opportunistic reasons.[13] Given disparities in information and expertise, beneficiaries may also lack the requisite knowledge or abilities to monitor or control the fiduciary's conduct.[14] To mitigate these risks and prevent domination, the law imposes a duty of loyalty on the fiduciary and requires them to act in the beneficiary's best interests.[15]

Fiduciary relationships notably arise in private law, such as in the law of trusts, property law, and corporate law.[16] Various relationships are fiduciary in nature, such as the relationship between parent and child, attorney and client, and doctor and patient.[17] Parents have fiduciary duties to act in the best interests of their children. And a doctor has a fiduciary duty to act in the best interests of their patient.

A fiduciary relationship can form through consent. In some cases, the beneficiary and trustee expressly consent to a fiduciary relationship, and the former authorizes the latter to act on their behalf.[18] For instance, a client may mandate a lawyer to represent them in legal proceedings, and a patient may consent to care by their physician.

But consent is not necessary to form a fiduciary relationship.[19] A parent can consent to a contract on a child's behalf, and a doctor can treat an unconscious patient.[20] A parent exercises fiduciary authority over their child, even though the child neither consented to being born nor authorized the parent to act for them.[21] A doctor has the authority to administer treatments to an unconscious patient who did not – and could not – expressly consent to care.[22]

7.2 FIDUCIARY RELATIONSHIPS IN PUBLIC LAW

Fiduciary relationships also exist within public law – an important consideration that underpins the fiduciary relationship between the State and individuals.[23] Three

12 Fox-Decent and Criddle, "The Fiduciary Constitution of Human Rights" at 311.

13 Fox-Decent, *Sovereignty's Promise* at 110.

14 Evan Criddle, "Fiduciary Foundations of Administrative Law" (2006) 54:1 *UCLA L Rev* 117 at 126; Ribstein, "Fencing Fiduciary Duties" at 907.

15 Robert Natelson, "The Constitution and the Public Trust" (2004) 52 *Buff L Rev* 1077 at 1083–85.

16 Paul Miller, "Justifying Fiduciary Duties" (2012) 58:4 *McGill LJ* 969 at 971–72; Paul Miller, "Fiduciary Representation" in Evan Criddle, Evan Fox-Decent, Andrew Gold et al. (eds.), *Fiduciary Government* (Cambridge University Press, 2018) at 24–25.

17 Fox-Decent, *Sovereignty's Promise* at 104. These examples are provided by Fox-Decent.

18 Miller, "Fiduciary Representation" at 25.

19 Fox-Decent, *Sovereignty's Promise* at 56, 67.

20 *Ibid.* at 56, 67, 90, 92.

21 *Ibid.*

22 *Ibid.* at 108.

23 Max Schanzenbach and Nadav Shoked, "Reclaiming Fiduciary Law for the City" (2018) 70:2 *Stan L Rev* 565 at 575–76. For a useful summary of fiduciary political theorists, see Ethan Leib, David Ponet, and Michael Serota, "Mapping Public Fiduciary Relationships" in Andrew Gold and Paul Miller (eds.), *Philosophical Foundations of Fiduciary Law* (Oxford University Press, 2014) at 395–99; Paul Miller, "The Fiduciary Relationship" in Andrew Gold and Paul Miller (eds.), *Philosophical Foundations of Fiduciary Law* (Oxford University Press, 2014) at 88.

examples illustrate the State's fiduciary duties in public law contexts: the fiduciary relationship between the State and Indigenous peoples in Canada, the public trust doctrine in natural resource law in the United States, and the State's fiduciary guardianship over public property in both countries.

First, the Supreme Court of Canada recognizes a *sui generis* fiduciary relationship between the State and Indigenous peoples.[24] This relationship stems from Canada's colonialist legacy, and how the State unilaterally asserted sovereignty over Indigenous persons' rights, interests, and land.[25] These acts deprived Indigenous individuals and communities of the power of self-government, and the protection of their rights and interests became dependent on the Government's decision-making.[26] The relationship between Indigenous persons and the State exemplifies vertical domination.[27] The Government's fiduciary duties towards Indigenous persons aim to mitigate that domination.[28]

Various Supreme Court of Canada decisions elucidate this point. In *Mitchell* v. *Minister of National Revenue*, the majority of the Court explained: "The common law status of aboriginal rights rendered them vulnerable to unilateral extinguishment, and thus they were 'dependent upon the good will of the Sovereign'."[29] Similarly, in *Wewaykum Indian Band* v. *Canada*, Justice Binnie alluded to how the State's discretionary power over Indigenous persons results in domination and remarked: "The fiduciary duty, where it exists, is called into existence to facilitate supervision of the high degree of discretionary control gradually assumed by the Crown over the lives of aboriginal peoples."[30] This fiduciary relationship imposes a duty on the State to act in the best interests of Indigenous peoples when it makes

24 Fox-Decent, *Sovereignty's Promise* at 59, *Guerin* v. *The Queen* [1984] 2 SCR 335 at 376 (per Dickson J.); *R* v. *Sparrow* [1990] 1 SCR 1075 at 1108; Paul Miller, "The Idea of Status in Fiduciary Law" in Andrew Miller and Paul Gold (eds.), *Contract, Status, and Fiduciary Law* (Oxford University Press, 2016) at 46–47.

25 *Southwind* v. *Canada*, 2021 SCC 28 at para. 55; *Mitchell* v. *MNR*, 2001 SCC 33 at para. 9; *Mikisew Cree First Nation* v. *Canada (Governor General in Council)*, 2018 SCC 40 at para. 57; *Williams Lake Indian Band* v. *Canada (Aboriginal Affairs and Northern Development)*, 2018 SCC 4 at para. 43.

26 *See* Rauna Kuokkanen, *Restructuring Relations: Indigenous Self-Determination, Governance, and Gender* (Oxford: Oxford University Press, 2019) at 22–23; Aaron Mills, *Rooted Constitutionalism: Growing Political Community* in Michael Asch, John Borrows and James Tully (eds.), *Resurgence and Reconciliation: Indigenous–Settler Relations and Earth Teachings* (University of Toronto Press, 2018) at 135–36.

27 Evan Fox-Decent and Ian Dahlman, "Sovereignty as Trusteeship and Indigenous Peoples" (2015) 16:2 *Theor Inq L* 507 at 511, 515; Evan Fox-Decent and Evan Criddle, *Fiduciaries of Humanity: How International Law Constitutes Authority* (Oxford University Press, 2016) at 59–62.

28 *Southwind* v. *Canada*, 2021 SCC 28 at paras. 54–64.

29 *Mitchell* v. *MNR*, 2001 SCC 33 at para. 11.

30 *Wewaykum Indian Band* v. *Canada*, 2002 SCC 79 at para. 79. The Court also noted at para. 80: "This *sui generis* relationship had its positive aspects in protecting the interests of aboriginal peoples historically . . . but the degree of economic, social and proprietary control and discretion asserted by the Crown also left aboriginal populations vulnerable to the risks of government misconduct or ineptitude."

discretionary decisions that affect their interests.[31] As part of this fiduciary duty, the State must consult Indigenous persons and accommodate them.[32]

Second, in certain US jurisdictions, the State has fiduciary duties related to natural resource law. Courts affirm that the State is a trustee over certain types of common property – such as navigable waters, shorelines, and public lands – and must maintain them.[33] Scholars such as Joseph Sax and Richard Lazarus observe that the public trust doctrine in natural resource law has deep historical roots that date to the Roman empire.[34]

The US Supreme Court case *Illinois Central Railroad Company* v. *Illinois* remains one of the most notable decisions in this regard.[35] The State had statutorily granted certain land to the Illinois Central Railroad Company – land that was located adjacent to the Chicago River and beneath the waterbed of Lake Michigan.[36] When the State subsequently repealed the statute, the corporation continued to construct railway tracks on the land that the State had previously granted.[37] The Attorney General brought a suit so that the corporation would halt construction and remove the structures and infrastructure that it had built.[38] The issue was whether the state of Illinois or the railway corporation owned the contested land.[39]

The Court concluded that the land in question could not be lawfully alienated because it belonged to the State and was held in trust for the public.[40] In particular, the Court observed that the trustee relationship required the State to protect that common property against interference from private parties.[41] Similar to how the State cannot abdicate its police power, it cannot, in principle, "abdicate its trust over property in which the whole people are interested."[42]

William Araiza notes that since 1970, nearly half of all US state courts have accepted the public trust doctrine in some form or another and it has been employed

31 *Haida Nation* v. *British Columbia (Minister of Forests)*, 2004 SCC 73 at paras. 16–20.

32 *Ibid.*

33 Richard Lazarus, "Changing Conceptions of Property and Sovereignty in Natural Resources: Questioning the Public Trust Doctrine" (1986) 71:3 *Iowa L Rev* 631 at 633–41; *Martin* v. *Lessee of Waddell*, 41 US 367 at 419–20 (1842); *Illinois Central R Co.* v. *Illinois*, 146 US 387 at 456–57 (1892); *State* v. *Cleveland & Pittsburgh RR*, 113 NE 677 at 682 (Ohio Supt Ct 1916); *Brickell* v. *Trammel*, 77 Fla 544 at 559 (Sup Ct 1919). All these cases are cited in and taken directly from Joseph Sax, "The Public Trust Doctrine in Natural Resource Law: Effective Judicial Intervention" (1970) 68:3 *Mich L Rev* 471.

34 Lazarus, "Changing Conceptions of Property and Sovereignty" 33 at 634–35.

35 *Illinois Central R Co.* v. *Illinois*, 146 US 387; William Araiza, "Democracy, Distrust, and the Public Trust: Process-Based Constitutional Theory, the Public Trust Doctrine, and the Search for a Substantive Environmental Value" (1997) 45:2 *UCLA L Rev* 385 at 396.

36 *Illinois Central R Co.* v. *Illinois*, 146 US 387 at 449.

37 *Ibid.*

38 *Ibid.* at 439.

39 *Ibid.* at 433, 439.

40 *Ibid.*

41 *Ibid.*

42 *Ibid.* at 453–54.

in various contexts.[43] The public trust doctrine helps ensure that individuals cannot acquire certain common property because others would become dependent on the rightsholder to access and use it.[44] In this way, the public trust doctrine prevents horizontal domination between persons.

Third, US and Canadian law acknowledge that the State holds certain types of public property – such as streets, public parks, and public squares – in trust for the public.[45] As part of its fiduciary duty, the State is responsible for safeguarding public property's shared value. For instance, in the 1939 US Supreme Court decision *Hague* v. *Committee for Industrial Organization*, Jersey City's mayor Frank Hague attempted to use a city ordinance to prevent a labor union from holding public meetings in any hall without acquiring a permit.[46] The mayor also sought to prohibit individuals from distributing pamphlets on public property.[47] The ordinance was enforced to suppress the activities of labor unions that the city alleged were Communist or tied to communist ideology.[48] The Court decided that the ordinance was unconstitutional because it violated the First Amendment right to free speech and freedom of association.[49] In a passage that has been cited in subsequent Supreme Court decisions,[50] the justices explained that the State held certain public spaces in trust for the public:

> Wherever the title of streets and parks may rest, they have immemorially been held in trust for the use of the public and, time out of mind, have been used for purposes of assembly, communicating thoughts between citizens, and discussing public questions. Such use of the streets and public places has, from ancient times, been a part of the privileges, immunities, rights, and liberties of citizens.[51]

43 Araiza, "Democracy, Distrust, and the Public Trust" at 401.

44 Sax, "The Public Trust Doctrine in Natural Resource Law" at 474 (note 14 in the text), 490–92; David Takacs, "The Public Trust Doctrine, Environmental Human Rights, and the Future of Private Property" (2008) 16:3 *NYU Env't LJ* 711 at 714–16; Charles Wilkinson, "The Public Trust Doctrine in Public Land Law" (1980) 14 *UC Davis L Rev* 269 at 286–87, 299.

45 Schanzenbach and Shoked, "Reclaiming Fiduciary Law for the City" at 602–09; Sarah Hamill, "Private Rights to Public Property: The Evolution of Common Property in Canada" (2012) 58:2 *McGill LJ* 365 at 390–91; Sarah Hamill, "Private Property Rights and Public Responsibility: Leaving Room for the Homeless" (2011) 30 *Windsor Rev Leg Soc Issues* 9 at 99–100; Carol Rose, "Joseph Sax and the Idea of the Public Trust" (1998) 25 *Ecology LQ* 351 at 351; *Hague* v. *Committee for Industrial Organization*, 307 US 496 at 515 (1939); *Friends of Van Cortlandt Park* v. *City of New York*, 232 F (3d) 324 at 326 (2nd Circ 2000); *Ackerman* v. *Steisel*, 104 (2d) 940 at 941 (NY Sup Ct App Div 1984).

46 *Hague* v. *Committee for Industrial Organization*, 307 US 496 at 500–01 (1939).

47 *Ibid.*

48 *Ibid.*

49 *Ibid.* at 516–18.

50 *Kunz* v. *New York*, 340 US 290 at 293–94 (1951); *Frisby* v. *Schultz*, 487 US 474 at 481–82 (1988); *Perry Ed Assn* v. *Perry Local Educators' Assn*, 460 US 37 at 45–46 (1983); *International Soc. for Krishna Consciousness, Inc.* v. *Lee*, 505 US 672 at 679 (1992).

51 *Hague* v. *Committee for Industrial Organization*, 307 US 496 (1939).

Supreme Court of Canada justices have also recognized that the State holds public property in trust for the public.[52] In *Committee for the Commonwealth of Canada* v. *Canada*, the claimants challenged the constitutionality of a regulation that prohibited individuals from distributing flyers in an airport.[53] A police officer who was patrolling the airport saw that the claimants were distributing pamphlets.[54] The officer ordered them to stop and took them to the airport's assistant manager, who confirmed that a regulation prohibited their activities.[55] The claimants challenged the regulation's constitutionality and argued that it violated their constitutional right to freedom of expression.[56]

The majority of the Court agreed and decided that the constitutional violation could not be justified in a free and democratic society.[57] Citing the US Supreme Court's decision in *Hague*, Justice L'Heureux-Dubé explained that the Government has an ownership right of public property that is "quasi-fiduciary in nature" and that the State holds this property for the public's benefit.[58] In other judicial decisions, such as *Abbottsford* v. *Shantz* discussed in previous chapters, the British Columbia Supreme Court observed that "Although public property is held in trust for the public, the right to access and use public spaces is not absolute."[59]

Notice two important features of the Government's fiduciary status in these public law contexts – features that also characterize the fiduciary bond between the State and the people as discussed in the next section. First, each of these fiduciary relationships – the fiduciary relationship between the State and Indigenous peoples in Canada, the public trust doctrine in the United States, and the State's fiduciary guardianship of public property in both countries – arises without consent. The Government's relationship with Indigenous people does not stem from actual or hypothetical consent.[60] Rather, it arises *sui generis* because Indigenous persons are uniquely vulnerable to State power due to colonialism and its legacy.[61] The public trust doctrine acknowledges that the State holds certain natural resources in trust for the people and must manage them for the common good – a fiduciary relationship to which the parties did not consent.[62] The duty exists to protect some individuals

52 Kevin Gray and Susan Francis Gray, "Private Property and Public Propriety" in Janet McLean (ed.), *Property and the Constitution* (London: Hart, 1999) at 28–29.

53 *Committee for the Commonwealth of Canada* v. *Canada* [1991] 1 SCR 139 at 167.

54 *Ibid.*

55 *Ibid.*

56 *Ibid.* at 174.

57 June Ross, "Committee for the Commonwealth of Canada v. Canada – Expression on Public Property" (1990–91) 2:4 *Const* F 107 at 109.

58 *Committee for the Commonwealth of Canada* v. *Canada* [1991] 1 SCR 139 at 174.

59 *Abbotsford (City)* v. *Shantz*, 2015 BCSC 1909 at para. 197. *See also City of Surrey* v. *Lewis*, 2016 BCPC 44 at para. 35; *Hussain* v. *Toronto (City)*, 2016 ONSC 3504 at paras. 39–41.

60 *Delgamuukw* v. *British Columbia* [1997] 3 SCR 1010; Fox-Decent, *Sovereignty's Promise* at 56, 67.

61 *Southwind* v. *Canada*, 2021 SCC 28 at para. 55.

62 Joseph Sax, "Liberating the Public Trust Doctrine from its Historical Shackles" (1980) 14:2 *UC Davis L Rev* 185 at 185–86; Alexandra Klass, "Modern Public Trust Principles: Recognizing Rights and Integrating Standards" (2006) 82:2 *Notre Dame L Rev* 699 at 699.

from appropriating land and depriving others from its use and resources – a form of horizontal domination that the State's fiduciary duty mitigates.[63] The State's duty to maintain public property's role and value arises without consent for similar reasons.[64]

Second, the State's fiduciary duties exist to rectify both vertical and horizontal forms of domination. Its fiduciary duty towards Indigenous peoples aims primarily to counteract vertical domination that stems from colonialism and the Government's deprivation of Indigenous persons' sovereignty and power of self-government.[65] And the State's fiduciary duties related to natural resource law and the regulation of public space both aim to protect individuals against horizontal domination by others.[66]

7.3 REPUBLICANISM AND THE STATE'S FIDUCIARY DUTIES

The State's three fiduciary relationships discussed in Section 7.2 may appear to be distinct and unrelated. But they flow from a single overarching fiduciary bond between the State and individuals that underpins the republican theory of government. Furthermore, this overarching fiduciary relationship bears the same three characteristics that support its existence. First, the fiduciary relationship between the Government and the people involves an asymmetric power dynamic that results in domination. Second, this fiduciary relationship arises without express or implied consent between the parties. Third, like other fiduciary obligations in public law, the State's fiduciary duties towards the people aim to counteract horizontal and vertical forms of domination.

The republican theory of government construes the State as a trustee and the people as its beneficiaries.[67] The fiduciary relationship arises from individuals' unilateral vulnerability to governmental power.[68] Public officials can exercise public powers that individuals lack, such as powers of criminalization, punishment, legislation, adjudication, taxation, expropriation, and more.[69] Individuals' vulnerability to public power – and their lack of reciprocal powers against the State – grounds the fiduciary relationship between the State and

63 *See* note 45 above.

64 *Abbotsford (City)* v. *Shantz*, 2015 BCSC 1909 at paras. 198–99.

65 *Southwind* v. *Canada*, 2021 SCC 28 at para. 55.

66 Sax, "The Public Trust Doctrine in Natural Resource Law" at 474 (note 14 in the text), 490–92; Takacs, "The Public Trust Doctrine" at 714–16.

67 Fox-Decent, *Sovereignty's Promise* at 26–28; Natelson, "The Constitution and the Public Trust" at 1086. Pettit, *Republicanism* at 147–48; Criddle and Fox-Decent, *Fiduciaries of Humanity* at 13–14; Daryl Levinson and Richard Pildes, "Separation of Parties, Not Powers" (2006) 119:8 *Harv L Rev* 2312 at 2318–19; Evan Criddle, "Fiduciary Administration: Rethinking Popular Representation in Agency Rulemaking" (2009) 88:3 *Tex L Rev* 441 at 446–48; Jean-Fabien Spitz, "The Twilight of the Republic" in Daniel Weinstock and Christian Nadeau (eds.), *Republicanism: History, Theory, and Practice* (New York: Routledge, 2004) at 55–56.

68 Fox-Decent, *Sovereignty's Promise* at 89, 103.

69 *Ibid.* at 103.

individuals.[70] Evan Fox-Decent notes that the State's fiduciary relationship arises without consent much like a parent's fiduciary relationship with their children; it is formed without express or implicit agreement due the asymmetric power dynamic between the parties.[71]

The fiduciary relationship between the State and the people aims to counteract domination.[72] Lawmakers can abuse their authority. Power can corrupt them. They may place their personal interests or aspirations above the long-term interests of the community.[73] They may exercise their discretion inappropriately or arbitrarily.[74] Democratically elected lawmakers can still produce a tyranny of the majority and violate marginalized individuals and groups' interests.[75] The State's fiduciary duty to act in the people's best interests aims to neutralize domination by the State and control its discretionary power over individuals.[76]

Republicanism also justifies this fiduciary relationship on the ground that the State derives its power from the people.[77] Individuals delegate power to the State and its public officials through the democratic process.[78] The conferral of power further explains why the State and its public officials are trustees who must act in the best interests of their beneficiaries: the people.[79]

For instance, in the *Federalist Papers*, James Madison describes how State authority derives from the people and must be exercised on their behalf and for the common good.[80] He explained that "The genius of Republican liberty seems to demand on one side not only that all power should be derived from the people but that those entrusted with it should be kept in dependence on the people."[81] Madison remarked that political constitutions aim to ensure that public officials exercise their powers "for the common good of society" and that they hold this power in the public trust.[82]

70 *Ibid.*
71 *Ibid.*
72 Criddle, "Liberty in Loyalty" at 1002.
73 Philip Pettit, "The General Will, the Common Good, and the Democracy of Standards" in Yiftah Elazar and Geneviève Rousselière (eds.), *Republicanism and the Future of Democracy* (Cambridge University Press, 2019) at 39. Pettit's exact quote is: "The commitment to their ends, and to attaining or keeping the power needed to realize them, may lead participants to bend the rules of the system in their own short- term interest but to the long-term detriment of the common good."
74 Pettit, *Republicanism* at 250, 265.
75 Annelien de Dijn, "Republicanism and Democracy: The Tyranny of the Majority in Eighteenth Century Political Debate" in Yiftah Elazar and Geneviève Rousselière (eds.), *Republicanism and the Future of Democracy* (Cambridge University Press, 2019) at 59.
76 *Ibid.*
77 Criddle, "Liberty in Loyalty" at 1002.
78 Theodore Rave, "Politicians as Fiduciaries" (2013) 126:3 *Harv L Rev* 671 at 708–11.
79 *Ibid.*
80 James Madison, "Federalist No. 37" in Ian Shapiro (ed.), *The Federalist Papers* (New Haven: Yale University Press 2009) at 181. This excerpt cited in Jack Balkin, "Republicanism and the Constitution of Opportunity" (2016) 94 *Tex L Rev* 1427 at 1433, fn. 57 in the text.
81 Madison, "Federalist No. 37" at 181.
82 James Madison, "Federalist No. 57" in Shapiro (ed.), *The Federalist Papers* at 290.

Drawing on the work of republican theorists such as Cicero, John Locke, and the Federalists, Theodore Rave observes that the fiduciary conception of State authority is embedded within republican theory.[83] Republicanism construes the State as a fiduciary that has a duty to act in the people's best interests.[84] Like other republican theorists, he suggests that the fiduciary duty's source is that individuals confer power to the State through the democratic process.[85] Individuals suffer domination when they lack a power of self-government and are ruled by an external will.[86] This also explains why Indigenous peoples suffer a unique form of domination that arises from colonialism.[87]

The overarching fiduciary relationship between the State and individuals gives rise to the State's overarching fiduciary duty to counteract vertical and horizontal domination that flow from that relationship.[88] The fulfilment of this duty aims to ensure that individuals can enjoy freedom vis-à-vis the State and vis-à-vis others.[89] Since individuals are both vulnerable to State authority and confer power to the State through the democratic process, the State's duty of loyalty requires it to act in individuals' best interests and protect them against vertical domination.[90]

But the State also has a fiduciary duty to protect individuals against horizontal domination that stems from its laws, policies, and conduct. Public institutions and their officials are necessary to secure freedom against private domination.[91] Individuals lack the public powers to legislate, regulate, govern, and adjudicate because they would unilaterally limit others' freedom without authority.[92] The State and its public institutions prevent that form of private domination.[93] Yet this very justification for creating public institutions – preventing private domination – is undermined when the State's laws, policies, or inaction permit some individuals to dominate others. Furthermore, the State does not act in individuals' best interests when it permits private domination because nondomination is a shared interest.

The State must also fulfil its overarching fiduciary duty to counteract domination to secure political equality.[94] Individuals lack the status of free and equal persons if they are subject to uncontrolled unilateral threats of interference by the State or by others.[95]

83 Rave, "Politicians as Fiduciaries" at 711–12.
84 *Ibid.*
85 *Ibid.*
86 Fox-Decent and Criddle, "The Fiduciary Constitution of Human Rights" at 333.
87 *Ibid.*
88 Pettit, *On the People's Terms* at 76–77.
89 *Ibid.*
90 Criddle, "Liberty in Loyalty" at 1002.
91 Arthur Ripstein, *Force and Freedom* (Cambridge: Harvard University Press, 2009) at 238–39, 255–56.
92 *Ibid.*; Jacob Weinrib, *Dimensions of Dignity: The Theory and Practice of Modern Constitutional Law* (Cambridge University Press, 2016) at 48, 59.
93 Ripstein, *Force and Freedom* at 255–56.
94 Pettit, *Republicanism* at 31–32, 63–64.
95 *Ibid.*; Cecile Laborde, "Republicanism" in Michael Freeden, Lyman Tower Sargent, and Marc Stears (eds.), *The Oxford Handbook of Political Ideologies* (Oxford University Press, 2013) at 525.

Rather than be their own masters, dominated individuals remain subjugated to an external will. Freedom from horizontal and vertical domination promotes political equality because individuals are mutually constrained by a system of rights and a system of laws that bind them reciprocally.[96] In a society where individuals enjoy nondomination, they possess similar power and antipower, such that they can interact with one another from a position of equal strength.[97]

The political ideal of expressive egalitarianism exemplifies the State's fulfilment of its overarching fiduciary duty to counteract both forms of domination.[98] The term "expressive egalitarianism" connotes laws, policies, and decisions that express equal respect and consideration for individuals.[99] Expressively egalitarian laws and policies track individuals' interests and strive to treat each person as though they matter equally, such that they are protected against domination by the State and by others.[100]

The State's laws, policies, and actions are increasingly expressively egalitarian when they respect two requirements that counteract domination and safeguard political equality: political legitimacy and social justice.[101] While political legitimacy implies that the State counteracts vertical domination optimally, social justice connotes that the State counteracts horizontal domination optimally.[102]

To be clear, the State's laws, policies, and actions may satisfy political legitimacy and social justice to greater or lesser extents. Furthermore, in some contexts, the State may increasingly respect the first requirement of political legitimacy but not the second requirement of social justice, or vice versa.[103] Yet the State increasingly respects its overarching fiduciary duty to counteract domination where its laws, policies, and decisions are increasingly expressively egalitarian, such that individuals can enjoy nondomination and political equality on a par with others.

The State's fiduciary duties described previously – in the contexts of Crown and Indigenous relations, the public trust doctrine, and the regulation of public property – are distinct fiduciary duties that flow from the State's overarching fiduciary duty to counteract domination. But the State's specific fiduciary duties are not confined to these public law contexts exclusively. As discussed in Section 7.4, the State also has three specific fiduciary duties related to homelessness and public property.

96 Fox-Decent, *Sovereignty's Promise* at 139.

97 Philip Pettit, "Freedom as Anti-Power" (1996) 106:3 *Ethics* 576 at 588; Pettit, *On the People's Terms* at 82.

98 Pettit, *On the People's Terms* at 77–79, 82–92 (describing the connection between expressive egalitarianism and non-domination). The term "expressive egalitarianism" is used by Pettit.

99 *Ibid.* at 76–77.

100 *Ibid.* at 68, 110–11.

101 *Ibid.* at 3.

102 *Ibid.* at chs. 2 and 3.

103 On the possibility for the State to respect the first and second requirement, see Pamela Pansardi, "Republican Democracy and the Priority of Legitimacy over Justice" (2015) 5 *Phil & Pub Issues* 43 at 44–45.

These fiduciary duties exist because the State fails to accommodate unhoused persons within two systems of mutual coercion that the State creates to secure freedom: the private property system and laws that govern public property. The State's fiduciary duties related to homelessness and public property aim to counteract this domination.

7.4 PROPERTY, HOMELESSNESS, AND THE STATE'S THREE FIDUCIARY DUTIES

Together, republicanism and fiduciary theories of legal authority demonstrate why the State has three interrelated fiduciary duties pertaining to homelessness and public property, each of which are discussed in Sections 7.4.1, 7.4.2, and 7.4.3. First, the State has a fiduciary duty to end homelessness and treat unhoused persons with equal concern and respect. Second, as public property's trustee, the State has a fiduciary duty to protect its shared value and safeguard liberty in the public sphere. Third, the State has a fiduciary duty to legitimize coercion and punishment associated with laws that govern public property. Laws that govern public property are increasingly expressively egalitarian when the State increasingly fulfils these three fiduciary duties.

7.4.1 *The Duty to End Homelessness*

First, the State has a fiduciary duty to end homelessness and treat unhoused persons with equal concern and respect. The justification for this duty can be summarized as follows. Previous chapters showed why the State creates a system of private property rights to protect individuals against horizontal domination.[104] Yet unhoused persons suffer domination because the State fails to accommodate them within that system, and prohibits them from resorting to self-help to secure their liberty.[105] For this reason, people experiencing homelessness are exposed to unilateral and uncontrolled interference by others and are uniquely vulnerable to laws that govern public property.[106] The State's fiduciary duty to end homelessness aims to neutralize the vertical and horizontal domination to which unhoused persons are subject.

To illustrate this point, consider first why the State creates a system of private property rights to reduce horizontal domination. Private property rights safeguard individuals against domination for two interrelated reasons.[107] First, rightsholders can exercise their power of exclusion to protect themselves against the threat of

[104] *See* Chapter 4 of this book; Christopher Essert, "Property and Homelessness" (2016) 44 *Phil & Pub Aff* 266 at 266.

[105] Terry Skolnik, "Homeless Encampments: A Philosophical Justification" (2023) 36 *JL & Soc Pol'y* 97 at 100–01, 111.

[106] Terry Skolnik, "How and Why Homeless People Are Regulated Differently" (2018) 43 *Queen's LJ* 297 at 313–23.

[107] Ripstein, *Force and Freedom* at 154–55; Essert, "Property and Homelessness" at 266.

interference by others – a power that is backed by the State.[108] Second, private property rights insulate rightsholders against others' power of exclusion.[109] Without a system of private property rights, individuals would face horizontal domination because they would lack legal protection against potential interference by others.[110]

The State establishes a private property regime that binds all, and that changes individuals' normative situation vis-à-vis others by creating new rights, powers, duties, and liabilities.[111] The State exercises a public power when it creates and maintains a private property system and backs it by governmental coercion.[112] Individuals lack a comparable public power to establish a private property system that binds all because they would unilaterally limit others' freedom without authority.[113] To be clear, certain collectivities – such as Indigenous communities, religious groups, or cooperatives – may also establish binding property schemes. However, the State's creation of a private property system – and its assumption of control over it – represents the exercise of a public power that binds individuals.

Although the State creates a system of private property rights to secure liberty, it fails to accommodate unhoused persons within that system, which results in their domination.[114] The private property system allocates property rights based primarily on market exchanges rather than individual need.[115] Unhoused persons are de facto excluded from the private property system when they lack the financial capacities to acquire private property rights that would safeguard their liberty. Furthermore, they cannot lawfully appropriate public or private property based on individual need.[116] Leaving aside rare cases of adverse possession,[117] courts reject poverty and homelessness as a justification for such appropriation.[118] Unhoused persons thus cannot resort to self-help to secure nondomination for themselves.

Unhoused persons' de facto exclusion from this necessary system of private property rights subjects them to a unique form of double domination that manifests itself in different ways. Chapters 3 and 4 showed why unhoused persons are consistently vulnerable to others' power of exclusion.[119] Additionally, others exert control over unhoused persons' opportunities to obey laws that govern public property.[120]

108 Skolnik, "Homeless Encampments" at 99–100.
109 *Ibid.*
110 Essert, "Property and Homelessness" at 266.
111 Ripstein, *Force and Freedom* at 90, 154–55.
112 *Ibid.* at 154–57.
113 *Ibid.*; Weinrib, *Dimensions of Dignity* at 48–49.
114 Andy Yu, "Equity and Homelessness" (2020) 33:1 *Can JL & Jur* 245 at 250–51.
115 Jeremy Waldron, "Why Indigence Is Not a Justification" in William Kleinig and John Heffernan (eds.), *Indigence and Criminal Justice* (Oxford University Press, 2000) at 107.
116 Skolnik, "Homeless Encampments."
117 Henry Smith, "Self-Help and the Nature of Property" (2005) 1 *JL Econ & Policy* 69 at 80–85.
118 Waldron, "Why Indigence Is Not a Justification" at 109; *London Borough of Southwark* v. *Williams & Anor* [1971] 2 All ER 175.
119 Essert, "Property and Homelessness" at 266.
120 Skolnik, "How and Why" at 313–23.

Unlike people with access to housing, people experiencing homelessness must also make nonegalitarian trade-offs to obey laws that govern public property.[121] And as discussed in Chapter 5, the State has greater power to regulate and police unhoused persons compared to people with access to housing.[122]

The State's fiduciary duty to end homelessness aims to counteract these forms of domination.[123] The private property system cannot achieve its objective to secure freedom if the State fails to accommodate certain individuals within that system.[124] But the State cannot abolish its private property system, as it would result in private domination. If the State did so, it would abdicate its overarching fiduciary duty to counteract domination. The duty to end homelessness rectifies certain individuals' exclusion from a system of private property rights – a system that is necessary to secure freedom.[125]

This account also explains why the duty to end homelessness falls principally on the State rather than on private individuals. The State is the body that creates and assumes control over a system of private property rights, which aims to secure freedom between persons without constituting a form of private domination. Moreover, the State is responsible for the private property system's establishment, architecture, and operation. The State's simultaneous action – establishing a private property system – and inaction – failing to accommodate people experiencing homelessness within that system – results in unhoused persons' domination. For this reason, the State bears responsibility for creating the conditions that give rise to unhoused persons' unfreedom.[126] And for this same reason, the State has a specific fiduciary duty to end that domination; one that flows from its overarching duty to protect liberty.

As part of the fiduciary duty to end homelessness, the State must address the risk factors associated with homelessness – such as poverty, mental illness, and substance use disorder – and ensure that individuals have access to housing. Chapter 9 explores the fulfilment of this duty and analyzes it more in depth. But its content can be summarized as follows. First, the fiduciary duty to end homelessness is primarily ameliorative in nature and seeks to avoid coercion and punishment. The ameliorative nature of this duty allows the State to end homelessness in a manner that does not produce domination, and that treats unhoused persons with greater consideration and respect. Second, this fiduciary obligation gives rise to a correlative right to be protected against homelessness and the domination that flows from it.

121 *Ibid.*

122 *Ibid.*

123 *See, e.g.*, Ernst Weinrib, "Poverty and Property in Kant's System of Rights" (2003) 78 *Notre Dame L Rev* 795 at 816–17.

124 Laura Underkuffler, "Fiduciary Theory: The Missing Piece for Positive Rights" in Evan Criddle, Evan Fox-Decent, Andrew Gold et al. (eds.), *Fiduciary Government* (Oxford University Press, 2018) at 109–15.

125 Yu, "Equity and Homelessness" at 250–51.

126 *Ibid.*

This second feature explains why the State's fiduciary obligation to end homelessness is both preventive and reactive in nature. Notably, the State must address the risk factors associated with homelessness so that individuals do not lose access to housing or remain unhoused. And it must provide access to housing, emergency shelters, and other services when individuals lose access to housing that they once enjoyed. Third and interrelatedly, the State's fiduciary duty to end homelessness results in a right to access to housing, which can be fulfilled through several means, such as housing vouchers, public housing, and Housing First programs. More on these points in Chapter 9.

7.4.2 *The Duty to Protect Public Property's Role and Value*

The State's second fiduciary duty related to homelessness is that it must protect public property's shared value and secure liberty in the public sphere, meaning outside of one's home.[127] The State's second fiduciary duty is justified by two considerations: land's immovability and public property's vulnerability to collective action problems. Land's immovability explains why the State establishes a public property system that helps secure liberty in the public sphere. Public property's vulnerability to collective action problems, on the other hand, justifies why the State regulates public property to secure nondomination outside of one's home. Notably, the State must enact and enforce norms that govern public property to protect its role and value.

Consider land's immovability first. Given that individuals are interdependent, they must leave their private property for various reasons: work, socialization, shopping, and more.[128] And they must pass through land to do these things. Land, however, is immovable, and individuals must inevitably use it to travel between places.[129] Recall Essert's observation that individuals must be granted permission to access private property to lawfully do any act in that space.[130] If all land was privatized, individuals would constantly have to secure others' authorization to travel between spaces and engage in certain conduct outside of their homes – they would suffer horizontal domination.[131]

Public property resolves this problem. As an open-access space, public property helps ensure that individuals can freely move and act outside of their homes without the risk of unilateral interference by others.[132] In theory, without public property, individuals could contract out a series of arrangements with other rightsholders, such that they could move between places without having to constantly secure others' permission.[133] Beyond its inefficiency, this type of regime would still

127 *See, e.g.*, Ripstein, *Force and Freedom* at 238–39, 244–45.
128 Gregory Alexander, *Property and Human Flourishing* (Oxford University Press, 2018) at 7.
129 Ripstein, *Force and Freedom* at 238–39, 244–45.
130 Essert, "Property and Homelessness" at 275–76.
131 *Ibid.*; Ripstein, *Force and Freedom* at 238–39, 244–45, 255–56.
132 *Ibid.*
133 *Ibid.*

undermine liberty and equality. Some rightsholders would exercise their freedom of contract and deny entry to their land.[134] Others could charge exorbitant prices for such private arrangements. Less affluent individuals would be unable to purchase the permission to travel and would lack the freedom to move between places that others enjoy. This type of contractual scheme would result in horizontal domination. Public property counteracts horizontal domination because it constitutes a space where individuals are free from others' private power of exclusion and agenda-setting authority.[135]

Together, private property rights and public property foster nondomination. Private property rights protect individuals' liberty, security, and autonomy within the private sphere.[136] These rights help secure nondomination because they confer the rightsholder a power to exclude others and insulate the rightsholder from others' power of exclusion.[137] Public property, on the other hand, helps secure freedom because it ensures that people can travel and engage in conduct outside of their homes without being subject to others' power of exclusion.[138] The State thus creates, authorizes, and enforces two systems of mutual coercion – the private property and public property regimes – to secure freedom in a manner that avoids private domination.

The second consideration that justifies the State's fiduciary duty to protect public property is its vulnerability to collective action problems – problems that undermine public property's value and limit liberty in the public sphere.[139] Chapter 5 demonstrated how public property is an open-access space that is susceptible to a tragedy of the commons.[140] A tragedy of the commons occurs when each person's rational attempt to maximize public property's benefits results in collectively irrational outcomes – namely, that public property's value declines for all.[141] Unregulated public property can lead to rivalry between persons, overexploitation, congestion, and usages that are inconsistent with public property's role and worth.[142] A tragedy of the commons also undermines freedom outside of one's home. Individuals may engage in conduct that restricts others' liberty in the public sphere or that constrains others' freedom to use public property on equal terms. These considerations explain why the

134 *Ibid.*

135 *Ibid.*

136 Benjamin Barros, "Home as a Legal Concept" (2006) 46 *Santa Clara L Rev* 255 at 259–75.

137 Terry Skolnik, "Freedom and Access to Housing: Three Conceptions" (2018) 35 *Windsor YB Access Just* 226 at 233, 236.

138 Ripstein, *Force and Freedom* at 238–39, 255–56.

139 Robert Ellickson, "Controlling Chronic Misconduct in City Spaces: Of Panhandlers, Skid Rows, and Public-Space Zoning" (1996) 105 *Yale LJ* 1165 at 1168–70.

140 Sheila Foster, "Collective Action and the Urban Commons" (2011) 87:1 *Notre Dame L Rev* 57 at 64–70.

141 Elinor Ostrom, *Governing the Commons* (Cambridge University Press, 1990) at 5. Ostrom's original quote is: "individually rational strategies lead to collectively irrational outcomes" (*ibid.*).

142 Foster, "Collective Action and the Urban Commons" at 67; Sheila Foster and Christian Iaione, "The City as a Commons" (2016) 34:2 *Yale L & Pol'y Rev* 281 at 288–89; Brett Frischmann, "An Economic Theory of Infrastructure and Commons Management" (2005) 89 *Minn L Rev* 917 at 984.

State establishes mutually binding norms of conduct that govern public property, and that help secure nondomination between individuals in the public sphere.

Though the State creates a system of public property that prevents some types of horizontal domination, it also enacts mutually binding laws that protect public property's value and that mitigate collective action problems.[143] The State exercises a public power when it enacts laws that regulate public property and that mutually bind all.[144] Private individuals lack a comparable public power because they would limit others' freedom without authority.[145]

Together, land's immovability and public property's vulnerability to collective action problems underpin the State's fiduciary duty to protect public property's collective worth and safeguard liberty in the public sphere. And the State fulfils this duty when it enacts and enforces laws that govern public property that promote those ends.

But the State's attempt to fulfil its fiduciary duty to safeguard public property's role reduces some forms of domination but produces others. Although laws that govern public property aim to mitigate horizontal domination in the public sphere, these laws subject unhoused persons to vertical domination and nonegalitarian coercion.[146] Furthermore, unhoused persons cannot appropriate others' private property to use public property on equal terms with others.[147] Nor can unhoused persons freely access others' private property in a manner that decreases their contribution to a tragedy of the urban commons, meaning a tragedy of the commons on public property. Just as the State fails to accommodate unhoused persons within a necessary system of private property rights that helps secure liberty in the private sphere, the State fails to accommodate unhoused persons within its system of laws that govern public property and that safeguard liberty in the public sphere.

7.4.3 *The Duty to Legitimize Laws That Govern Public Property*

Third, the State has a fiduciary duty to legitimize the coercion and punishment associated with laws that govern public property. It must fulfil this duty to ensure that it regulates public property – and respects its second fiduciary obligation to safeguard the shared value of public space – in a manner that does not constitute domination and does not entrench individuals in homelessness.

7.4.3.1 The Duty to Legitimize Coercion

There are two main reasons why the coercion associated with laws that govern public property is more legitimate when individuals enjoy the undominated choice to obey

143 Ripstein, *Force and Freedom* at 238–39, 255–56.
144 *Ibid.*
145 *Ibid.*
146 Skolnik, "How and Why" at 313–23.
147 Skolnik, "Homeless Encampments" at 100, 111.

them: respect for human agency and political obligation. Consider first the relationship between undominated choice to obey the law, respect for human agency, and coercion.[148] Building on the work of scholars such as H. L. A. Hart, Chapters 4 and 6 showed how coercion and punishment are justified by choice-based conceptions of culpability.[149] Recall how Hart conceptualized the law as a choosing system that aims to demonstrate respect for human agency.[150] According to this conception, the State enacts laws that communicate which conduct is prohibited and the punishments for breaching these laws.[151] Yet the choice of law-abidingness is left up to the individual.[152] This system respects human agency because it treats individuals as rational agents who weigh the pros and cons of obeying the law, and punishes them for their rational choice to break it.[153]

The law withholds blame and punishment when individuals lacked a free choice to obey the law.[154] More specifically, the law excuses an individual's legal transgression when they either lacked the physical or mental capacity to obey the law, or, did not have a fair opportunity to do so given the circumstances.[155] In these contexts, it is unfair for the law to blame and punish an actor whose freedom of choice to obey the law was constrained by external factors: threats, compulsion, emergency, or others' control over the defendant's opportunity to obey the law.[156] Coercion demonstrates greater respect for persons when it is imposed on individuals who enjoyed undominated choice to obey the law, rejected available alternatives to violating it, and transgressed it culpably.

Consider next how undominated choice to obey the law promotes political obligation, meaning individuals' moral duty to obey the law.[157] Some contend that the principle of fair play justifies political obligation.[158] The fair play conception of political obligation construes the law as a system that protects mutually shared

148 Antony Duff, "Choice, Character, and Criminal Liability" (1993) 12:4 *Law & Phil* 345 at 346–48; Michael Moore, "Choice, Character, and Excuse" (1990) 7 *Soc Phil & Pol'y* 29 at 29; Michael Moore, *Placing Blame: A Theory of the Criminal Law* (Oxford University Press, 2010) at 48; *R* v. *Ruzic*, 2001 SCC 24 at para. 45: "The treatment of criminal offenders as rational, autonomous and choosing agents is a fundamental organizing principle of our criminal law"; *Perka* v. *The Queen* [1984] 2 SCR 232 at 250.

149 H. L. A Hart and John Gardner, *Punishment and Responsibility* (Oxford University Press, 2008) at 22–23.

150 *Ibid.*

151 *Ibid.*

152 *Ibid.*

153 *Ibid.*

154 George Fletcher, *Rethinking Criminal Law* (Oxford University Press, 2000) at 802–04.

155 Hart and Gardner, *Punishment and Responsibility* at 152–53.

156 *Ibid.*

157 Richard Dagger, "What Is Political Obligation?" (1977) *Am Pol Sci Rev* 86 at 86–88, 94.

158 *See, e.g.*, H. L. A. Hart, "Are There Any Natural Rights?" (1955) 64:2 *Phil Rev* 175 at 185, 190–91; Richard Dagger, *Playing Fair: Political Obligation and the Problems of Punishment* (Oxford University Press, 2018) at 42–45; George Klosko, *Political Obligations* (Oxford University Press, 2005) at 102.

interests through cooperation.[159] Under this system, an individual can enjoy their fundamental interests only if others abide by laws that safeguard their same interests. Since the individual benefits from others' cooperation and compliance with the law, the individual is also bound to obey the law and respect others' shared interests as a matter of fairness or fair play.[160]

The moral duty to obey the law thus ensures that individuals mutually respect each other's legally protected rights.[161] An individual's rights impose legally binding duties of noninterference on others, which others respect when they obey the law.[162] The individual must also obey the law to fulfil their duty to respect others' rights.[163] The duty to obey the law is not simply an impersonal obligation that individuals owe to the State.[164] It is justified by the interpersonal duties that members of a community owe to one another as a matter of mutual respect, cooperation, and reciprocity.[165] In these ways, the moral duty to obey the law helps secure nondomination between persons.

Fairness is essential to fair play conceptions of political obligation.[166] The notion of fairness implies that individuals retain similar benefits and are imposed similar burdens as part of the cooperative scheme.[167] Fairness is breached when some individuals must either do unreasonably more than others to sustain the cooperative scheme or enjoy the scheme's benefits unreasonably less than others.[168] Such unfair schemes fail to treat these individuals as political equals.[169] Notably, unfair cooperative schemes instrumentalize individuals by using them as a means to secure benefits for others. Furthermore, unjust schemes treat individuals' shared interests in the scheme's benefits as less important. The duty to obey the law is imposed less fairly in contexts where its benefits and burdens are allocated disparately.

The principle of fair play explains why the undominated choice to obey laws that govern public property legitimizes them. The benefits and burdens of compliance are distributed relatively evenly amongst persons who control their own law abidingness and need not make egalitarian trade-offs to comply with the law. Under such

159 Dagger, *Playing Fair* at 42–45; Klosko, *Political Obligations* at 102.

160 Richard Dagger, "Authority, Legitimacy, and the Obligation to Obey the Law" (2018) 24:2 *Leg Theory* 77 at 101–02.

161 Richard Dagger, "Membership, Fair Play, and Political Obligation" (2000) 48:1 *Pol Stud* 104 at 115.

162 Wesley Hohfeld, "Fundamental Legal Conceptions as Applied in Judicial Reasoning" (1917) 26 *Yale LJ* 710 at 710 (describing rights and duties as jural correlatives).

163 Dagger, "Membership, Fair Play, and Political Obligation" at 115.

164 *Ibid.*; Richard Dagger, "Republican Citizenship" in Engin Isin and Bryan Turner (eds.), *Handbook of Citizenship Studies* (Thousand Oaks: Sage, 2002) at 150.

165 Richard Dagger, *Civic Virtues: Rights, Citizenship, and Republican Liberalism* (Oxford University Press, 1997) at 47.

166 Klosko, *Political Obligations* at 4–6, 115.

167 *Ibid.* at 4–6, 115 (noting that benefits and burdens must be evenly distributed); Dagger, *Playing Fair* at 52–53, 101–02, 105–06; George Klosko, *The Principle of Fairness and Political Obligations* (New York: Rowman & Littlefield, 1992) at 63–64.

168 Dagger, *Playing Fair* at 105–06.

169 *Ibid.*

a scheme, all individuals can maximally enjoy public property and can respect each other's shared interests in a manner that impacts their freedom similarly.

Since all persons have an interest in enjoying public property on equal terms, it is only fair that they play their part to obey laws that regulate public property. And they do so when comply with laws that govern public space and engage in need-alleviating acts in private. Access to housing, in turn, provides the greatest undominated choice to obey these laws because it affords a default private place where individuals can freely alleviate their needs and obey the law.[170]

Together, unhoused persons' de facto exclusion from the private property system and their unique vulnerability to laws that govern public property violate the principle of fair play. Chapter 3 demonstrated how the private property regime distributes benefits and burdens disparately, which systematically disadvantages unhoused persons.[171] Unhoused persons have a legal duty to respect others' private property rights and can be excluded by them.[172] But others owe no reciprocal duty of noninterference to unhoused persons because they do not have private property rights.[173] For this reason, unhoused persons enjoy few benefits from the private property system but are encumbered with its burdens – a disparity that undermines the private property regime's fairness.[174]

These background disadvantages explain why laws that govern public property violate the principle of fair play for unhoused persons for two interrelated reasons. First, laws that govern public property violate fair play because they impose additional affirmative duties to act on unhoused persons that are subject to others' control.[175] Chapter 5 showed how unhoused persons have a supplementary duty to secure access to private property to lawfully alleviate their needs and obey the law.[176] In contrast, people with access to housing are imposed no comparable duty because they have default access to private property to alleviate their needs.[177] This disparate allocation of burdens to comply with laws that govern public property undermines fairness. This unfairness is exacerbated by the fact that others exert control over unhoused persons' fulfilment of their duty to secure access to private property to alleviate their needs and obey the law.

Second, these laws violate the principle of fair play because they impose nonegalitarian trade-offs on unhoused persons, which render their obligation to obey the law more onerous compared to others.[178] Unhoused persons alone must make

170 Skolnik, "Freedom and Access to Housing" at 236.
171 Jane Baron, "Homelessness as a Property Problem" (2004) 36 *Urb Law* 273 at 287.
172 Jeremy Waldron, "Property and Community: For Those Who Have Neither" (2009) 10:1 *Theor Inq L* 161 at 165–66.
173 *Ibid.*
174 Jane Baron, "Property and 'No Property'" (2006) 42:5 *Hous L Rev* 1425 at 1429.
175 Skolnik, "How and Why" at 313–23.
176 *Ibid.*
177 *Ibid.*
178 *Ibid.*

nonegalitarian sacrifices to comply with laws that regulate public property to sustain its coordinating function.[179] They must disproportionately endanger their interests to safeguard public property and help secure liberty in the public sphere.[180]

The duty to obey laws that govern public property is imposed less fairly for unhoused persons because it instrumentalizes them – they suffer domination to secure others' freedom in the public sphere. Furthermore, by imposing nonegalitarian trade-offs, these laws violate fair play constraints because they treat unhoused persons' shared interests in security, privacy, and dignity as less important – interests they must sacrifice to obey the law.

7.4.3.2 Legitimizing Punishment

Beyond legitimizing coercion, the State also has a fiduciary duty to legitimize the punishments associated with laws that govern public property. The State must fulfil this duty to ensure that its sanctions do not constitute domination and do not entrench individuals in homelessness. As discussed further in this section, punishments are more legitimate when they are consistent with its two main rationales: retributivism and consequentialism.[181] Moreover, the State must respect the basic requirements of proportionality and instrumental rationality to ensure that its sanctions are consistent with retributive and consequentialist rationales for punishment.

Retributivism is more legitimate when individuals enjoyed the greatest undominated choice to obey the law. Chapter 6 discussed how retributivism justifies punishment based on defendants' free and culpable choice to commit an offense.[182] Individuals do not deserve punishment when they lacked the fair opportunity to comply with the law and thus did not freely choose to break it.[183] The lack of fair opportunity to obey the law undermines freedom of choice, culpability, and ultimately, punishment's deservedness.[184] For this reason, the defendant alone

179 *Ibid.*

180 *Ibid.*

181 Terry Skolnik, "Socially Deprived Offenders" in Jesper Ryberg (ed.), *Oxford Handbook of Punishment Theory and Philosophy* (Oxford University Press, 2024) (forthcoming). Draft on file with author. *See also* David Dolinko, "Retributivism, Consequentialism, and the Intrinsic Goodness of Punishment" (1997) 16:5 *Law & Phil* 507 at 507–08 (describing retributivism); David Dolinko, "Punishment" in John Deigh and David Dolinko (eds.), *The Oxford Handbook on the Philosophy of the Criminal Law* (Oxford University Press, 2011) at 405–07 (describing consequentialism). This does not suggest that retributivism and consequentialism are the only legitimate justifications for punishment. Punishments that are justified by other theories – such as mixed theories of punishment, expressivism, or unfair advantage – are more legitimate when individuals enjoy undominated choice to obey the law and are not subject to nonegalitarian trade-offs.

182 Moore, "Choice, Character, and Excuse" at 29; Duff, "Choice, Character, and Criminal Liability" at 346–48; Peter Aranella, "Convicting the Morally Blameless: Reassessing the Relationship between Legal and Moral Accountability" (1992) 39:6 *UCLA L Rev* 1511 at 1517–18.

183 *Ibid.*

184 *Ibid.*; Terry Skolnik, "Homelessness and the Impossibility to Obey the Law" (2016) 43:3 *Fordham Urb LJ* 741 at 745.

should control their law-abidingness so that coercion and punishment can be fairly attributed to them.[185] Punishment is more deserved when individuals enjoyed the greatest freedom to comply with the law's requirements. In such contexts, punishments more closely reflect the fact that individuals exercised their human agency to break the law and rejected available alternatives.

Furthermore, retributive justifications for these punishments are more legitimate when the State considers the defendant's personal circumstances and avoids entrenching them in homelessness.[186] Harsh punishments can enmesh individuals in homelessness where they will continue to suffer domination and are more likely to alleviate their needs on public property.[187] The State abdicates all three of its fiduciary duties – ending homelessness, protecting public property's value and securing liberty in the public sphere, and legitimizing laws that govern public property – when it imposes excessive sanctions that entrench persons in homelessness. Although individuals may deserve punishment for culpably violating laws that regulate public property, they do not deserve to become enmeshed in a condition that undermines their freedom and political equality.

This book's final chapter illustrates why day fines (or graduated economic sanctions) better ensure proportionate financial penalties that also consider unhoused persons' unique personal circumstances.[188] Day fines impose financial penalties that are calculated according to the gravity of the offense and a portion of the defendant's daily adjusted income.[189] They have been implemented successfully in European countries and in some US jurisdictions.[190] The final chapter demonstrates why graduated economic sanctions are a vital means to ensure that financial penalties do not entrench individuals in homelessness and to respect proportionality in sentencing.

The consequentialist justifications for unhoused persons' punishments are more legitimate when these sanctions are instrumentally rational. Consequentialist theories of punishment justify sanctions based on their future consequences, such as deterrence.[191] Similar to retributivism, human agency and free choice are central to consequentialism.[192] Deterrence is premised on the notion that individuals are

185 *Ibid.*

186 Terry Skolnik, "Rethinking Homeless People's Punishments" (2019) 22:1 *New Crim L Rev* 73 at 76.

187 *Ibid.*

188 Sally Hillsman, "Fines and Day Fines" (1990) 12 *Crime & Just* 49 at 76; Beth Colgan, "Graduating Economic Sanctions According to Ability to Pay" (2017) 103:1 *Iowa L Rev* 53 at 56.

189 Tapio Lappi-Seppälä, "Sentencing and Punishment in Finland: The Decline of the Repressive Ideal" in Michael Tonry and Richard Frase (eds.), *Sentencing and Sanctions in Western Countries* (Oxford University Press, 2001) at 94.

190 Susan Turner and Joan Petersilia, "Day Fines in Four U.S. Jurisdictions" (1996) at xv, www.ojp.gov/pdffiles1/pr/163409.pdf [perma.cc/9MUF-J9U9]; Beth Colgan, "Fines, Fees, and Forfeitures" (2017) 18 *Criminology, Crim Just L & Soc'y* 22 at 31.

191 Christopher Russell, "Deterring Retributivism: The Injustice of Justice Punishment" (2002) 96 *NW U L Rev* 843 at 857.

192 Antony Duff, *Punishment, Communication, and Community* (Oxford University Press, 2001) at 3–5; Andrew von Hirsch, *Censure and Sanctions* (Oxford University Press, 1991) at 13.

rational agents who consider the threat of punishment to guide their conduct.[193] The law excuses wrongdoing in contexts where the individual either lacked the capacity or fair opportunity to obey the law because the threat of punishment could not deter such conduct.[194]

The principle of instrumental rationality (or means–end proportionality) ensures that punishment is a rational means to achieve its consequentialist end.[195] Means–end proportionality typically focuses on whether the burdens of punishment outweigh its benefits.[196] The constraint of instrumental rationality is particularly important for punishments associated with laws that govern public property given their potential to entrench individuals in homelessness.[197] Since unhoused persons must alleviate their needs but lack free access to a private place to do so, even harsh punishments cannot deter their biologically necessary conduct when they lack reasonable alternatives to alleviating their needs on public property.[198] Moreover, punitive entrenchment can increase the risk that individuals alleviate their needs on public property rather than in private, which undermines the consequentialist justifications for such sanctions.[199]

Excessive sanctions violate both proportionality and instrumental rationality constraints for laws that govern public property and delegitimize consequentialist justifications for punishment. Disproportionate sanctions that entrench individuals in homelessness invites – rather than deters – recidivism associated with these laws.[200] Severe financial penalties also limit access to housing, and thus, reduce one's sphere of undominated choice to obey laws that regulate public property and increase the likelihood of future legal transgressions.[201] Excessive punishments are not a rational means to prevent unhoused persons from alleviating their needs on public property.

The State legitimizes coercion and punishment associated with laws that govern public property when it fulfils its other two fiduciary duties related to homelessness and public property. By fulfilling its first fiduciary duty to end homelessness, the State maximizes individuals' undominated choice to obey the law, which legitimizes coercion, political obligation, and retributive and consequentialist justifications for punishment.

Furthermore, when the State attempts to end homelessness and regulate public property, the State fulfils its second fiduciary duty to safeguard public property's

193 Duff, *Punishment, Communication, and Community* at 3–5; Von Hirsch, *Censure and Sanctions* at 13.
194 Sanford Kadish, "Excusing Crime" (1987) 75:1 *Cal L Rev* 257 at 263.
195 Richard Frase, "Limiting Excessive Prison Sentences under Federal and State Constitutions" (2008) 11:1 *U Pa J Const L* 39 at 43; Hamish Stewart, "*Bedford* and the Structure of Section 7" (2015) 60:3 *McGill LJ* 575 at 581 (discussing instrumental rationality as means–ends rationality).
196 Colton Fehr, "Instrumental Rationality and General Deterrence" (2019) 57:1 *Alta L Rev* 53 at 54.
197 Skolnik, "Rethinking Homeless People's Punishments" at 76.
198 Maria Foscarinis, "Downward Spiral: Homelessness and Its Criminalization" (1996) 14:1 *Yale L & Pol'y Rev* 1 at 58.
199 Skolnik, "Freedom and Access to Housing" at 236.
200 Skolnik, "Rethinking Homeless People's Punishment" at 76.
201 *Ibid.*

shared value and protect liberty in the public sphere. Individuals who have access to housing enjoy the undominated choice to obey the law and can freely alleviate their needs on private property rather than on public property, which maximizes its shared worth. Individuals who have access to housing create fewer negative externalities on public property and can use it on equal terms with others, such that all persons enjoy greater freedom in the public sphere.

Lastly, the State fulfils its first two fiduciary duties more optimally when it legitimizes the coercion and punishment associated with laws that govern public property. The State can more effectively end homelessness when it ensures that its punishments do not entrench individuals in that condition. By preventing punitive entrenchment, fewer individuals will alleviate their needs on public property, which safeguards its communal value and fosters liberty in the public sphere.

All three of these specific fiduciary duties related to homelessness and public property stem from the State's overarching fiduciary duty to counteract domination; a duty that flows from its fiduciary relationship with the people. And the fulfilment of this overarching duty is necessary to secure both liberty and political equality in the private and public spheres.

7.5 CONCLUSION

Building on the insights of republicanism and fiduciary theories of legal authority, this chapter demonstrated why the State and the people are in a fiduciary relationship with one another – a relationship that has been recognized in other areas of public law. It showed why this relationship justifies the State's three interrelated fiduciary duties related to homelessness and public property. Notably, the State has a fiduciary duty to end homelessness and treat unhoused persons with equal concern and respect, protect public property's shared value to secure liberty in the public sphere, and legitimize the coercion and punishment associated with laws that govern public property.

The next chapter demonstrates why this book's overarching theory is preferable to other coercive and ameliorative governmental mechanisms related to homelessness, such as increased shelter spaces, zoning modifications, concentration strategies, and dispersal tactics. It also shows why this book's fiduciary theory is more desirable and legitimate compared to encampments as a private self-help strategy.

8

In Defense of the State's Fiduciary Duties

The previous chapter demonstrated why the State has three fiduciary duties related to homelessness and public property: ending homelessness, protecting public property's role, and legitimizing coercion and punishment associated with laws that govern public property. It showed why these three duties flow from the State's overarching fiduciary obligation to prevent and counteract domination.

This chapter demonstrates why the State's fulfilment of its three fiduciary duties is preferable to other governmental and private mechanisms that address homelessness. The State may resort to ameliorative or coercive mechanisms to address homelessness, such as shelter space increases, zoning strategies, concentration tactics, and dispersal schemes. Yet each of these governmental mechanisms either exacerbates domination or fails to alleviate it. The State abdicates its three fiduciary obligations related to homelessness and public property – and its overarching fiduciary duty to redress domination – when it resorts to these alternatives.

This chapter then explores how unhoused persons have established tent encampments as a private self-help mechanism to protect themselves against domination and enjoy something that resembles a private property right. But as discussed further in Section 8.3, encampments cannot constitute a permanent and complete justification for appropriating public property.[1] Encampments are inconsistent with the core tenets of a property law regime. They undermine the potential of both private property and public property to neutralize domination. However, encampments can be temporarily and partially justifiable in certain contexts. Ultimately, the fact that individuals cannot justifiably establish permanent encampments as a self-help mechanism further underpins the State's fiduciary duty to end homelessness.

[1] These arguments were initially advanced in Terry Skolnik, "Homeless Encampments: A Philosophical Justification" (2023) 36 *JL & Soc Pol'y* 97.

8.1 SHELTER SPACE INCREASES

First, one might claim that cities can simply provide more shelters spaces and washrooms to redress homelessness and treat unhoused persons with greater concern and respect. According to this argument, individuals would enjoy greater freedom to obey laws that govern public property if they had more access to resources that promote law-abidingness and that constitute reasonable alternatives to lawbreaking. Chapter 2 demonstrated how this argument underpins certain successful constitutional challenges to laws that govern public property. For instance, courts have struck down laws that prohibit urban camping or sleeping on public property when there were too few shelter spaces to accommodate the city's unhoused population.[2] Conversely, courts have upheld these laws provided that sufficient shelter space was available.[3]

There are four important limitations to this argument. First, the argument construes homelessness as a reductive condition where individuals' needs are limited to survival and law-abidingness.[4] Purely quantitative assessments of available shelter space construe homelessness as a form of bare-life, which overlooks unhoused persons' wider needs and interests related to self-actualization, human flourishing, and independence.[5] Shelters may ensure that individuals are protected against the elements and can obey the law. Yet many shelters cannot provide the requisite privacy and safety that are necessary for human flourishing.[6] Moreover, many cannot accommodate couples and families, which limits individuals' intimacy and capacity to forge deeper relationships.[7] The claim that more shelter spaces and public washrooms can resolve homelessness tends to construe unhoused persons' liberty in purely negative terms.

Second, quantitative assessments regarding shelter availability may ignore the quality of resources that the State provides to unhoused persons.[8] Chapter 4 demonstrated how shelters may be unsanitary, dangerous, or overcrowded.[9] Individuals

2 *Pottinger* v. *City of Miami*, 810 F Supp 1551 (SD Fla 1992); *Jones* v. *City of Los Angeles*, 444 F (3d) 1118 (9th Circ 2006); *Martin* v. *City of Boise*, 902 F (3d) 1031 (9th Circ 2018); *Victoria (City)* v. *Adams*, 2009 BCCA 563; *Abbotsford (City)* v. *Shantz*, 2015 BCSC 1909.

3 *Joel* v. *City of Orlando*, 232 F (3d) 1353 at 1362 (11th Circ 2000).

4 Margaret Kohn, *Brave New Neighborhoods: The Privatization of Public Space* (New York: Routledge, 2004) at 136.

5 *Ibid.*; Leonard Feldman, *Citizens without Shelter: Homelessness, Democracy, and Political Exclusion* (Ithaca: Cornell University Press, 2004) at 58–59, 69.

6 Sara Rankin, "Hiding Homelessness: The Transcarceration of Homelessness" (2021) 109 *Cal L Rev* 559 at 585; Caryl Patrick, "Aboriginal Homelessness in Canada: A Literature Review" (2014) at 54, www.homelesshub.ca/sites/default/files/AboriginalLiteratureReview.pdf [perma.cc/8DXH-5MQM].

7 Amy Donley and James Wright, "Safer Outside: A Qualitative Exploration of Homeless People's Resistance to Homeless Shelters" (2012) 12:4 *J Forensic Psych Prac* 288 at 299.

8 Terry Skolnik, "How and Why Homeless People Are Regulated Differently" (2018) 43:2 *Queen's LJ* 297 at 317.

9 *See, e.g.*, Sara Rankin, "Punishing Homelessness" (2019) 22:1 *New Crim L Rev* 99 at 117; Michelle Moffa, Ryan Cronk, Donald Fejfar et al., "A Systematic Scoping Review of

may be reluctant to use public washrooms for similar reasons.[10] A strict emphasis on providing more shelter spaces and washrooms to unhoused persons may ignore the problem of nonegalitarian trade-offs that limit individual freedom.[11]

Third, individuals who must stay in a shelter still experience domination without interference. Individuals who must use shelters continue to depend on others' permission to access these spaces. They still lack a private power to exclude others and the authority to set the agenda over a private space in a manner that fosters autonomy. Individuals who have access to a shelter space may suffer less interference. But they continue to experience domination.

Fourth, the mere provision of more shelter spaces and public washrooms fails to secure unhoused persons' egalitarian status. Unhoused persons may feel stigmatized because they lack access to housing and must stay in a shelter.[12] Conversely, individuals may harbor stereotypes and prejudices against shelter residents.[13] Community members may also oppose homeless shelters due to fears that they increase disorder or crime in the neighborhood.[14] Opposition to homeless shelters is typically associated with concepts such as NIMBY (not in my back yard) and LULU (local undesirable land use).[15] Although shelters may confer important benefits to unhoused persons and to society more generally, a community's residents may oppose them because their costs are concentrated amongst few rightsholders.[16] Individuals may mobilize politically to block the construction or expansion of homeless shelters within the community.[17] Organizations may not receive zoning approval due to political and legal pressure from community groups.[18]

Environmental Health Conditions and Hygiene Behaviors in Homeless Shelters" (2019) 222:3 *Int'l J Hygiene & Env't Health* 335 at 345.

10 *See, e.g.*, Los Angeles Central Providers Collaborative, Skid Row Community Residents and Partners, "No Place to Go: An Audit of the Public Toilet Crisis in Skid Row" (2017) at 30–40, https://lafla.org/wp-content/uploads/2017/08/No-Place-To-Go-final.pdf [perma.cc/9FAR-H9A3].

11 Terry Skolnik, "Freedom and Access to Housing: Three Conceptions" (2018) 35 *Windsor YB Access Just* 226 at 241.

12 *See, e.g.*, Rachel Rayburn and Nicholas Guittar, "'This Is Where You Are Supposed to Be': How Homeless Individuals Cope with Stigma" (2013) 33:2 *Socio Spectrum* 159 at 160–62, 167 (providing an overview of the relationship between homelessness and stigma).

13 *See, e.g.*, Sarah Brinegar, "The Social Construction of Homeless Shelters in the Phoenix Area" (2003) 24:1 *Urb Geo* 61 at 62–63; John Belcher and Bruce R. DeForge, "Social Stigma and Homelessness: The Limits of Social Change" (2012) 22:8 *J Hum Behav in the Soc Env't* 929 at 930–31.

14 Vincent Lyon-Callo, "Making Sense of NIMBY: Poverty, Power and Community Opposition to Homeless Shelters" (2001) 13: 2 *City & Soc'y* 183 at 183, 189–91; Michael Gerrard, "The Victims of Nimby?" (1994) 21:3 *Fordham Urb LJ* 495 at 496.

15 Nicole Stelle Garnett, "Relocating Disorder" (2005) 91:5 *Va L Rev* 1075 at 1116; Carissa Schively, "Understanding the NIMBY and LULU Phenomena: Reassessing Our Knowledge Base and Informing Future Research" (2007) 21:3 *J Plan Literature* 255 at 256.

16 Vicki Been, "What's Fairness Got to Do with It? Environmental Justice and the Siting of Locally Undesirable Land Uses" (1993) 78:6 *Cornell L Rev* 1001 at 1001–02.

17 Deirdre Oakley, "Housing Homeless People: Local Mobilization of Federal Resources to Fight NIMBYism" (2002) 24:1 *J Urb Aff* 97 at 98.

18 *Ibid.*

These considerations demonstrate why individuals may view homeless shelters and their residents as problematic – a hallmark that unhoused persons lack the status of political equals. The simple provision of shelter spaces and public washrooms neither protects unhoused persons against domination nor treats them with equal concern and respect.

8.2 ZONING, CONCENTRATION, AND DISPERSAL STRATEGIES

8.2.1 *Zoning*

Others claim that zoning strategies can protect public property's communal worth – an approach that places greater emphasis on the regulation of public space rather than the alleviation of homelessness. Robert Ellickson has advanced a zoning scheme that attempts to confine low-level incivilities and nuisances to certain parts of the city.[19] He offers a thought experiment where cities could divide public property into three zones, each of which tolerate conduct that is prohibited by municipal ordinances to different degrees.[20] A small portion of the city's public spaces – roughly 5 percent – would be designated as a Green Zone that prohibits incivilities such as noise, panhandling, or sleeping on a park bench.[21] Most of the city's public property – approximately 90 percent – would be designated as Yellow Zones that allow periodic noise, public intoxication, or panhandling, but proscribe them in most contexts.[22] Lastly, a small portion of the city – roughly 5 percent – would be designated as a Red Zone that generally permits sleeping on a park bench, public intoxication, panhandling, and noise.[23]

Scholars have critiqued Ellickson's zoning strategy on various grounds. Jeremy Waldron notes that it would segregate unhoused persons to certain parts of the city and treat them as second-class citizens.[24] The dichotomy between Green Zones and Red Zones would reinforce rank-ordering between individuals.[25] Others, such as Stephen Munzer, posit that Ellickson's proposed zoning strategy can increase risks of violence to unhoused persons because unruly conduct would be concentrated within certain parts of the city.[26] Furthermore, Ellickson's proposed zoning scheme

19 Robert Ellickson, "Controlling Chronic Misconduct in City Spaces: Of Panhandlers, Skid Rows, and Public-Space Zoning" (1996) 105:5 *Yale LJ* 1165 at 1220–22.

20 *Ibid.*

21 *Ibid.* at 1221–22.

22 *Ibid.* at 1221.

23 *Ibid.*

24 Jeremy Waldron, "Property and Community: For Those Who Have Neither" (2009) 10:1 *Theor Inq L* 161 at 185.

25 *Ibid. See also* Sara Rankin, "The Influence of Exile" (2016) 76:1 *Md L Rev* 4 at 26–27.

26 Stephen Munzer, "Ellickson on 'Chronic Misconduct' in Urban Spaces: Of Panhandlers, Bench Squatters, and Day Laborers" (1997) 32:1 *Harv CR-CLL Rev* 1 at 28.

could be insulated against effective judicial review.[27] While municipal ordinances are frequently subject to constitutional review, formal and informal zoning schemes generally are not.[28] Lastly, Ellickson's proposed strategy could also exacerbate discrimination and the overpolicing of unhoused persons.[29] Police officers could selectively enforce certain laws against marginalized persons who are condensed within a confined area that is known to police.[30] For these reasons, the implementation of Ellickson's zoning proposal would increase various forms of domination that unhoused persons experience and fail to treat them with equal concern and respect.

8.2.2 *Concentration Strategies*

Consider concentration strategies next. Nicole Stelle Garnett observes that cities have employed concentration tactics and dispersal strategies to maximize public property's communal worth.[31] Historically, certain cities condensed a significant portion of the homeless population within a particular area of the city, such as Skid Row in Los Angeles.[32] The city concentrated services for unhoused persons within Skid Row to promote the downtown district's development.[33] Other cities have implemented homeless campuses that agglomerate various services within a small part of the city, such as shelter spaces, meals, showers, treatment facilities, and more.[34]

Like zoning policies that segregate unhoused persons to certain parts of the city, concentration strategies are objectionable for several reasons. For one, these strategies can be sited disproportionately within racialized or lower-income communities, which disparately impacts their residents and worsens inequality.[35]

27 Don Mitchell, *The Right to the City: Social Justice and the Fight for Public Space* (New York: Guilford Press, 2003) at 218.

28 Garnett, "Relocating Disorder" at 1087.

29 *See, e.g.*, Sheila Foster, "Collective Action and the Urban Commons" (2011) 87:1 *Notre Dame L Rev* 57 at 73.

30 *Ibid.*

31 Garnett, "Relocating Disorder" at 1077.

32 *Ibid.* at 1085–86.

33 *See, e.g.*, Alex Vitale, "The Safer Cities Initiative and the Removal of the Homeless: Reducing Crime or Promoting Gentrification on Los Angeles' Skid Row" (2010) 9:4 *Criminology & Pub Pol'y* 867 at 870–71; Deshonay Dozier, "Contested development: Homeless property, police reform, and resistance in Skid Row, LA" (2019) 43:1 *Int'l J Urb & Reg'l Rsch* 179 at 180–81; Bernard Harcourt, "Policing L.A.'s Skid Row: Crime and Real Estate Redevelopment in Downtown Los Angeles (An Experiment in Real Time)" (2005) *U Chicago Legal F* 325 at 391–92, citing Mike Davis, "Afterword – A Logic Like Hell's: Being Homeless in Los Angeles" (1991) 39:1 *UCLA L Rev* 325 at 328.

34 Garnett, "Relocating Disorder" at 1086; Nicole Stelle Garnett, *Ordering the City: Land Use, Policing, and the Restoration of Urban America* (New Haven: Yale University Press, 2010) at 101–02.

35 *See, e.g.*, Craig Anthony Arnold, "Planning Milagros: Environmental Justice and Land Use Regulation" (1998) 76:1 *Denv U L Rev* 1 at 24 (noting how certain types of local undesirable land uses may be confined to lower-income or racialized communities); Schively, "Understanding the NIMBY and LULU Phenomena" at 262; Madeline Halimi, "Siting Homeless Shelters in New York City: Fair Share versus Borough-Based" (2020) 47:5 *Fordham Urb LJ* 1519 at 1531.

Furthermore, tragedies of the commons can occur within areas that are subject to a concentration strategy.[36] Negative externalities – such as garbage, syringes, and human waste – can accumulate within areas that employ confinement tactics.[37] Concentration strategies impose significant costs on a limited number individuals who are within or near the concentration area: unhoused persons, business owners, and others.[38] Lastly, concentration strategies are problematic because they instrumentalize unhoused persons to safeguard others' liberty and to maximize the value of public property. Unhoused persons are disproportionately burdened with the negative externalities within areas so that these costs are not imposed on others.[39] For these reasons, confinement tactics fail to express equal concern and respect for unhoused persons because they treat them as means to an end. These strategies ignore that unhoused persons have a shared interest to enjoy equal liberty on public property, and to enjoy public space on equal terms with others.

8.2.3 *Dispersal Strategies*

Some cities attempt to safeguard public property's shared value through dispersal strategies. These strategies spread unhoused persons throughout the city rather than confine them to a particular area.[40] Dispersal strategies exist in various forms, such as trespass ordinances, exclusion orders, intensive ticketing practices, transjurisdictional transport, area restrictions (or Red Zones), and police sweeps.[41]

36 Munzer, "Ellickson on 'Chronic Misconduct' in Urban Spaces" at 28–29.

37 *See, e.g.*, Maylin Tu, "Skid Row's Toilet Crisis: How a Basic Necessity Became a Political Battle," The Guardian (December 12, 2022), www.theguardian.com/us-news/2022/dec/12/skid-row-toilets-los-angeles-homelessness [perma.cc/HXZ9-6JTX]; Los Angeles Central Providers Collaborative, "No Place to Go" at 8, 10; Steve Lopez, "The People Who Clean Skid Row Find Needles, Rats, the Occasional Corpse – and Deep Gratitude," LA Times (May 22, 2021), www.latimes.com/california/story/2021-05-22/la-skid-row-cleaning-benefits-homeless-provides-jobs [perma.cc/6673-GRJV].

38 Been, "What's Fairness Got to Do with It?" at 1001–02.

39 Munzer, "Ellickson on 'Chronic Misconduct' in Urban Spaces" at 28–29.

40 *See, e.g.*, Garnett, "Relocating Disorder" at 1077; Barrett Lee and Townsand Price-Spratlen "The Geography of Homelessness in American Communities: Concentration or Dispersion?" (2004) 3:1 *City & Comty* 3 at 3–4; Ben Alexander-Eitzman, David Pollio, and Carol North, "The Neighborhood Context of Homelessness" (2013) 103:4 *Am J Pub Health* 679 at 679.

41 *See, e.g.*, Don Mitchell and Nik Heynen, "The Geography of Survival and the Right to the City: Speculations on Surveillance, Legal Innovation, and the Criminalization of Intervention" (2009) 30:6 *Urb Geo* 611 at 621–22 (describing trespass ordinances); Marie-Eve Sylvestre, William Damon, Nicholas Blomley et al., "Spatial Tactics in Criminal Courts and the Politics of Legal Technicalities" (2015) 47:5 *Antipode* 1346 at 1347 (describing area restrictions); Katherine Beckett and Steve Herbert, "Penal Boundaries: Banishment and the Expansion of Punishment" (2010) 35:1 *L & Soc Inq* 1 at 6–7 (discussing park exclusion orders). Transjurisdictional transport (or dumping) refers to the police practice of transporting and dropping a person outside of a particular area. *See* William King and Thomas Dunn, "Dumping: Police-Initiated Transjurisdictional Transport of Troublesome Persons" (2004) 7:3 *Police Q* 339 at 341–42.

Katherine Beckett and Steve Herbert observe that cities employ quasi-criminal trespass orders and exclusion orders to regulate homelessness.[42] For instance, Seattle has used trespass admonishments and park exclusion orders that forbid some individuals from using certain parts of the city.[43] A trespass admonishment is an agreement between an individual or entity and the police, which authorizes officers to exclude certain individuals from public property.[44] Once the agreement is concluded, officers can exclude a trespasser without having to secure permission from the property owner in a particular situation.[45] Trespass admonishments can prohibit individuals from accessing certain public spaces, such as transportation facilities, community centers, and commercial establishments.[46] Individuals who violate these admonishments can be convicted of criminal trespassing.[47]

Park exclusion orders, for their part, proscribe certain individuals from entering one, several, or all parks within a city.[48] These exclusion orders can be imposed when individuals violated a municipal ordinance related to a park; for instance, because they camped or urinated in it.[49] Some cities' park exclusion orders can last for up to one year.[50] Like the violation of a trespass admonishment, the violation of a park exclusion order is a criminal offense.[51]

These types of quasi-criminal orders raise various concerns. First, these orders constitute a form of individualized criminal law that results in nonegalitarian coercion.[52] Notably, the State more heavily regulates and coerces individuals who are subject to these orders.[53] These orders prohibit only some individuals from engaging in conduct that is lawful for others.[54]

Second, trespass admonishments and park exclusion orders are problematic because they can circumvent traditional criminal law and procedure safeguards.[55] Police officers require probable cause that someone engaged in unlawful conduct to

42 Katherine Beckett and Steve Herbert, *Banished: The New Social Control in America* (Oxford University Press, 2009) at 64–65.

43 *Ibid.*

44 *Ibid.* at 51.

45 *Ibid.*

46 *Ibid.* at 50–51.

47 *Ibid.* at 51.

48 *Ibid.* at 47; Beckett and Herbert, "Penal Boundaries" at 7.

49 Beckett and Herbert, "Penal Boundaries" at 7.

50 *Ibid.*

51 *Ibid.*

52 *See, e.g.*, Peter Ramsay, "The Theory of Vulnerable Autonomy and the Legitimacy of Civil Preventative Orders" in Bernadette McSherry, Alan Norrie and Simon Bronitt (eds.), *Regulating Deviance: The Redirection of Criminalisation and the Futures of Criminal Law* (London: Hart, 2009) at 114.

53 Andrew Cornford, "Criminalising Anti-Social Behaviour" (2012) 6:1 *Crim L & Phil* 1 at 19.

54 Ramsay, "The Theory of Vulnerable Autonomy and the Legitimacy of Civil Preventative Orders" at 114.

55 *See* Adam Crawford, "Governing through Anti-Social Behaviour: Regulatory Challenges to Criminal Justice" (2009) 49:6 *Brit J Crim* 810 at 818 (noting that two-step orders can be used to circumvent burdens of proof or facilitate convictions).

lawfully arrest them.[56] And the prosecution must prove beyond a reasonable doubt that the defendant engaged in some type of unlawful conduct to secure a conviction.[57] Two-step orders, such as trespass admonishments and park exclusion orders, facilitate arrests and convictions and circumvent these safeguards. At the first step, these orders may be granted based on some type of unlawful conduct. But at the second step, an individual's unlawful presence – irrespective of whether they engaged in illegal activity – suffices for an arrest and criminal conviction.[58] The police can more easily arrest persons – and the prosecution can more easily convict them – based on proof of unlawful presence compared to proof of other types of unlawful conduct that are more difficult to establish and that may incorporate a more demanding fault requirement.[59]

Some cities employ intensive ticketing practices to disperse unhoused persons from public space.[60] For instance, in the city of Montreal, the number of municipal ordinance citations increased by 700 percent between 1994 and 2004.[61] Common offenses included public intoxication, consumption of alcohol on public property, loitering, and lying down on a bench or seat on transportation authority property.[62] The conduct underlying these offenses – being intoxicated, consuming alcohol, loitering, and lying down – are all lawful on private property. However, unhoused persons may violate these laws because they lack a private place to engage in such behavior lawfully.[63]

Intensive ticketing practices are objectionable for several reasons. For one, they contribute to punitive entrenchment.[64] The fines, fees, surcharges, and collateral consequences associated with fines decrease access to housing and increase the likelihood that unhoused persons will continue to violate municipal ordinances.[65] Moreover, intensive ticketing practices are ineffective because they fail to address the underlying reasons why individuals violate certain municipal ordinances, for

56 Aisha Jain, "Arrests as Regulation" (2015) 67 *Stan L Rev* 809 at 818.

57 In the United States, *see* Louis Bilionis, "Process, the Constitution, and Substantive Criminal Law" (1998) 96:5 *Mich L Rev* 1269 at 1304, citing *In re: Winship*, 397 US 358 (1970). In Canada, *see R* v. *Lifchus* [1997] 3 SCR 320.

58 Andrew Simester and Andrew von Hirsch, "Regulating Offensive Conduct through Two-Step Prohibitions" in Andrew Von Hirsch and Andrew Simester, *Incivilities: Regulating Offensive Behaviour* (London: Hart, 2006) at 175.

59 *See, e.g.*, Steve Herbert and Katherine Beckett, "'This Is Home for Us': Questioning Banishment from the Ground Up" (2010) 11:3 *Soc & Cultural Geo* 231 at 235.

60 *See, e.g.*, Catherine Chesnay, Céline Bellot, and Marie-Eve Sylvestre, "Taming Disorderly People One Ticket at a Time: The Penalization of Homelessness in Ontario and British Columbia" (2013) 55:2 *Can J Criminology & Crim Just* 161 at 162.

61 Céline Bellot and Marie-Eve Sylvestre, "La Judiciarisation de l'itinérance à Montréal: les dérives sécuritaires de la gestion pénale de la pauvreté" (2017) 47 *RGD* 11 at 20.

62 *Ibid.* at 23.

63 For an overview of this problem, see Chapters 3 and 4 of this book.

64 For an overview of this problem, see Chapter 6 of this book.

65 Terry Skolnik, "Rethinking Homeless People's Punishments" (2019) 22:1 *New Crim L Rev* 73 at 76, 82–83.

instance, because they lack of access to housing or suffer from substance use disorder.[66] Lastly, unhoused persons may move to more isolated locations to avoid being fined, which can result in various problems.[67] They may lack access to sanitation infrastructure, be unable to access resources that are designated for unhoused persons and become more vulnerable to physical or psychological harm.[68]

In some contexts, police officers engage in transjurisdictional transport – also referred to as "dumping" or "starlight tours" – to disperse unhoused persons.[69] As part of this unlawful and informal practice, police officers transport an individual outside of the jurisdiction and leave them in that location.[70] Transjurisdictional transport has been used in various provinces, such as Quebec, British Columbia, and Saskatchewan.[71] In Canada, Indigenous persons have been subject to transjurisdictional transport in various contexts.[72]

Transjurisdictional transport raises an array of concerns. It may subject unhoused persons to trauma, injury, or death.[73] Individuals who are transported to remote locations – especially in a state of intoxication – are vulnerable to being harmed, kidnapped, or killed by others. Moreover, the unlawful nature of transjurisdictional transport constitutes a form of tortious conduct – such as false imprisonment – or a criminal act – such as unlawful confinement, kidnapping, or criminal negligence.[74] And police officers have notoriously subjected Indigenous persons to starlight tours, which combine the wrongfulness of forcible confinement, displacement, and discrimination.[75]

Area restrictions (or Red Zones) raise other problems. These restrictions can be imposed as a bail condition pending trial for individuals who are charged with a crime.[76] Marie-Eve Sylvestre, Céline Bellot, and Nicholas Blomley have shown

66 *See, e.g.*, Terry Skolnik, "Homelessness and the Impossibility to Obey the Law" (2016) 43:3 *Fordham Urb LJ* 41 at 749–50. Although the article focuses primarily on need-alleviating conduct that is biologically necessary, similar arguments apply to other types of acts, especially those associated with substance use disorder.

67 *Abbotsford (City)* v. *Shantz*, 2015 BCSC 1909 at para. 213.

68 *Ibid.*

69 King and Dunn, "Dumping" at 341–42.

70 *Ibid.*

71 Public Inquiry Commission on Relations between Indigenous Peoples and Certain Public Services in Québec, *Listening, Reconciliation, and Progress: Final Report* (Quebec: Government of Quebec, 2019) at 15, 282–83, www.cerp.gouv.qc.ca/fileadmin/Fichiers_clients/Rapport/Final_report.pdf; Pamela Palmater, "Shining Light on the Dark Places: Addressing Police Racism and Sexualized Violence against Indigenous Women and Girls in the National Inquiry" (2016) 28:2 *Can J Women & L* 253 at 265; David Tanovich, "E-Racing Racial Profiling" (2004) 41:4 *Alta L Rev* 905, note 17 in the text.

72 Tanovich, "E-Racing Racial Profiling," note 17 in the text.

73 *Ibid.*

74 *See, e.g.*, Laura Brown, "He Who Controls the Mind Controls the Body: False Imprisonment, Religious Cults, and the Destruction of Volitional Capacity" (1991) 25:3 *Val U L Rev* 407 at 421; Criminal Code, RSC 1985, c. C-46, ss. 279(1) (kidnapping) and 219 (criminal negligence).

75 Tanovich, "E-Racing Racial Profiling," note 17 in the text.

76 Sylvestre et al., "Spatial Tactics in Criminal Courts and the Politics of Legal Technicalities" at 1360–61.

that unhoused defendants may be prohibited from entering a certain perimeter within a city – or can be excluded from an entire city – as a bail condition.[77] Like trespass admonishments and park exclusion orders, Red Zones result in nonegalitarian coercion because only some individuals cannot engage in conduct that is lawful for others. Area restriction orders also result in nonegalitarian sacrifices. People experiencing homelessness may not be able to access resources or services – such as safe injection sites, shelters, or treatment centers – that are within the prohibited perimeter.[78] Furthermore, the violation of these orders can exacerbate punitive entrenchment. Bail breaches may result in additional criminal charges, convictions, or punishment.[79]

Lastly, cities may employ sweeps (or crackdowns) to safeguard public property's value.[80] For instance, cities have dismantled homeless encampments, which disperses people experiencing homelessness to other parts of the city.[81] Encampment sweeps raise a host of concerns. Police officers may confiscate or destroy unhoused persons' property during these sweeps, including government issued identification, sleeping bags, tents, and medication.[82] Individuals may have difficulty renting an apartment, opening a bank account, or securing employment without governmental identification.[83] They must also pay the costs to replace their lost, confiscated, or destroyed property, which detracts from their money to pay rent.

Furthermore, certain studies indicate that encampment sweeps are not an effective deterrent. Scholars conducted a survey study of homeless encampment residents in Honolulu that evaluated how police sweeps affected their decision to stay at a homeless shelter.[84] Roughly 21 percent of respondents reported that they were less

77 Marie-Eve Sylvestre, Nicolas Blomley and Céline Bellot, *Red Zones: Criminal Law and the Territorial Governance of Marginalized People* (Cambridge University Press, 2019) at 12 (providing an overview of red zones); Marie-Eve Sylvestre, Nicolas Blomley, and Céline Bellot, "Une Peine avant judgement? La mise en liberté provisoire et la réforme du droit pénal canadien" in Julie Desrosiers, Margarida Garcia and Marie-Ève Sylvestre (eds.), *Réformer le droit criminel au Canada: défis et possibilités* (Cowansville: Éditions Yvon Blais, 2017) at 195–96.

78 Sylvestre, Blomley, and Bellot, *Red Zones* at 4, 170.

79 *Ibid.* at 107.

80 Mila Sahoni, "Crackdowns" (2017) 103 *Va L Rev* 31 at 33–34 (defining crackdowns and their core features); Garnett, "Relocating Disorder" at 1102; Farida Ali, "Limiting the Poor's Right to Public Space: Criminalizing Homelessness in California" (2014) 21:2 *Geo J Poverty L & Pol'y* 197 at 215–16; Marc Roark, "Homelessness at the Cathedral" (2015) 80 *Mo L Rev* 53 at 103.

81 *See, e.g.*, Eric Tars, Heather Maria Johnson, Tristia Bauman et al., "Can I Get Some Remedy: Criminalization of Homelessness and the Obligation to Provide an Effective Remedy" (2014) 45:3 *Colum HRLR* 738 at 747–48, citing *Kincaid* v. *City of Fresno* (ED Cal 2008).

82 Rankin, "Punishing Homelessness" at 112–14; Sara Rankin, "Civilly Criminalizing Homelessness" (2021) 56:2 *Harv CR-CLL Rev* 367 at 394; Chris Herring, Dilara Yarbrough, and Lisa Marie Alatorre, "Pervasive Penality: How the Criminalization of Poverty Perpetuates Homelessness" (2020) 67 *Soc Probs* 131 at 140; Ben McJunkin, "Homelessness, Indignity, and the Promise of Mandatory Citations for Urban Camping" (2020) 52:3 *Ariz St LJ* 955 at 965.

83 *See, e.g.*, Jennifer Darrah-Okike, Sarah Soakai, Susan Nakaoka et al., "'It Was Like I Lost Everything': The Harmful Impacts of Homeless-Targeted Policies" (2018) 28:4 *Hous Pol'y Debate* 635 at 646.

84 Tai Dunson-Strane and Sarah Soakai, *The Effects of City Sweeps and Sit-Lie Policies on Honolulu's Houseless* (Minoa: Department of Urban and Regional Planning, University of Hawai'i at Mānoa,

inclined to stay at a shelter following a sweep, while 68 percent reported that the sweep did not impact their decision to sleep on public property.[85] Sweeps and the dismantling of encampments – especially when cities do not offer support to encampment residents – displace unhoused persons to a new location rather than alleviate homelessness.[86] Outreach workers may be unable to locate and assist unhoused persons who are displaced following a sweep.[87] Emotionally salient dispersal strategies may decrease individuals' trust in the police and in local governments.[88] Yet unhoused persons' trust in outreach workers and other personnel is an important factor that can help them secure access to housing.[89] Police sweeps worsen domination and fail to treat unhoused persons with concern and respect.

8.3 ENCAMPMENTS

Others contend that homeless encampments – or tent cities – are a viable temporary solution to homelessness while individuals lack access to housing.[90] To be clear, these scholars do not suggest that encampments are a permanent solution to homelessness or a substitute for housing. Instead, they posit that encampments confer various benefits to unhoused persons and acknowledge that encampments also result in various problems.[91]

This section shows how encampments cannot constitute a complete justification for appropriating public property because they result in various problems and are inconsistent with the property law regime.[92] The term "justification" implies that acts which are normally wrong are morally acceptable in the

2015) at 19, www.yumpu.com/en/document/read/55342338/honolulus-houseless-tai-dunson-strane-and-sarah-soakai [perma.cc/44J4-CEE5].

85 *Ibid.*

86 Rebecca Cohen, Will Yetvin, and Jill Khadduri, "Understanding Encampments of People Experiencing Homelessness and Community Responses: Emerging Evidence as of Late 2018" (2019) at 13, www.huduser.gov/portal/sites/default/files/pdf/Understanding-Encampments.pdf [perma.cc/4ZG6-VV7C].

87 Erika Smith, "He Had to Leave Echo Park Lake and He's Still Homeless. Is This What L.A. Wants?" LA Times (March 26, 2022), www.latimes.com/california/story/2021–03–27/echo-park-homeless-camp-gone-la-crisis [perma.cc/99QG-2UT4].

88 Chris Herring, "Complaint-Oriented Policing: Regulating Homelessness in Public Space" (2019) 84:5 *Am Socio Rev* 769 at 775; Ombudsman Toronto, "Ombudsman Toronto Interim Report: Investigation into the City's Process for Clearing Encampments in 2021" (July 2022) at 10, 18, www.ombudsmantoronto.ca/Investigative-Work/Early-Recommendations-to-Improve-City-Response-to.aspx [perma.cc/ALV2-884D].

89 Christopher Weare, "Housing Outcomes for Homeless Individuals in Street Outreach Compared to Shelter" (2021) 25:6 *J Poverty* 543 at 556.

90 *See, e.g.*, Zeo Loftus-Farren, "Tent Cities: An Interim Solution to Homelessness and Affordable Housing Shortages in the United States" (2011) 99:4 *Cal L Rev* 1037 at 1040; Samir Junejo, "No Rest for the Wary: Why Cities Should Embrace Homeless Encampments" (2016) at 1, https://digitalcommons.law.seattleu.edu/cgi/viewcontent.cgi?article=1006&context=hrap [perma.cc/KS5L-329Q].

91 Loftus-Farren, "Tent Cities" at 1040; Junejo, "No Rest for the Wary" at 1, 10.

92 *Ibid.* This argument was first advanced in Skolnik, "Homeless Encampments" at 110–16.

circumstances.[93] A complete justification would connote that unhoused persons can appropriate property permanently when they lack other reasonable alternatives.[94]

But encampments can operate as a partial justification in some circumstances. A partial justification denotes that unhoused persons can establish temporary encampments when no other reasonable options exist and the encampment's benefits outweigh its burdens.[95] The partially justifiable nature of encampments – a concept acknowledged by judicial decisions – limits the State's capacity to lawfully displace, coerce, or punish encampment residents who lack adequate alternatives in certain circumstances.[96]

The partial justifiability of encampments also underpins the State's fiduciary duty to end homelessness; a duty that must be fulfilled for the State to regulate public property and legitimize laws that govern public space. The State must end homelessness because individuals cannot justifiably establish permanent encampments as a self-help mechanism.

8.3.1 *The Benefits of Encampments for Unhoused Persons*

Encampments can be partially justifiable because they protect unhoused persons fundamental interests when the State abdicates its fiduciary duty to end homelessness. Tent encampments confer various benefits to people experiencing homelessness.[97] For one, in contrast to shelters or sleeping alone on public property, encampments may better protect unhoused persons' safety and property.[98] Encampments provide "safety in numbers" that residents would not otherwise enjoy.[99] Encampments may also devise governing rules and regulations that aim to safeguard their inhabitants.[100] They may also use security guards – or impose

93 *Perka* v. *The Queen* [1984] 2 SCR 232 at 247, citing Herbert Packer, *The Limits of the Criminal Sanction* (Stanford University Press, 1968) at 113. *See also* Albin Eser, "Justification and Excuse" (1976) 24:4 *Am J Comp L* 621 at 622; Mitchell Berman, "Justification and Excuse, Law and Morality" (2003) 53:1 *Duke LJ* 1 at 3–4, citing George Fletcher, "The Right and the Reasonable" (1985) 98 *Harv L Rev* 949 at 954–55; George Fletcher, *Rethinking Criminal Law* (Oxford University Press, 2000) at 759.

94 Skolnik, "Homeless Encampments" at 110–16.

95 *Ibid.* at 98.

96 *Ibid.*

97 Many scholars have advanced these arguments. *See, e.g.*, Skolnik, "Homeless Encampments" at 107–08. *See also* Junejo, "No Rest for the Wary" at 7–14; Cohen, Yetvin, and Khadduri, "Understanding Encampments of People Experiencing Homelessness and Community Responses" at 4–6; Loftus-Farren, "Tent Cities" at 1050–57.

98 *See, e.g.*, Chris Herring and Manuel Lutz, "The Roots and Implications of the USA's Homeless Tent Cities" (2015) 19:5 *City* 689 at 695.

99 *Ibid.*

100 *Ibid.* at 697.

security duties on residents – to maximize residents' safety.[101] These security mechanisms allow encampment residents to store more property in a tent city compared to in other public spaces.[102]

Second, encampments provide a degree of stability, predictability, and autonomy that unhoused persons may not otherwise enjoy.[103] Whereas some unhoused persons must find a new place to sleep each night, encampment residents may consistently stay in the same place surrounded by friends and acquaintances.[104] Furthermore, some cities provide sanitation infrastructure and other resources to assist encampment residents, such that they have free access to a place to alleviate their basic needs.[105] Whereas shelters may impose strict rules and regulations, reach capacity limits, or refuse entry to individuals, encampment residents may be subject to fewer regulations and may benefit from greater autonomy.[106]

Third, encampments offer a sense of belonging and community.[107] Encampment residents may mutually assist one other and offer vital social and emotional support.[108] They may form strong friendship bonds because they are experiencing a similar situation.[109] Samir Junejo notes that certain self-governing aspects of encampments aim to promote a sense of community.[110] Notably, residents may be required to sign an agreement that they will abide by the encampments' rules and regulations, which aim to foster mutual respect, cooperation, and cohesion.[111] Furthermore, some encampments mandate that residents perform various duties – security, maintenance, cleaning – as part of their individual and communal responsibilities.[112] And unlike shelters, encampments may allow individuals to stay with their partners and pets.[113]

Fourth, compared to homeless shelters, individuals may enjoy more positive, negative, and republican liberty within encampments. Despite their informality and impermanent nature, encampments aim to provide many of the same benefits

101 Herring and Lutz, "The Roots and Implications of the USA's Homeless Tent Cities" at 695; Tony Sparks, "Citizens without Property: Informality and Political Agency in a Seattle, Washington Homeless Encampment" (2017) 49:1 *Env't & Plan* 86 at 94–95.

102 Junejo, "No Rest for the Wary" at 12.

103 Chris Herring, "The New Logics of Homeless Seclusion: Homeless Encampments in America's West Coast Cities" (2014) 13:4 *City & Comty* 285 at 296.

104 Junejo, "No Rest for the Wary" at 11.

105 Cohen, Yetvin, and Khadduri, "Understanding Encampments of People Experiencing Homelessness and Community Responses" at 5.

106 Junejo, "No Rest for the Wary" at 12–13.

107 *Ibid.* at 11–12; Jessie Speer, "The Rise of the Tent Ward: Homeless Camps in the Era of Mass Incarceration" (2018) 62 *Pol Geog* 160 at 166.

108 Junejo, "No Rest for the Wary" at 11–12.

109 Jamie Suki Chang, Philip Boo Riley, Robert Aguirre et al., "Harms of Encampment Abatements on the Health of Unhoused People" (2022) 2 *SSM-Qualitative Rsch in Health* 1 at 4.

110 Junejo, "No Rest for the Wary" at 11–12.

111 *Ibid.*

112 *Ibid.*

113 *Ibid.*

of housing.[114] As discussed earlier, individuals may benefit from more privacy, security, and stability within encampments, all of which promote positive liberty as self-actualization. In contrast to individuals who sleep alone on public property, encampment residents may suffer less interference from police officers and from others, which secures negative liberty. They can lawfully do certain things within their tent that are prohibited in public, such as engaging in intimate acts or consuming alcohol. And given the stable nature of encampments, residents may enjoy something akin to an informal power to exclude others from their tent, and to be safeguarded against others' private power of exclusion.

8.3.2 *Problems Associated with Encampments*

Encampments also raise important concerns and result in various problems that militate against their justifiability. First, encampments can generate public health concerns.[115] Human waste, garbage, and syringes can accumulate within and around encampments.[116] For instance, sanitation and environment workers cleared an encampment in Echo Park, Los Angeles, that was comprised of roughly 160 tents.[117] The workers cleared approximately 35 tons of trash from the area.[118] This included roughly 700 lbs of biological waste, including 180 lbs of feces and 564 lbs of urine.[119] The workers also cleared 300 lbs of hazardous waste and 30 lbs of drug paraphernalia.[120] Volunteers have recovered thousands of syringes from areas that were used as an encampment in Everett, Washington.[121] Feces and garbage have also

114 David Jenkins and Kimberley Brownlee, "What a Home Does" (2022) 41 *L & Phil* 441 at 465; Skolnik, "Homeless Encampments" at 107–08.

115 Anna Gorman and Kaiser Health News, "Medieval Diseases Are Infecting California's Homeless," The Atlantic (March 8, 2019), www.theatlantic.com/health/archive/2019/03/typhus-tuberculosis-medieval-diseases-spreading-homeless/584380/ [perma.cc/PA8N-43GJ].

116 *See, e.g.*, Benjamin Oreskes, "After Personal Effects Were Retrieved, Workers Collected 35 Tons of Trash at Echo Park Lake," LA Times (May 6, 2021), www.latimes.com/homeless-housing/story/2021–05–06/sanitation-workers-amass-35-tons-trash-echo-park-lake [perma.cc/AQ9U-E3AY]; Karena Walter, "'I'm a Gardener. I Wasn't Hired to Clean up Human Waste': Societal Issues Taking Toll on St. Catharines Municipal Workers," St. Catharines Standard (May 18, 2022), www.stcatharinesstandard.ca/news/council/2022/05/18/im-a-gardener-i-wasnt-hired-to-clean-up-human-waste-societal-issues-taking-toll-on-st-catharines-municipal-workers.html [perma.cc/9M6X-QGL8]; Heather Knight, "Poop. Needles. Rats. Homeless Camp Pushes SF Neighborhood to the Edge," San Francisco Chronicle (June 24, 2018), www.sfchronicle.com/news/article/Neighbors-disgusted-over-despair-on-block-hit-13015964.php [perma.cc/RNQ2-QMYJ].

117 Oreskes, "After Personal Effects Were Retrieved."

118 *Ibid.* For an overview of these statistics, see LA Sanitation, "CD-13: Echo Park Metrics: Total Solid Waste Collected," https://ca-times.brightspotcdn.com/8d/82/069134a548b0a39b1ea57b2d7c88/cd-13-echo-park-metrics-mar-26-27-2021.pdf [perma.cc/D9L4-WT8U].

119 Oreskes, "After Personal Effects Were Retrieved." As the Los Angeles Times notes, these amounts do not include "feces and urine from portable or stationary restrooms at the park."

120 *Ibid.*

121 Caleb Hutton and Diana Hefley, "Recovering Addicts Bag Thousands of Needles at Everett Camp," HeraldNet (October 24, 2017), www.heraldnet.com/news/some-damage-undone-thousands-of-heroin-needles-removed/ [perma.cc/M39V-USNQ].

accumulated in other homeless encampments.[122] Infectious diseases may propagate within tent cities that lack adequate sanitation infrastructure and resources.[123] Diseases such as Hepatitis A, Typhus, and Shigella bacteria outbreaks have occurred within encampments.[124] Vermin infestations may also occur in tent cities.[125] Certain infectious diseases may spread to encampment residents through infected fleas who feed on rats.[126]

Second, encampments can be dangerous.[127] Encampment residents may experience violence, threats, or harassment during their stay.[128] And other individuals may be subject to these same realities from encampment residents.[129] Some cities have experienced a rise of shootings in homeless encampments.[130] Encampments can also pose fire risks for their residents and for individuals in surrounding areas.[131] Some unhoused persons have died from fires that occurred within an encampment.[132] Others risk carbon monoxide poisoning when they heat their

122 Thomas Fuller, "San Francisco Wants Homeless to Leave Tent Camp, but Some Vow to Fight," NY Times (February 26, 2016), www.nytimes.com/2016/02/27/us/san-francisco-wants-homeless-to-leave-tent-camp-but-some-vow-to-fight.html [perma.cc/XJ6N-AVRW].

123 Gorman and Kaiser Health News, "Medieval Diseases Are Infecting California's Homeless"; Michael Cousineau, "Health Status of and Access to Health Services by Residents of Urban Encampments in Los Angeles" (1997) 8:1 *J Health Care for the Poor and Underserved* 70 at 80.

124 Gorman and Kaiser Health News, "Medieval Diseases Are Infecting California's Homeless"; Karen Bartko, "Shigella Outbreak Spreading through Edmonton's Homeless Population: 'We've Got 3rd-World Conditions'," Global News (October 19, 2022), https://globalnews.ca/news/9212073/edmonton-inner-city-shigella-outbreak-2022/ [perma.cc/3GDT-TC9Y].

125 The Canadian Press, "Halifax Prepared to Use Police to Clear Park Encampment after Other Efforts Fail," CTV News (August 5, 2022), https://halifax.citynews.ca/nova-scotia-news/halifax-prepared-to-use-police-to-clear-park-encampment-after-other-efforts-fail-5659369 [perma.cc/PG6Z-RFCJ].

126 Gorman and Kaiser Health News, "Medieval Diseases Are Infecting California's Homeless."

127 Adam Zivo, "Crime at Homeless Encampments Is Becoming a National Problem," National Post (July 23, 2022), https://nationalpost.com/opinion/adam-zivo-crime-at-homeless-encampments-is-becoming-a-national-problem [perma.cc/P6ZG-2A44]; *Black et al.* v. *City of Toronto*, 2020 ONSC 6398 at para. 105.

128 *Black et al.* v. *City of Toronto*, 2020 ONSC 6398 at para. 209; *British Columbia* v. *Adamson*, 2016 BCSC 1245 at paras. 79–80.

129 *Poff* v. *City of Hamilton*, 2021 ONSC 7224 at para. 209; Gary Wrath, "'Our Hands Are Tied.' Incidents of Homeless Violence Raise Concerns," San Diego Tribune (January 8, 2023), www.sandiegouniontribune.com/news/homelessness/story/2023-01-08/philanthropic-group-adds-homeless-mans-violent-attack-to-list-of-shipwrecks [perma.cc/7UPN-WSAW].

130 Greg Kim, "Shootings in Seattle Are Increasing. Shootings Connected to Homelessness Are Increasing Faster," Seattle Times (June 30, 2022), www.seattletimes.com/seattle-news/homeless/shootings-in-seattle-are-increasing-shootings-connected-to-homelessness-are-increasing-faster/ [perma.cc/EC29-48XR].

131 *Poff* v. *City of Hamilton*, 2021 ONSC 7224 at paras. 192, 198, 208; *Saanich (District)* v. *Brett*, 2018 BCSC 1648 at paras. 111–16.

132 Isaac Callan, "Encampment Fire at Toronto Cell Tower Leaves One Dead: Police, Fire Officials," Global News (January 7, 2023), https://globalnews.ca/news/9394266/liberty-village-encampment-fire-toronto/ [perma.cc/LD68-V4RY].

tents during winter months.[133] Police officers have also seized firearms and stolen property from encampments.[134]

Third, encampments can generate negative economic repercussions for businesses, cities, and other individuals. Encampments in urban areas can adversely impact local business and tourism.[135] Customers may be less willing to frequent businesses that are difficult to access due to tents, tarps, and other objects that obstruct sidewalks.[136] Encampments residents may occupy the spaces in front of businesses and engage in conduct – such as drug use, loitering, or sidewalk sitting – that disincentivizes patrons from frequenting them.[137] Some business owners that are in proximity to encampments have experienced property damage, vandalism, threats, and harassment.[138]

Cities bear financial costs related to encampments. The price to clean up encampment sites can be high.[139] St. Catharines, Ontario – a city of roughly 136,000 people – paid approximately $128,000 of cleaning fees related to

133 Jack Morse, "Charlottetown Homeless Encampment Set to Be Knocked Down," CTV News (January 24, 2023), https://atlantic.ctvnews.ca/charlottetown-homeless-encampment-set-to-be-knocked-down-1.6244588 [perma.cc/NQ38-CVRC]; The Associated Press, "Delaware State Police: 4 Found Dead in Tent at Homeless Camp," (February 19, 2020), www.thestar.com/news/world/us/2020/02/19/delaware-state-police-4-found-dead-in-tent-at-homeless-camp.html [perma.cc/D4T5-V8W6].

134 *See, e.g.*, Kendra Mangione, "'Guns Infiltrate Tent City', Vancouver Police Say Amid Controversial Teardown," CTV News (August 22, 2022), https://bc.ctvnews.ca/guns-infiltrate-tent-city-vancouver-police-say-amid-controversial-teardown-1.6037561 [perma.cc/74VJ-7RCU]; Doyle Potenteau, "Weapons, Stolen Property Seized in Homeless Camp by Kelowna RCMP," Global News (September 13, 2022), https://globalnews.ca/news/9126043/homeless-camp-weapons-stolen-property-kelowna/ [perma.cc/6XXQ-LT74]; Felicia Alvarez, "$100,000 in Stolen Tools, Guns Found in San Jose Homeless Bunker," LA Times (July 14, 2022), www.latimes.com/california/story/2022–07–14/san-jose-police-discover-homeless-bunker-with-100k-in-stolen-guns-tools [perma.cc/8YDX-KXEL].

135 Sharon Chamard, "Homeless Encampments," Problem-Oriented Guides for Police Problem-Specific Guides Series No. 56 at 9, https://popcenter.asu.edu/sites/default/files/problems/pdfs/homeless_encampments.pdf [perma.cc/EGE3-NAN2]; Sarah Grochowski, "Concerns Flare about Vancouver Tent City Scaring Away Tourism from Local Businesses," Vancouver Sun (July 22, 2022), https://vancouversun.com/news/local-news/concerns-flare-about-vancouver-tent-city-scaring-away-tourism-from-local-businesses [perma.cc/96UX-XG6H].

136 Chamard, "Homeless Encampments" at 9.

137 *Ibid.*, citing Blair Berkley and John Thayer, "Policing Entertainment Districts" (2009) 23:4 *Policing: Int'l J Police Strategy & Mgmt* 466 at 476; Kaitlin Miller, "South Nashville Businesses Dealing with Trash, Glass, and Human Feces Daily," WZTV Nashville (December 6, 2022), https://fox17.com/features/high-cost-of-homelessness/south-nashville-businesses-dealing-with-trash-glass-and-human-feces-daily-high-cost-of-homelessness-middle-tennessee-nashville-feature-news [perma.cc/FKW8-REJ4].

138 Kate Bueckert, "Business Owners Near Kitchener Encampment Call on Region to Provide More Security," CBC News (July 19, 2022), www.cbc.ca/news/canada/kitchener-waterloo/business-owners-kitchener-encampment-more-security-call-1.6533964 [perma.cc/UQX8-SYUH].

139 Lauren Dunton, Jill Khadduri, Kimberly Burnett et al., "Exploring Homelessness among People Living in Encampments and Associated Cost: City Approaches to Encampments and What They Cost" (2020) at 31–32, www.huduser.gov/portal/sites/default/files/pdf/Exploring-Homelessness-Among-People.pdf [perma.cc/HKN2-H8GZ] [Dunton, Khadduri, Burnett et al., "Exploring Homelessness"].

encampments in 2021.[140] While the City of Chicago paid approximately $3.4 million to address encampments during the 2019 fiscal year, San Jose paid roughly $8.6 million to do so.[141]

Fourth, encampments can limit others' use of public property. Encampments in urban areas may block sidewalks, which can create dangers and difficulties for individuals with mobility issues.[142] Individuals may be unable to use public parks, squares, or other areas that are occupied by encampments.[143] Encampment residents who reside in public parks may also engage in conduct that undermines the park's use as an inclusive space for all, such as public urination and defecation, indecent exposure, public intercourse, and so on.[144]

Fifth, encampments can generate environmental risks and cause damage that necessitates remediation. An unhoused man who unlawfully camped in the Uncompahgre National Forest, Colorado, generated roughly 8,500 lbs of garbage.[145] The clean-up required a helicopter and forty-eight volunteers.[146] The individual was eventually sentenced to six months' imprisonment.[147] Unlawful encampments in Chilliwack resulted in similar consequences. Twenty-five helicopter loads were required to remove the garbage that accumulated at the encampment.[148] The encampments created environmental threats. Garbage and

140 Walter, "I'm a Gardener"; City of St. Catharines, "Demographics," www.stcatharines.ca/en/business-and-economic-development/demographics.aspx [perma.cc/BP4H-T9AS]. The City's website lists St. Catharines' population at 136,803 in 2021.

141 Kriston Capps, "The High Cost of Clearing Tent Cities," Bloomberg News (April 12, 2021), www.bloomberg.com/news/articles/2021–04–12/the-high-cost-of-clearing-homeless-encampments [perma.cc/BRM3-FNEA]; Dunton, Khadduri, Burnett et al, "Exploring Homelessness" at 31–32.

142 *See, e.g.*, Frances Bula, "Vancouver Tent Encampment Leaves City to Figure Out Better Way to Confront Housing Crisis," Globe and Mail (September 24, 2022), www.theglobeandmail.com/canada/british-columbia/article-vancouver-tent-encampment-leaves-city-to-figure-out-better-way-to/ [perma.cc/QS8P-AMSV].

143 *See, e.g.*, Rosie DiManno, "Homelessness Is a Complex Issue, and Encampment Dwellers Deserve Sympathy – but Parks Are for Public Use, Not Tents," Toronto Star (July 19, 2022), www.thestar.com/opinion/star-columnists/2022/07/19/homelessness-is-a-complex-issue-and-encampment-dwellers-deserve-sympathy-but-parks-are-for-public-use-not-tents.html [perma.cc/N6LA-5GL2].

144 The San Diego Tribune Editorial Board, "Opinion: The Closure of a Chula Vista Park that Became a Homeless Camp Needs to Be a Campaign Issue," San Diego Tribune (September 1, 2022), www.sandiegouniontribune.com/opinion/editorials/story/2022–09–01/chula-vista-harborside-park-elementary-school-homeless-camp-sex-drugs-defecation [perma.cc/385P-87TT].

145 Lee Cerveny and Joshua Baur, "Homelessness and Nonrecreational Camping on National Forests and Grasslands in the United States: Law Enforcement Perspectives and Regional Trends" (2020) 118:2 *J Forestry* 139 at 140.

146 *Ibid.*

147 Janet Oravetz, "Man Dumps 8,500 Pounds of Trash in National Forest," USA Today (September 18, 2015), www.usatoday.com/story/news/nation-now/2015/09/18/man-dumps-8500-pounds-trash-national-forest/72392102/ [perma.cc/7W6M-TX6J]. Oravetz notes that the individual was convicted of "residing on National Forest System Lands."

148 Glenda Luymes, "'Frustration': Volunteers Clean Up One Abandoned Chilliwack Encampment as Another Pops Up," Vancouver Sun (December 30, 2022), https://vancouversun.com/news/merry-go-round-of-frustration-volunteers-clear-garbage-at-one-abandoned-encampment-and-another-pops-up [perma.cc/CSQ7-HZQC].

waste risked polluting the river and traveling downstream.[149] Encampments in forests can create fire safety risks in environmentally sensitive areas.[150] Volunteers cleared over 6,000 lbs of garbage from an abandoned homeless encampment along the James Lake Forest Service Road in British Columbia.[151] Human waste from encampment residents can also contaminate adjacent waterways and creeks.[152]

8.3.3 *Encampments, Justification, and Necessity*

Although encampments protect unhoused persons' fundamental interests, they cannot operate as complete justification for appropriating property permanently.[153] Encampments operate much like the necessity defense in criminal justice contexts – a defense that is conceptualized as a justification in jurisdictions such as the United States and England and Wales.[154] Three general conditions must be satisfied for a defendant to invoke the necessity defense successfully.[155] First, the individual violated the law to avoid impending harm or death.[156] Second, the individual lacked a reasonable lawful alternative to violating the law.[157] Third, the harm inflicted through lawbreaking must be comparable or less serious than the harm that the individual averted if they would have obeyed the law.[158]

There are two principal reasons why encampments cannot operate as a complete justificatory defense in contexts of extreme need. First, as Jeremy Waldron argues, the necessity defense applies in contexts where individuals challenge the

149 *Ibid.*; Shannon Paterson, "Garbage from Homeless Camps Could End Up in Chilliwack River," CTV News (November 6, 2019), https://bc.ctvnews.ca/garbage-from-homeless-camps-could-end-up-in-chilliwack-river-1.4673765 [perma.cc/L3W3-67US].

150 Luymes, "Frustration."

151 Victoria Femia, "Task Force Undertakes Clean-Up at Abandoned Homeless Camp," CTV News (July 9, 2022), https://globalnews.ca/news/8978850/task-force-undertakes-clean-up-at-abandoned-homeless-camp/ [perma.cc/2YFB-6W2G].

152 Nichole Fiore, Will Yetvin, Kimberly Burnett et al., "San Jose, California: Community Encampment Report" (US Department of Housing and Urban Development, 2020) at 2, www.huduser.gov/portal/sites/default/files/pdf/SanJose-Encampment-Report.pdf [perma.cc/H66F-ST5A].

153 Skolnik, "Homeless Encampments" at 113–14.

154 *Ibid.* In the United States, *see, e.g.*, Berman, "Justification and Excuse, Law and Morality" at 6; Model Penal Code, § 3.02 (1985). In England and Wales, *see* David Ormerod and Karl Laird, *Smith, Hogan, and Ormerod's Criminal Law*, 16th ed. (Oxford University Press, 2021) at 398. Note that other jurisdictions, such as Canada, conceptualize necessity as an excuse, which concedes the wrongfulness of the conduct but absolves the defendant from conviction and punishment because they lacked the free choice to obey the law. *See, e.g.*, *Perka* v. *The Queen* [1984] 2 SCR 232 at 248.

155 Note that Canadian and American law impose similar requirements for the necessity defense. In Canada, *see Perka* v. *The Queen* [1984] 2 SCR 232 at 260; David Paciocco, "No-One Wants to Be Eaten: The Logic and Experience of the Law of Necessity and Duress" (2010) 56:3 *Crim LQ* 240 at 254. In the United States, see Model Penal Code, § 3.02(1) and 2 (1985); Paul Robinson and Markus Dubber, "The American Model Penal Code: A Brief Overview" (2007) 10:3 *New Crim L Rev* 319 at 337–38.

156 *Perka* v. *The Queen* [1984] 2 SCR 232 at 260.

157 *Ibid.*

158 *Ibid.*

overinclusiveness of legal rules rather than a distributive justice scheme.[159] For instance, the law prohibits individuals from breaking and entering into others' private property.[160] Yet the necessity defense can succeed where a lost hiker breaks into another's cabin so that they do not suffer hypothermia or die.[161] The necessity defense applies to mitigate the crime of breaking and entering's overinclusiveness; namely, that it does not create an exception for individuals who break and enter into another's private property to avoid serious harm during an emergency.

Permanent encampments, however, challenge the property law system's distributive justice scheme rather than the overinclusiveness of a particular rule.[162] The complete justifiability of encampments would modify the property law system's allocative scheme from market-based transactions to appropriation based on individual need.[163] This explains why the necessity defense is generally restricted to one-off emergencies that exemplify a rule's overinclusiveness rather than chronic situations where necessity can be invoked repeatedly to counteract a distributive scheme's unjustness.[164] Although a lost hiker can invoke the necessity defense successfully when they break into another's cabin during an acute emergency, the defense will be rejected if they appropriate another's cabin due to chronic poverty.[165]

Second, encampments cannot constitute a complete justification for appropriating public property because they unilaterally limit others' liberty without consent or authority.[166] If encampments operated as a complete justification, an individual could unilaterally confer themselves a private property right over public space replete with a private power to exclude others.[167] In doing so, they would attempt to exercise public powers that individuals lack. Notably, encampment residents would unliterally dictate which land does and does not constitute public property in a manner that binds all – a public power that the State exercises as part of its fiduciary duty to safeguard public property.[168] Furthermore, encampment residents would also attempt to exercise the equivalent of a public power to confer themselves a need-based private property right that binds all and that operates in parallel with

159 Jeremy Waldron, "Why Indigence Is Not a Justification" in William Kleinig and John Heffernan (eds.), *From Social Justice to Criminal Justice: Poverty and the Administration of Criminal Law* (Oxford University Press, 2000) at 105–06.

160 *See, e.g.*, Criminal Code, RSC 1985, c. C-46, s. 348.

161 *Perka* v. *The Queen* [1984] 2 SCR 232 at 249; Terry Skolnik, "Three Problems with Duress and Moral Involuntariness" (2016) 63 *Crim LQ* 124 at 128.

162 Waldron, "Why Indigence Is Not a Justification" at 109.

163 *Ibid.*

164 Ian Howard Dennis, "On Necessity as a Defence to Crime: Possibilities, Problems and the Limits of Justification and Excuse" (2009) 3:1 *Crim L & Phil* 29 at 35 (noting that necessity applies to one-off emergencies); Skolnik, "Homelessness and the Impossibility to Obey the Law" at 777–78.

165 Skolnik, "Homelessness and the Impossibility to Obey the Law" at 777–78.

166 Skolnik, "Homeless Encampments" at 112–13.

167 *Ibid.*

168 *Ibid. See also* Arthur Ripstein, "Private Order and Public Justice: Kant and Rawls" (2006) 92:7 *Va L Rev* 1391 at 1427.

a market-based property system.[169] In doing so, encampment residents would unilaterally limit others' freedom to use public property without consent or authority. Yet as discussed in the previous chapter, the State has the public power to establish a mutually binding system of property rights that binds all and does not constitute domination.[170]

These types of concerns explain why courts have rejected the necessity defense when individuals appropriated property due to extreme need. The English Court of Appeal decision *Southwark London Borough Council* v. *Williams* is the most notable example.[171] In *Williams* a group of unhoused individuals appropriated unused housing that belonged to the city's borough council.[172] The individuals repaired some of the housing units.[173] Approximately 9,000 individuals were on a waiting list to access the borough's housing.[174] The city sought possession of the housing units. In response, the defendants invoked the necessity defense.[175] The court rejected the claim for various reasons. Lord Denning noted that the necessity defense would result in a slippery slope that undermines the property law system's allocative function.[176] He suggested that the expansion of the necessity defense could invite anarchy and disorder.[177] In his view, some individuals would argue that their needs were greater than those of others to appropriate their property.[178] He posited that others could create situations of need to acquire property through means other than market exchanges.[179] The court rejected the defendant's claims for these reasons.

8.3.4 *Homeless Encampments As a Partial Justification*

Although encampments cannot constitute a complete justification for permanently appropriating public property, they may be temporarily and partially justifiable in certain circumstances.[180] A partial justification connotes that unhoused persons can establish temporary encampments in certain places when they lack adequate alternatives, provided the benefits of encampments outweigh their burdens.[181] Furthermore, certain judicial decisions acknowledge how encampments can be

169 Skolnik, "Homeless Encampments" at 112–13.
170 *See, e.g.*, Arthur Ripstein, "Property and Sovereignty: How to Tell the Difference" (2017) 18:2 *Theor Inq L* 243 at 256–57.
171 *Southwark London Borough Council* v. *Williams* [1971] 2 WLR 467. *See also* Eduardo Moises Penalver and Sonia K. Katyal, "Property Outlaws" (2007) 155:5 *Pa L Rev* 1095 at 1174–75.
172 *Southwark London Borough Council* v. *Williams* [1971] 2 WLR 467 at 470–71.
173 *Ibid.*
174 *Ibid.*
175 *Ibid.* at 472–73.
176 *Ibid.* at 473.
177 *Ibid.*
178 *Ibid.*
179 *Ibid.*
180 Skolnik, "Homeless Encampments" at 110–16.
181 *Ibid.*

partially justifiable on a temporary basis when no other reasonable alternatives exist.[182]

Several interrelated considerations explain why encampments may be partially justifiable in certain contexts.[183] First, they are partially justified in response to the State's failure to accommodate unhoused persons within the property system and protect them against domination.[184] Unhoused persons are unilaterally vulnerable to others' power of exclusion and to threats of interference by others, including risks of theft and violence.[185] Yet individuals who reside in encampments enjoy something like an informal power of exclusion and informal protection against others' exclusionary power, both of which strive to protect their fundamental interests and counteract horizontal domination.[186] For instance, encampment residents may protect one another's physical safety, guard each other's property, and exclude individuals from the encampment because they violated its rules.[187]

Similarly, encampments safeguard their residents against vertical forms of domination. Encampment residents may enjoy greater freedom to alleviate their basic needs in tent cities without having to rely on others' permission to access private property. Individuals who reside in encampments may also be subject to fewer nonegalitarian trade-offs. In contrast to shelter residents, encampment residents may be able to alleviate their basic needs without having to risk their health, safety, or property.[188] They may enjoy more freedom because cities may not enforce certain laws that govern public property within encampments.[189]

Encampments can be partially justifiable in certain circumstances because the State abdicates both its overarching duty to protect individuals against domination, and its specific fiduciary duty to end homelessness.[190] Encampments may help safeguard individuals against domination because the State does not fulfil its duty to do so.[191] Individuals establish encampments to redress the State's failure to

182 *Ibid.*

183 *Ibid.*, where these arguments were initially advanced.

184 *Ibid.*

185 Christopher Essert, "Property and Homelessness" (2016) 44 *Phil & Pub Aff* 266 at 266.

186 Skolnik, "Homeless Encampments."

187 Cohen, Yetvin, and Khadduri, "Understanding Encampments of People Experiencing Homelessness and Community Responses" at 5; Sparks, "Citizens without Property" at 94–95 (describing security duty within encampments); Loftus-Farren, "Tent Cities" at 1053, 1056–57; Justin Patrick Jones, Khalia Parish, Peter Radu et al., "Alternatives to Unsanctioned Homeless Encampments: A Report for the City of Oakland from the Goldman School of Public Policy" (2015) at 50, https://gspp.berkeley.edu/assets/uploads/page/15-13160_-_Goldman_Student_Report_-_Final_Draft_-_May_11_2015_reduced_size.pdf.pdf [perma.cc/Q7QY-LK5F]; *The Regional Municipality of Waterloo* v. *Persons Unknown and to be Ascertained*, 2023 ONSC 670 at para. 23.

188 Loftus-Farren, "Tent Cities" at 1055–56.

189 Herring, "The New Logics of Homeless Seclusion" at 294–25; Herring and Lutz, "The Roots and Implications of the USA's Homeless Tent Cities" at 694.

190 Skolnik, "Homeless Encampments" at 110–11.

191 *Ibid.*

accommodate unhoused persons within two systems of mutual coercion that secure liberty: the private property system and the public property system.[192]

Second and interrelatedly, encampments may be partially justifiable in certain circumstances because they informally redistribute some of the property law system's benefits and burdens.[193] Previous chapters demonstrated how unhoused persons disproportionately bear the property law system's burdens but enjoy few of its benefits.[194] Notably, they must constantly fulfil duties not to interfere with others' private property and are constantly subject to others' power of exclusion.[195] Yet others owe no reciprocal duty of noninterference to unhoused persons because they lack private property rights.[196] By conferring something like an informal power to exclude others and informal protection against others' power, encampments may unofficially confer benefits and powers to unhoused persons that they would otherwise lack.[197] To be clear, this power and protection is both limited and informal. But it may be more than what unhoused persons enjoy when they do not stay in encampments.

Third, the primacy of human life over property may partially justify temporary encampments in certain contexts. Encampments may be the only way for individuals to protect their most fundamental needs – such as health, safety, and well-being – because they lack other reasonable alternatives. Like the defense of necessity, the partial justifiability of encampments acknowledges that the sanctity of human life is more important than property.[198] In some contexts, public property's role and communal value must temporarily yield to the sanctity of human life where individuals lack access to alternatives that protect their most basic interests.

The partial justifiability of an encampment is conditional to various factors: the availability of adequate shelter space, the placement of the encampment, and a proportionality assessment regarding the benefits and burdens associated with the encampment for its residents and for others.[199] In other words, encampments can be more or less justifiable depending on the totality of the circumstances. The partial justifiability of encampments is conditional because it applies only in contexts where individuals lack access to alternatives, such as access to housing or to

192 *Ibid.*

193 *Ibid.*

194 Jane Baron, "Homelessness as a Property Problem" (2004) 36:2 *Urb Law* 273 at 287; Jane Baron, "Property and No Property" (2006) 42:5 *Hous L Rev* 1425 at 1427, 1448; Jeremy Waldron, "Community and Property – For Those Who Have Neither" (2008) 10:1 *Theor Inq L* 161 at 164–67; Jeremy Waldron, "Property, Justification and Need" (1993) 6:2 *Can JL & Jur* 185 at 193.

195 Waldron, "Community and Property – For Those Who Have Neither" at 189.

196 *Ibid.*

197 Skolnik, "Homeless Encampments."

198 *See, e.g.*, Abraham Maslow, "A Theory of Human Motivation" (1943) 50 *Psych Rev* 370 at 372–85; Andrew von Hirsch and Nils Jareborg, "Gauging Harm: A Living Standards Analysis" (1991) 11:1 *Oxford J Leg Stud* 1 at 17.

199 *Ibid.* See Sections 8.3.1 and 8.3.2 (discussing the benefits and burdens of encampments).

adequate shelter space.[200] This partial justifiability is temporary because encampments cannot constitute a complete and permanent justification for appropriating public property for the reasons discussed above.[201] And the right is circumstantial because encampments are more justifiable in some locations – such as in parks or lots – rather than others – on busy city streets or in locations that block access to essential services.[202]

Two interrelated consequences flow from the partial justifiability of encampments in certain circumstances. First, partial justifications may limit the State's capacity to displace, coerce, or punish unhoused persons who establish encampments because they lack adequate alternatives.[203] Second and interrelatedly, the partial justifiability of encampments may confer a conditional, temporal, and limited right to set up tents on public property when no other alternatives are available, provided the encampment's benefits outweigh its burdens.[204]

Courts have recognized that encampments can constitute a partial and temporary justification for occupying public property when unhoused persons lack other reasonable alternatives.[205] Certain examples illustrate this point. Some courts invalidate laws that comprehensively prohibited urban camping when there was insufficient shelter space for a city's unhoused population.[206] In doing so, these courts recognized that individuals enjoy a conditional and limited right to establish encampments to protect their fundamental interests when no other reasonable options were available.[207] For instance, some judicial decisions permitted unhoused persons to erect tents during nighttime but required these tents to be dismantled during daytime.[208] More recently, certain courts have struck down an urban camping ban and decided that unhoused persons can maintain encampments during daytime when they lacked access to other alternatives.[209] Other courts have refused to grant an injunction to clear an encampment in contexts where individuals lacked access to other alternatives, and where the encampment's benefits outweighed its detrimental effects.[210]

200 *See, e.g., Victoria (City)* v. *Adams*, 2009 BCCA 563 at paras. 75, 129; *Abbotsford (City)* v. *Shantz*, 2015 BCSC 1909 at paras. 82, 131–32; *The Regional Municipality of Waterloo* v. *Persons Unknown and to be Ascertained*, 2023 ONSC 670 at paras. 92–94.

201 Section 8.3.3.

202 *Victoria (City)* v. *Adams*, 2009 BCCA 563; *Abbotsford (City)* v. *Shantz*, 2015 BCSC 1909.

203 *See, e.g., Victoria (City)* v. *Adams*, 2009 BCCA 563; *Abbotsford (City)* v. *Shantz*, 2015 BCSC 1909; *The Regional Municipality of Waterloo* v. *Persons Unknown and to be Ascertained*, 2023 ONSC 670.

204 Skolnik, "Homeless Encampments" at 115–16; *The Regional Municipality of Waterloo* v. *Persons Unknown and to be Ascertained*, 2023 ONSC 670 at para. 82.

205 Skolnik, "Homeless Encampments" at 114–16.

206 *Victoria (City)* v. *Adams*, 2009 BCCA 563; *Abbotsford (City)* v. *Shantz*, 2015 BCSC 1909.

207 *The Regional Municipality of Waterloo* v. *Persons Unknown and to be Ascertained*, 2023 ONSC 670 at paras. 81–82.

208 *Ibid.*

209 *Ibid.* at para. 105.

210 *British Columbia* v. *Adamson*, 2016 BCSC 584.

These types of decisions exemplify the partial, temporary, and circumstantial justifiability of encampments in certain contexts. These decisions limit the State's capacity to prohibit encampments when the State abdicates its fiduciary duty to end homelessness, such that there are too few shelter spaces for the city's unhoused population. Conversely, these types of decisions recognize a conditional, temporal, and limited right to establish encampments when the State does not fulfil its fiduciary duty to end homelessness.

Ultimately, the partial justifiability of encampments further underpins the State's duty to end homelessness. The State must fulfil this obligation because individuals cannot unconditionally establish permanent encampments to protect their interests and safeguard themselves against domination. The next chapter shows how the State fulfils this fiduciary duty when it addresses the risk factors associated with homelessness, improves access to housing, and provides emergency shelters and other interim resources until individuals become housed.

8.4 CONCLUSION

This chapter demonstrated why certain ameliorative and coercive mechanisms related to homelessness fail to alleviate domination. These mechanisms include shelter space increases, zoning proposals, concentration strategies, dispersal tactics, and encampments. It showed why the State fails to fulfil its fiduciary duties related to homelessness and public property when it employs these mechanisms.

The concluding parts of this chapter showed why encampments are not a complete and permanent justification for appropriating public property due to extreme need. Although encampments safeguard unhoused persons' fundamental interests, tent cities result in various problems and are inconsistent with the property system. Yet encampments can be partially and temporarily justifiable in certain circumstances when the State abdicates its fiduciary duty to end homelessness, such that individuals lack access to housing or to adequate shelter spaces.

Ultimately, the fact that individuals cannot justifiably establish permanent encampments as a self-help mechanism further supports the State's fiduciary duty to end homelessness. Against this backdrop, the following chapter advances concrete proposals for how the State can better fulfil its three fiduciary duties related to homelessness and public property: the duties to end homelessness, safeguard public property's role and value, and legitimize laws that govern the urban commons.

9

Fulfilling the State's Fiduciary Duties

How can the State fulfil its three fiduciary duties related to homelessness and public property? How can the State end homelessness and treat unhoused persons with equal respect, protect public property's communal worth, and legitimize laws that govern public space? And how can the State safeguard unhoused persons against domination?

This chapter aims to answer these questions. The opening parts of this chapter highlight the connection between the State's fiduciary duty to end homelessness and its fiduciary duties to safeguard public property and legitimize the laws that govern it. It then sets out why the duty to end homelessness and treat unhoused persons with equal respect is comprised of three interrelated elements: the obligations to address the risk factors associated with homelessness, improve access to housing, and provide shelters and other interim resources until individuals become housed.

Later parts of the chapter provide a set of concrete proposals that illustrate how the State may attempt to fulfil its three fiduciary duties related to homelessness and public property. Laws that govern public property treat individuals with greater respect when the State alleviates homelessness and mitigates nonegalitarian coercion and punitive entrenchment. In doing so, the State can increasingly fulfil its three fiduciary duties discussed above, and ultimately, better respect its overarching fiduciary obligation to redress domination.

9.1 THE RELATIONSHIP BETWEEN THE STATE'S THREE FIDUCIARY DUTIES

The State's three fiduciary duties related to homelessness and public property are inextricably intertwined. The fiduciary duty to end homelessness and treat unhoused persons with equal respect must be fulfilled for the State to satisfy its other fiduciary obligations to protect public property's value and to legitimize the laws that regulate it. The interconnection between the State's three fiduciary duties related to homelessness and public property – and its overarching duty to counteract domination – can be summarized as follows.

First, the State must end homelessness and treat unhoused persons with equal respect to prevent and neutralize domination. Individuals who have access to housing are subject to less horizontal and vertical domination.[1] Housed persons are protected against others' private power of exclusion and are safeguarded against the disparate enforcement of laws that govern public property.[2] They do not consistently depend on others to obey laws that regulate public space and are subject to fewer nonegalitarian trade-offs as the price to comply with these laws.[3] Ultimately, individuals who enjoy access to housing are better safeguarded against nonegalitarian coercion and punitive entrenchment.[4]

Second, the State must end homelessness and treat unhoused persons with equal respect to fulfil its fiduciary duty to maintain public property's shared value.[5] Individuals who have access to housing enjoy greater freedom to alleviate their needs on private property rather than on public property, which increases public property's shared worth and reduces negative externalities in public spaces.[6]

Access to housing is fundamental because it optimally absorbs negative externalities that would otherwise occur on public property.[7] Individuals who alleviate their needs in public enjoy the benefits of their conduct, bear little to none of its costs, and diffuse these costs onto many other persons.[8] In contrast, individuals who alleviate their needs within their home enjoy the benefits of that conduct and impose no negative externalities onto others.[9] Individuals are encouraged to alleviate their needs properly within their homes – for instance, by performing their bodily functions in their bathrooms rather than elsewhere in their homes – because they will principally bear the costs of such conduct. For these reasons, a home can internalize the costs of need-alleviating conduct so that they are not imposed onto others. Access to housing encourages rightsholders to alleviate their needs within

1 *See, e.g.*, Terry Skolnik, "Freedom and Access to Housing: Three Conceptions" (2018) 35 *Windsor YB Access Just* 226 at 240–41.

2 *See, e.g.*, Terry Skolnik, "How and Why Homeless People Are Regulated Differently" (2018) 43:2 *Queen's LJ* 297 at 313–23; Christopher Essert, "Property and Homelessness" (2016) 44 *Phil & Pub Aff* 266 at 266, 276 (describing how private property rights protect individuals against horizontal domination).

3 Skolnik, "Freedom and Access to Housing" at 240–41.

4 *Ibid.*; Terry Skolnik, "Homelessness and Unconstitutional Discrimination" (2019) 15 *JL & Equal* 69 at 89; Terry Skolnik, "Rethinking Homeless People's Punishments" (2019) 22 *New Crim L Rev* 73 at 82–83.

5 Skolnik, "Freedom and Access to Housing" at 240.

6 *Ibid.* at 240.

7 *See, e.g.*, Harold Damsetz, "Towards a Theory of Property Rights" (1967) 57:2 *American Economic Rev* 347 at 348 (describing how private property internalizes externalities); Lee Anne Fennell, "Property and Half-Torts" (2007) 116:7 *Yale LJ* 1400 at 1442–43 (noting how private property contains the effects of certain conduct).

8 Robert Ellickson, "Controlling Chronic Misconduct in City Spaces: Of Panhandlers, Skid Rows, and Public-Space Zoning" (1996) 105:5 *Yale LJ* 1165 at 1177 (noting how certain conduct on public property can affect many other persons).

9 *See, e.g.*, Gideon Parchomovsky and Peter Siegelman, "Cities, Property, and Positive Externalities" (2012) 54 *Wm & Mary L Rev* 211 at 223.

their homes in a manner that imposes the fewest costs onto all persons. The State will better protect public property's value when it ensures access to housing that internalizes negative externalities that would otherwise occur on public property.[10] Housed persons can freely alleviate their needs on private property and are not required to do so in public space.

Third, access to housing ensures that individuals enjoy maximal freedom to comply with laws that regulate public space and avoid coercion and punishment, which legitimizes these laws.[11] Individuals who have access to housing have the greatest undominated choice to obey the law, and their law-abidingness is less subject to others' external control.[12] Housed persons may be subject to fewer nonegalitarian trade-offs as the price to obey laws that govern public property.[13] And they enjoy more protection against the State's capacity to regulate, police, and punish their need-alleviating acts.[14] As discussed in previous chapters, housing provides greater physical and legal protection against surveillance, searches, intrusions, and law enforcement actions.[15]

The State's fiduciary duty to end homelessness and treat unhoused persons with equal respect is a keystone fiduciary obligation that must be fulfilled so that the State respects its other fiduciary duties.[16] Individuals will continue to experience horizontal and vertical domination when they lack access to housing.[17] Furthermore, since individuals must alleviate their needs somewhere, the State cannot protect public property's role optimally unless it ensures that individuals are housed. Laws that govern public property will continue to lack legitimacy so long as they subject individuals to nonegalitarian coercion and punitive entrenchment. The fulfilment of the fiduciary duty to alleviate homelessness is a precondition to the fulfilment of the State's other fiduciary duties related to homelessness and public property.

9.2 THE STATE'S FIDUCIARY DUTY TO END HOMELESSNESS

9.2.1 *The Scope of the State's Fiduciary Duty to End Homelessness*

The State's first fiduciary obligation – the duty to end homelessness and treat unhoused persons with equal respect – is comprised of three elements, each of

10 *See, e.g.*, Skolnik, "Freedom and Access to Housing" at 240.

11 *See, e.g.*, Terry Skolnik, "Homelessness and the Impossibility to Obey the Law" (2016) 43:3 *Fordham Urb LJ* 741 at 742 (noting that laws are less legitimate when individuals lack the fair opportunity to obey them).

12 Skolnik, "Freedom and Access to Housing" at 240.

13 *Ibid.* at 241.

14 Skolnik, "How and Why Homeless People Are Regulated Differently" at 319–23.

15 *See* Chapter 5 of this book; Benjamin Barros, "The Home as a Legal Concept" (2006) 46 *Santa Clara L Rev* 255 at 263–69.

16 *See, e.g.*, Carol Rose, "Property as the Keystone Right" (1996) 71:3 *Notre Dame L Rev* 329 at 333–61 (discussing different reasons why property functions as a keystone right that protects other interests).

17 Skolnik, "Freedom and Access to Housing" at 240–41.

which secures freedom differently and protects individuals against domination in distinct ways. First, the State must address the risk factors associated with homelessness. The unhoused population is heterogeneous and has diverse needs.[18] Even if the State provides access to housing, many individuals require additional support to remain housed. For instance, individuals who obtain access to housing may require extensive mental health support.[19] Studies indicate that individuals with complex needs are more likely to remain housed when they have both access to housing and additional support mechanisms, such as Assertive Community Treatment that assists individuals with complex mental health needs.[20] Other studies suggest that individuals who are provided with access to housing may reexperience homelessness when they are not given necessary support, such as mental health care, treatment for substance use disorder, a primary physician, and greater income or employment opportunities.[21] Ending homelessness requires the State to respond to both a lack of access to housing and the risk factors associated with homelessness.

Second, the State must provide access to housing for individuals who lack the capacity to acquire it and who cannot safeguard themselves against domination. The State can fulfil this duty through different means. The State can provide rental housing subsidies – such as a housing voucher program – that secures access to housing and prevents many lower-income individuals from experiencing homelessness.[22] In other contexts, the State must do more to ensure that individuals can maintain access to housing and enjoy nondomination. More specifically, the State must provide access to some form of housing when voucher programs will not suffice to alleviate homelessness. Housing First programs may help individuals in such contexts.[23]

Third, the State must provide access to shelters and other resources to assist individuals who suddenly experience homelessness or who require interim

[18] Patrick Fowler, Peter Hovmand, Katherine Marcal et al., "Solving Homelessness from a Complex Systems Perspective: Insights for Prevention Responses" (2019) 40 *Ann Rev Pub Health* 465 at 467–68.

[19] *Ibid.*

[20] Tim Aubry, Sam Tsemberis, Carol Adair et al., "One-Year Outcomes of a Randomized Controlled Trial of Housing First with ACT in Five Canadian Cities" (2015) 66:5 *Psychiatr Serv* 463 at 463; Tim Aubry, Sam Tsemberis, Carol Adair et al., "Effectiveness of Permanent Supportive Housing and Income Assistance Interventions for Homeless Individuals in High-Income Countries: A Systematic Review" (2020) 5 *Lancet Pub Health* e342 at e344–47.

[21] Maryann Roebuck, Ayda Agha, Geoffrey Nelson et al., "Predictors of Housing Instability and Stability among Housing First Participants: A 24-Month Study" (2023) J Soc Distress & Homelessness 1 at 6–8.

[22] *See, e.g.*, Dallas Augustine and Margot Kushel, "Community Supervision, Housing Insecurity, and Homelessness" (2022) 701:1 *Annals AAPSS* 152 at 163; Michelle Wood, Jennifer Turnham, and Gregory Mills, "Housing Affordability and Family Well-Being: Results from the Housing Voucher Evaluation" (2008) 19:2 *Hous Pol'y Debate* 367 at 381–83.

[23] Aubry, Tsemberis, Adair et al., "Effectiveness of Permanent Supportive Housing and Income Assistance Interventions for Homeless Individuals in High-Income Countries" at e342, e356–57; Maria Raven, Matthew Niedzwiecki, and Margot Kushel, "A Randomized Trial of Permanent Supportive Housing for Chronically Homeless Persons with High Use of Publicly Funded Services" (2020) 55 *Health Serv Rsch* 797 at 804.

resources until they become housed. Shelters provide emergency services in contexts where individuals lose access to housing.[24] They also identify the need for various resources that can help individuals become housed, such as mental health services, treatment for substance use disorder, and access to housing and employment programs.[25] Studies indicate that homelessness is more frequently transitory than chronic.[26] Individuals may unexpectedly require access to an emergency shelter for various reasons.[27] For instance, they may experience homelessness due to interpersonal conflict, domestic violence, eviction, criminal charges or convictions, or health challenges.[28] The State better fulfils its fiduciary duty to end homelessness and treat unhoused persons with greater respect when it provides emergency shelter and interim resources that assist individuals until they become housed.

9.2.2 *Mechanisms That Address Risk Factors Associated with Homelessness*

The State can address certain risk factors associated with homelessness through different mechanisms, such as Assertive Community Treatment, outreach teams, Intensive Case Management, Critical Time Intervention, culturally sensitive and inclusive services, and reentry programs – many of which have been explored in depth by Carol Caton.[29] The mechanisms explored in this section draw significantly on her insightful scholarship. To be clear, these mechanisms are not intended to be exhaustive given the heterogeneity of the unhoused population, and given each unhoused person's distinct needs. Nor can these mechanisms address every risk factor related to homelessness. Other useful services, programs, and resources also assist people experiencing homelessness. Yet these mechanisms exemplify different ways in which the State can address homelessness and its risk factors.

24 Elizabeth Hopper, Ellen Bassuk, and Jeffrey Olivet, "Shelter from the Storm: Trauma-Informed Care in Homelessness Services Settings" (2010) 3 *Open Health Serv Pol'y J* 80 at 81.

25 Jon Erickson and Charles Wilhelm, "Introduction" in John Erickson and Charles Wilhelm (eds.), *Housing the Homeless* (New York: Routledge, 2017) at xxviii.

26 Amy Donley, Denise Crisafi, Alyssa Mullins et al., "How Stable Is the Condition of Family Homelessness?" (2017) 54 *Soc'y* 46 at 46–47; Christopher Weare, "Housing Outcomes for Homeless Individuals in Street Outreach Compared to Shelter" (2021) 25:6 *J Poverty* 543 at 557.

27 Barrett Lee, Marybeth Shinn, and Dennis Culhane, "Homelessness as a Moving Target" (2021) 693:1 *Annals AAPSS* 8 at 15.

28 *See, e.g.*, Elisa Fisher and Amanda Stylianou "To Stay or to Leave: Factors Influencing Victims' Decisions to Stay or Leave a Domestic Violence Emergency Shelter" (2019) 34:4 *J Interpersonal Violence* 785 at 787; Richard Tessler, Robert Rosenheck, and Gail Gamache, "Gender Differences in Self-Reported Reasons for Homelessness" (2001) 10:3 *J Soc Distress & Homelessness* 243 at 248 (describing self-reported reasons why individuals experience homelessness).

29 David Ponka, Eric Agbata, Claire Kendall et al., "The Effectiveness of Case Management Interventions for the Homeless, Vulnerably Housed and Persons with Lived Experience: A Systematic Review" (2019) 15:4 *PLoS One* 1 at 3; Carol Caton, *The Open Door: Homelessness and Severe Mental Illness in the Era of Community Treatment* (Oxford University Press, 2017) at 74–82. Note that Caton discusses each of these mechanisms described in this chapter.

First, the State may provide Assertive Community Treatment (ACT), which is a model of care that combines outreach, access to community resources, integrated services, and continuity of care for individuals who have complex mental health needs.[30] Research indicates that mental illness is an important risk factor for homelessness, and many individuals who experience chronic homelessness struggle with mental illness.[31] ACT teams are comprised of professionals such as psychiatrists, nurses, social workers, substance use counselors, vocational counselors, and others.[32] They adopt a holistic approach to address the specific needs of unhoused persons.[33] These teams have relatively low caseloads to maximize their effectiveness.[34] Some studies suggest that ACT can improve access to housing for unhoused persons with mental health challenges more effectively than other forms of case management.[35] Research also indicates that the combination of ACT and Housing First programs can help house individuals with mental illness more effectively than traditional treatment models.[36]

Second, local governments can provide interdisciplinary outreach teams that assist unhoused persons with complex needs. The city of Toronto offers a Multi-Disciplinary Outreach Team (MDOT) comprised of nonpolice specialists who streamline access to housing, social services, medical services, and mental health treatment.[37] Toronto's MDOT incorporates a housing specialist, a nurse, outreach workers, and psychiatrists.[38] The team works closely with the healthcare system and with Housing First programs.[39] As a low-barrier program, there are no

30 Gary Bond and Robert Drake, "The Critical Ingredients of Assertive Community Treatment" (2015) 14:2 *World Psychiatry* 240 at 240.

31 Stefan Gutwinski, Stefanie Schreiter, Karl Deutscher et al., "The Prevalence of Mental Disorders among Homeless People in High-Income Countries: An Updated Systematic Review and Meta-Regression Analysis" (2021) 18:8 *PLoS Medicine* 1 at 12, 14.

32 Sandra Johnson, *Assertive Community Treatment: Evidence-Based Practice or Managed Recovery* (New York: Routledge, 2017) at 1.

33 Bond and Drake, "The Critical Ingredients of Assertive Community Treatment" at 241.

34 Johnson, *Assertive Community Treatment* at 1.

35 Renée de Vet, Maurice van Luijtelaar, Sonja Brilleslijper-Kater et al., "Effectiveness of Case Management for Homeless Persons: A Systematic Review" (2013) 103:10 *Am J Pub Health* e13 at e23–24; Craig Coldwell and William Bender, "The Effectiveness of Assertive Community Treatment for Homeless Populations with Severe Mental Illness: A Meta-Analysis" (2007) 164 *Am J Psych* 393 at 397–98; Caton, *The Open Door* at 77–78. Note, however, that others observe that findings are mixed. *See* Kevin Pottie et al., "Clinical Guideline for Homeless and Vulnerably Housed People, and People with Lived Homelessness Experience" (2020) 192:10 *CMAJ* e240 at e244.

36 Tim Aubry, Paula Goering, Scott Veldhuizen et al., "A Multiple-City RCT of Housing First with Assertive Community Treatment for Homeless Canadians with Serious Mental Illness" (2016) 67:3 *Psychiatr Serv* 275 at 279–80.

37 Manal Guirguis-Younger, Ryan McNeil, and Stephen Hwang, "Collaborative Approaches to Community-Based Mental Health Care for Homeless People: Toronto's Inner-City Health Associates" in Ryan McNeil, Manal Guirguis-Younger, and Stephen Hwang (eds.), *Homelessness & Health in Canada* (University of Ottawa Press, 2014) at 283–84.

38 B. H. Lettner, R. J. Doan, and A. W. Miettinen, "Housing Outcomes and Predictors of Success: The Role of Hospitalization in Street Outreach" (2016) 23 *J Psychiatr & Mental Health Nursing* 98 at 99.

39 *Ibid.*

preconditions – such as sobriety or taking medication – to be assisted by Toronto's MDOT team.[40] Some studies indicate that MDOT helped unsheltered unhoused persons receive necessary mental health care and obtain stable access to housing.[41]

Third, the State can offer Intensive Case Management (ICM) to address risk factors associated with homelessness. Intensive case managers connect unhoused persons with healthcare providers, direct them to community services and treatment programs, advocate on their behalf, and assist them during crises.[42] ICM is less intensive than ACT.[43] Furthermore, there are differences between both treatment models.[44] The members of an ACT team provide direct treatment to unhoused persons, whereas intensive case managers do not.[45] Certain studies suggest that ICM can reduce the duration of homelessness.[46] Furthermore, as Carol Caton notes, research suggests that ICM can improve quality of life more effectively when combined with access to housing.[47]

Fourth, governments can provide Critical Time Intervention (CTI) programs that aim to rapidly house individuals who enter the shelter system.[48] CTIs are short-term programs – generally between six to nine months – that assist unhoused persons while they transition from a shelter to community care.[49] Case workers provide continuity of care so that unhoused persons can access certain resources in the community and obtain access to housing.[50] Some research studies suggest that CTIs reduced the likelihood of homelessness and decreased the duration of homelessness more effectively than standard care.[51]

Fifth, the State can support more inclusive and culturally sensitive resources that prevent homelessness, increase access to housing, and improve well-being for certain populations with specific needs. Indigenous persons are overrepresented in

40 Guirguis-Younger, McNeil, and Hwang, "Collaborative Approaches" at 284.

41 Lettner, Doan, and Miettinen, "Housing Outcomes and Predictors of Success" at 103–04.

42 *See, e.g.*, Heather Menzies Munthe-Kaas, Rigmor Berg, and Nora Blaasvær, "Effectiveness of Interventions to Reduce Homelessness: A Systematic Review and Meta-Analysis" (2018) 3 *Campbell Systematic Revs* 1 at 104; Caton, *The Open Door* at 76–77.

43 Vicky Stergiopoulos, Stephen Hwang, Agnes Gozdzik et al., "Effect of Scattered-Site Housing Using Rent Supplements and Intensive Case Management on Housing Stability Among Homeless Adults With Mental Illness: A Randomized Trial" (2015) 313:9 *JAMA* 905 at 906.

44 Munthe-Kaas, Berg, and Blaasvær, "Effectiveness of Interventions to Reduce Homelessness" at 12.

45 *Ibid.*; de Vet et al., "Effectiveness of Case Management for Homeless Persons" at e13–e14.

46 Pottie et al., "Clinical Guideline for Homeless and Vulnerably Housed People, and People with Lived Homelessness Experience" at e244.

47 Caton, *The Open Door* at 76–77.

48 *Ibid.* at 78–79.

49 Stephen Hwang and Tom Burns, "Health Interventions for People who are Homeless" (2014) 384 *Lancet* 1541 at 1541; Pottie et al., "Clinical Guideline for Homeless and Vulnerably Housed People, and People with Lived Homelessness Experience" at e247 (noting that the CTI last between six to nine months).

50 Hwang and Burns, "Health Interventions for People who are Homeless" at 1541; Caton, *The Open Door* at 78–79.

51 Pottie et al., "Clinical Guideline for Homeless and Vulnerably Housed People, and People with Lived Homelessness Experience" at e244.

Canada's unhoused population.[52] They face unique barriers to housing due to the impacts of colonization and the legacy of residential schools.[53] These realities resulted in increased rates of substance use, suicide, social dislocation, post-traumatic stress disorder, foster care, and unemployment.[54] Some research indicates that the risk factors associated with homelessness – and the pathways out of it – are different for Indigenous and non-Indigenous people.[55]

Culturally sensitive programs and services can better prevent and address homelessness amongst Indigenous persons.[56] Studies show that cultural continuity is associated with improved health and wellness outcomes for Indigenous persons.[57] Brittany Bingham and colleagues note that traditional treatment models for substance use – an important risk factor for homelessness – are less effective for Indigenous persons than for non-Indigenous persons.[58] They explain that "approaches that create reconnection to community, culture and traditions have been shown to have a positive impact on substance use."[59]

Some jurisdictions have culturally sensitive and inclusive programs that aim to improve Indigenous persons' access to housing and well-being, and reconnect them with their culture and traditions.[60] For instance, Anishnawbe Health Toronto (AHT) provides a range of services to support Indigenous persons.[61] These services

[52] Julia Christensen, "Indigenous Homelessness: The Canadian Context" in Julia Christensen and Evelyn J. Peters (eds.), *Indigenous Homelessness: Perspectives from Canada, Australia, and New Zealand* (Winnipeg: University of Manitoba Press, 2016) at 17.

[53] *Ibid.* at 15–17.

[54] *Ibid.*; Sandeep Agrawal and Celine Zoe, "Housing and Homelessness in Indigenous Communities of Canada's North" (2021) *Hous Pol'y Debate* 1 at 4; Brittany Bingham, Akm Moniruzzaman, Michelle Patterson et al., "Indigenous and Non-Indigenous People Experiencing Homelessness and Mental Illness in Two Canadian Cities: A Retrospective Analysis and Implications for Culturally Informed Action" (2019) 9 *BMJ Open* 1 at 4–6.

[55] Bingham et al., "Indigenous and Non-Indigenous People Experiencing Homelessness and Mental Illness in Two Canadian Cities" at 4–6.

[56] *Ibid.*

[57] Monique Auger, "Cultural Continuity as a Determinant of Indigenous Peoples' Health: A Metasynthesis of Qualitative Research in Canada and the United States" (2016) 7:4 *Int'l Indigenous Pol'y J* 1 at 10–13. In the United States, *see* James Allen, Lisa Wexler, and Stacy Rasmus, "Protective Factors as a Unifying Framework for Strength-Based Intervention and Culturally Responsive American Indian and Alaska Native Suicide Prevention" (2022) 23 *Prevention Sci* 59 at 65–67.

[58] Bingham et al., "Indigenous and Non-Indigenous People Experiencing Homelessness and Mental Illness in Two Canadian Cities" at 6, citing Rod McCormick, "Aboriginal Traditions in the Treatment of Substance Abuse" (2000) 34:1 *Can J Counselling* 25 at 26.

[59] Bingham et al., "Indigenous and Non-Indigenous People Experiencing Homelessness and Mental Illness in Two Canadian Cities" at 6, citing McCormick, "Aboriginal Traditions in the Treatment of Substance Abuse" at 26–27; *see also* Michelle Firestone, Mark Tyndall, and Benedikt Fischer, "Substance Use and Related Harms among Aboriginal People in Canada: A Comprehensive Review" (2015) 26: 4 *J Health Care for the Poor and Underserved* 1110 at 1121.

[60] Firestone, Tyndall, and Fischer, "Substance Use and Related Harms among Aboriginal People in Canada" at 1121.

[61] *Ibid. See* Allison Reeves and Suzanne Stewart, "Exploring the Integration of Indigenous Healing and Western Psychotherapy for Sexual Trauma Survivors Who Use Mental Health Services at Anishnawbe Health Toronto" (2014) 48:4 *Can J Counselling & Psych* 57 at 61.

include access to physical and mental healthcare, traditional teachings, Indigenous supportive housing, support from elders, a circle of care, substance use support, a mobile healing unit, and programs for Two-Spirit and transgender persons.[62] The State better fulfils its fiduciary duty to alleviate homelessness when it supports inclusive programs that address the distinct needs of communities who are overrepresented in the unhoused population.

Sixth, the State can devise reentry programs that increase access to housing for unhoused persons who had prior contact with the criminal justice system. *Ready, Willing, and Able* is a New York City-based initiative that offers various resources for unhoused persons. The program offers paid employment opportunities, physical and mental health support, career training, and housing.[63] Many individuals who complete the program secure access to housing.[64] Furthermore, those who completed the program tend to have less contact with the police, are less likely to reoffend, and have higher rates of stable employment.[65] *Ready, Willing, and Able* also saves New York City significant financial costs that would be spent on the criminal justice system.[66] Other cities, such as Boulder, Philadelphia, Washington, and Atlanta have adopted similar programs.[67]

9.2.3 *Access to Housing*

The State must also ensure access to housing to fulfil its fiduciary duty to end homelessness and treat unhoused persons with equal respect. Cities can implement two notable mechanisms that improve access to housing: Housing First programs and housing vouchers.[68] Housing First programs offer private market accommodations with no preconditions, such as sobriety, mental health treatment, or

62 *See* Allison Reeves and Suzanne Stewart, "Healing the Spirit: Exploring Sexualized Trauma and Recovery among Indigenous Men in Toronto" (2017) 24:1 *Am Indian and Alaska Native Mental Health Rsch* 30 at 35; Anishnawbe Health Toronto, "Our Services" and "Our Programs," https://aht.ca [perma.cc/3M55-V5AH].

63 The Doe Fund, "Ready, Willing, and Able: A Balanced, Proven Approach to Reducing Recidivism and Restoring Civic Life" (2016) at 1, www.doe.org/wp-content/uploads/2016/10/ReadyWillingandAble.pdf [perma.cc/V86K-ZXCK].

64 *See, e.g.*, The Doe Fund, "A Working Way Home for the Men in Blue: 2019 Annual Report" (2019) at 15, www.doe.org/wp-content/uploads/2020/05/The-Doe-Fund-2019-Annual-Report-and-Impact-Report.pdf [perma.cc/YD3J-Q9UK]; The Doe Fund, "A Blueprint for Recovery: 2021 Annual Report" (2022) at 8, www.doe.org/wp-content/uploads/2022/04/The-Doe-Fund-2021-Annual-Report_DIGITAL.pdf [perma.cc/KL6K-N7WJ].

65 Catherine Sirois and Bruce Western, "An Evaluation of 'Ready, Willing, and Able'" (May 14, 2010) at 73–74, 83–85, online (pdf): https://prisonstudiesproject.org/wp-content/uploads/2011/07/RWA_evaluation.pdf [perma.cc/F5VV-PJKW].

66 The Doe Fund, "Ready, Willing, and Able" at 3.

67 *Ibid.* at 6.

68 *See, e.g.*, Julia Woodhall-Melnik and James R. Dunn, "A Systematic Review of Outcomes Associated with Participation in Housing First Programs" (2016) 31:3 *Hous Stud* 287 at 287; Kelly Doran, Callan Elswick Fockele, and Marcella Maguire, "Overdose and Homelessness – Why We Need to Talk About Housing" (2022) 5:1 *JAMA Open Network* 1 at 2 (noting the effectiveness of housing vouchers).

employment.[69] People experiencing homelessness can be given access to housing through a private landlord without having to initially pass through the shelter system or transitional housing.[70] By employing a harm-reduction approach, Housing First users are not required to abstain from alcohol or drug use as a condition to obtain housing.[71] Individuals in Housing First programs are provided additional community-based support for mental health challenges, substance use disorder, and more.[72]

Housing First programs are typically contrasted with traditional Treatment First models. Treatment First models require unhoused persons to first seek care for substance use or mental illness to obtain housing.[73] Case managers then allocate available housing spaces based on an individual's adherence to treatment and readiness to be housed.[74]

Some empirical studies suggest that Housing First can reduce homelessness and improve housing stability more effectively compared to Treatment First models.[75] Furthermore, certain research indicates that Housing First can produce other benefits, such as fewer hospitalizations and emergency room visits.[76]

Different cities have employed Housing First models. Beginning in 2008 in Canada, the federal government implemented the *At Home/Chez Soi* Housing First program and conducted a study to evaluate its effectiveness.[77] As part of this program, the government offered a Housing First program in five major Canadian

69 Tim Aubry, Geoffrey Nelson, Sam Tsemberis et al., "Housing First for People with Severe Mental Illness Who Are Homeless: A Review of the Research and Findings from the At Home–Chez Soi Demonstration Project" (2015) 60:11 *Can J Psych* 467 at 468–69; Paula Goering and David Steiner, "Putting Housing First: The Evidence and Impact" (2015) 60:11 *Can J Psych* 465 at 465.

70 Marybeth Shinn and Jill Khadduri, *In the Midst of Plenty: Homelessness and What to Do about It* (London: Blackwell, 2020) at 82.

71 *Ibid.* at 83.

72 James Lachaud, Cilia Mejia-Lancheros, Anna Durbin et al., "The Effect of a Housing First Intervention on Acute Health Care Utilization among Homeless Adults with Mental Illness: Long-term Outcomes of the At Home/Chez-Soi Randomized Pragmatic Trial" (2021) 98 *J Urb Health* 505 at 506; Lisa Wood, Nicholas Wood, Shannen Vallesi et al., "Hospital Collaboration with a Housing First Program to Improve Health outcomes for People Experiencing Homelessness" (2019) 22:1 *Hous, Care & Support* 27 at 28.

73 Deborah Padgett, Victoria Stanhope, Ben Henwood et al., "Substance Use Outcomes among Homeless Clients with Serious Mental Illness: Comparing Housing First with Treatment First Programs" (2011) 47 *Comty Mental Health J* 227 at 227–28.

74 *Ibid.*

75 Andrew Baxter, Emily Tweed, Srinivasa Vittal Katikireddi et al., "Effects of Housing First Approaches on Health and Well-Being of Adults Who Are Homeless or at Risk of Homelessness: Systematic Review and Meta-Analysis of Randomised Controlled Trials" (2019) 73 *J Epidemiol Comty Health* 379 at 384–85; Yinan Peng, Robert Hahn, Ramona Finnie et al., "Permanent Supportive Housing with Housing First to Reduce Homelessness and Promote Health among Homeless Populations with Disability: A Community Guide Systematic Review" (2020) 26:5 *J Pub Health Mgmt Prac* 404 at 408.

76 Baxter et al., "Effects of Housing First Approaches on Health and Well-Being of Adults Who Are Homeless or at Risk of Homelessness" at 384–85; Nick Kerman, John Sylvestre, Tim Aubry et al., "The Effects of Housing Stability on Service Use among Homeless Adults with Mental Illness in a Randomized Controlled Trial of Housing First" (2018) 18:190 *BMC Health Serv Rsch* 1 at 6–8.

77 Kathleen Worton, Geoffrey Nelson, Tim Aubry et al., "The Development of Regional Networks to Promote Housing First Implementation in Canada" (2019) 10:3 *Global J Cmty Psych Prac* 1 at 4.

cities: Montreal, Moncton, Toronto, Winnipeg, and Vancouver.[78] The study lasted a period of five years. Its results were compared to traditional programs designed to reduce homelessness.[79] Results indicated that the combination of Housing First and other mechanisms – such as ACT or ICM – improved quality of life more significantly than other forms of treatment.[80]

Certain studies observe that the costs of Housing First are not entirely offset by reductions in other financial costs associated with homelessness, such as fewer emergency room visits, fewer hospitalizations, increased use of social programs, and more.[81] However, some research suggests that Housing First can offset roughly two-thirds of the costs associated with traditional programs and initiatives to reduce homelessness.[82] As some scholars note, this cost disparity can be justified because Housing First may result in better outcomes compared to other programs.[83]

To be clear, given the heterogeneity of the unhoused population, Housing First is not a one-size-fits-all solution. Given the costs of implementation, Housing First programs may be difficult to scale. Furthermore, as discussed above in Section 9.2.2, the State must provide resources that address the risk factors associated with homelessness, such as treatment for mental illness and substance use disorder, and that allow individuals to secure access to housing while avoiding dependency on the State.

Housing vouchers – meaning government issued financial support for private market accommodation – are another mechanism that can improve access to housing.[84] Carol Caton notes that in the United States, Section 8 housing voucher recipients pay roughly 30 percent of their income to rent.[85] The State, subsidies, or private charities pay the remaining portion of rental costs.[86] Studies suggest that housing vouchers are an effective means to reduce homelessness.[87] Furthermore, systematic reviews indicate that these vouchers also improve housing stability and food security.[88] Housing vouchers have also been shown to produce more positive outcomes for certain subpopulations of people experiencing homelessness, such as unhoused families and pregnant women.[89]

78 *Ibid.*
79 *Ibid.*
80 *Ibid.*
81 Angela Ly and Eric Latimer, "Housing First Impact on Costs and Associated Cost Offsets: A Review of the Literature" (2015) 60:11 *Can J Psychiatry* 475 at 486.
82 Eric Latimer, Daniel Rabouin, Zhirong Cao et al., "Cost-Effectiveness of Housing First with Assertive Community Treatment: Results from the Canadian At Home/Chez Soi Trial" (2020) 71:10 *Psychiatr Serv* 1020 at 1025–29.
83 *Ibid.*
84 Ingrid Gould Ellen, "What Do We Know about Housing Vouchers" (2020) 80 *Reg'l Sci & Urb Econ* 1 at 1–2.
85 Caton, *The Open Door* at 93.
86 *Ibid.*
87 *Ibid.*
88 Aubry et al., "Effectiveness of Permanent Supportive Housing and Income Assistance Interventions for Homeless Individuals in High-Income Countries" at e342, e356–57.
89 *Ibid.* at e357.

Various studies highlight the effectiveness of housing vouchers. In a New York City study, families living in a homeless shelter who received a housing voucher were roughly four times more likely to be housed compared to families who received no voucher.[90] More specifically, 80 percent of unhoused families who received the voucher were housed at that five-year period compared to 18 percent of participants who received no voucher.[91] Similarly, in a study that evaluated the impact of housing vouchers in a dozen sites across the United States – the Family Options study – individuals who received vouchers were significantly more likely to be housed compared to individuals who did not receive them.[92] These outcomes highlight the importance of housing vouchers as a mechanism to alleviate homelessness.[93]

9.2.4 *Inclusive Emergency Shelter and Interim Resources*

The State's duty to end homelessness and treat unhoused persons with equal respect requires it to provide access to shelters and to other interim resources until individuals become housed. The State better fulfils this duty when it allocates resources that respond to the general needs of all unhoused persons and to the distinct needs of subsets of the unhoused population. In terms of general needs that are shared by all unhoused persons, the State must provide access to resources that fulfil basic subsistence needs in emergency contexts, such as access to food, clothing, sanitation infrastructure, and safe shelter.[94]

The State better fulfils its fiduciary duty to end homelessness when it also addresses the discrete needs of subsets of the unhoused population. Chapter 1 explained how certain individuals are more likely to experience homelessness compared to the general population. Examples include survivors of domestic violence, members of the LGBTQ community, immigrants, veterans, individuals with prior criminal justice system involvement, and racialized and Indigenous persons.[95]

90 Shinn and Khadduri, *In the Midst of Plenty* at 71–72.

91 *Ibid.*

92 *Ibid.*; Claudia Solari, Douglas Walton, and Jill Khadduri. "How Well Do Housing Vouchers Work for Black Families Experiencing Homelessness? Evidence from the Family Options Study" (2021) 693:1 *Annals AAPSS* 193 at 203–05.

93 Matthew Desmond, *Evicted: Poverty and Profit in the American City* (New York: Random House, 2016) at 308–11.

94 *See, e.g.*, Robert Rodriguez, Jonathan Fortman, Chris Chee et al., "Food, Shelter, and Safety Needs Motivating Homeless Persons' Visits to an Urban Emergency Department" (2009) 53:5 *Annals of Emergency Med* 598 at 601–02 (describing these basic necessities).

95 Myra Piat, Lauren Polvere, Maritt Kirst et al., "Pathways into Homelessness: Understanding How Both Individual and Structural Factors Contribute to and Sustain Homelessness in Canada" (2015) 52:13 *Urb Stud* 2366 at 2368–69, 2371; Sandra Feodor Nilsson, Merete Nordentoft, and Carsten Hjorthø, "Individual-Level Predictors for Becoming Homeless and Exiting Homelessness: A Systematic Review and Meta-Analysis" (2019) 96 *J Urb Health* 741 at 747; Zachary Giano, "Forty Years of Research on Predictors of Homelessness" (2020) 56 *Cmty Mental Health J* 692 at 703; Marian Moser Jones, "Does Race Matter in Addressing Homelessness? A Review of the Literature" (2016) 8:2 *World Med & Health Pol'y* 139 at 140.

The State better fulfils its fiduciary duty to end homelessness and treat unhoused persons with equal respect when it offers resources that are inclusive, culturally sensitive, and capable of accommodating the distinct needs of subsets of the unhoused population.

Two examples illustrate this point. First, domestic violence shelters offer specific resources and support that can help individuals leave abusive relationships, prevent revictimization, secure access to housing, and increase employment stability.[96] Such specialized shelters aim to counteract a unique type of horizontal domination – domestic violence – that other unhoused persons may not experience. The State alleviates and counteracts homelessness more effectively when it allocates shelters and other resources that address the unique needs of domestic violence survivors.

Second, homeless shelters and other programs can better accommodate the specific needs of members of the LGBTQ community.[97] For instance, transgender persons who stay in conventional homeless shelters are vulnerable to distinct type of domination based on their personal characteristics. Research indicates that transgender persons are more likely to be victims of violent crimes compared to the general population, and that they report feeling unsafe in conventional shelters due to risks of harassment, discrimination, and violence.[98] Yet cities may create more inclusive transitional housing and shelters that better accommodate transgender persons.[99] Shelters may also provide inclusive policies, outreach, training, and support services for unhoused members of the LGBTQ community that aim to decrease discrimination, harassment, and violence.[100]

Jurisdictions can implement other types of inclusive services for members of the LGBTQ community. Some studies suggest that unhoused male members of the LGBTQ community are more at risk to contract HIV compared to the general population, which highlights the need for specific services to address this reality.[101]

96 *See, e.g.*, Amanda Stylianou and Changnary Pich, "Beyond Domestic Violence Shelter: Factors Associated with Housing Placements for Survivors Exiting Emergency Shelters" (2021) 36 *J Interpersonal Violence* NP9440 at NP9441-2.

97 John Ecker, Tim Aubry, and John Sylvestre, "A Review of the Literature on LGBTQ Adults Who Experience Homelessness" (2019) 66:3 *J Homosexuality* 297 at 316–17 (discussing certain specific needs of LGBTQ persons).

98 Michelle Johns, Richard Lowry, Jack Andrzejewski et al., "Transgender Identity and Experiences of Violence Victimization, Substance Use, Suicide Risk, and Sexual Risk Behaviors Among High School Students – 19 States and Large Urban School Districts, 2017" (2019) 68:3 *Morbidity and Mortality Weekly Report* 67 at 67–68 (describing increased violent victimization of transgender students); Brodie Fraser, Nevil Pierse, Elinor Chisholm et al., "LGBTIQ+ Homelessness: A Review of the Literature" (2019) 16 *Int'l J Env't Rsch & Pub Health* 1 at 7 (describing how transgender persons report feeling unsafe in shelters); Edward McCann and Michael Brown, "Homeless Experiences and Support Needs of Transgender People: A Systematic Review of the International Evidence" (2021) 29 *J Nursing Mgmt* 85 at 90–91 (same).

99 Geoff Bardwell, "The Impact of Risk Environments on LGBTQ2S Adults Experiencing Homelessness in a Midsized Canadian City" (2019) 31:1 *J Gay & Lesbian Soc Serv* 53 at 61.

100 *Ibid.*

101 Ecker, Aubry, and Sylvestre, "A Review of the Literature on LGBTQ Adults Who Experience Homelessness" at 315.

Some jurisdictions have implemented preventive HIV case management programs for transgender women – a population that disproportionately experiences homelessness.[102] Some research suggests that this program reduced homelessness and improved participants' quality of life.[103] These are just some examples, but they highlight how inclusive shelters and services may help reduce homelessness and address the unique needs of unhoused members of the LGBTQ community.

9.3 REDUCE NONEGALITARIAN COERCION AND PUNITIVE ENTRENCHMENT

The State must also decrease nonegalitarian coercion and punitive entrenchment to fulfil its three fiduciary duties related to homelessness and public property. Laws that govern public property treat individuals with greater concern and respect when the State counteracts domination associated with these laws. Furthermore, by avoiding punitive entrenchment, the State can better fulfil its duty to end homelessness. Different mechanisms can help achieve these aims, such as avoiding incarceration, graduating economic sanctions (or day fines), collateral consequence minimalism, automatic criminal record expungements, and criminal justice debt absolution.

9.3.1 *Avoiding Incarceration*

The State can reduce punitive entrenchment – and treat individuals with greater respect – when it avoids incarcerating unhoused persons because they violated laws that govern public property or could not afford to pay their fines.[104] Previous chapters illustrated how incarceration can enmesh individuals in the condition of homelessness.[105] Furthermore, incarceration can result in financial difficulties, physical or psychological harm, lower income, and unemployment.[106]

102 Cathy Reback, Steven Shoptaw, and Martin Downing, "Prevention Case Management Improves Socioeconomic Standing and Reduces Symptoms of Psychological and Emotional Distress among Transgender Women" (2012) 24:9 *AIDS Care* 1136 at 1136, 1139–42, cited in John Ecker, Tim Aubry, and John Sylvestre, "Experiences of LGBTQ Adults Who Have Accessed Emergency Shelters in a Large Urban City in Canada" (2002) 37:2 *Soc Work in Pub Health* 168 at 169.

103 Reback, Shoptaw, and Downing, "Prevention Case Management Improves Socioeconomic Standing … among Transgender Women" at 1139–42.

104 It is important to note that many scholars, lawyers, and civil society groups have advanced similar suggestions. *See, e.g.*, Harvard Law School Criminal Justice Policy Program (CJPP), "Proportionate Financial Sanctions: Policy Prescriptions for Judicial Reform" (September 2019) at v, 16–23, perma.cc/UJ3P-2SJT.

105 *See* Chapter 6 of this book.

106 Nils Jareborg, "Criminalization as Last Resort (*Ultima Ratio*)" (2005) 2 *Ohio St J Crim L* 521 at 526; Bruce Western, Jeffrey Kling, and David Weimen, "The Labor Market Consequences of Incarceration" (2001) 47:3 *Crime & Delinquency* 410 at 424 (noting that incarceration results in lower wages); Zoe Feingold, "The Stigma of Incarceration Experience: A Systematic Review" (2021) 27:4 *Psych Pub Pol'y & L* 550 at 550 (noting that incarceration increases the prospect of unemployment); Danielle Wallace and Xia Wang, "Does In-Prison Physical and Mental Health Impact

The relationship between homelessness, criminal justice debt, and incarceration underpins the need to avoid incarceration in the contexts described above.[107] Homelessness is associated with a greater likelihood of incarceration.[108] Studies indicate that individuals who have been incarcerated are more likely to experience homelessness compared to individuals who have not been imprisoned.[109] Some research suggests that approximately 23 percent of incarcerated persons were unhoused when they were sentenced to prison.[110] A Public Health Agency of Canada survey study observed that most unhoused youth have been incarcerated or have spent time in youth-detention.[111] The John Howard Society estimates that roughly 45 percent of people discharged from prison are either unhoused or are at risk of experiencing homelessness upon release.[112]

Other studies have highlighted the connection between criminal justice debt and homelessness.[113] Some research indicates that criminal justice debt is associated with longer periods of homelessness.[114] Furthermore, this research suggests that criminal justice debt increased the duration of homelessness in ways that other types of debt – such as student loans or credit card debt – did not.[115]

This does not mean that the State can never incarcerate unhoused persons because they violated a law that governs public property. As a general principle,

Recidivism?" (2020) 11 *SSM Population Health* 1 at 1 (providing an overview of studies on the connection between incarceration and poor health outcomes).

107 *See, e.g.*, Stephen Metraux and Dennis Culhane, "Homeless Shelter Use and Reincarceration Following Prison Release" (2004) 3 *Criminology & Pub Pol'y* 139 at 140; Marianne Quirouette, Tyler Frederick, Jean Hughes et al., "'Conflict with the Law': Regulation & Homeless Youth Trajectories toward Stability" (2016) 31 *Can JL and Soc'y* 383 at 387; Stephen Gaetz and Bill O'Grady, "Homelessness, Incarceration, and the Challenge of Effective Discharge Planning: A Canadian Case" in David Hulchanski, Philippa Campsie, Shirley Chau et al. (eds.), *Finding Home: Policy Options for Addressing Homelessness in Canada* (Toronto: Cities Centre Press, 2009) ch. 7.3, at 20.

108 Ahmad Bashir, Noreen Moloney, Musaab Elzain et al., "From Nowhere to Nowhere. Homelessness and Incarceration: A Systematic Review and Meta-Analysis" (2021) 17:4 *Int J Prisoner Health* 452 at 452–53.

109 *Ibid.* at 459; Julie Moschion and Guy Johnson, "Homelessness and Incarceration: A Reciprocal Relationship?" (2019) 35 *J Quantitative Criminology* 855 at 878–79.

110 Bashir et al., "From Nowhere to Nowhere" at 458.

111 Stephen Gaetz, "Coming of Age: Reimagining the Response to Youth Homelessness in Canada" (2014), at 12, www.homelesshub.ca/sites/default/files/ComingOfAgeHH_0.pdf [perma.cc/WUH6-JM42], citing Public Health Agency of Canada, "Street Youth in Canada: Findings from Enhanced Surveillance of Canadian Street Youth, 1999–2003" (March 2006) at 6, www.phac-aspc.gc.ca/std-mts/reports_06/pdf/street_youth_e.pdf [perma.cc/FY7R-6R4D].

112 John Howard Society, "Homeless and Jailed: Jailed and Homeless" (2010) at 27, https://johnhoward.ca/wp-content/uploads/2016/12/Amber-Kellen-Homeless-and-Jailed-Jailed-and-Homeless.pdf [perma.cc/4W5K-Z2XH].

113 *See, e.g.*, Mary Patillo, Erica Banks, Brian Sargent et al., "Monetary Sanctions and Housing Instability" (2022) 8:2 *Russell Sage Foundation J Soc Sci* 57 at 71–72.

114 Jessica Mogk, Valerie Shmigol, Marvin Futrell et al., "Court-Imposed Fines as a Feature of the Homelessness–Incarceration Nexus: A Cross-Sectional Study of the Relationship between Legal Debt and Duration of Homelessness in Seattle, Washington, USA" (2020) 42:2 *J Pub Health* 1 at 6.

115 *Ibid.*

the State can more justifiably resort to imprisonment in such contexts as a last resort and when no others reasonable alternatives are appropriate.[116] For instance, incarceration can be more legitimate in situations where an unhoused person repeatedly or deliberately engages in conduct that harms or endangers others, creates meaningful public health or safety risks, or violates basic norms of public order (for instance, engaging in sexual acts in public), and where harm-reduction strategies and alternative sanctions are ineffective. In such contexts, incarceration may be an appropriate sanction.

9.3.2 *Graduating Economic Sanctions (Day Fines)*

Second, the State can replace fixed financial penalties with graduating economic sanctions (or day fines) to mitigate punitive entrenchment.[117] Jurisdictions in Canada and the United States tend to impose fixed financial penalties (or tariff fines) irrespective of the defendant's income or financial capacities.[118] Tariff-fines disproportionately impact impecunious persons and result in additional fees and consequences due to nonpayment, which are referred to as "poverty penalties."[119] In contrast, day fines impose financial penalties that are proportionate to the defendant's daily adjusted income and to the gravity of the offense.[120] Countries such as Sweden, Finland, and Denmark use day fines.[121] Some US jurisdictions have also experimented with day fines.[122] Staten Island (New York), Maricopa County (Arizona), Polk County (Iowa), Bridgeport (Connecticut), and several counties in Oregon implemented day fines as part of a pilot project.[123]

The quantum of a day fine is calculated through a two-step process.[124] First, the State determines the number of days for a particular offense.[125] The number of "days" represents a numerical value (or number of points) that increases according

[116] *See, e.g.*, Jeffrey Fagan and Aaron Kupchik, "Juvenile Incarceration and the Pains of Imprisonment" (2011) 3:1 *Duke FL & Soc Change* 29 at 58 (advancing a similar argument in the context of juveniles and imprisonment).

[117] Sally Hillsman, "Fines and Day Fines" (1990) 12 *Crime and Just* 49 at 76.

[118] Beth Colgan, "Graduating Economic Sanctions According to Ability to Pay" (2017) 103 *Iowa L Rev* 53 at 55; Alec Schierenbeck, "The Constitutionality of Income-Based Fines" (2018) 85:8 *U Chi L Rev* 1869 at 1874; Lindsay Bing, Becky Pettit, and Ilya Slavinski, "Incomparable Punishments: How Economic Inequality Contributes to the Disparate Impact of Legal Fines and Fees" (2022) 8:2 *Russell Sage Foundation J Soc Sci* 118 at 119.

[119] Neil Sobol, "Charging the Poor: Criminal Justice Debt and Modern-Day Debtors' Prisons" (2016) 75:2 *Md L Rev* 486 at 516, 518; Tia Lee Kerkhof, "Small Fines and Fees, Large Impacts: Ability-to-Pay Hearings" (2021) 95:2 *S Cal L Rev* 447 at 449 (describing poverty penalties).

[120] Beth Colgan, "Fines, Fees, and Forfeitures" (2017) 18 *Criminology, Crim Just L & Soc'y* 22 at 31.

[121] Tapio Lappi-Seppala, "Penal Policy in Scandinavia" (2007) 36 *Crime & Just* 217 at 223.

[122] Michael Tonry and Mary Lynch, "Intermediate Sanctions" (1996) 20 *Crime & Justice* 99 at 129–30.

[123] Susan Turner and Joan Petersilia, "Day Fines in Four U.S. Jurisdictions" (1996) at xv, Santa Monica: Rand Institute, www.ojp.gov/pdffiles1/pr/163409.pdf [perma.cc/MS8Z-8N7V].

[124] Elena Kantorowicz-Reznichenko, "Day-Fines: Should the Rich Pay More?" (2015) 11 *Rev L Econ* 481 at 482.

[125] *Ibid.*

to the gravity of the offense.[126] Second, the State determines the number of units that apply to the offender.[127] The number of "units" represents a fraction of the offender's daily adjusted income which considers personal and family living expenses.[128] The total cost of the fine is calculated by multiplying the number of days by the number of units.[129] A day fine cannot exceed a certain proportion of the offender's daily adjusted income. In Finland, for example, the amount of the fine cannot be greater than one-third of the offender's daily adjusted income.[130]

Some object to day fines on the grounds that these financial penalties impact affluent offenders disproportionately. For instance, an affluent motorist in Finland received a €110,000 fine for speeding.[131] However, certain mechanisms can prevent excessive day fines. The State can impose a statutory cap (or ceiling) on the severity of fines that resembles the current maximum fine imposed by statute.[132] This ensures that individuals do not pay exorbitant amounts for minor offenses, and that individuals will not pay more than they did prior to the implementation of a day fine scheme.[133]

Day fines may also benefit cities and local governments. Although the quantum of day fines tends to be lower than tariff fines, certain studies suggest that defendants who received day fines paid higher amounts compared to defendants who received fixed financial penalties.[134] Furthermore, some research suggests that defendants were more likely to pay their day fines within a year compared to those who received fixed financial penalties.[135] Increased complete payment rates, for their part, can reduce the costs that cities expend to issue bench warrants for unpaid fines and to hold collection hearings.[136]

Certain measures may also improve defendants' payment and compliance rates without increasing cities' expenditures significantly. The justice system can develop flexible and longer payment plans for more expensive day fines.[137] Cities can remove mandatory court appearances for missed payments, avoid warrants for nonpayment, and send phone or text message reminders to defendants who do not pay on time.[138]

126 *Ibid.*
127 *Ibid.*
128 *Ibid.*; Colgan, "Graduating Economic Sanctions According to Ability to Pay" at 56.
129 *Ibid.*
130 Tapio Lappi-Seppälä, "Sentencing and Punishment in Finland: The Decline of the Repressive Ideal" in Michael Tonry and Richard Frase (eds.), *Sentencing and Sanctions in Western Countries* (Oxford University Press, 2001) at 94.
131 Joe Pinsker, "Finland, Home of the $103,000 Speeding Ticket," The Atlantic (March 12, 2015), www.theatlantic.com/business/archive/2015/03/finland-home-of-the-103000-speeding-ticket/387484/ [perma.cc/GF5T-LVQH].
132 Colgan, "Graduating Economic Sanctions According to Ability to Pay" at 96–99.
133 *Ibid.* at 99.
134 *Ibid.* at 67.
135 *Ibid.* at 70–71.
136 *Ibid.* at 71.
137 *Ibid.* at 89.
138 CJPP, "Proportionate Financial Sanctions" at 36–40.

Furthermore, as Beth Colgan notes, some cities employ supportive collection methods – such as self-addressed and stamped envelopes and clear payment instructions – that reduce administrative burden and may increase collection rates.[139]

9.3.3 *Collateral Consequence Minimalism*

Third, the State can minimize collateral consequences for unpaid fines that entrench individuals in homelessness. The collateral consequences of unpaid fines include additional fees and penalties, driver's license suspensions, civil asset forfeiture, parole revocation, loss of public benefits, disclosure of unpaid fines to consumer reporting agencies, and default civil judgments against defendants, amongst others.[140]

Chapter 6 demonstrated how these collateral consequences exacerbate nonegalitarian coercion and punitive entrenchment in different ways.[141] Defendants who cannot afford to pay their fines must pay additional fines, fees, and penalties rather than their rent.[142] Furthermore, individuals who owe criminal justice debt are less able to save money, qualify for a mortgage, and buy a home.[143] Unpaid fines may result in a loss of social assistance – such as public housing or social security – that result in homelessness.[144] Suspended driver's licenses, for their part, can lead to unemployment and lower income.[145] Unpaid fines can be disclosed to a credit agency, which can decrease an individuals' credit rating and capacity to rent an apartment.[146] Collateral consequence minimalism may help decrease punitive entrenchment, safeguard individuals against domination, and legitimize laws that govern public property.

The State can reduce the collateral consequences of criminal justice debt in different ways. Jurisdictions can establish independent commissions to review and modify the consequences of unpaid fines.[147] Governments can abolish driver license

139 Colgan, "Graduating Economic Sanctions According to Ability to Pay" at 106.

140 *See, e.g.*, Beth Colgan, "The Excessive Fines Clause: Challenging the Modern Debtors' Prison" (2018) 65 *UCLA L Rev* 2 at 6–8; Brandon Garrett, Sara Greene, and Marin Levy, "Foreword: Fees, Fines, Bail, and the Destitution Pipeline" (2020) 69:7 *Duke LJ* 1463 at 1464; Neil Sobol, "Fighting Fines & Fees: Borrowing from Consumer Law to Combat Criminal Justice Debt Abuses" (2017) 88:4 *U Colo L Rev* 841 at 844, 876; Skolnik, "Rethinking Homeless People's Punishments" at 80.

141 Skolnik, "Rethinking Homeless People's Punishments" at 80. *Ibid.* at 81.

142 Patillo et al., "Monetary Sanctions and Housing Instability" at 69.

143 *Ibid.* at 62.

144 Beth Colgan, "Reviving the Excessive Fines Clause" (2014) 102 *Cal L Rev* 277 at 293.

145 *See, e.g.*, Colgan, "The Excessive Fines Clause" at 64–65 and note 338 in the text; Colleen Chien, Alexandra George, Srihari Shekhar et al., "Estimating the Earnings Loss Associated with a Criminal Record and Suspended Driver's License" (2022) 64:3 *Ariz L Rev* 675 at 717.

146 Karin Martin, "Monetary Sanctions: Legal Financial Obligations in US Systems of Justice" (2018) 1 *Ann Rev Criminology* 471 at 475; Catherine Chesnay, Céline Bellot, and Marie-Eve Sylvestre, "Taming Disorderly People One Ticket at a Time: The Penalization of Homelessness in Ontario and British Columbia" (2013) 55 *Can J Corr* 161 at 176–78.

147 Ilya Slavinski and Kimberly Spencer-Suarez, "The Price of Poverty: Policy Implications of the Unequal Effects of Monetary Sanctions on the Poor" (2021) 37:1 *J Contemp Crim Just* 45 at 59, citing Martin, "Monetary Sanctions: Legal Financial Obligations in US Systems of Justice."

suspensions associated with criminal justice debt.[148] For instance, states such as New York and Montana have limited driver's license suspensions for unpaid fines.[149] Other jurisdictions, such as Texas, mandate judges to hold ability-to-pay hearings for fines and offer alternative options to indigent persons, such as fee-waivers or community service.[150] Statutes can require fees and surcharges to be imposed proportionally to individuals' income, or eliminate them entirely for impecunious persons.[151] Although these are just some examples, they show how cities and states may attempt to mitigate punitive entrenchment.

Courts may also attempt to counteract collateral consequences that function as poverty penalties. For instance, judges may determine that mandatory collateral consequences – such as additional fees and surcharges – violate the Excessive Fines Clause in the United States or the constitutional right to be free from cruel and unusual punishments in Canada.[152] As discussed in Section 9.3.5, the Supreme Court of Canada has decided that mandatory surcharges impose a cruel and unusual punishment on indigent persons.[153] Together, cities and courts may counteract the collateral consequences of criminal justice debt and reduce punitive entrenchment.

9.3.4 *Automatic Criminal Record Expungements*

Fourth, jurisdictions can adopt automatic criminal record expungement schemes to reduce punitive entrenchment.[154] Jurisdictions typically require defendants to apply for a criminal record expungement (also referred to as a "pardon" or "criminal record suspension").[155] Individuals may have to wait many years until they become

148 Criminal Justice Policy Program (CJPP), "Confronting Criminal Justice Debt: A Guide for Policy Reform" (2016) at 17, National Consumer Law Centre, www.nclc.org/wp-content/uploads/2022/10/confronting-criminal-justice-debt-3.pdf [perma.cc/A7Y5-PYFA].

149 Fines and Fees Justice Center, "Driver's License Suspension Reform Act" (June 2021), https://finesandfeesjusticecenter.org/content/uploads/2021/06/Updated-FAQ_Drivers-License-Suspension-Reform-Act_7.5.21.pdf [perma.cc/W59G-LHX5]; Prison Policy Initiative, "Winnable Criminal Justice Reforms" (December 2021) at 8, https://static.prisonpolicy.org/reports/winnable2022.pdf [perma.cc/DR7Z-7RAF].

150 Matthew Menendez, Michael Crowley, Lauren-Brooke Eisen et al., "The Steep Costs of Criminal Justice Fines and Fees" (2019) at 26, www.brennancenter.org/sites/default/files/2019–11/2019_10_Fees%26Fines_Final5.pdf [perma.cc/A3A2-D3DU].

151 Slavinski and Spencer-Suarez, "The Price of Poverty" at 58.

152 *See, e.g.*, Colgan, "The Excessive Fines Clause" at 38–39 (suggesting that fees can fall within the Excessive Fines Clause); *R* v. *Boudreault*, 2018 SCC 58 (striking down a mandatory victim surcharge).

153 *R* v. *Boudreault*, 2018 SCC 58.

154 *See, e.g.*, Terry Skolnik, "Two Criminal Justice Systems" (2023) 56:1 UBC L Rev 286 at 325–31. *See also* Cass Sunstein, "Default Rules Are Better than Active Choosing (Often)" (2017) 21:8 *Trends in Cognitive Sci* 600 at 600–04 (discussing the differences between automatic enrollment and opt-in schemes).

155 *See, e.g.*, Sonja Starr, "Expungement Reform in Arizona: The Empirical Case for a Clean Slate" (2020) 52:3 *Ariz St LJ* 1059 at 1066.

eligible for a criminal record expungement.[156] In Canada, the criminal record suspension ineligibility period is five or ten years following the conclusion of one's punishment.[157]

Criminal records can contribute to homelessness.[158] Individuals who have a criminal record can become ineligible for public housing.[159] Landlords tend to screen for prospective renters' criminal records.[160] Furthermore, research suggests that landlords are less willing to rent private accommodations to individuals with prior convictions compared to individuals with no criminal record.[161] Prior convictions can also reduce employment opportunities and result in public benefit ineligibility, both of which limit access to housing.[162]

The criminal record expungement application process can be complex and may impose heavy administrative burdens.[163] For instance, jurisdictions may require individuals to ascertain eligibility requirements, fill out complex forms, pay application fees, obtain copies of fingerprints, visit police stations, and mail an application package.[164] Eligible individuals may not apply for a criminal record expungement due to these administrative burdens.[165] Furthermore, indigent persons may not request a record suspension due to expensive applications costs and fees.[166]

The uptake rate for criminal record expungements is low.[167] Research suggests that fewer than 20 percent of eligible persons in certain US states apply for a criminal record expungement (note that fewer than 10 percent apply in other states).[168] Similarly, following the decriminalization of simple possession of marijuana in Canada, the uptake rate for criminal record suspensions for that offense was

156 J. J. Prescott and Sonja Starr, "Expungement of Criminal Convictions: An Empirical Study" (2020) 133:8 *Harv L Rev* 2460 at 2472.

157 Criminal Records Act, RSC 1985, c. 47, s. 4(1). Notably, a five-year ineligibility period applies for summary convictions offenses, and a ten-year ineligibility period applies for indictable offenses.

158 Claire Herbert, Jeffrey Morenoff, David Harding et al., "Homelessness and Housing Insecurity among Former Prisoners" (2015) 1:2 *Russell Sage Foundation J Soc Sci* 44 at 45, 48, 74.

159 Prescott and Starr, "Expungement of Criminal Convictions" at 2471.

160 Peter Leasure and Tara Martin, "Criminal Records and Housing: An Experimental Study" (2017) 13 *J Experimental Criminology* 527 at 527–28.

161 *Ibid.*

162 *See, e.g.*, Amanda Agan and Sonja Starr, "The Effect of Criminal Records on Access to Employment" (2017) 105:5 *Am Econ Rev* 560 at 563–64 (noting how criminal records decrease employment prospects); Alexander Burton, Francis Cullen, Justin Pickett et al., "Beyond the Eternal Criminal Record: Public Support for Expungement" (2021) 20:1 *Criminology & Pub Pol'y* 123 at 124–25; Naomi Sugie, "Criminal Record Questions, Statistical Discrimination, and Equity in a Ban the Box Era" (2017) 16:1 *Criminology & Pub Pol'y* 167 at 167.

163 Prescott and Starr, "Expungement of Criminal Convictions" at 2501–05.

164 Brian Murray, "Insider Expungement" (2023) 2023:2 *Utah L Rev* 337 at 346.

165 Prescott and Starr, "Expungement of Criminal Convictions" at 2502–04.

166 *Ibid.* at 2504.

167 *See, e.g.*, Cassie Chambers Armstrong, "The Price of Fundamental Rights: Criminal Convictions, Expungement Fees, and Constitutional Concerns" (2022) 74;3 *Rutgers UL Rev* 1167 at 1181–82; Colleen Chien, "America's Paper Prisons: The Second Chance Gap?" (2020) 119:3 *Mich L Rev* 519 at 524, 556–57.

168 *See, e.g.*, Chien, "America's Paper Prisons?" at 524, 556–57.

low.[169] Roughly 10,000 persons were estimated to be eligible for a criminal record suspension for simple possession of marijuana.[170] However, only 780 people applied over a two-year period, and only 484 of those individuals received a criminal record suspension.[171]

More recently, some jurisdictions have implemented automatic criminal record expungement schemes that avoid many of the problems associated with traditional expungement applications.[172] Some European jurisdictions also expunge individuals' criminal records automatically after a fixed period.[173] Automatic expungements models eliminate complexity, administrative burdens, and fees that discourage individuals from criminal record expungement applications.[174] Furthermore, automatic expungements may be a relatively simple and cost-effective way to increase uptake rates, and ultimately, counteract punitive entrenchment and domination.

9.3.5 *Criminal Justice Debt Absolution*

Fifth, criminal justice debt absolution may also help reduce punitive entrenchment and domination. The term "criminal justice debt absolution" implies that individuals have a right to be released from criminal justice debts that entrench them in homelessness and poverty.[175]

Individuals enjoy a constitutional right to be protected against excessive fines in the United States, and a right to be protected against cruel and unusual punishments in Canada.[176] In *Timbs* v. *Indiana*, the US Supreme Court decided that the Eighth Amendment right to be free from cruel and unusual punishments – including the Excessive Fines Clause – is incorporated into the states through the Fourteenth Amendment.[177] The Excessive Fines Clause also applies to municipal ordinances,

169 Peter Zimonjic, "Only 484 Marijuana Pardons Have Been Granted since Program Started in 2019," CBC News (October 31, 2021), www.cbc.ca/news/politics/pot-pardons-still-low-484-1.6230666 [perma.cc/GS5D-NP7Q].

170 *Ibid.*

171 *Ibid.*

172 Brian Murray, "Retributive Expungement" (2021) 169:3 *U Pa L Rev* 665 at 671, 709; Brian Murray, "A New Era for Expungement Law Reform: Recent Developments at the State and Federal Levels" (2016) 10:2 *Harv L & Pol'y Rev* 361 at 371; Prescott and Starr, "Expungement of Criminal Convictions" at 2464; Burton et al., "Beyond the Eternal Criminal Record" at 141–42 (citing Pennsylvania, Utah, California, and New Jersey); Jeffrey Selbin, Justin McCrary, and Joshua Epstein, "Unmarked: Criminal Record Clearing and Employment Outcomes" (2018) 108:1 *J Crim L & Criminology* 1 at 53–54.

173 Burton et al., "Beyond the Eternal Criminal Record" at 141–42 (citing Pennsylvania, Utah, California, and New Jersey), citing James Jacobs, *The Eternal Criminal Record* (Cambridge: Harvard University Press, 2015) at 119 (see footnote in the text).

174 Skolnik, "Two Criminal Justice Systems."

175 *See, e.g.*, Skolnik, "Rethinking Homeless People's Punishments" at 91–95.

176 In the United States, *see* US Const amend VIII; Colgan, "The Excessive Fines Clause" at 10; *Timbs* v. *Indiana*, 139 US 682 (2019) (US). In Canada, *see* Canadian Charter of Rights and Freedoms, s. 7, Part 1 of the Constitution Act, 1982, being Schedule B to the Canada Act 1982 (UK), 1982, c. 11, s. 12; *R* v. *Bissonnette*, 2022 SCC 23 at paras. 59–70.

177 *Timbs* at 686–91.

including laws that govern public property.[178] Canadian law also offers some protection against excessive fines. In *R* v. *Boudreault*, the Supreme Court of Canada concluded that a mandatory $100 or $200 victim surcharge constituted a cruel and unusual punishment due to its impact on unhoused and impecunious persons.[179] The Court reasoned that the fine violated section 12 of the Canadian Charter because it imposed the equivalent of an indeterminate sentence, resulted in civil and administrative collection efforts, and impacted indigent offenders disparately.[180] These constitutional provisions provide some protection against excessive fines.

Yet individuals may have accumulated significant criminal justice debt even when courts determine that a particular fine is cruel and unusual.[181] Research indicates that some unhoused persons in Montreal have accumulated over $10,000-worth of unpaid fines.[182] Beth Colgan notes that in the United States in 2016, individuals owed $110 billion-worth of restitution for financial penalties, $100 billion-worth of which the federal government estimated will not be recouped because individuals cannot afford to pay them.[183] Although defendants may successfully challenge a particular fine's excessiveness, the right to be free from cruel and unusual punishments does not absolve their past criminal justice debts that flow from other offenses.

Some jurisdictions have implemented criminal justice debt relief programs. The city of Montreal's Programme d'Accompagnement Justice-Itinérance à la Cour Municipale (PAJIC) – which works together with the municipal court and the Droits Devant community organization – offers a criminal justice debt relief initiative to unhoused persons.[184] Between 2015 and 2016, roughly 150 people completed the PAJIC program and the municipal court absolved roughly 2,400 unpaid fines.[185] Other cities, such as Los Angeles, decided to void a significant number of fines

178 *See, e.g.*, *Pimentel* v. *City of Los Angeles*, 974 F (3d) 917 (9th Circ 2020); *Blake* v. *City of Grants Pass* (D Or 2020).

179 *R* v. *Boudreault*, 2018 SCC 58 at paras. 1–6.

180 *Ibid.* at paras. 65–79.

181 Skolnik, "Rethinking Homeless People's Punishments" at 91.

182 *See, e.g.*, Céline Bellot and Marie-Eve Sylvestre, "La Judiciarisation de l'itinérance à Montréal: les dérives sécuritaires de la gestion pénale de la pauvreté" (2017) 47 *RGD* 11 at 31–35.

183 Beth Colgan, "Wealth Based Penal Disenfranchisement" (2019) 72 *Vand L Rev* 55 at 81–82. Colgan's full quote is: "In Fiscal Year 2016, for example, the federal courts sentenced over fifteen thousand people to pay economic sanctions totaling over $9 billion, adding to the $110 billion in outstanding restitution alone, $100 billion of which the federal government deems uncollectable because debtors lack the financial resources to pay."

184 Véronique Fortin and Isabelle Raffestin, "Le Programme d'Accompagnement Justice-Itinérance à la Cour Municipale de Montréal (PAJIC): un tribunal spécialisé ancré dans le communautaire" (2017) 47 *RGD* 177 at 183–200; Quebec Department of Justice, "Programme de procureur désigné et de percepteur désigné pour les personnes en situation d'itinérance (Programmes PAJIC et PAPSI)" (July 1, 2011), www.justice.gouv.qc.ca/fileadmin/user_upload/contenu/documents/Fr__francais_/centredoc/publications/couple-famille/prog_procureur.pdf [perma.cc/U692-2J3A].

185 Clinique Droits Devant, "Bilan Annuel: 2015–2016" (2016) at 21, www.cerp.gouv.qc.ca/fileadmin/Fichiers_clients/Documents_deposes_a_la_Commission/P-212.pdf [perma.cc/5NLQ-36DE].

issued to unhoused persons and relieved them of their criminal justice debts.[186] These programs can help counteract punitive entrenchment and reduce domination. But unhoused and impecunious persons lack a statutory or constitutional right to be absolved of their criminal justice debts that they cannot pay – an important step to obtain access to housing.

In the future, courts or lawmakers may recognize a right to criminal justice debt absolution.[187] A judicially recognized constitutional right to criminal justice debt absolution – a right to be freed from cruel and unusual criminal justice debts – would confer stronger protection against punitive entrenchment.

9.4 CONCLUSION

This chapter argued that the State's three fiduciary duties – ending homelessness and treating unhoused persons with equal respect, protecting public property's value, and legitimizing laws that govern the urban commons – are interconnected. It demonstrated why the State must alleviate homelessness to fulfil its other fiduciary duties. It explained the three components of the State's fiduciary duty to alleviate homelessness: addressing the risk factors associated with homelessness, improving access to housing, and providing emergency shelter and interim resources until individuals become housed.

The later parts of this chapter offered a set of concrete proposals for how the State can better fulfil its fiduciary duties related to homelessness and public property, and ultimately, counteract nonegalitarian coercion, punitive entrenchment, and domination. The implementation of these proposals can better ensure that the State regulates public property in a manner that treats unhoused persons with greater respect and consideration.

186 Mark Puente and Richard Winton, "L.A. Vows to Void 2 Million Court Citations and Warrants: Homeless People Will Benefit Most," LA Times (October 2, 2019), www.latimes.com/california/story/2019%9610-02/homeless-housing-erase-citation-fine-fees [perma.cc/WVB8-7HVM].

187 *See, e.g.*, Skolnik, "Rethinking Homeless People's Punishments" at 91–95.

Conclusion

This book advances a theory of the State's fiduciary duties to end homelessness, maintain public property's shared value, and legitimize laws that govern public space. It argues that republicanism provides new insight into homelessness and the regulation of public property – insights that existing constitutional theory and legal philosophy typically overlook. This book's overarching argument, original contributions, and advantages can be described as follows.

Chapter 1 provided an overview of homelessness in the United States and in Canada, the risk factors associated with homelessness, and the overrepresentation of certain groups in the unhoused population. It described the evolution of laws that regulate public property and unhoused persons. It also detailed the rise and fall of vagrancy laws and the emergence of municipal ordinances in the United States and in Canada.

Chapter 2 explored how constitutional law has approached homelessness and the regulation of public property in these jurisdictions. It discussed the principal constitutional challenges to laws that regulate public property, and highlighted the successes and shortcomings of those claims. It analyzed the arguments that municipal ordinances that govern public property are unconstitutionally vague or overbroad, violate the fundamental right to travel, contravene the right to equality (or equal protection), or impose cruel and unusual punishments. The second chapter also explained why US and Canadian courts have not yet recognized a positive right to housing.

Chapter 3 analyzed some of the principal legal philosophical approaches to homelessness, liberty, and property that are based on the positive conception of freedom as self-actualization and the negative conception of freedom as noninterference. The chapter showed how housing protects both forms of freedom, and it illustrated why unhoused persons enjoy less positive and negative freedom compared to people with access to housing.

Chapter 4 introduced the republican theory of liberty as nondomination. It distinguished between three forms of domination: horizontal domination by other individuals, vertical domination by the State, and double domination by the State and by others. It also highlighted the connection between nondomination and political equality. The chapter demonstrated why unhoused persons face two forms of double domination associated with laws that govern public property. First, others exert control over unhoused persons' opportunities to obey these laws. Second, unhoused persons must make nonegalitarian sacrifices as the price of law-abidingness. Chapter 4 elucidated why unhoused persons lack positive, negative, and republican liberty, and ultimately, political equality.

Chapter 5 explained how people experiencing homelessness suffer double domination because they are subject to nonegalitarian coercion, meaning that the State has more power to regulate and to police unhoused persons compared to people with access to housing. It distinguished the respective roles of private property and public property. And it showed why the State can more justifiably regulate need-alleviating conduct on public property than on private property. More specifically, the State's justifications for regulating such conduct on public property either do not apply to private property, are mitigated when individuals alleviate their needs on private property, or are outweighed by a person's privacy and dignitary interests within the home. The concluding parts of Chapter 5 explained why law enforcement can more easily surveil and police unhoused persons' need-alleviating conduct compared to the need-alleviating acts of people with access to housing – a form of vertical domination that disparately affects people experiencing homelessness.

Chapter 6 showed why unhoused persons are subject to punitive entrenchment which exacerbates nonegalitarian coercion. It explained how fines, fees, surcharges, and collateral consequences enmesh individuals in homelessness. It discussed how excessive punishments violate proportionality constraints and are inconsistent with retributivist and consequentialist justifications for punishment. The final parts of the chapter elucidated how excessive financial penalties fail to satisfy instrumental rationality constraints. Rather than deter unhoused persons from alleviating their needs on public property, harsh financial penalties entrench individuals in homelessness, such that they are more likely to sleep, shelter themselves, or urinate in public spaces.

Chapter 7 justified the State's fiduciary duties related to homelessness and public property. It argued that the government and individuals are in a fiduciary relationship, which gives rise to the State's overarching fiduciary duty to counteract domination. Drawing on the insights of republicanism and fiduciary theory, the chapter contended that the State's overarching fiduciary obligation to redress domination results in three specific fiduciary duties. First, the State must end homelessness to counteract the domination to which unhoused persons are subject. Second, the State must safeguard public property's value and protect liberty in public space. Third, the State must legitimize the coercion and punishment associated with laws that govern public property. Chapter 7 explained why the State bears these fiduciary duties. Notably, the State creates a private and public property system to secure liberty in both spheres. Yet the State de facto excludes unhoused persons from these systems of mutual coercion, which results in domination. The State's three fiduciary duties related to homelessness and public property aim to rectify that domination and secure individuals' liberty and equality.

Chapter 8 demonstrated why the State's fulfilment of its fiduciary duties is preferable to other public and private mechanisms that address homelessness. It argued that certain existing ameliorative and coercive mechanisms either fail to reduce unhoused persons' domination or exacerbate it. These mechanisms include shelter space increases, zoning proposals, concentration strategies, dispersal tactics, and encampments. The final part of the chapter explained why encampments cannot constitute a complete and permanent justification to appropriate public property. However, encampments can be partially and temporarily justifiable in certain contexts when unhoused persons lack other reasonable alternatives and the benefits of encampments outweigh their burdens. The fact that encampments can only constitute a partial justification further underpins the State's fiduciary duty to end homelessness and supports a right to housing.

Chapter 9 offered a set of concrete proposals for how the State can better fulfil its three fiduciary duties related to homelessness and public property. The opening parts of the chapter highlighted the connection between these duties. It showed how the State better fulfils its fiduciary duties when it helps ensure that individuals enjoy access to housing. It described the components of the State's first fiduciary duty to end homelessness. More specifically, the State must address the risk factors associated with homelessness, improve access to housing, and provide shelters and other interim resources until individuals become housed. Chapter 9 then set out various mechanisms for how the State can alleviate homelessness, reduce nonegalitarian coercion, and decrease punitive entrenchment.

This book's overarching theory refines our understanding of homelessness, property, and the regulation of public space. The republican theory of freedom deepens our knowledge about why people experiencing homelessness lack freedom and political equality that others enjoy. This book provides new insight into how access to housing protects republican liberty in ways that positive and negative liberty theory can overlook. By uniting republicanism and fiduciary theory, it enhances our comprehension of why the State has obligations to end homelessness, regulate public property, and legitimize laws that govern public space.

There are several advantages to the theory advanced in this book. Its arguments provide new insight into homelessness, criminal law, property law, and fiduciary theories of legal authority even if one disagrees with republicanism. One can reject republicanism as a theory of freedom or government or disagree that the State has a duty to counteract domination. Yet one can accept that republicanism offers a deeper understanding of homelessness, liberty, property, and their interrelationship. Furthermore, one may accept many of the final chapter's concrete proposals even if one rejects republicanism or disagrees with this book's theoretical framework. For instance, a reader can accept the final chapter's proposals for reform because they treat unhoused persons with greater respect and consideration, regulate public space more effectively, or cost less than existing mechanisms. This book's law and public policy proposals are advantageous because they can be justified on various grounds and can be implemented across jurisdictions.

This book's arguments can play an important role with respect to homelessness and the regulation of public property. Society will face new challenges that can exacerbate homelessness and create new challenges for the regulation of public space, such as climate change, automation, pandemics, and increased costs of living. More than ever, cities will be forced to address homelessness and manage public property effectively. And they must do so in a way that treats individuals with the dignity, respect, and concern they deserve, irrespective of whether they have access to housing. This book offers a framework and a set of law and public policy reforms that may help achieve those aims.

Ultimately, this book raises a more basic question about what it means to be free and what it means to be treated as an equal. Indeed, the nature of homelessness and the regulation of public property is more than a story about who can be where and who can do what. It is fundamentally a story about our liberty, political equality, and the extent to which some individuals wield power over others. This book not only shows us why that is. It also provides a roadmap to safeguard the liberty and equality of all persons in the private and public spheres.

Index